Philosophy
FOR
DUMMIES®
UK EDITION

by Martin Cohen

WILEY

A John Wiley and Sons, Ltd, Publication

Philosophy For Dummies®, UK Edition

Published by
John Wiley & Sons, Ltd
The Atrium
Southern Gate
Chichester
West Sussex
PO19 8SQ
England

E-mail (for orders and customer service enquires): cs-books@wiley.co.uk

Visit our Home Page on www.wiley.com

For general information on our other products and services, please contact our Customer Care Department within the U.S. at 877-762-2974, outside the U.S. at 317-572-3993, or fax 317-572-4002.

For technical support, please visit www.wiley.com/techsupport.

Wiley also publishes its books in a variety of electronic formats. Some content that appears in print may not be available in electronic books.

British Library Cataloguing in Publication Data: A catalogue record for this book is available from the British Library

ISBN: 978-0-470-68820-5

Printed and bound in Great Britain by TJ International, Padstow, UK.

10 9 8 7 6 5 4 3 2 1

WILEY

About the Author

Martin Cohen is a full-time writer and editor of philosophical books. He has both taught and researched philosophy at a number of universities in the UK and Australia but is best known for his books advocating and developing a method of teaching philosophy sometimes known as *modularity*. This is a technique, (which is very appropriate to the 'Philosophy for Dummies' style) in which big complex problems are broken down into bits, each part of which is (as much as possible) independent and self-standing. He was originally encouraged in the approach by George MacDonald Ross, for whom he was a researcher on an ambitious project to change the way philosophy is taught in UK universities in the 1980s, and to make it less 'stuffy' and more practical.

Martin's earlier books include: *101 Philosophy Problems*, *101 Ethical Dilemmas*, *Political Philosophy*, *Wittgenstein's Beetle and Other Classic Thought Experiments*, *Philosophical Tales*, and *Mind Games*.

As well as having been a lecturer and researcher, Martin is also a professional school teacher, who in the distant past taught in schools in Yorkshire and Staffordshire, with children from ages as young as seven. He remains an advocate of 'philosophy for children' and his '101' books are popular with many teachers.

Although his book *Philosophical Tales* paints rather an unkind picture of Karl Marx, Martin sees the 'point of philosophy', as Marx once said, to be not merely to interpret the world but to change it, and he has been active on many ethical and environmental issues.

Author's Acknowledgments

For Dummies style does not allow footnotes (which is surely right – out, out damned footnote!) nor even end notes. However, that can be a little bit of an invitation to borrow without acknowledgement. So this section is an effort to catch up with some of the many people who really ought to be acknowledged, as indeed this book is not all my own ideas, but merely my distillation of reading, research, and discussions with others. Here are just some of those philosophical folk whose ideas I have benefited from and attempted to communicate to a new audience:

Brenda Almond, Gideon Calder, Anna Cohen, James Danaher, Pierre-Alain Gouanvic, Wendy Hamblet, Trevor Jordan, Colin Kirk, Mary Lenzi, Yuli Liu, George MacDonald Ross, Tom Morris, Chris Onof, Andrew Porter, John Sellars, Daniel Silvermintz, Dean D'Souza, Stephen Thornton, Zenon Stavrinides and Brad Weslake.

On the production side, I should also like to thank all those 'professional Dummies' at Wiley – notably Nicole Hermitage, who introduced me to the idea of *For Dummies*, and Simon Bell, who coped very patiently with my occasional incredulity at the requirements of 'Dummies Style'. I would also like to thank the various readers of the manuscript, especially Zenon, for their careful comments, corrections and advice.

Publisher's Acknowledgments

We're proud of this book; please send us your comments through our Dummies online registration form located at www.dummies.com/register/.

Some of the people who helped bring this book to market include the following:

Commissioning, Editorial, and Media Development

Project Editor: Simon Bell

Content Editor: Jo Theedom

Commissioning Editor: Nicole Hermitage

Assistant Editor: Ben Kemble

Copy Editor: Charlie Wilson

Technical Editor: Dr Zenon Stavrinides

Publisher: David Palmer

Production Manager: Daniel Mersey

Cover Photos: © Sly/Fotolia

Cartoons: Ed McLachlan

Composition Services

Project Coordinator: Lynsey Stanford

Layout and Graphics: Ashley Chamberlain, Joyce Haughey, Stephanie Jumper

Proofreader: Laura Albert

Indexer: Sharon Shock

Contents at a Glance

Table of Contents

Introduction

*P*hilosophy For Dummies! How about that! Actually, it doesn't sound quite
right. *Philosophy For Thoughtful People,* maybe. *Philosophy For Geniuses.*
yes, I like that. But *Philosophy For Dummies,* no. Because philosophy has a
certain *cachet*: it has a certain, rather grand, status. You don't think so? How
many ancient geographers or chemists or astronomers are lovingly quoted
everyday, not just for historical interest, but as *authorities*? But philosophers
certainly are. How many subjects can survive simply reprinting old essays
without having to come up with we material? But philosophy is like that.
We'd much rather read the words of an ancient philosopher or at least a very
highly respected dead one, than listen to the latest ideas of some still living
professor who quite likely won't even be remembered in a thousand years.

So yes, philosophy has a bit of a weighty, serious side, and suits weighty
serious types. But that's just one way to loo at it. It's also a surprisingly sexy
subject. After all, how many Geography Cafés are there? Informal gatherings
of young people discussing geography in public bars? Not many. But there
are philosophy ones. And how many people rush to take courses in teaching,
say, chemistry to very young children – calling it Chem4Children, perhaps?
But Philosophy for Children (meaning the under sevens by and large) has
really taken off – and the little ones love it!

What's more remarkable, is the 'little ones' are pretty good at it. And that's
why *Philosophy For Dummies* is actually not such a Dumb Idea. The real
issues, and the real ideas of philosophy belong to everyone, and if philosophy has traditionally been stuck a little bit too much on its pedestal, a
little too full of its obscure jargon, Latin terms and so on, then that's all the
more reason to bring it down a peg or two, and return it to where actually it
started, the public arena as a pursuit for everyone. I hope by the end of this
book to have convinced you that you too can 'do philosophy' – and equally
importantly, that maybe some of those philosophical experts whose boring
books might have put you off before, aren't quite as on top of the subject as
they think they are. Subversive? Well, yes. But that's philosophy. That's why
it matters. And that's why everyone should have a go at it.

About This Book

Philosophy For Dummies provides you with two things. First, the essential facts – the nuts and bolts – of 3000 years of people philosophising. And secondly, it provides you with a toolbox of methods and techniques for dealing with problems and tricky questions. These tools are really what makes philosophy valuable. For they can be used equally well throughout life, not just on traditional philosophical problems.

Conventions Used in This Book

To help you get the most from this book, I follow a few conventions:

- *Italic* emphasises and highlights new words or strange terms that I go on to define. . . .

- *Sidebars* (the grey boxes you come across from time to time) contain tasty extracts from classic philosophical works are typically based on the standard contemporary translations, but occasionally slightly reworded, to make them read more naturally.

- I don't give *dates* all the time, for example for philosophers or their books, except where I feel it is directly useful to the passage.

What You're Not to Read

The book is divided into five parts, plus the usual *For Dummies* 'Part of Tens'. These, like the chapters themselves, can be read in any order. Similarly, within each chapter, extensive use of sidebars, headings and sub-headings both invites you and enables you to dip in and out of the text. There's no need to plough through this book, just take it idea by idea, debate by debate. And do a lot of pausing to think, of course!

You'll also see plenty of icons above text which you can take or leave: I hope you'll enjoy the 'Lousy Idea' icon, which of course is a little bit tongue-in-cheek, and check out the 'Thought Experiments' whenever the icon appears.

Foolish Assumptions

In writing this book, I made a few assumptions about who you are:

- You're curious and motivated to find out more about philosophy, even though you may not be 100 per cent sure how to go about it.
- You have an open mind, and have not already filled it up with rigid options – especially philosophical ones.
- You're interested in hearing about the links between different philosophical traditions and ideas.
- You're open to the idea that philosophy is a pretty broad field, sweeping across natural science and sociology as well as the traditional pursuits of standard college courses.

Beyond those, I've not assumed too much, I hope. This book is for you whether you're seven or seventy, a PhD or a Member of Parliament.

How This Book Is Organised

A bit more now about the six parts of *Philosophy For Dummies*.

Part I: What Is Philosophy?

Great place to start! But honestly, 'what philosophy is' is harder to pin down than it really ought to be. My interpretation is not like most of the others 'philosophers' versions, although I'm far from alone in arguing that philosophy is actually a practical tool for dealing with real issues. This part sketches out the overall aims and 'scope' of philosophy, making sure that what we now call 'science' is put back where it belongs – at the heart of the subject. And Part I closes by setting out some of the techniques you'll need to actually start 'doing' philosophy, practising philosophy as an activity.

Part II: The History of Philosophy

This part covers everything you need to know about what philosophers' have said and argued and indeed done in the past. From the origins of many of philosophy's debates in both Ancient Greece and China, to the latest confusing philosophical isms (like existentialism and utilitarianism) this part spells the debates out clearly and puts it all in context

Part III: The Nuts and Bolts of Philosophy

This is the 'How to section' - How to use 'logic' effectively, how to find things out (rather than just think you have found something out and be mistaken!) and how to step back from everything you just found out and realise that you still don't really know it. That might sound more like undoing the nuts and bolts of your philosophical go-kart, but hey, that's kind of useful too. Trouble is, no one knows (yet) how to put everything 'we used to know' back together again.

Part IV: Exploring the Mind, Consciousness and Morality

This is without doubt the most valuable part of the book. Why do I say that? Because it is to do with values. And although that sounds a bit 'preachy' – go home Vicar! – by the time you've read this, I think you'll maybe want to call the Vicar back again, sit him down for tea and biscuits and discuss many of the issues raised here, from 'What is art?' to whether economic forces always work for the best.

Part V: Philosophy and Science

Philosophers are a bit sniffy about Science. In fact, most philosophy introductions and quite a few universities consider 'philosophy of science' to be not proper philosophy at all – and maybe to belong in a separate book (or classroom) a long, long way away. That's a pretty dumb view, as this part will show. And indeed, science nowadays is increasingly at the cutting edge of philosophy, with trad philosophers struggling to join in with their supposedly practical colleagues. Don't you get left behind – read this and join in the big new debates!.

Part VI: The Part of Tens

Every _For Dummies_ book has one. The Part of Tens offers two bite-sized chapters filled with tempting philosophical puzzles and tasty morsels of philosophical texts.

Icons Used in This Book

Sprinkled through the book you'll see various icons to guide you on your way. Icons are a For Dummies way of drawing your attention to important stuff, interesting stuff, and stuff you really need to know to watch out for.

Key pieces of information which repay, well, a closer look.

This is stuff you may want to add to your memory bank – the very best bits of philosophy.

Philosophers love their obscure terminology and exclusive lingo. This icon points you to clear, straightforward translations.

And the other side of the coin – this is stuff you may want to delete from your memory bank – but don't be tempted to do so, these ideas are still influential and still part o the history of philosophy.

These are imaginary scenarios that investigate those philosophy problems in a more 'scientific' manner.

Little nuggets of information to smooth your understanding.

Take careful note of the advice under this icon, and you'll avoid calamities.

Where to Go from Here

I've organised this book so that you can just dip in and out of it as you like. It isn't specifically written to be read from start to finish, although you can do that if you want. In general, though, you'll probably find that you look up what you want to read about in the Table of Contents or the index and dive straight in at that section. Or, if you prefer to read in a more conventional way, reading Part I will still give you the basics for getting started in philosophy from scratch, and point you towards places later in the book where you can hop to for more detailed information on topics in which you're particularly interested.

Best of luck, and . . . happy philosophising!

Part I
What Is Philosophy?

In this part . . .

Philosophy is a pretty posh name for a pretty posh
subject. Not one most of us need know anything
about, you'd think. Gardening, how to drive cars, maybe a
bit of computers these days – but philosophy? Wake me
up when the professor's gone!

But philosophy's not boring or useless at all. This part
explains why you actually just might find it incredibly useful to read the rest of the book, and why you really might
enjoy finding out all about those strange philosophical
questions, puzzles and ideas. Ready? Now get stuck in!

Chapter 1

What's Philosophy All About?

In This Chapter

▶ Making light work of some common misunderstandings of philosophy

▶ Getting a handle on some of the big ideas

▶ Delving back into ancient history and exploring the origins of key philosophical ideas

n this chapter we find out 'what philosophy is' – and what I used to be too (which are not quite the same thing). We immediately solve one of philosophy's biggest problems – the problem of knowledge – and we look at the experiences of a greedy chicken and a sock with a hole in it too.

Defining the Job

> *Philosophy is the 'no-man's land' between science and theology, under attack from both sides.*

> – Bertrand Russell

Or, as philosophers might prefer to put it, science and religion are really two slices of bread, with philosophy the tasty bit in the middle. Scientists reduce the world to 'matter', make the world into a machine and destroy free will and purpose. On the other hand, spiritual types, who are searching for a purpose and the freedom to find it, are attracted to religions and to all those 'irrational' activities, such as astrology and watching TV. And they don't feel the need to get anything done. Between the two camps, it seems there's not much room left for philosophy!

But then, from the outside, philosophy seems to be a rather peculiar, not to say pointless, subject full of unanswerable riddles and questions like 'Is the King of France bald' or 'Does that table exist' that no one in their right minds would ask anyway.

Indeed, philosophy courses often start off (as if determined to disprove the point, but inadvertently just reinforcing it) by asking, 'What is philosophy?' – a question that no self-respecting study would normally need to ask. What is chemistry? What is cooking? What is geography? Yet philosophers certainly seem to like asking these 'what is' questions, and asking it about their own subject seems to them to be quite the right thing to do. The point for them, after all, is to ask questions, not to answer them.

So what is philosophy?

Philosophy is a subject that has no particular content and covers no particular area. It is, rather, a kind of intellectual cement that attempts to stick the rest of the (rather grand sounding) intellectual edifice together.

Or put another way (less grand sounding), philosophy is a kind of manure. Pile it high, in a few places, and it simply rots and stinks. But spread it around and it becomes surprisingly useful. That was the view of some of philosophy's defenders at the end of the last century. At the same time, people all over the Western World were asking the question 'what's the point of philosophy?' and had decided there wasn't one. People were beginning to see philosophy departments that were training people to ask strange unanswerable questions or to repeat obscure chunks of ancient texts as wasting their time. In the cold light of economic downturns, critics considered the efforts of serious philosophers to investigate the following sacred problems of philosophy and the like as a waste of money:

- How do I know I exist?
- How do I know God exists?
- How do I know the world exists?
- Is snow white?
- If a tree falls in a forest and there' no one there to hear it, does it make any sound?

So what is the point of philosophy?

But, on the other hand, the efforts of practical people to make sense of their useful subjects – doctors, lawyers, astronomers, physicists, chemists, historians, linguists; you name it, they need to do it – always seemed to come back to certain paradoxical or tricky questions that are, essentially, well, philosophical. So even as philosophy as a hobby of the leisured classes went out one door, in came philosophy as a practical study – in the form of mini philosophy courses for medical ethics or business ethics or critical thinking and (for the scientists) theories of space and time.

And this in a way was a return to the roots of philosophy – because for the Ancient Greeks (who invented the word, but certainly not the activity – whatever you may read elsewhere!) , philosophy is fundamentally a guide to action – helping to answer the perennial question 'what should I do'?

Loving Wisdom

It makes good sense for a lot of philosophically-minded people today to avoid the use of the word *philosophy* and study practical questions instead.

Medical folk may want to look at questions like:

- ✔ When does 'life' begin?
- ✔ What is consciousness?

Business types may want to ponder puzzles like:

- ✔ When do successful companies become monopolies?
- ✔ Are organisations obliged to spread wealth?

And physicists and chemists ask themselves:

- ✔ Can time flow backwards?
- ✔ Is there a form of water on Mars made up of three hydrogen atoms to two oxygen atoms (H_3O_2 instead of H_2O) – and if so, is that still water?

Eventually, everyone begins to wonder:

- ✔ Do unicorns have one or two horns?
- ✔ Are all bachelors (really) unmarried men?

But hang on! Isn't this all becoming a bit like the old, traditional courses in philosophy? The questions aren't practical at all! What's changed? And the answer is, of course, nothing's changed. Philosophers, after all, don't like change. They like truth and certainty. They like problems they can be the sole experts on. Yet even if 'professional philosophers' are reluctant to change, when practical people take a look at the subject the fundamentals of philosophy become clearer.

Recent guides on 'what philosophy is'

Wondering what philosophy really is? These four writers offer some of the most popular answers:

> 'What is philosophy? This is a notoriously difficult question. One of the easiest ways of answering it is to say that philosophy is what philosophers do, and then point to the writings of Plato, Aristotle , Descartes . . . and other famous philosophers.'

– Nigel Warburton in *Philosophy: the Basics*

> 'Philosophy, noun. The topic of this dictionary. Those who study it disagree to this day on how they should define their field.'

– Geoffrey Vesey and Paul Foulkes in their *Dictionary of Philosophy*

> 'Philosophy is thinking about thinking.'

– Richard Osborne in *Philosophy for Beginners*

> 'What is philosophy? Many people who have been studying and teaching the subject for years wouldn't agree on a definition . . . Just as you can learn to swim only by getting in the water, you can only find out what goes on in philosophy by engaging in it. Nevertheless, to describe philosophy, let's try at least one plausible suggestion which covers most if not all of what people that are engaged in thinking and writing about the subject are constantly doing. The suggestion is that philosophy is the study of justification.'

> – John Hospers in *An Introduction to Philosophical Analysis*

Of them all, the first is just what real philosophers call a *circular argument* – it immediately raises the question: if philosophy is what philosophers do, then what is it that makes someone a philosopher? And that's clearly by doing philosophy. And the only possible answer to that question is, the thing that makes someone into a philosopher is their doing philosophy. Certainly, it looks plausible, but actually the answer just leads you round in a circle.

The second answer is frankly a cop-out. But it saves the writer a lot of bother! (I opted for this answer when I edited a dictionary too.)

The third response is more artistic but is just wrong.

The fourth answer is more complicated but is basically saying philosophy is the study of the reasons people have for thinking as they do think – for delving a bit deeper into every other subject. And so maybe, unfashionable as it looks, this last answer may still be the best. That's because it's the only answer left standing after the rest have been knocked down.

Philosophy isn't a body of knowledge with a set of 'answers' to common questions to be learned. Philosophy is a technique, a way of teasing apart and examining reality so not only do you understand it a little bit better, but you can act more effectively, achieve your aims more completely, live a little bit better. And it's no contradiction that increasingly these days you find the true philosophers not in dusty philosophy departments poring over the misleadingly named 'philosophy' journals full of language chopping (arguing about definitions of words) and not very good maths (philosophical logic), but in the hospitals, the appeal courts, the physics laboratories – anywhere but up there in the ivory towers.

Deciding What Counts as 'Real' Knowledge

Of course, professional philosophers *can* help find answers too – when they want to. In fact, philosophers can have a special role as a kind of umpire or referee in disputes emerging from the nitty-gritty of research or practice in all other subjects and areas. They can come into an area unencumbered by too many presumptions and clarify the fundamentals. And what could be more fundamental than deciding what counts as knowledge as opposed to mere belief or superstition? Because no one likes thinking that he knows something if there's a chance that someone may later shown him up as being wrong. Lots of 'facts' are like this – they're things you think you know but actually you just take them on trust from the person (or book, or TV show) that tells you, rather than really know. Very few things exist that you can know directly, for yourself.

For example, take 'knowing' that you can bite into an apple because it's crisp and crunchy, unlike a rock, which is very hard, or knowing that the sun will come up tomorrow. Both of these seem pretty safe to count as 'things you know', but wouldn't you guess it, the philosophers dispute even these. Their complaint is that both assumptions rely on nothing more than past experience, and past experience is an unreliable guide.

The 20th-century British philosopher Bertrand Russell tells a nice story about some chickens to illustrate this problem. These domesticated birds have a little coop outside the farmhouse and each morning the farmer's wife comes and throws a handful of grain to them. Each morning, therefore, it makes sense for the birds to rush to leave the coop and get the first cluck at the tasty grain. Such is the chicken's theory of the matter anyway. But one day (not that the chickens know it) the farmer's wife is intending to make chicken soup. Does it make sense to rush out of the chicken coop towards the farmer's wife that morning?

In fact, it doesn't make sense for the chicken to do anything but hide in the very deepest recesses of the coop that morning, but there is no evidence drawn from the past that could point the chicken away from its assumption, and indeed plenty of evidence that would support the assumption! This is what philosophers call the *problem of induction*, which is a complicated sounding way of reasoning that's based on assuming that what you've already seen tells you about what you'll find next. People do this all the time, but philosophically it's not valid; indeed, it's straightforwardly illogical.

A dialogue between chickens

Imagine a conversation between two chickens who are wondering whether to leave the safety of their chicken coop one morning.

Chicken 1: I'm not going out there (for the grain); I don't trust those farmers.

Chicken 2: Why not? I trust them. Yesterday they gave us grain, the day before they gave us grain, the day before that they give us grain . . . They've given us grain for as long as I can remember! Chicken, I think they're going to give us some grain today!

Chicken 1: Well, I dunno, those are just facts about the past. They prove nothing about what's going to happen this time. It's not any kind of logical proof, is it?

Chicken 2: I seem to recall hearing somewhere that the British philosopher John Locke once said: 'The man that, in the ordinary affairs of life, would admit of nothing but direct plain demonstration would be sure of nothing in the world but of perishing quickly.'

Chicken 1: (Impressed.) Well, yes, but I have a hunch that today the farmers are planning to kill us! I'm not going out until you can persuade me there's no doubt that it's safe.

Chicken 2: Well, now, my cowardly friend, I have a theory I call 'the Principle of Belief Conservation', which says that you can accept certain basic beliefs without absolute proof if discarding them would require throwing away many of your other beliefs. Beliefs are your indispensable map of reality that guides us through the day. Knowledge, on the other hand, is very much a bolt-on extra.

(Chicken 2 leaves the coop and is throttled by the farmer's wife, who's making Sunday lunch.)

Why do people follow illogical lines of thinking? The answer is, because (as John Locke says) people have no choice. If you acted only on things that you 'really, really know' to be the case, you wouldn't act on many things at all.

In practice, many people would say that, given human frailty, it's enough to say that you know something if:

  ✔ You believe it to be the case

  ✔ You have a good, relevant reason for your belief and

  ✔ The thing you believe you know is actually as you believe – you're right!

A few famous philosophers deciding what counts for 'real' knowledge

The French philosopher René Descartes distinguished 'clear and distinct' beliefs from other ones and called these *knowledge*. A more recent Oxford philosopher of language, J.L. Austin, suggested that to say you know something is to give your word that it's so, to make a special kind of promise. On the other hand (and philosophers always try to look at the other side of any question), Francis Bacon, the English philosopher credited with coining the phrase 'knowledge is power' (thinking of practical knowledge), once said: 'If a man will begin with certainties, he shall end in doubts – but if he will be content to begin with doubts, he shall end in certainties.'

This is knowledge as what philosophers call knowledge as 'justified, true belief'. It's called that because you believe it, that's the 'belief bit'; you have a reason for our belief, that's the justification bit, and (what else?) it's true. That's the 'true' bit. Sorting out knowledge is easy! However, in many cases, like that of Chicken Two (see the nearby sidebar), some claims satisfy all three conditions and yet you still might feel they don't really count as real knowledge – that you need something more to make it absolutely certain. (In Chapter 9 I look at what that 'something else' might be.)

Crunching Up Three Types of Knowing

Many different ways of knowing something exist. You can know a fact, know a friend, and you can know how to paint or how to tie your shoelace:

- ✔ **To know that** this fruit is tasty, that two plus two makes four, that the weather will be good tomorrow

- ✔ **To know how** to ride a bicycle, read, check logical proofs

- ✔ **To know by acquaintance** the best way to get to town in the rush hour, a very good cheese shop, the neighbours

It's the first type of knowledge that interests philosophers most, even if they fall out over just what counts as knowledge as opposed to mere belief or value judgement.

Reasons for action

Facts are all very well, but everyone knows that what motivates you in everyday life is anything but. Rather than following some grand and logically valid system of deductions, people follow their whims and their prejudices. Your actions are affected by a complex mixture of emotion, suspicion and plain prejudice. Can philosophy help improve on this? Don't you believe it.

A lot of complicated-sounding nonsense is written about this, but the bottom line, according to one fairly standard view, as professional (read dull) philosophers like to say, is that your beliefs and desires determine the reasons for your actions. No room for facts!

belief + desire → action

For example, the belief that 'money makes people happy' plus the desire 'I want to be happy!' might lead to the action 'I'm going to rob a bank'.

But what if you *also* believe robbing banks is wrong? Then you have a conflict in your belief system that you need to resolve. And this is where that other great use for philosophy comes in: deciding the 'right' thing to do. (I explore this in Chapter 13.) Just a pity people don't use this aspect of philosophy more!

You might think separating facts from opinion is pretty simple, but wait until you've read today's newspaper, let alone some more philosophy. For example, you might think that your location in space and time is pretty certain, but many physicists would say, strictly speaking, that there isn't any absolute or true answer, and it's more a matter of convention. Or you might think that the weather forecaster who says it will rain tomorrow doesn't really know whether it will or not – but if he's right, what then? Did he really know?

Philosophers are inclined to narrow down the task of defining knowledge to just the simplest claims, even if it turns out that they're little more than tautologies (the same thing said twice). They prefer people to say things like 'Apples are apples'. Depart from these simple claims and you may make mistakes. For example, 'Apples are fruits' is only safe to say because everyone agrees that, well, apples are fruits, but woe betide you if you say 'strawberries are fruits'! Stick to 'strawberries are strawberries and you won't go wrong . . .

When it comes down to it, the search for knowledge is really about making sense of different kinds of beliefs. And put that way, it's clear that that there are different kinds of knowledge just as there are different kinds of belief. Perhaps the most important distinction for philosophy is between facts and opinions – or to use some often heard jargon, between objective and subjective claims:

✔ *Objective claims* are about things 'out there' in the world that you know about through sense perception, through experience and through measurement. This is what philosophers call *empirical knowledge*.

✔ *Subjective claims* are based on things like your personal opinions, your values, your judgements and your preferences. These are the claims that give your life purpose and meaning, although, typically, philosophers ever since Plato have given subjective claims rather lower status than those supposedly objective ones.

Exploring the Physical World Around You

People often think of philosophers as being concerned only with ideas and abstractions, and leave the physical world to less brainy folk like, well, the scientists. And you can easily trace this prejudice (for that's what it is, really) back to the most important figure of ancient philosophy: Plato himself. But Plato didn't manage to persuade Aristotle, who spent nearly 20 years studying under him, that being only concerned with ideas was the case. Instead, Aristotle's method for obtaining knowledge was to start by looking around him both at the physical evidence and at the conventional opinion of the time (something his boss, Plato, particularly despised!).

One of Aristotle's most influential experiments was to decide whether the Earth was – or wasn't – fixed immovably at the centre of the universe.

Actually, 2,000 or so years ago, everyone said the Earth was flat and fixed in space. Why did they think that? Well (wouldn't you guess) it's because the philosophers had convinced them of it through their arguments. Now everyone says the Earth is a sphere whirling around the Sun. If you think this is right, you must count this at least as an example of how 'everyone' can be wrong. And it shows how incredibly influential philosophy can be, *for good or bad*.

But in fact, there'd been some debate about all this amongst the ancients, with one, Archimedes, noting (in *The Sand Reckoner*) that he'd heard a chap called Aristarchus had brought out a book consisting of certain hypotheses including amazing notions like these:

✔ The stars and the Sun are motionless.

✔ The Earth rotates around the Sun in a circle, with the Sun lying in the middle of its orbit.

✔ The distance from the Earth to the fixed stars is enormous.

Aristrachus's book, however, lost out in the battle of ideas, even if his moving Earth theory was influential enough for a former boxer called Cleanthes, who, amongst other things, was the head of the Stoics in ancient Greece (the Stoics were a group philosophers whose name has ended up in everyday language meaning people who are good at enduring pain!). Cleanthes recommended the prosecution of Aristarchus on . . .

> . . . the charge of impiety for putting in motion the hearth of the universe [and] supposing the heaven to remain at rest and the earth to revolve in an oblique circle, while it rotates, at the same time, about its own axis . . .

Happily, Aristarchus was never prosecuted, although his book seemed to disappear. Instead, it was the muddled theory of another lot of ancient philosophers – the Pythagoreans – that had both the Earth and the Sun orbiting a 'central fire' that had to challenge the everyday impression that humans lived on a motionless rock which the heavens and Sun whirled around. Plato was very influenced by the Pythagoreans, and even hints (in the *Timaeus*) at the then rather racy idea that the Earth might be rotating on its axis.

Testing whether the Earth is moving

Aristarchus's idea that the Earth might move was clearly catching on! Of course, you know that Aristarchus was right, and Cleanthes and everyone else down the centuries was wrong. The story of how philosophy led people to think that the Earth (and thus humanity itself) really was fixed immovably at the centre of the universe is a cautionary one.

It all comes down to a simple philosophical argument posed by Aristotle in a particularly rambling account called 'On the Heavens'. He starts by reminding his readers that those 'Pythagoreans' think

> . . . that at the centre there is fire, whilst the earth, which is seen as one of the stars, moves around it in a circle which produces night and day . . .

Then he quickly dismissing the idea as 'impossible'. You can see this, Aristotle explains, by considering the evidence of the eyes, notably that a rock thrown vertically upward falls vertically downward, rather than slightly to one side, as it would if the Earth was in any kind of motion. In fact, all objects instead behave in a similarly very sensible way and make no movements other than that diligent effort to return to the centre of the universe. For Aristotle this proved 'that it so happens that the Earth and the universe have the same centre', and he deduced the Earth must be not only motionless in space, but also motionless on its axis.

Of course, rocks (and other things) do fall straight down – but not for the reason Aristotle gives. It's to do with momentum – but that concept hadn't even been invented then! This illustrates the important philosophical principle that what you observe depends not just on what's 'out there' (the facts) but on what's 'in there', in your head – that is, what you observe depends on your concepts and yes, your beliefs too. This is an idea you keep coming back to in whatever part of philosophy you're looking into.

Suffice to say here, for the moment, that when (some 400 years later) the astronomer Ptolemy constructed his cosmological picture, the Earth was placed securely at the centre, immovable as a rock, just as it appears to be in ordinary life. And there it remained for thousands of years until another philosopher–astronomer, Galileo, stirred things up by arguing the opposite.

It might seem easy to laugh at the people who put the Earth at the centre of the universe and made the Sun and the stars trot obediently around it, but in many ways this is the sensible way to proceed. After all, consider for a moment your own position in the universe. One minute ago where were you exactly? In the same place? Perhaps if you're on a train you might (cunningly) say, 'No, I was a 20 kilometres away!' But if you're instead sitting quietly somewhere, it seems odd to say, 'Why, I was 100 kilometres away due to the Earth's rotation spinning me around.' And stranger still, you could say, 'Why, I was 1,000 kilometres away due to the Earth's rotation around the Sun.' And that's leaving aside the solar system's rotation around the centre of the galaxy and the galaxy's headlong rush away from the original site of the Big Bang!

In fact, over the centuries, this Earth-centered model proved itself a valuable tool for ships and navigators, and even for predicting celestial phenomena, such as eclipses. Indeed, scientifically speaking, to make sense of planets circling the sun you have to accept all sorts of strange ideas to do with what the great 20th-century physicist Albert Einstein described as heavenly objects falling through 'curved space time' – not in itself an immediately commonsensical supposition!

You can read more about some of Aristotle's impressive and not so impressive conclusions in Chapters 4 and 8, but the idea that real knowledge has to be ultimately based on sense perception wasn't just Aristotle's. One of Britain's most sensible philosophers, John Locke, writing in the 17th century in England, held equally sensible views. The sensible son of a sensible, middle-class family of Somerset merchants, he was particularly influenced and impressed by the new discoveries in natural philosophy (which is what we now call physics) – especially those of his fellow Englishman Isaac Newton.

How Newton's philosophy shapes our world

Isaac Newton's great idea was that the physical world is made up of lots of objects bouncing around and hitting each other – reacting to forces like momentum and gravity. Everyone knows his invention of a new – gravity – to explain why apples fall from trees. It's hard to think how people managed without gravity before him! Yet, pause a minute and you'll see that the idea is really rather odd, because gravity acts instantaneously, invisibly and across vast empty voids of space. It's philosophy, not science, that comes up with stuff like that.

One of Locke's common sense views was that you gather 'all the materials of human knowledge' (that is, all the facts and opinions you share about the world and how it works) from the world around you via sense perception, or indirectly from the same sources via your internal, mental world through *introspection* – that is, by thinking about (or half remembering) things you've seen, smelt or tasted earlier. But is that right? You can take a look at some reasons to think knowledge gathering isn't that simple after all in Chapters 10 and 11. But for Locke, it's all plain sailing. He believed your brain is a kind of blank tablet of wax on which external objects continually make marks. Locke puts it this way:

> *All those sublime thoughts which tower above the clouds, and reach as high as heaven itself, take their rise and footing here; in all that great extent wherein the mind wanders in those remote speculations it may seem to be elevated with, it stirs not one jot beyond these ideas which sense or reflection have offered for its contemplation.*

Locke's ideas have been influential. For example, look at the distinction he made between primary and secondary qualities:

- ✔ The *primary* qualities are somehow fundamental and inseparable from the object, being solidity, extension, figure, whether the object's at rest or in motion, and number.

- ✔ The *secondary* qualities, on the other hand – colours, smells, sounds and so on – are 'in truth', as Locke puts it in Book II of his philosophical classic, the Essay on Human Understanding, nothing in the objects themselves but merely 'powers to produce various sensations in us'. A secondary quality of fire, for example, is that it produces pain. (Under certain circumstances; it may be warmth under others.) Pain isn't an essential part of fire, nor is (wait for it, philosophers *adore* this example!) being white an essential part of being snow.

Secondary qualities are prone to error, due to blue spectacles, a cold or whatever. (Hey, everything looks blue today, and my apple crumble doesn't smell right . . .) But as another Great Briton (Irish, to be precise), Bishop George Berkeley, soon pointed out, you can say the same of the primary qualities, like size and weight. For example, objects can seem smaller when further away, or a bag can feel heavier when you're tired.

The bishop's aim was to remind people that common sense is often wrong. Nevertheless, Locke's view that the physical word consists only of matter in motion became the accepted basis of theories of sound, heat, light and electricity. And even today, when quantum mechanics works on completely different principles, much of people's understanding follows his way of thinking, wrong (based on false beliefs!) or not.

Looking for Locke's Sock

But common sense only goes so far.

John Locke recognised this when he proposed a scenario regarding a favourite sock that develops a hole. He pondered whether the sock would still be the same after a patch was applied to the hole. If yes, then would it still be the same sock after a second patch or even a third was applied? Indeed, would it still be the same sock many years later, even after all of the material of the original sock had been replaced with patches?

The sock problem worried him, at least a bit, because if the sock was the same despite all those practical changes, it could only be because something above and beyond the physical 'sense perception' sock existed, defined by its location in space and time.

Reading Locke's theory not long afterwards, Berkeley wrote (in the *Principles of Human Knowledge*) that

> . . . *upon the whole, I am inclined to think that the greater part, if not all, of those difficulties which have hitherto amused philosophers, and blocked up the way to knowledge, are entirely owing to ourselves – that we have first of all raised up a dust and then complain that we cannot see.*

It was in a bid to dispel some of this 'philosophical dust' that the good bishop came up with one of the weirdest, most quoted – and least understood – philosophical theories of them all. He devised the doctrine that *esse est percipi* ('to be is to be perceived'). In other words, material objects – everything in the world around you – exists only through being perceived by conscious beings. To the objection that in that case a tree in a forest, for instance, would cease to exist when no one was around, he replied that God always perceived everything. In his opinion, this was a clinching argument, but then he *was* a bishop.

Being mystical with Bishop Berkeley

George Berkeley's best writings are dialogues in the style of Plato, and he wrote them while still in his 20s. In a book called *Dialogues of Hylas and Philonous* (published in 1713) his argument against the scientists and their world of dull, inert matter is set out best. The book starts with two blokes arguing in a 'talking to the taxi driver' style: Hylas, who sounds like a 'cabbie' and speaks up for scientific common sense, and Philonous (like a hapless passenger), who puts forward Berkeley's own view. After some amiable remarks in the manner of Plato and Socrates, Hylas says he's heard that his friend holds the view that there's *no such thing as matter.* Can anything be 'more fantastical, more repugnant to common sense or a more manifest piece of scepticism, than this', he exclaims!

Philonous tries to explain that sense data are in fact mental, as is shown by the everyday experience of lukewarm water. Put a cold hand in the water and it appears warm; put a hot hand in it and it appears cold. Hylas accepts this point, but clings to the reality of other everyday cases of sense experience. Philonous then says that tastes are either pleasant or unpleasant, and are therefore mental, and the same can be said of smells.

Hylas valiantly rallies at this point, and says that sounds don't travel through a vacuum. From this, he concludes, they must be 'motions of air molecules', not mental thingumajigs, as his friend is trying to persuade him. Philonous responds that if this is indeed real sound, it bears no resemblance to what he knows as sound, so in that case sound may as well the mental phenomenon after all! The same argument fells Hylas when it comes to a discussion of colours, when he realises that they too disappear under certain conditions, such as when you see a golden cloud at sunset but close up it's just a grey mist.

Even something like size varies depending on the observer's position. Here, Berkeley's convenient straight-man, Hylas, obligingly tries to defend common sense by saying that you should distinguish the object from the perception, allowing that maybe the act of perceiving is all in the mind, but that a material object still exists out there. Philonous quickly pounces, replying: 'Whatever is immediately perceived is an idea: and can any idea exist out of the mind?' In other words, the perception, say of a tree, exists only in the mind – not 'out there'. Even Hylas's brain, Philonous cheekily suggests, 'exists only in the mind'!

Are colours real?

For philosophers at least, there are (at least) two fairly tricky problems about colour. One is whether it really is 'out there', or is only 'in here'? Is it in the mind of the beholder, or made up of little electromagnetic vibrations? Anyway, what difference exists between a real sensation of colour and an imaginary one? (Are the grey blobs in the image below, known as *The Grid Illusion* real or imaginary?) Not to forget colour-blind people who see green as red, and animals, which hardly see colours at all. Worse still, what's true of colours is also true for all the other sense perceptions, even if John Locke *et al* have tried to mark colour off as a special case of unreliable knowledge.

Berkeley's own conclusion is that compelling, logical grounds exist for concluding that the physical world is an illusion and only minds and mental events really exist. However, if you're beginning now to think this is all just too mad to take seriously and it's better to stick to science, you might be interested to hear that the 20th century's greatest scientist Albert Einstein himself explained (in 1938) that he'd come to realise that:

> . . . *physical concepts are free creations of the human mind, and are not, however it may seem, uniquely determined by the external world.*

Einstein went on to offer his own metaphor of a ticking watch to explain the problem of making sense of the world:

> *In our endeavour to understand reality we are somewhat like a man trying to understand the mechanism of a closed watch. He sees the face and the moving hands, even hears its ticking, but he has no way of opening the case. If he is ingenious he may form some picture of a mechanism which could be responsible for all the things he observes, but he may never be quite sure his picture is the only one which could explain his observations. He will never be able to compare his picture with the real mechanism and he cannot even imagine the possibility or the meaning of such a comparison.*

In fact, as Einstein says, the only way to approach the core truths of reality is through philosophy. The world really is more complex than people normally think it is. It's not just the philosophers creating mysteries.

Chapter 2

Discovering Why Philosophy Matters

> *'And what, Socrates, is the food of the soul?'*
>
> *'Surely,' said Socrates, 'knowledge is the food of the soul.'*
>
> – Plato

*U*ntil late in the 18th century, what we now call science was merely a branch of philosophy, the philosophy of nature, studied by people like Copernicus, Kepler, Galileo, Bacon and Descartes. Nowadays, only the last two of these feature in philosophy books, and the first three are called astronomers – but they all did a bit of both.

Equally (if confusingly) what people then called 'science' they now call philosophy, or 'knowledge of what's necessarily true'. Indeed, in many ways science only began with Isaac Newton, who as well as making several excellent discoveries drew up a new system of ways to categorise and name things that was in its way as influential as Aristotle's 2,000 years earlier. It's because of Newton that today the world has not only 'physiks' (as Newton spelt it) but science too.

Laying the Foundations for Science

The central assumption of science is that the world follows rules that you can investigate and identify. The most important of these rules is that of cause and effect. The world is orderly and consistent, and people assume that identical conditions will produce identical outcomes. But all this is really philosophical theory. The idea is that when you identify a rule or law of nature, you can make accurate predictions. The prediction of such phenomena as the appearances of comets and tides was regarded as a great achievement of applied philosophy.

Thales gets his hands dirty

One of the things people like to say about philosophy is that it seems to offer a chance to get away from the dreary detail and the disappointing reality of the everyday world. People often use the word that way – they say points are more philosophical than practical, or that someone who's ignoring some misfortune is being philosophical. And if you read their books and articles, you'll think that today's paid philosophers in universities are almost entirely preoccupied only with abstract ideas and obscure distinctions. But philosophy's roots were firmly in the everyday world – the natural world – and the Ancient Greek philosophers were clear that they were talking not just about abstractions but were trying to really get to grips with reality and understand practical matters.

A good example of this ancient taste for applied philosophy is Thales. Thales lived around 2,500 years ago in what's now Turkey, and is often described as the first 'true' philosopher (although that is a rather debatable claim). But he certainly has the honour of being counted by later writers as one of the Seven Wise Men of the Ancient World, admired in particular for his mathematical and astronomical wisdom, which he put to good, practical use.

Amongst his achievements was predicting the eclipse of 585 BCE, which left the region in almost total darkness and, what's more, took place during a battle – doubtless confusing soldiers' aims in mid-hack. Another feat, recounted by Aristotle, tells how Thales once used philosophy to predict a good growing season and then hired in advance all the olive presses in Miletus. When indeed there was a bumper crop of olives that year, he was able to rehire the presses out at a considerable profit.

But philosophers admire Thales less for his weather-forecasting and more for having pioneered the study of *essences*. In other words, he started the philosophical fashion for defining things by essential features, rather than by often misleading and unreliable surface appearances. Both Thales, and a bit later, Aristotle, shared a preference for identifying natural properties, rather than for creating grand new theoretical entities. For instance, Thales concluded that the essential quality of the world was water, and the essence of the human soul was its ability to act like a kind of magnet, exerting an invisible pull over the body and causing it to move.

Considering causation

Understanding what causes things isn't only the primary goal of scientific enquiry but is essential to philosophical theories of perception (how do you see?) and ethics. A related and very thorny question (that still perplexes metaphysicians) is how it can be that something non-physical like 'mind' can affect matter. Take free will, for example. Is someone *really* freely making a choice, say, to have a meal if her body chemistry is forcing her towards wanting something to eat? Or put another way – is someone on a diet really free to go without pudding if her body chemistry is *forcing* her to have some more apple tart!

No wonder one of the first philosophers, Democritus, said that he'd rather discover 'one true cause' than gain the kingdom of Persia! More recently too, Samuel Alexander (1859–1938) suggested that causation was the essence of existence itself, adding that 'to be real' is to have 'causal powers'. Like a witch!

The notion of *essences* is connected with the importance accorded by Plato and his followers to the search of the definitions of things. Thales and other ancient natural philosophers focused their efforts on working out the 'constitution' of things, that is, on what the world was *made of*. The constitution of the world was thought to explain the visible workings of the world. (There's more on this in Chapter 17). However, Plato tells a rather different story in the *Theaetetus*, one of his playlets, of a much less practical Thales. He describes the wise man as having been so busy staring up at the stars one evening that he fell down a well, where he was seen and laughed at by a passing Thracian serving girl! This is the caricature most people today have of philosophers. But it's a caricature – in fact, philosophical reflection is an inseparable part of life.

Philosophers running out of Time and finding Nothingness

Another important concept much debated by philosophers, that we'd certainly have trouble doing without is time. Because when you think about it (not that many of us normally do; too little time . . .), it *is* rather an odd thing.

In the words of the 20th-century writer, T.S. Eliot, there's something strange about time in that it consists of a 'pattern of timeless moments'. Everything hinges on that infinitely brief moment of the present, the fountain where the river of time gushes out of nothingness, producing the bottomless lake of the past. Events, having swum into being and floated away, are eternally real, and the future doesn't exist at all.

Plato rather poetically called time 'a moving image of eternity', which although rather nice as a phrase isn't very helpful. However, Aristotle discussed the nature of time in more detail, saying that time is the result of change in the material world. Since objects around you change in a smoothly continuous way (plants grow, have flowers, fade and die – and then start all over again), so, he deduced, time must also flow smoothly and continuously. Of course, as Plotinus, a Roman philosopher, pointed out a few centuries later, this definition of time involves reference to the thing being discussed in the process, a feature of a bad definition. (That is, Aristotle used the notion of 'change', which is by definition over time.)

Finding some space

If time remains a slippery creature then what about that other strange entity – space? Not outer space, particularly, full of stars and galaxies – just plain, empty space. Nothingness. The void. If philosophy of space is a neglected area of study in philosophy departments these days, it's had its important followers in the past.

Back in Ancient Greece, Democritus had said simply the void was what 'was not'. Aristotle said space was only a feature to be inferred from the presence of real objects. Plato, who as usual had the definitive word on this as on so many other matters, thought that space was a very special kind of thing, neither made of matter like the rest of the universe, nor entirely abstract like ideas and concepts. It was something in between. Or so says Socrates' friend, Timaeus, in the dialogue Plato named after him: 'an invisible and characterless thing, that receives all things and shares in a perplexing way all that is intelligible'.

The only way to investigate the properties of space is by 'a kind of *fatherless reasoning* (by *fatherless* Timaeus means that the thinking lacks any rational basis) that does not involve sense perception' – for example, through a dreamlike trance.

Exploring space with dream power

That's not the method that springs to mind for many researchers today! This method is generally avoided by other philosophers and indeed physicists up to (but not necessarily including) Einstein. Einstein got his best ideas while dreaming – or in the bath.

On the contrary, Descartes thought that pure reason was good enough to tell you about space. In fact, in the 17th century, at the start of the scientific age, Descartes proposed that space itself was really a kind of physical object, a real object made out of an unusual form of matter lacking any of the usual qualities of matter such as being solid or having dimensions.

Space-time

Our modern conception of space, based on Einstein's Theory of General Relativity, actually dispenses altogether with the elegant truths of geometry that so impressed the ancients such as Plato. Instead, his theory proposes that the geometry or curvature of space (or more precisely, space-time) depends on the bodies immersed in it. Confused? You will be!

Einstein proposed that although space is the raw material underlying reality, it's not independent and absolute but flexible and dynamic, enmeshed with time and relative. So you no longer think of space as being independent from time. Space and spatial relations are mere manifestations of space-time, depending on the point of view of the observer. Put another way, space is relative, but space-time is absolute: it's a *something*.

About a century later Immanuel Kant also thought that pure reason was the way to explore space, even if some of his findings – such as his theory that intelligent life existed on all the planets with the intelligence decreasing the farther out from the Sun you went – weren't very impressive. (But most of the other philosophers looking at the question also had their cosmic hobby horses.) However, Kant also had some rather more influential ideas. One was about whether space was fixed and absolute (providing a framework for the rest of reality), or subjective and relative (depending on what objects were in space and on any observer's point of view). Put another way, relative to the Sun and stars, the Earth goes around the Sun in a big circle. But relative to the Earth, the Sun and stars are the ones wheeling around. Is there anything in the universe that's not relative to something else?

Kant examined this question by imagining a universe consisting of just one thing – a glove. Nothing else exists. Now the crucial thing about gloves is that they're exactly the same if you measure them – they have four fingers and a thumb, and all the proportions are identical. But, as Kant says, although you can turn a glove around as much as you like, if it's a left-hand glove it always stays a left-hand glove. Try it out yourself with a glove! Kant's challenge is that in the universe that consists of just one glove it will still be possible to say whether it is one for a left hand or one for a right hand – or won't it? If Kant's right, then his thought experiment shows that at least *some* things aren't relative and dependent on other things or on the observer's point of view.

Yet Plato's original approach has outlived both Descartes' and Kant's versions of space as invisible but reassuringly permanent and fixed. That's because Plato's idea has elements of relativity in it. When objects are impressed onto the flux, as Plato puts it rather mysteriously (but in language that fits comfortably with bang-up-to-date notions like energy fields) it in turn changes, and in changing affects the objects again. 'It sways irregularly in every direction as it is shaken by those things, and being set in motion it in turn shakes them.' Matter acts on space and space acts on matter. Plato's idea is pretty much Einstein's Theory of General Relativity in a nutshell, 2,000 years before Einstein came up with his theory!

Zeno's space-time riddles

One of the most accessible philosophers of space and time was Zeno of Elea who lived in the fifth century BC, just in time to know Socrates (that is, a generation earlier than Plato). Zeno's philosophy was set out in a book that included all those funny stories that people still talk about. One of these stories was about an unlikely race between Achilles and a tortoise.

In the race, the tortoise has a head start. Achilles, the famous athlete, then runs to where the tortoise was, doubtless going very fast. But while he's doing this, the tortoise moves a bit farther on. So Achilles must run a bit farther too. But while he's doing *that*, the tortoise again moves on a little bit farther. In fact, to Achilles' amazement, it seems that no matter how fast he runs to where the tortoise was, he can never quite catch up.

Of course, reality isn't like that. But Zeno's point is that people's dearly held assumptions about space and time lead to contradictions and logical impossibilities. So people need to rethink some of their assumptions.

Getting to Know the Physical World

Naturally, philosophy isn't just about physical theories and understandings of space and time and the like – it's behind theories of biology and society too. Consider the influence of Darwin's Theory of Natural Selection, the biological theory that sees the world as a kind of battleground in which the fastest and strongest survive and the rest must perish. If you want to understand how science and philosophy are intricately tied up together, this is a great place to start.

This theory is so practical that it's rarely considered 'philosophical' at all nowadays. Indeed, in the US it's highly controversial for schools and colleges to even treat it as a theory rather than as absolute, incontrovertible fact. Yet theory it is, subject in the past to significant revision and likely (in the best traditions of science) to be amended and revised in the future too, or even thrown out completely! Equally, natural selection as a theory is more a testament to the power of philosophical ideas than to the power of methodical observation – although Darwin did also do excellent pioneering work in that area, hoping to provide evidence in support of his theory.

Imposing order on a disorderly world

Another part of the philosophical quest to make sense of the universe is the effort to discover the laws that govern it (or at least, the ones people think jolly well should govern it). These are called the laws of nature. They're supposed to be absolutely true, *ceteris paribus*.

Darwin (and Darwinism)

Charles Darwin (1809–82) was born in Shrewsbury, England, and his first love was rocks and chemistry, not biology. He became interested in how animals change after studying not-very-interesting marine invertebrates at Edinburgh University and went on to travel widely, discovering not only giant tortoises but what were to him curiously different kinds of human beings. He recorded his findings in his celebrated account *On the Origin of Species, by Means of Natural Selection or the Preservation of Favoured Races in the Struggle for Life* (1859).

In his work he used many examples of newly discovered or little-known species to try to expand on an already existing theory and demonstrate that related species had at some point had a common ancestor. His theory was that by a process of either successfully adapting to circumstances and therefore flourishing, or by failing to adapt and therefore dying out, the species slowly evolved into the myriad forms you see today.

Darwin openly extended his theory to cover the human race, challenging many of the assumptions of his time. He even included moral values as just another form of randomly generated behaviour whose effect was to improve the chances of species preservation. To some philosophers this application of the Theory of Natural Selection to human society and culture is inappropriate. But whether inappropriate or not, the theory certainly has often been so applied, and often for the worst motives. Hitler used it to justify his 'ethnic cleansing' in Europe, and as late as the 1970s the United States' government used it to justify sterilisation of American Indians.

'Set-er-what?' I hear you ask. *Ceteris paribus* is Latin for 'other things being equal'. All scientific laws have a 'ceteris paribus' clause implied.

Actually, debate exists over whether any laws of nature really exist. Newton certainly made up a few, such as the law of gravitation, which seemed to work, but this required a bit of creative invention on his part, notably the concepts of absolute space and absolute time. Without these, his theory of mechanics couldn't function.

Over in Germany, his contemporary rival, the polymath (know all) Gottfried Leibniz, mocked this approach (that of inventing things to make the theory work), writing to Newton's secretary, Samuel Clarke:

> *To conclude. If the space (which the author fancies) void of all bodies is not altogether empty; what is it then full of? Is it full of extended spirits perhaps, of material substances, capable of extending and contracting themselves; which over therein, and penetrate each other without inconveniency, as the shadows of two bodies penetrate one another upon the surface of a wall . . . The principle of the want of a sufficient reason does alone drive away these spectres of the imagination. Men easily run into fictions, for want of making a right use of that great principle . . .*

Nowadays, ever since Einstein's Theory of General Relativity, no one thinks Newton's 'fictions' really exist. Mind you, despite the name 'Theory of General Relativity', Einstein's aim still was (like so many of the philosophers) to impose order on the universe. He too started, after all, by making the speed of light the same everywhere and at all times, and his theory concludes by offering up a new theoretical entity called *space-time*. Space-time is just as absolute as anything in classical science.

Free will and determinism

Determinists think that events, including people's actions, don't happen by chance but rather are caused, or predetermined, by something already decided. The chain of events leads back until eventually you need a first cause, which people generally think is divine in character. The theory implies, of course, that the future is all decided. The Greeks had the notion of the *fates*, the white-robed personifications of destiny usually depicted as cold, remorseless and unfeeling old crones or hags (which is both sexist and ageist, but this is Ancient Greece).

However, Epicurus offered one glimmer of hope for people. He modified the atomism of Democritus to include the random undetermined swerve of the particles of life. But after Newton (in the 18th century) elegantly demonstrated that you could both explain and anticipate the mysterious movements of the cosmos by measurements coupled with mathematics, the universe was reduced, it seemed, to a clockwork toy and with it humanity again seemed to lose its freedom to act.

These days, quantum mechanics aims to explore whether there might really be something in Epicurus's swerve. But on the wider issues of determinism, the debate about what is and what is not really possible to do otherwise remains firmly a philosophical question and not a scientific one.

Inventing Systems and Logic

The rise of Greek philosophy was carried skywards on the wings of mathematics, so to speak, and mathematics has continued to fascinate philosophers ever since, not least the efforts of the logicians to reduce human thought to a kind of symbolic notation. Pythagoras taught that all learning was ultimately about numbers, and Euclid's *Elements*, in which he sets out definitions and axioms to demonstrate a wealth of geometrical facts, became for 1,000 years the shining example of pure knowledge so desired by philosophers.

Euclid sets the rules out

Euclid invented not so much geometry but a mathematical system for proving claims. As such, he's responsible for a lot of suffering in school classrooms.

Euclid's axioms, based on Egyptian theories, offered just five necessary assumptions upon which you could build a pretty good geometry:

✔ Things that are equal to the same thing are equal to one another.

✔ If you add equals to equals the wholes are equal.

✔ If you subtract equals from equals the remainders are equal.

✔ Things that coincide with one another are equal to one another.

✔ The whole is greater than the part.

If you don't think much of these, you won't like the formal proofs a whole lot either! But Euclid's approach of setting out his assumptions, then demonstrating why some mathematical claims were true, line by painful line, was *very* attractive to many subsequent philosophers – not to mention all subsequent school maths teachers.

The Greeks imagined Euclid's geometry to be the exemplar of pure knowledge, with its inviolable rules such as 'parallel lines never meet' and 'the angles of a triangle always add up to 180 degrees' and so on. Yet Euclidian geometry is really just one possible kind of geometry and you can look at things in other ways so that parallel lines *do* meet and the angles of a triangle add up to rather more than 180 degrees. Think about flying around the Earth, for example. The angles of triangles drawn on a globe do add up to more than 180 degrees, and two planes flying parallel courses run a considerable risk that they'll eventually collide!

The facts of mathematics aren't so certain after all. Philosophers with mathematical interests, such as Henri Poincaré, have accepted that not only are the many different geometries possible, but they're mutually incompatible and impossible to choose between other than by convention.

The Greek word *axioma* literally means 'worthy of respect', and axioms claim to be that. Logic, mathematics and philosophical arguments in general all rely on certain underlying assumptions without which no progression can occur. Unfortunately, these assumptions are often anything but certain.

Take numbers, for example. What are those silly things? You can't touch them, see them, let alone eat them . . . Well, it seems that the first numbers people wrote down were the positive integers, I, II, III, IIII, IIIII derived from heaps of pebbles or marks on sticks, expressed only later in Arabic notation as 1, 2, 3 and so on. Positive integers are very useful and practical for keeping records, such as how many sheep you have, and for measuring out fields and buildings. The Egyptians and Mesopotamians soon complicated things by deciding that they needed fractions, also called *rational numbers*, with the inevitable consequence that not long afterwards Pythagoras and his followers discovered the *irrational numbers*. These are numbers you can't express exactly either as a fraction or as a decimal no matter how long you let the number run on, such as the square root of two. Legend has it that a member of the school was drowned for revealing the existence of such untidy numbers to the horrified public.

Mathematics couldn't advance much before the invention of zero, which is indeed a strange number. It was Indian mathematicians who systematised its use around the seventh century, and shortly afterwards it became possible to work with negative numbers and even the first *imaginary numbers* (the square root of a negative number is called an imaginary number). Newton and Leibniz conjured up numbers so small you can't express them (*infinitesimals*), in order to create the mathematics of calculus. And the manipulation of infinity, soon split into countable and uncountable varieties, took place in the 19th century largely as a result of the work of another mathematical philosopher, Georg Cantor.

Most of Zeno's paradoxes (see the earlier sidebar on Zeno) and quite a lot of the philosophy of space and time involves number theory. And just as Zeno challenged the assumptions of his time with his paradoxes of motion, much of the orthodoxy of modern philosophy and mathematics rests on certain agreed numerical conventions that are certainly not as ancient or indeed perhaps as inevitable as people have become accustomed to thinking. For example, in maths the number of points on a line is always the same, no matter how long the line is! In physics, motion is a complicated mix of three things: position, time and place, the exact recipe for which is still not settled.

The laws of thought

Western philosophy to a very large extent has been founded upon laws of thought. People believe that their thinking should strive to eliminate ideas that are vague, contradictory or ambiguous, and the best way to accomplish this, and thereby ground your thinking in clear and distinct ideas, is to strictly follow laws of thought.

So what are the laws of thought? They're logical rules like:

- ✔ The law of identity (A equals A).
- ✔ The law of non-contradiction (A does not equal not-A).
- ✔ The law of the excluded middle (either A or not A but not both A and not-A).

Phew! What an indigestible intellectual recipe! But put another way, the laws are saying:

- ✔ All apples are apples.

- ✔ If something isn't an apple, then you can't consider it to be an apple.

- ✔ Something can't both be an apple and be 'not an apple' at the same time.

In spite of how little these laws of thought seem to say, they've not been without their critics, and philosophers from Heraclitus to Hegel have lev-elled powerful arguments against them. Going back to their origins, it was Parmenides, one of the pre-Socratic philosophers in the fifth century BC, who first dreamt up the law of non-contradiction: 'Never will this prevail, that what is not is.' Plato noted this view in his dialogue the *Sophist*: 'The great Parmenides from beginning to end testified . . . "Never shall this be proved that things that are not are." ' Say again? Certainly. Something can't both be an apple and be 'not an apple' at the same time.

It may seem strange that the principle of non-contradiction needed invent-ing, but it seems that before Parmenides the natural way of thinking *was* that everything was a bit of both. As Heraclitus put it: 'Cold things grow warm; warm grows cold; wet grows dry; parched grows moist.'

Making everything a bit of both made sense for Heraclitus because he thought that in order for something to be able to change, it had to already contain within it the seeds of what it would become. For example, water isn't hard like a rock, but it's hard when it becomes ice. Thus water is both hard and not hard, depending on the temperature. However, Plato and Parmenides had their sights on better things than earthly water – they wanted to talk about the 'true' water, essence of water. And that assuredly is wet and watery and not hard.

Searching for 'real' knowledge with Plato

The Pythagoreans, the ancient school of philosophers, also thought that true knowledge had to be about things that didn't change. They wanted objects of thought that were pure, fixed and eternal. And they thought they'd found them in the abstract world of mathematics. The Pythagoreans worked out the essential qualities of the numbers from zero to ten with religious zeal, decid-ing that nothing could stop one from being about wholeness, two from being about duality and so on.

It was their notion that numbers existed in a parallel, higher reality that inspired Plato to seek similar 'perfect and unchanging' entities in the abstract world of the forms (or ideas). In fact, in the *Republic*, one of his most cele-brated dialogues, Plato has Socrates firmly pronounce: 'It is obvious that the same thing will never do or suffer opposites in the same respect in relation to the same thing and at the same time.' Thus, Plato put his very considerable authority behind two more of the laws – the laws of non-contradiction and of excluded middle.

Don't ask what philosophy is 'for'

A story told of Plato reveals him as both harsh and dogmatic, but also idealistic. Asked by a student to explain the practical application of the courses he was being taught, Plato instead simply instructed another boy to give the student a small coin 'so that he might appreciate better the value of the knowledge' – and then threw him out of the school!

But Plato's no fool. He understood the problems with the laws in practice. In another of his dialogues, this time the *Euthydemus*, Dionysodorus (think *dinosaur*) mocks one of the laws by saying that if it were true, then Socrates must be the father of a dog! This is how he 'proves' that.

1. **According to the laws of thought, something can't be both a particular thing and not that thing (be both A and not-A) at the same time.**

2. **Socrates is a father.**

3. **The dog has a father.**

4. **Something can't both be a father and not be a father at the same time.**

5. **Conclusion: Socrates must be the father of the dog.**

Actually, in case you're wondering, Socrates wasn't the father of the dog, but that's where the laws take you. It's not obvious quite where the flaw is either. Plato attempts to sort it out by saying that the law is correct, but in our earthly reality objects are all tangled up. So the problem here is that the type of father Socrates was is different from the type of father that the dog had. Two kinds of father, in short. Messy, though.

The search for essences

Like Plato, Aristotle believed in the laws of thought, and considered them to provide solid foundations for all right thinking. He tried to tidy the laws up a bit and make them more rigorous so that they only applied to certain contexts and certain times. He suggested a new way of thinking about the different kinds of things in the world – like the different kinds of animals – which involved a better grasp of their elusive essences. In fact, about a quarter of Aristotle's writing seems to have been concerned with categorising nature, in particular animals. Man, in Aristotle's mind, is a particular kind of animal – a rational animal, because a person is a kind of an animal, and what's unique about a person is their rationality. Well, that's what Aristotle thought. In fact, many people would say animals are often rational too – they know what's in their interests and use this knowledge to run away from predators or make little shelters – and so you need a different essence. (Some have said that man is a *moral* animal, for example.)

With the development of machines in the 17th century, and the philosophical fashion for seeing the universe in such terms, the search for these essential characteristics took a slightly different direction. In his *Essay Concerning Human Understanding*, John Locke takes up the question again of essences using the example of a strawberry.

What's important about strawberries? A nice taste? A bright red colour? Their scent? But Locke wouldn't have any of that. He thought the important characteristic about a strawberry shouldn't be anything to do with how it tastes, or its colour, or its smell, because all these things are *subjective* – that is, they depend on the viewer. Some people think strawberries smell sweet and tasty; others might think they smell like sour grapes. On the other hand, the shape of the strawberry (minus its colour) Locke thought was *objective* – everyone should agree on its shape.

The inflexible logic of the laws of thought thus brought philosophers to try to create a new kind of world in which they could have undisputed authority and rule. But what sort of world was it?

Understanding the mysterious forms

Plato's Theory of Forms is one of the most important ideas in the history of philosophy. Strange, though, that it's not really very well understood. Or maybe that's why it's so influential.

The best way to come to terms with the theory is to realise that Plato was saying people are aware of two kinds of reality:

- ✔ One that's shifting and imprecise, which is the world of things around you conveyed by sense impressions.

- ✔ One that's fixed and eternal, if also rather imprecise, which is your concepts or ideas.

Plato uses many examples to try to explain this, but perhaps beauty is the easiest one to get a handle on. You may see many beautiful things – say flowers or some wooded hillsides – but inevitably, these 'real' things are imperfect. The flowers wilt, and the hillside has a power line running across it. And anyway, what do the two things have in common; what is it that makes them beautiful? So Plato says you have to have in mind something separate to which you compare the sense impressions, something that you see – Plato prefers to say *recognise* – in both the flowers and the hillsides. This is the quality of being beautiful. Plato calls it a *form*, but sometimes people refer to it as an idea or a concept. But the one thing for sure about the form is that it doesn't exist in any everyday, material sense – it's only in an eternal realm which can be accessed only by reason, or what Plato calls *intellection* or *noesis*.

Plato on maths

Above the doorway to Plato's Academy was famously written: 'Let no one ignorant of mathematics enter here'. For that reason, the story (in the *Meno* dialogue; see Chapter 3 for an extract) of Socrates teasing out Pythagoras's theorem from an apparently ignorant slave boy is an important social comment. It offers a more subtle, inclusive definition of educational competence, demonstrating that even a slave who'd never been to school was born with important mathematical concepts imprinted in his mind!

Plato's dialogue the *Timaeus* echoes this perspective, with five geometrical shapes – or solids – representing the four elements of fire, air, water and earth, plus the universe, taken as a whole. The Greek astronomers made plenty of observations (without, of course, telescopes) but they assumed the heavens were to exhibit the geometry of the gods, which was why it was necessary to insist on the stars and planets circling the Earth on perfect crystal spheres, making music as they turned (that's where the phrase 'the music of the spheres' comes from) long after observations undermined the hypothesis.

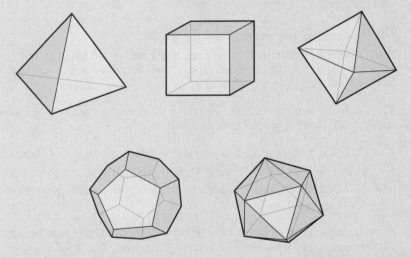

But here too Plato deplores the fact that 'the great mass of mankind' regard geometrical and mechanical descriptions of phenomena 'as the sole causes of all things'. For such causes are 'incapable of any plan or intelligence for any purpose'. He believes he must seek the deeper truths in the mysterious, parallel world of the forms.

What's the point of things that don't exist in any material sense but only in this airy-fairy way? Aren't scientists doing very well without such things? But in fact, they're even more reliant on these imagined entities to bind together and make sense of everything than everyone else. Ideas like time and space, and mathematical concepts like numbers or infinity are all as mysterious and directly unknowable as anything in Plato's strange parallel universe of the forms.

Western intellectual history has been intent upon creating an understanding that's founded upon universal laws. In order to create such universal laws, people have attempted to eliminate all objects of thought to which such laws don't universally apply. And that is itself irrational because there often are exceptions to even our very shiniest, bestest rules. For example, the rule that the same cause always results in the same effect does not really apply to events in both science and social life. Take a doctor who successfully treats a patient with cancer with a course of aspirin – this would be an example of the 'placebo effect', because aspirin does not really cure cancer, but just the psychological boost of being given some pills (research has often confirmed) can make people better! Things like the Placebo effect are 'irrational', yes, but real.

In the 18th century the laws were still causing the philosophers so many problems that Immanuel Kant was prompted to publish 'An attempt to introduce the concept of negative quantities into science'. In his book, Kant tried to identify internal contradictions in several very abstract, very metaphysical theories derived from pure logic (that is, theories dealing with things that could never be seen or measured). Essentially, Kant points out that although in logic either A or not-A is true, in reality something can be both A and not-A. For instance, a body can be both in motion and not-in-motion because it depends who's looking at it. Trains today offer a good example of this. Sit on a train and put your cup of coffee on the table. To you, the cup isn't in motion. But to someone watching the train whiz past, it certainly is!

Hegel, Kant's German successor, also saw the problem, and returned to Heraclitus's position, which was that change, and in particular contradiction and conflict, was the true reality, and the static, unchanging world of the laws of thought was the false one.

Hegel even specifically attacked the law of identity, pointing out that the law says very little in itself. The fact is, he says, that 'A equals A' is no more than a tautology and has little meaning. (A *tautology*, after all, is the same thing said twice.) Knowing that something is *exactly* the same as something tells us almost nothing about it. The only way a thing truly takes on identity is through its *otherness* or *what it's not.*

Doubting Everything You Don't Know

Searching for certainty and looking for things you know for sure is an old preoccupation of philosophy. But so is running down everyone else's claims to know things.

Even during the heady days of Plato and Aristotle, the Greeks had always been sceptical, both about the knowledge they had (was it really any good?) and about the possibility of ever knowing things. Two schools, the *Sceptics* and the *Cynics*, became preoccupied with unsolvable riddles and paradoxes and started to teach that it was impossible to find truth. You can find more detail on the Sceptics in the nearby sidebar 'Scepticism and the Sceptics', and on the two schools in Chapters 7 and 10.

One of the most cynical of the Cynics was Diogenes (of Sinope – there were three famous Diogenes at this time) who tried to shock fellow Greek aristocrats out of their complacency by living life 'like a dog'. This involved wearing rags and sleeping in a wine barrel, and on one notorious occasion masturbating in the public square while explaining 'that life would be much better if only it were as easy to be rid of the desire for food by rubbing his stomach'! Other philosophical demonstrations involved standing in the cold hugging a bronze statue (in order to train his body to ignore cold), and provoking people to insult him in order to harden his emotions. All of this led Plato to call Diogenes a 'Socrates gone mad', by which he probably implied a little bit of a criticism of Socrates too.

But the greatest doubter of them all in philosophy is undoubtedly René Descartes, 2,000 years later. Descartes says that in order to separate out real knowledge from unreliable hearsay, optical illusions and tricks by other people (including evil demons) you have to assume everything you're told, everything you see or hear and everything you can't be absolutely sure of is a trick. I look at some of his influential thought experiments to explore his doubts in Chapter 10.

But Descartes admits that he was only playing at doubting everything in order to find certainty. It was the Ancient Greek Sceptics who really specialised in doubting, and their conclusion was that no one can really be sure of anything at all. That's why they're called *Sceptics*. Descartes is famous because, at the moment when all human knowledge seems to have been reduced to mere optimistic guesses and convention, he brought forward with a dramatic flourish something that he said *is* absolutely reliable and certain – something you can really be sure of! This is the most famous titbit in philosophy probably (see Chapter 5 for plenty more on it).

Scepticism and the Sceptics

Scepticism derives from the Greek word *skepsis* for careful *consideration*, but nowadays scepticism implies not believing in things. The evidence of the senses has always been particularly suspect. Ancient Greek Sceptics such as Arcesilaus of Pitane and Carneades of Cyrene went so far as to say that you can't justify claiming knowledge about anything in the world, you can only make naive and optimistic assertions.

Another group of ancients known as the Stoics insisted that there *were* ways of dividing knowledge and sense data up and distinguishing arrant nonsense from well-founded evidence. But this was never the view of the true Sceptics. The debate carries on today in philosophy, with the conventional position being that knowledge is 'justified true belief'. Plato himself is pretty sceptical, offering many reasons for not believing in things, and specifically rejecting this view of knowledge.

Chapter 3

Becoming a Philosophical Thinker

As for me, I know that I know nothing. But others know still less.

– Socrates

So what is the secret recipe of the great philosophers? They're a mixed bunch, and there is no common route or method followed. Some raise up logic and rationality – other s decry all that as myth and illusion. Some are really scientists, who start with observations of the world, while others deliberately set all that aside and look inwards for insights. Plato had great contempt for the followers of 'common sense', although Aristotle considered it the essential starting point. In the eighteenth century, out of two more of the undoubtably 'great' philosophers, one, David Hume, used common sense to guide his celebrated enquiries, while the other, Georg Hegel, elaborately spurned it.

In this Chapter, I look at some of the ways philosophers use arguments, pose questions and explore puzzles as part of developing their ideas. In the process, I'll indicate the similarities and differences between Plato and Socrates' approaches, appreciate the importance of imagination in even the most 'abstract' thinking, and take note of some of the many intellectual pitfalls on the way.

Having a Philosophical Conversation

Ever since people started studying anything, let alone philosophy, a tension has existed between two different ways of approaching the search for knowledge. In Ancient Greece, the two competing approaches are summed up by the different styles of its two great foundational figures, Plato and Socrates. Confusingly, most people know Socrates through Plato's accounts of him, as the 'star' of his dialogues. But Socrates certainy did have his own views, and there are other historical sources describing his ideas, such as the writings of Xenophon (435–354 BCE).

Debating with Socrates

Socrates' style was that of the Ancient Greek Sophists who were experts in the arts of rhetoric, public speaking and debate. Unlike Socrates, the Sophists generally expected to be paid for sharing their skills, with their main market being well-off citizens hoping to improve their performance – either as politicians or lawyers – in the public assemblies that were a central feature of life in Ancient Greece. So Socrates method is a bit like that of a lawyer in court or a politician in a debate. He picks up the points his 'opponents' make, and expands on them, usually trying to show that they have ridiculous consequences, or conflict with something else that they have already said. Socrates himself often uses the analogy of combat sports (like boxing) for the practice of philosophical debate – through sparring, the aim is not really to hurt the other person, but to improve their defences and raise their skills. The best outcome for Socrates is when the pupil can outfox the master!

Another important aspect to the *Socratic Method* is that what is said is not so important as how it is said – the debate is not concerned with particular facts or cases (thought they may be raised) but is free-flowing and essentially unpredictable in terms of what topics may or may not come up. The Sophists, and Socrates, did not have much use for reading and writing, but valued quickness and agility in speaking. Socrates, as far as anyone knows, never wrote anything down, and indeed is supposed to have frowned on the practice, considering it to blunt the mind and make it lazy.

Another name for 'Socratic Method' is *elenchus,* which is one of those bits of Latin philosophers cling to, and yet another term used it *dialectical reasoning.* However, all of them describe the technique exemplified by Plato in his description of Socrates's debates with the other Athenians. The characteristics of it are that both parties on a joint quest for truth, with the inquiry proceeding by one person putting forward an idea, and the other person challenging it by suggesting a fault or problem with it. This obliges the first person to refine, or improve their original suggestion.

In medieval Europe, this sort of debate was very popular. Audiences eagerly watched skilled debaters tackling philosophical questions until one of the debaters contradicted himself, at which point the audience deemed him to have lost.

One example, from medieval times, is that of a debate over why a lance continues rushing through the air after someone throws it. The problem seemed to be that, after it has left the thrower's hand, the lance continues with nothing pushing it. Nowadays we are comfortable with the idea of *momentum* which says that things continue moving unless something stops them, but in the medieval period, Aristotle's influence made this problem controversial, as he said things stop moving immediately things stop pushing them. So in one debate an 'Aristotelian' tried to suggest that lances keep moving through the air (after they are released from the hand) because air molecules press harder on the blunt end than on the tip – creating a kind of push. The response to this was to simply ask the audience to imagine someone throwing a lance sharpened at both ends. Now the Aristotelian asks whether such a lance would be unable to fly and fall immediately to the ground instead, because clearly the air molecules would then press equally on both ends. And the argument, like the most best arguments, is both immediately comprehensible and and compelling. Modern day 'debates', by contrast are really pre-rehearsed speeches, in which questions are ignored in preference for delivering little potted speeches.

Imagining things with Galileo

Another way to use questions effectively to make your point, is to offer imaginary examples or 'thought experiments'. One of the most important in intellectual history were by the astronomer Galileo. Here, he effectively demonstrates just through the power of words and ideas the fundamental principal of relativity – that is that all motion is 'relative' to a stable background.

The aim of Galileo's ship experiment, set out in his *Dialogue Concerning the Two Chief World Systems*, (which you may not have heard of, but is actually one of the most important books in the history of science – and still quite fun to read!) was to explain why, if the world really is a sphere whizzing round on its axis in space, we are unaware of it. Back in 1632, the idea that we lived on rock hurtling around the Sun was still rather hard to swallow, and the now commonplace experience of smooth constant motion in one direction (for example, on a train, if not so much in a car) was still something of a rarity.

'Galileo's ship' illustrates that is only by stepping outside the 'local framework', that is, in this case, the ship, that we can make sense of claims about what is motionless and what is moving. To detect the motion of the ship, for example, we would have to look through the porthole at the receding cliffs, or the sun. To see the motion of the Earth itself, we must look at the night sky and the movement of the stars. (Of course, the cliffs might be shrinking, or the stars rotating on crystal spheres . . .)

The thought experiment has been resurrected in various similar forms subsequently by other physicists to make further useful intuitions about the nature of the universe. In 1907 Einstein realised that extending the same principles to a spaceship steadily accelerating would demonstrate in similar manner the impossibility of distinguishing between the push of constant acceleration and the pull of gravity, and hence arrived at the General Theory of Relativity.

Socrates and the art of philosophical conversation

In this extract from Plato's Republic, we see Socrates engaged in an unusually robust debate over the nature of Justice.

THRASYMACHUS: Behold! The wisdom of Socrates; he refuses to teach himself, and goes about learning of others, yet never even says 'thank you'!

SOCRATES: To say that I learn of others is quite true; but to say that I am ungrateful I wholly deny. I don't have any money, and therefore I pay people in praise, which is all I have:. How ready and willing I am to praise anyone who appears to me to speak well you will very soon find out when you answer; for I expect that you will give me a fine answer to my question.

THRASYMACHUS: Listen, then. I proclaim that justice is nothing else than the interest of the stronger. And now why do you not praise me? But predicatbably you refuse to.

SOCRATES: Well, let me first understand you. Justice, you say, is the 'interest of the stronger'. What, Thrasymachus, do you mean by this? You cannot mean to say that because Polydamas, the wrestler, is stronger than we are, and finds the eating of beef conducive to his bodily strength, that to eat lots of beef is therefore right and just for us?

THRASYMACHUS: That's abominable of you, Socrates; you take the words in the sense which is most damaging to the argument.

SOCRATES: Not at all, my good chap. I am trying to understand them; and I wish that you would be a little clearer.

THRASYMACHUS: Well, have you never heard that forms of government differ; there are tyrannies, and there are democracies, and there are aristocracies?

SOCRATES: Well, yes, I know all that.

THRASYMACHUS: And the government is the ruling power in each state?

SOCRATES: Certainly.

THRASYMACHUS: And that the different forms of government make their laws democratic, aristocratic, or tyrannical, depending on their calculation of their own particular interest; and that these laws, made by them for their own interests, are the 'justice' which they deliver to their subjects, and anyone who transgresses their laws they punish in the interests of what they call 'justice' And that is what I mean when I say that in all states there is the same principle of justice, which is the interest of the government. And as governments must be supposed to have power, the only reasonable conclusion is, that everywhere there is one principle of justice, which is the interest of the powerful.

SOCRATES: Now I understand you; but whether you are right or not I will still have to investigate a bit more to try to discover.

At this point, Plato has put a strong argument forward, and we wonder how Socrates will deal with it. Characteristically, Socrates does so less by addressing the 'issue' than by trying to make it look like his opponent has a view that is flawed by contradictions. Of course, this makes his opponent look silly too!

SOCRATES: Now we are both agreed that justice is interest of some sort, but you go on to say 'of the stronger'; about this addition I am not so sure, and must therefore consider further.

THRASYMACHUS: Proceed.

SOCRATES: I will; and first tell me, Do you say that it is justice when citizens obey their rulers?

THRASYMACHUS: I do.

SOCRATES: But are the rulers of states absolutely infallible, or are they sometimes liable to err?

THRASYMACHUS: To be sure, they are liable to make mistakes sometimes.

SOCRATES: Then in making their laws they may sometimes make them rightly, and sometimes make mistakes?

THRASYMACHUS: True.

SOCRATES: When they make them rightly, they make them to work in their interest; and when they are mistaken, they make them contrary to their interest; you admit that?

THRASYMACHUS: Yes.

SOCRATES: And the laws which they make must be obeyed by their subjects, – because that is what you call justice?

THRASYMACHUS: Doubtless.

SOCRATES: Then justice, according to your argument, is not only obedience to the interest of the stronger but obedience to that which is not in the interest of the stronger?

THRASYMACHUS: What is that you are saying?

SOCRATES: I am only repeating what you said, I believe.

Socrates wins – as usual. But notice the method – he asks questions, aiming to lead his 'opponent' into a contradiction.

(Salvatius explains the experiment in Galileo's elegant dialogue quoted in the nearby sidebar 'Galileo's ship'.)

Taking it step-by-step with Plato

In the extract below, drawn from one of Plato's dialogues called the *Meno*, after the main character in it, Plato has Socrates adopt a quite different style, in order to illustrate that certain knowledge is 'built in' to all of us, although we may need help to rediscover or 'recollect' it. No one knows whether Plato's version of these Socratic conversations is accurate, or just made-up to illustrate Plato's own views. But certainly the style here is much more of a lecturer or class-room teacher.

The important thing about it though, is that the learning is broken down into small steps, each of which has to be fully understood and accepted. The nearby sidebar 'Socrates and Plato give a geometrical demonstration'

Galileo's Ship demonstrates the Principles of Relativity

As part of a kind of 'Socratic conversation, Salvatius asks his friend to try a kind of 'thought experiment'.

'Shut yourself up with some friend in the main cabin below decks on some large ship, and have with you there some flies, butterflies, and other small flying animals. Have a large bowl of water with some fish in it; hang up a bottle that empties drop by drop into a wide vessel beneath it.

'With the ship standing still, observe carefully how the little animals fly with equal speed to all sides of the cabin. The fish swim indifferently in all directions; the drops fall into the vessel beneath; and, in throwing something to your friend, you need to throw it no more strongly in one direction than another, the distances being equal; jumping with your feet together, you pass equal spaces in every direction.

'When you have observed all of these things carefully (though there is no doubt that when the ship is standing still everything must happen this way), have the ship proceed with any speed you like, so long as the motion is uniform and not fluctuating this way and that. You will discover not the least change in all the effects named, nor could you tell from any of them whether the ship was moving or standing still. In jumping, you will pass on the floor the same spaces as before, nor will you make larger jumps toward the stern than towards the prow even though the ship is moving quite rapidly, despite the fact that during the time that you are in the air the floor under you will be going in a direction opposite to your jump. In throwing something to your companion, you will need no more force to get it to him whether he is in the direction of the bow or the stern, with yourself situated opposite.

'The droplets will fall as before into the vessel beneath without dropping towards the stern, although while the drops are in the air the ship runs many spans. The fish in the water will swim towards the front of their bowl with no more effort than toward the back, and will go with equal ease to bait placed anywhere around the edges of the bowl. Finally the butterflies and flies will continue their flights indifferently toward every side, nor will it ever happen that they are concentrated toward the stern, as if tired out from keeping up with the course of the ship, from which they will have been separated during long intervals by keeping themselves in the air. . . .'

From *Dialogues Concerning the Two Chief World Systems* (1632)

Plato's Academy

Socrates was certainly a great talker, but Plato, on the other hand, was both a great writer, and a keen 'lecturer', anxious to expound on his own theories and share his discoveries. He invented the 'Academy', a kind of college situated in a park just outside the city walls of Athens, which is often said to be the archetype of all modern collages of higher education. (It's where we get the term 'academic' from too.) In Plato's Academy, the main form of teaching was the lecture, which was listened to passively by the students. Plato's books are intended to be a kind of lecture notes.

Although they are all written as dialogues, many of the 'debates' are little more than monologues in which Socrates (confusingly, given Socrates rather different educational style!) is made the 'star', dispensing an expert view, and various points of view are only represented by other characters in order to be quickly dismissed.

In Plato's dialogue the *Republic*, teaching philosophy is placed at the top of a hierarchy of educational training, which starts in youth with physical activities (such as sport and also military training) and only ends up at philosophy by the time individuals are in their fiftieth year! The philosophy teacher is expected to still older, and indeed has something of the air of a 'greybeard' as the Chinese call them, or wise old sage.

Where Socrates hoped to improve the way people active in public life thought about issues, Plato aims to lead the 'best minds' away from practical concerns and point them instead at abstract philosophical truths. It is in no small part Plato's influence that has left education with a prejudice against practical skills and in favour of pure theory. Socrates' offers his skills for everyone, but Plato imagines contemplation of 'truth, beauty and goodness' to be possible only for a highly educated elite.

Blending the two approaches

Nowadays, universities contain elements of both Socrates' and Plato's educational philosophies. There are lectures, given by 'experts' accompanied by rote learning and memorisation – but there are also 'seminars' and opportunities for discussion and interaction. This pattern emerged in the Middle Ages, in medieval universities and has persisted ever since. However, over the centuries, there has been a steady shift away from *oracy*, in favour of *literacy*. Put another way, away from those skills of listening and speaking that Socrates held so dear, and towards the production of written material. Students of philosophy nowadays are expected to obtain all their most important ideas from books, and to 'learn them' by summarisation in the form of essays. Debate hardly comes into it. The consequence is that 'professional' philosophers are both oral debaters and writers of windy discussions of philosophical issues. At least, that is how philosophy is taught in universities. In schools, it is (happily) rather more active.

Of course, until the invention of the printing press, and indeed for quite a long time after, books were laboriously hand written and only for the libraries of monasteries and the most wealthy aristocrats. So philosophy had to be studies through debates and dialogue. But another shift in favour of Plato and away from Socrates is harder to explain by mere technological changes – the increasing emphasis on individual 'excellence' at the expense of co-operative activity and a shared search for answers.

Socrates and Plato give a geometrical demonstration

SOCRATES: I told you, Meno, just now that you were a rogue! Now you ask me to teach you something, even though my point is that there is people are not taught things, but rather helped to remember them. Doubtless you imagine that you will thus involve me in a contradiction.

MENO: Indeed, Socrates, I protest that I had no such intention. I only asked the question from habit; but if you can prove to me that what you say is true, I wish that you would.

[A slave boy is summoned . . .]

Socrates: Tell me, boy, do you know that a figure like this is a square?

Boy: I do.

Socrates: And you know that a square figure has these four lines equal?

Boy: Certainly.

Socrates: And do you agree that these lines which I have drawn through the middle of the square are also equal?

Boy: Yes.

Socrates: And that a square may be of any size?

Boy: Certainly.

Socrates: And that if one side of our square is two units and the other sideis also two units , how much will the whole be? Let me explain: if in one direction the space was of two units, and in other direction of one unti, the whole would be of two units taken once?

Boy: Yes.

Socrates: But since this side is also of two, there are twice two units?

Boy: There are.

Socrates: Then the square is of twice two?

Boy: Yes.

Socrates: And how many are twice two? count and tell me.

Boy: Four, Socrates.

Socrates: And might there not be another square twice as large as this, and having like this the lines equal?

Boy: Yes.

Socrates: And how many units will that be?

Boy: Eight.

Socrates: And now try and tell me the length of the line which forms the side of that double square: this is two what will that be?

Boy: Clearly, Socrates, it too will be double.

Socrates (*aside*): Observe, Meno, that I am not *teaching* the boy anything, but only asking him questions; yet already he knows how long a line is necessary in order to produce a figure of eight square feet; does he not?

Some of the most important differences between the two main approaches to turning ordinary folk into 'philosophical thinkers' are set out in Table 3-1.

Table 3-1	Two different approaches to philosophy	
	Active Learning	*The Academy*
Historical origins	The Greek Sophists demonstrating skills and having scientific debates	Plato's original Academy in Athens with Plato as the Head.
Teaching methods	Active learning through open-ended discussion – the so-called Socratic Method Students and teachers are equals, with no hierarchy Aim is for students and teachers to discuss and explore issues together.	Passive learning. Plato was In turn influenced by the secretive and monastic style of Pythagoras and his disciples, who are obliged to rote learn much-prized mathematical and philosophical truths – in complete silence. The focus is on individual progress.
Techniques	Conversation, discussion and arguments	Copying, memorisation and learning of methods and facts.

Peeking Inside the Philosopher's Mind

So what does go in in a philosopher's mind? Do they think differently from the rest of us – do they really see the world differently?

The first thing to appreciate about the great philosophers is that they are not so very different from the rest of us. They are egotists, they are dogmatic, they are plain ignorant. But to some extent they are people who have tried to rise above this common human inheritance, and to employ in their lives some powerful thinking techniques.

And if philosophical facts (who was Hegesias of Cyrene? What is the definition of a 'clear and distinct idea'?) are not in much demand anywhere – except in philosophy departments – philosophical skills are another matter. Table 3-2 shows some of those that philosophers *claim* to be capable of. We might have some doubts though!

Table 3-2	Philosophical Skills
Reasoning skills	*Social skills*
analysis and synthesis of concepts and ideas (breaking them down into little bits or alternatively putting fragments of ideas together to make new ones)	listening to and making sense of different points of view *(well, this is what philosophers claim to do . . .)*
identifying key ideas, and hidden assumptions	working co-operatively in teams, yet also being able to work independently
spotting flaws in reasoning or in the 'logic' of arguments	reflecting on their own ideas and assumptions
abstracting information, and identifying the structure of arguments	stepping back from issues and suggestions and placing them in a wider social and ethical context
inventing and thinking through tricky cases and 'counter examples' to test out ideas	

The Three 'As'

Another way to think of philosophical thought is as a set of tools. We might sum them up as the 'Three As':

- *Analysis* – breaking down complicated issues and examining the bits carefully to better understand the issue or the problem. When it works, it is a great tool capable of 'untying mental knots' and separating out what's important from what's not – from irrelevant clutter and side-issues.

- *Assessment* – particularly once an issue has been broken down into its constituent bits, philosophers also need to set about assessing and evaluating claims and choosing between rival and opposed explanations. Today's world is full of such rival claims and conflicting sources of information – we need to take special care in dealing with them.

- *Argument* – probably what most of us associate with philosophers. I know many examples of groups of professional philosophers failing to take simple decisions like where to go for a drink, because they can't help but turn it into an argument. But 'arguing' is where it's at, this is how ideas develop. And philosophical arguments should not be mere shouting matches, but rather occasions where people present clear reasons for their beliefs and demonstrate how conclusions either do, or (which is equally important to know) *do not* from their assumptions.

It's a lot easier though to teach people 'facts' than to teach people to think. Yet even if philosophy could be reduced to being about one set of historical-technical facts to be poured into students, (perhaps to enable them to pass the exam a month later) it would still be a very inefficient and counterproductive tactic to do it this way. Philosophers of education know, as research studies have often demonstrated, that in terms of learning, telling people is extraordinarily ineffective. Done the right way, philosophy can be a great antidote to the usual ways of both thinking and learning, which almost invariably involve passive listening as information is delivered. Consider this: after lectures, only five per cent of the information given out has been retained. That is, if their lecture is an hour long, only three minutes of it has been digested or taken in!

Even worse, much of it did not go in one ear and out of the other, it never went in at all. Much of philosophical conversation is like this: the ideas leave the speakers mouth and float directly up to philosophical heaven without being intercepted by any of the audience.

But what about if the speaker uses OHPs, little anecdotes, music, video clips, celebrity guests – *Philosophy For Dummies* books as aids? The evidence is that the best and most skilled speakers, teachers, lecturers, can raise the 'delivery' rate of their information to about 25 per cent. That means three-quarters of the time the audience are not following it or are asleep.

The reality is, only active participation has any chance of achieving more than 50 per cent retention or understanding of philosophical debates. So that is why the approach to philosophy centered around real questions, paradoxes, ethical dilemmas, personal issues, real world problems and mysteries, is more effective than philosophy as a collection of disassociated technical terms and historical trivia. Which, alas, is how it is almost universally taught, and yes, examined.

When fear stalks the philosophy classroom

Wittgenstein, that celebrated philosophical icon, once punched recalcitrant girl student, causing her nose to bleed, for failing to understand one of his points. That's an extreme example, but how often have I seen philosophical terms used as weapons to intimidate or even humiliate others? Fear indeed, used to stalk the lecture rooms of a certain university I was teaching in, when it was time for 'logic class'. In the huge lecture room, the students all crowded into the ten or so rows of seats furthest from the lectern, for fear of being 'picked on' by the lecturer and asked questions. Of course, the safest thing to do was to skip class entirely!

Real philosophers – like Socrates – always welcome different points of view.

The quality of questions

Even when a 'teacher' is leading a student through something which there is no debate really related to (like Socrates leading Meno and his servant boy through Pythagoras' famous theorem), the rights sort of question is a great help. They should be not too simple and not too tricky either, so that the student can share in a sense of discovery.

Sometimes the best sorts of questions are those which are open-ended and with the widest possible range of responses – not ones which the 'teacher' already know s the answer to! They're ones where the teacher or lecturer should also be able be surprised and finish the day with their view too changed.

That is why the best approach to philosophy is not as a body of knowledge, but is centred around questions and questioning. This, after all, was the style of Ancient Greek and Ancient Chinese philosophy, and lies at the heart of most of the great works of philosophy, from Plato's dialogues onward.

Perplexing people with paradoxes

The Ancient Greek's loved puzzles (such as the Liar, which essentially asks 'Can we believe someone who tells us that they lie all the time?' Not to forget Zeno's various efforts – mentioned in Chapter Two) which they used as starting points for debates about the great issues, and they are invariably to be found at the heart of the great works of philosophy. Plato and Descartes alike wrestled with the strange cases of things that seem to stay the same in one sense – but change radically in another. Like, say wax which loses its 'shape' so easily when it melts or water that looks very different when it either freezes or boils. These change their physical form yet we are happy to say they are stil the same thing – wax or water. Thinking about these odd cases encouraged both philosophers to suppose that 'mind' was more fundamental than physical matter. And other philosophers too have used riddles and puzzles to make their cases. The rather dry, and technical arguments of Kant include at their heart four puzzles or 'antinomies' and a similar kind of thing is at the heart of David Hume's sceptical philosophy.

True paradoxes – by their very nature – are irresolvable, but philosophers value them anyway, partly as 'exercises' and partly for their role in triggering new ideas. As Bertrand Russell once said: 'A logical theory maybe tested by its capacity for dealing with puzzles, and it is a wholesome plan, in thinking about logic, to stock the mind with as many puzzles as possible'.

Similarly, in ethics (see Chapter 13 for a detailed account), and more generally in defining terms and concepts, paradoxes can be employed to re-examine terms and definitions. Take, for example, the case of the captain of an overloaded lifeboat sinking slowly in the waves – is it his duty to throw one or two of the passengers overboard? The paradox is that if he does nothing he is responsible for everyone in the boat drowning, which is bad, yet if he acts he is still responsible for killing innocents which also seems pretty bad. In this case, some people might say the 'interests of the greater number' make a lesser evil acceptable, but others might argue that that certain principles and values cannot be compromised.

Many cases can be clarified by coming up with tricky cases – or *boundary cases,* as philosophers sometimes call them.

This, Schopenhauer explains, is due to our 'innate vanity, which is particularly sensitive with regard to our intellectual powers'. Of course, one way out of this conflict of interests is to ensure that our statements are well established and sound. But that, as Schopenhauer observes, would require people to think before they spoke. And as for most people "innate vanity is accompanied by loquacity and innate dishonesty", they must speak well before they think, and even if soon afterwards they begin to perceive that what they have just said is wrong, they will want it to seem the contrary. 'So, for the sake of vanity, what is true must seem false, and what is false must seem true.'

Searching for patterns in the data

One of the most interesting ideas of philosophy is that the world comes to us as a great flood of 'sense impressions', themselves meaningless, which we then have to sort out through intellectual means. Specialists in neuroscience (or the science of how brains work) agree these days – shapes, colours, smells, all are intricately connected to the way our brains work, so that when something goes wrong (say after a tree falls on someone's head) people can start to 'interpret the data' in the most bizarre ways. In a famous case described by Oliver Sacks, one man even began to have trouble distinguishing his wife from his *hat*. No, literally: he tried to put his wife on his head!

How can you confuse a person with a hat? It seems that both were round, and clothed in black cloth. Such cases highlight how the brain works, and it is much more of a matter for philosophers than commonsense might allow.

The Art of Being Right

'If human nature were not base', wrote the German philosopher, Arthur Schopenhauer, in his iconoclastic little book 'The Art of Always Being Right', 'we should in every debate have no other aim than the discovery of truth'. We should not in the least care whether finding the truth favours our position, or that of our adversary in debate. Whether we win or not, 'we should regard as a matter of no importance, or at any rate, of very secondary importance. Yet, as things are, it is the main concern'.

Today, not only philosophers but biologists and physicists assume that the conceptual structures that we call 'knowledge' are themselves constructed by active learners who shape their thinking in reaction both to what they experience – and what they think they experience. The world each of us perceives – for better or for worse – is unique to us. And the implications are more general than just individuals having problems doing particular things – like remembering facts or recognising people – or walking straight!

To become a philosophical thinker, we have to try first of all realise that everything we know, everything we see and everything we 'think we think', is mediated through a series of built-in, automatic mental processes, which in turn are affected by 'whatever is really out there'. This willingness to 'step back' from our values and beliefs is the first step towards arriving at new ideas and new insights.

Part II
The History of Philosophy

'Don't go out — it's that Darwin again.'

In this part . . .

Ah, *history:* that's always a good way to look at something that seems complicated. Because most things started off simple and then got steadily bogged down with extra details, complications and add-ons (call 'em what you will). But strangely enough, philosophy's not like that. It's been complicated and confusing from the word go! If you can understand what the Ancient Greeks were arguing about, then you can understand what the most recent philosophy scholars are doing now or – more like – trying to.

In fact, the history of philosophy is a lot more important than, say, the history of chemistry, or the history of film, or the history of history. The history of philosophy is also the absolutely bang-up-to-date subject matter of philosophy. Knowing what philosophers used to think and say is knowing what the present issues are, and many of what the possible arguments and strategies for dealing with the issues are too.

And in this part, having done the usual wander about the old stones in Greece, we make a special trip to the Far East to see how a lot of philosophical ideas *really* originated there. Then I draw a kind of philosophical map of those mind-blowing pieces of gobbledegook – the philosophical 'isms' to avoid exactly that: having our minds blown!

Chapter 4

Looking at Ancient Philosophies

• •

• •

The farther backward you can look, the farther forward you are likely to see.

– Winston Churchill

*P*hilosophy is a peculiar thing in that it doesn't really have a timeline – part of the charm of the subject is the timeless quality of the discussions. Where else would you study ancient texts, written by hippies and weirdos 3,000 years ago, with as much respect – indeed more – than the latest books top university professors churn out? Well, I suppose there *are* places, not to forget whole religions.

But philosophy is unlike religion and nearer to the sciences in that it does – sort of – build upon itself. And even if so many philosophical debates have no obvious answers, just possible viewpoints, it always makes good sense for philosophers to remember what people have said in the past. In this chapter, I cover what the ancients thought about life and the universe because it's a crucial starting point for later philosophies.

Laying the Groundwork with the First Greek Philosophers

One of the funny things about philosophy is that the further you go back in time, the more interesting it gets. Of course, there are two very practical reasons to start with the Ancient Greeks:

✔ They invented the word *philosophy*, if not exactly the activity.

   ✔ Almost all of later philosophy refers back to their debates.

The word *philosophy* comes from the Greek *philia*, for love, and *sophia*, for wisdom.

But it's important to remember the Greeks weren't the only people to ask the big questions that make up philosophy. Oddly enough, about the time the Greeks started philosophising in Europe, the Indians and Chinese were doing the same thing too. (You can check this out in Chapter 6.)

The Ancient Greeks, although certainly ancient, weren't really Greeks. In fact, they were scattered all around the Mediterranean, from Turkey to North Africa to Italy. But wherever the first European philosophers lived, they were all linked by the flourishing Greek seafaring culture. *Ancient Greece* is a term covering a substantially larger area than Greece today. And on their travels, the Greeks would also have come into contact with all the latest ideas and inventions from all round the world – such as geometry from the Egyptians, astronomy from the Persians and philosophy from the Far East.

The philosophers described in the following sections all lived before Socrates and – guess what! – they're known as the *pre-Socratic philosophers*. They often came up with theories that were both interesting and (in Anaximander's case) well ahead of their time, but most of their writings have been lost. Just 'fragments' remain. It isn't until Plato and Aristotle (a century or so later) that you begin to find fully documented philosophical works and debates.

Introducing Thales and his apprentice, Anaximander

One of the first Ancient Greek philosophers was Thales, a politician and geometer in the port of Miletus, which is in modern-day Turkey. As well as the clever money-making things (mentioned in Chapter 2), he established his credentials as a lover of wisdom by correctly predicting the eclipse of 585 BC (no one knows how!). Starting off a long trend in grand, unifying theories in science, he claimed that *everything* in the world (by which he meant the universe) was made of . . . water. It might not sound like a detailed philosophical theory, but it does show how philosophers were thinking about the world long before science even got started.

Another important early philosopher was Anaximander, a kind of apprentice of Thales. He's remembered for suggesting that people had evolved from fish – which puts him some 2,000 years ahead of Charles Darwin's better known theory about evolution!

Being enigmatic with Heraclitus

Another important early philosopher was Heraclitus. He lived just after Anaximander (around 540–475 BC) and was an aristocrat who lived on the Ionian coast of Greece. His preference for composing short, almost contradictory philosophical sayings later earned him the nickname 'the Dark One'. Out of all his mysterious sayings it's the following one about rivers that's sparked the most debate ever since: 'You cannot step into the same river twice.' Sometimes this saying is put more precisely as: 'The waters that flow over those who step in the same river will be different.'

Anyway, what's so important about that? Well, some people say that it means that nothing in the physical world stays the same, because, for example, a flower soon wilts and dies while over there, say, a volcano appears. They say that this suggests that you need to ignore the world around you (perceived through the senses) if you want to find true knowledge. Whether Heraclitus meant this or not, his influence led Plato to reject information obtained in the everyday world of the senses, and hence to the Theory of Forms itself. (See Chapter 1 for more on his hugely important philosophical theory.)

And like many of the ideas of the otherwise rather obscure ancient philosophers, Heraclitus pops up again 2,000 years later, when the German philosopher Hegel found in Heraclitus's little saying the kernel of a new 'world philosophy'. (See Chapter 5 for more on this topic.)

Summing up Pythagoras

Probably the most famous pre-Socratic of them all is the man you've probably come across – perhaps unwillingly! – in algebra class: Pythagoras. Pythagoras was actually an influential philosopher, as well as being a mathematician.

Pythagoras was born on the island of Samos maybe around 570 BC (no one is sure really). He was a bit of an all-rounder – he not only made important contributions to music and astronomy, metaphysics, natural philosophy, politics and theology, but he was also the first person to bring the concepts of reincarnation and heaven and hell to the Western world. Pythagoras believed that these doctrines were a personal revelation to himself from God.

Unfortunately for him, a local ruler called Polycrates decided he was a subversive and forced Pythagoras and his followers to leave his island. So Pythagoras went to Italy, where he established a kind of philosophical community based on vegetarianism, poverty and chastity – so no meat, no money and no sex.

Dining with Pythagoras

One of Pythagoras's pupils recorded that Pythagoras considered the killing of animals murder and eating them cannibalism. This followed from Pythagoras's belief in reincarnation. Certainly he implored men not to eat animals. Instead, Pythagorean meals consisted of honeycomb, millet or barley bread, and vegetables. Pythagoras would actually pay fishermen to throw their catch back into the sea and apparently once even told a ferocious bear to eat barley and acorns rather than humans!

Pythagoras not only showed respect for animals, but also for trees, which he insisted people must not harm unless there was absolutely no alternative. Lesser plants too merited concern: on one occasion he ordered an ox not to trample a bean field. Whether the ox obeyed the order isn't recorded! Either way, you can see why Pythagoras might have been seen as a bit of an eccentric at the time . . .

The crucial event in Pythagoras's life was an invasion of Egypt in 525 BC while he was there on a visit, learning from priests, architects and musicians. He was taken to Babylon (what is now an area of modern-day Iraq) as a prisoner of war, but his experiences don't seem to have been too bad; while he was waiting for someone to pay his ransom, he was introduced to a rich tradition of geometrical and mathematical wisdom.

The significant thing about all this maths was the method of deduction. The modern tradition of mathematical proof, the basis for Western science, goes back in a fairly straight line (via Plato) to Pythagoras. If it hadn't been for them, philosophy and the search for knowledge would have stayed firmly in the hands of the mystics. But this new approach showed that even very specialised knowledge was accessible to everyone – if only they could learn to think systematically. And that's, of course, what philosophers pride themselves on doing.

From ancients like Pythagoras came the philosophical beliefs that you can investigate and explain the world using human reason, and that you can deduce the laws of nature purely by thought alone. Even the philosopher and scientist Isaac Newton in the 17th century referred back to Pythagoras. Philosophy is behind most of modern science – and modern physicists still debate strange Ancient Greek philosophy. The key idea is that philosophy is a rational (what later came to be termed *a priori*) inquiry.

Pythagoras was a mathematician, and this influenced his philosophies to a significant extent. He believed that mathematics offered a glimpse of a perfect reality, a realm of the gods that our own world imperfectly reflected. He believed that human souls were trapped within imperfect bodies in an imperfect world. Another core belief of the Pythagoreans was that numbers were the key to understanding all creation. He demonstrated this by showing how twanging different lengths of string made different sounds, and the same veneration of 'numbers' appears many times in the late works of Plato and Aristotle.

Plating Up Plato (and Serving Up Socrates)

People generally consider Plato (427–347 BC) to be the greatest philosopher of them all. Plato was born, studied, taught and died in Athens, albeit with plenty of travelling in between. As part of his travels he visited the Greek trading centres of Africa and Italy, absorbing the strange ideas of the Pythagoreans, such as that numbers were more real than sticks and stones, and then in 387 BC he returned to Athens.

One story has it that he was captured by pirates and held for ransom. Whether that's true or not, the second half of his long life is much more placid, with Plato establishing his famous Academy for the study of philosophy in the western suburbs of Athens. The Academy was an open-air park in which Plato would hold forth on his ideas. People today count the Academy as the first ever university.

Although Plato was primarily a scholar, rather than a politician, one exception to his scholarly existence occurred. During the 360s he travelled twice to Syracuse, the capital of Greek Sicily, to advise the new king, Dionysius II. This perhaps was his attempt to put the ideals sketched out in the *Republic* into practice. Yet the reality was disastrous. Plato fell out with the king, who preferred his own opinions, and only just managed to extricate himself from the situation to return to the relative tranquillity of life as head of the Academy. He's reported to have died in his sleep at the age of 80 after enjoying the wedding feast of one of his students.

Figuring out the Plato/Socrates connection

Socrates is in all Plato's little plays – he's the star. That's nice because the real Plato was taught philosophy by the real Socrates. But it's a bit of a stretch to think that Plato's actually recording Socrates' views.

In fact, no one knows much about the real Socrates; they mostly know only what Plato *said* Socrates said.

Philosopher kings

Plato's family was a distinguished Athenian one with political connections, and he had aristocratic lineage (perhaps even seeing himself as of 'kingly' stock). His real name was Aristocles, but in his school days he received the nickname 'Platon' (meaning broad) because of his broad shoulders, and that's how history has remembered him. As was normal at the time, Plato trained as a soldier as well as learning all about poetry. Indeed, he wrote some very good poems, but he is better remembered for having proposed that poetry be banned in his playlet, the *Republic*.

Plato certainly had political ambitions, and his *Republic* isn't only a central text in Western philosophical thought but also a political manifesto. In it, he makes clear his contempt for democracy, which he condemns as rule of the unwise. He explains instead that it's much better for a select elite of philosophers to rule society. As Athens was a 'democracy' at the time (that is, for well-off Greek males), this limited Plato's options at home and in 399 BC he left the city, declaring that things would never go right until either 'kings were philosophers or philosophers were kings'. I think it's fair to say that Plato was probably a pretty snooty philosopher!

Socrates didn't like writing – he thought it was the enemy of thinking – and so the only way to know about him is through other people's accounts. And comparing these you see quite a lot of disagreement. But because Plato made Socrates his mouthpiece for his debates, most people agree Socrates was the most influential philosopher of them all. This despite the fact that no one's quite sure what he said (let alone thought . . .)!

Historians consider Diogenes Laertius to be the most, indeed the only, reliable source for facts about the 'historical Socrates' – but Diogenes lived maybe 500 years afterwards, and so how reliable are his accounts? Yet otherwise, all the accounts say more about their author's preferences than they do about Socrates.

Anyway, over-shadowing all others who wrote about Socrates, it's the Platonic picture that's created the Socrates philosophers know and love. Plato, himself an idealist, offers up an idol, almost a philosophical saint, the prophet of 'the Sun-God', who's later condemned as a heretic for his teachings by the nasty Athenian government.

Discovering Plato's Republic and other works

Although many ancient philosophers' ideas have been lost to history, five large modern volumes of Plato's work still exist. Many subsequent scholars have seen these as not only the greatest philosophical work there is, but also one of the greatest works of literature.

From Plato's Republic – a bit of the debate on justice

Plato's unique style is amazingly timeless – and jargon free. Nonetheless, behind the chatter a lot's going on. A bit too much, in fact. No wonder professional philosophers still pore over the texts, trying to explain them! Here Plato recalls a supposed conversation between Socrates and a Greek aristocrat called Glaucon. The topic is broadly 'how to run society'.

Socrates: When two things, a greater and less, are called by the same name, are they like or unlike in so far as they are called the same?

Glaucon: They are alike.

Socrates: The just man then, if we regard the idea of justice only, will be like the just State?

Glaucon: He will.

Socrates: And a State was thought by us to be just when the three classes in the State severally did their own business; and also thought to be temperate and valiant and wise by reason of certain other affections and qualities of these same classes?

Glaucon: True.

Socrates: And so of the individual; we may assume that he has the same three principles in his own soul which are found in the State; and he may be rightly described in the same terms, because he's affected in the same manner?

Glaucon: Certainly.

Socrates: Once more then, my friend, we have alighted upon an easy question – whether the soul has these three principles or not?

Glaucon: An easy question! Nay, rather, Socrates, the proverb holds that hard is the good.

Socrates: Very true, and I do not think that the method which we are employing is at all adequate to the accurate solution of this question; the true method is another and a longer one. Still we may arrive at a solution not below the level of the previous enquiry.

Glaucon: May we not be satisfied with that? Under the circumstances, I am quite content.

The extract is from 'Book V' of the *Republic*. Very typically of Plato, the discussion just points at how *complicated* everything is!

Plato's works consist of a series of little playlets starring Socrates, in which he records conversations between Socrates and various other characters, often with wit, always with subtlety. Plato himself never appears in any of the dialogues as such, but it's impossible to say whose views are really being rehearsed in them, or where. Do the playlets convey Plato's view, or Socrates', or Pythagoras's or . . .? These days, the most famous of all Plato's dialogues is the *Republic*, sketching out a theory of government, and most experts think that this at least is Plato's own view – but whether it is his view or not, no one's ever taken the political recipe very seriously.

Plato's writings are so important in philosophy that people often refer not only to the particular dialogue in the book, but the section, the subsection – and the line number! It's interesting in fact how chatty the whole thing is, given that the book is now 2,300 years old! And the style of debate is rather chummy – not much of a debate at all! With one or two exceptions, Plato always has Socrates win all the 'arguments' too easily, and his opponents seem to spend most of their time agreeing with him. In fact, the characters, including Socrates, are just convenient mouthpieces for certain points of view that Plato wanted to bring across in a lively way.

His dialogues, apparently recording historical conversations between Socrates and various fellow citizens of the city, range widely from the distinction between mind and matter, echoed later by Descartes (see Chapter 5), to the strange theory of heavenly ideas or *forms*. This is made clear from the special place Plato gives to the 'form of the good', and his much quoted, but still rather ambiguous, metaphor of the cave (both in the *Republic)* that said shackled prisoners can only be set free when they let the light thrown out by knowledge of good illuminate their miserable earthbound existence.

Clever bods conventionally divide Plato's dialogues into three main periods:

- ✔ Philosophers believe the first, the *early dialogues*, to be the ones written in his youth, when he's supposed to be still reflecting Socrates' influence. They think these are the most 'actual accounts of Socrates' own views. The key dialogue from this period is the *Apology*, written apparently shortly after Socrates' execution.

- ✔ The second period, the *middle dialogues*, includes what philosophers now think are the most important philosophical works, with Plato at the peak of his brilliance. These are the dialogues of the *Republic*, the *Symposium* and the *Phœdrus*. The *Republic* deals not only with the design and organisation of the ideal state, but also with the nature of knowledge and the forms; the *Symposium* or 'Drinking Party' deals with the nature of beauty, love and the meaning of life, and the *Phœdrus*. deals with the question of immortality and the soul.

- ✔ The third period consists of dialogues in which Plato seems to change tack, entertaining criticisms of views put in the earlier works, and poor old Socrates gets shoved to one side. The late dialogues are said to be the Critias, the Laws, the Philebus, the Sophist, the Statesman and the Timaeus.

You can't take anything in Plato at face value. Although in *Republic* includes an apparently clear condemnation of poetry and even sex (in the ideal state children will be produced in a more controlled and logical way), in the *Symposium* Plato gives an entirely different view. Here, after describing the psychological fevers that the physical presence of a lover can create (the fevers grandly condemned in the *Republic* as a 'tyrant'), Plato has *this* Socrates saying that it's only love that prevents the 'wings of the soul' from becoming parched and dry, and proceeds, scandalously, to credit *eros* (sexual love) as a god!

The one thing that seems to be clear about Plato's own views is that he (like other Greeks, notably Pythagoras) had a hierarchy of knowledge in which ethics comes out on top, pure mathematics comes second and practical knowledge, obtained largely by experimentation, trails in last.

Plato's work actually included the thinking of several ancient philosophers, rather than simply presenting the opinions of the real Socrates. Plato's works include Pythagorean theories, as well as pulling together various ancient strands of thought. But don't forget that he contradicts himself and creates new ideas in each work, no single 'Platoian' theory exists.

Arguing with Aristotle

Aristotle (384–322 BC) was born just in time to know Plato. He tried to organise every subject under the sun with alarming zeal. Aristotle, like the other Greek philosophers, didn't make any distinction between scientific and philosophical investigations. Aristotle was particularly interested in observing nature; much later on his biology was much admired by Darwin, amongst others.

Substantial amounts of Aristotle's work have survived and have been very influential historically. He actually wrote even more than the works that exist now, including some apparently very lively dialogues in the manner of his illustrious predecessor. None of these remain, however, leaving only a dry pseudo-scientific collection of notes and theories. Despite this, he was certainly the most influential thinker in Europe during the Middle Ages – much more so than Plato or any of the other Greeks. He was so important that in the 13th century alone the pope in Rome banned his books no less than five times! Just like political movements today, quite why Aristotle's ideas offended is less important than the fact that people definitely considered them *worth* banning.

Everything has a purpose

Aristotle's pet theory was that everything in nature has a function or purpose, and if you work out what that is, then you can understand everything. For example, he said that if you see plant shoots bending towards the light, then the explanation is that they're 'seeking the light'. That sounds okay. But what about people? The function of mankind is, he suggests, to reason, because this is what people are better at than any other member of the animal kingdom. As he puts it, 'Man is a rational animal.' But this approach is in contrast to that of today's scientists who try to explain things by reference to mechanisms. They say instead that the plant bends towards the light because the cells on the sunny side shrink, causing the stem to bend and so on.

Aristotle's dodgy political theory

In many ways Aristotle's *Politics* strikes a dodgy note. He defined the state as a collection of a certain size of citizens participating in the judicial and political processes of the city. But his term *citizens* didn't include many inhabitants of the city. He didn't include slaves, nor (unlike Plato) women, whom he considered to be 'irrational' and whom he compared to domestic pets. 'Some men,' Aristotle wrote, 'belong by nature to others,' and so should properly be either slaves or *chattels* (things that you own, for example, a book or a pencil).

For Aristotle, liberty was fundamental for citizens, but it's a peculiar kind of freedom, even for these privileged members of society. He thought that the state should reserve the right to ensure efficient use of property, for its own advantage. He also agreed with Plato that the state should control the production of children to ensure the new citizens had 'the best physique'. (Plato puts it more generally, saying it should be used so as to 'improve on nature'.) And, again like Plato, Aristotle wanted everyone to be educated in the manner determined by the state. He said, 'Public matters should be publicly managed; and we should not think that each of the citizens belongs to himself, but that they all belong to the State.' Aristotle even produced a long list of ways in which the state should control the lives of citizens. For him, the government should be like the father in a well-regulated household: the children (the citizens) should have 'a natural affection and disposition to obey.'

Aristotle marks the zenith of Ancient Greek philosophy; after him it all went a bit downhill. He himself was born 15 years after the execution of Socrates (in 399 BC) and was lucky enough to be at the Academy in Athens under Plato. Although he'd hoped to become Plato's successor, in fact it was Plato's nephew, Speussippus, who took over instead.

Doubtless very indignant after this, Aristotle left Greece for Turkey, where for the next five years he concentrated on developing his philosophy and biology. He then returned to Macedonia, in the north of Greece, to be tutor to a young aristocrat – the later Alexander the Great (a military wizard who conquered much of Europe). This might have been an opportunity for him to spread his political views – set out in a long book called the *Politics* – but Alexander doesn't seem to have wanted to listen to too much philosophy.

Making a splash in the Islamic world

Although historians often treat Aristotle as Plato's right-hand man, during his lifetime and for many years afterwards he was considered a bit of a duffer. Indeed, the renowned sceptic Timon of Philus sneered at 'the sad chattering of the empty Aristotle', and another Ancient Greek, Theocritus of Chios, wrote a rather unkind rhyme about him in which he calls Aristotle empty-headed. Most likely these critics didn't agree with Aristotle's political views, rather than seeing the weaknesses of his scientific and logical theories. Or perhaps they simply noticed little mistakes he made, such as that women had fewer teeth than men, which of course anyone can check by simply counting.

Fortunately for Aristotle, his writings found their way to the Islamic world, where they were widely studied. There scholars hailed him as 'the wise man' or 'The Philosopher' (with a capital 'P'). Aristotle's views on the origins and workings of the universe fitted in well with Islamic teachings, and his second-rate status for women didn't harm his popularity there either. On the other hand, the Islamic philosophers also picked and chose from Aristotle's texts, using him as an authority when it suited their purposes, or rejecting his theories as 'foreign science' when it didn't. The one thing that's sure, though, is that it was because of these Islamic scholars that his ideas were still around to be rediscovered in the Middle Ages by the scholarly monks of the Catholic Church and become highly influential. And indeed, his ideas still are.

Writing his way to recognition

Philosophers generally say that Aristotle's greatest achievement was his laws of thought (see Chapter 2 for more on this), which were part of his attempt to put everyday language on a logical footing. Like many contemporary philosophers, he regarded logic as providing the key to philosophical progress. For Aristotle, *logic* is a set of rules that describe how to reason correctly and avoid mistakes. It's about *how* to argue, not about *what* to argue.

That all sounds reasonable – but don't you believe it! His book, called the *Prior Analytics*, is the first attempt to create a system of formal deductive logic, and the *Posterior Analytics* attempts to use this to systematise scientific knowledge.

Although the names of Aristotle's books sound grand, they're really quite simple. *Analytics* is like a collection of things he's analysed, with the *prior* meaning 'read this bit first' and the *posterior* bit meaning 'this bit follows on' – just like your posterior follows you as you walk around!

In fact, about a quarter of Aristotle's writing is concerned with creating systems and categories with his most successful efforts (that people still use today) concerning nature, in particular animals. Less usefully, he catalogued the different forms the soul takes in different creatures. Then there's a lot of influential stuff on the essence of space and time, but I leave that to Part V. Suffice to say that it was due to Aristotle that for 1,000 years people thought that the Earth stayed still while the Sun, the planets and all the stars whizzed around it.

Nowadays that seems laughable. But people still take Aristotle's views on right and wrong very seriously. They're set out in two books called the *Nicomachean* and the *Eudaemian Ethics*. The *Nicomachean Ethics* is one of the most influential books of moral philosophy, including accounts of what the Greeks considered to be the great virtues. In this, Aristotle featured a 'great souled man' who spoke with a deep and calm voice, who reminds readers wisely that 'without friends, no one would choose to live, though he had all other goods'. The main idea here is that being good is about behaving 'virtuously' – I look at this in more detail in Chapter 13.

Finding the truth

Aristotle says that the proper 'end of mankind' – that is, the one thing that people everywhere should be aiming at – is the pursuit of happiness. This sounds very satisfactory, but in fact, he uses the word *eudaimonia*.

Eudaimonia is Greek for a very particular kind of happiness. It has three aspects: as well as mere pleasure, there's political honour and the rewards of contemplation. What sort of contemplation? Crossword puzzles? TV? No. Only, of course, philosophy will do.

Many of the ideas that Aristotle gets the credit for, notably the merit of fulfilling your function, of cultivating the virtues and of the golden mean between two undesirable extremes are, actually, much older. Indeed, Plato puts all these ideas across too. Nonetheless, one important difference between Aristotle and Plato exists. It's the one summed up by a famous picture of the great philosophers painted by the Italian painter Raphael. In it Plato is pointing upwards, as if to indicate his heavenly forms. But Aristotle is gesticulating downwards, as if to say, 'No, we must look around us!' And Aristotle's greatest influence is in his idea that it's by observing and analysing the physical evidence all around that you can find out the truth of how the universe works.

Chapter 5

Moving from the Dark Ages to the Modern Day

In This Chapter

▶ Putting God through the philosophical hoops

▶ Putting philosophy through some sceptical hoops too

▶ Trying to turn philosophers into thinking machines

▶ Seeing how analytic philosophers turned to mathematics

The concept 'God' invented as the antithetical concept in life – everything harmful, noxious, slanderous, the whole mortal enmity against life brought into one terrible unity!

– Nietzsche

Ancient philosophy is pure philosophy, where thinking comes first, looking second, and it seems anything goes. That's why the 1,000 years that included the heyday of Ancient Greece are for many philosophers, the subject's golden age. But golden ages, like honeymoons, come to an end, and this chapter is about what happened next.

For 1,000 years after the collapse of the Roman Empire, life in Europe was much less orderly, those Roman roads were dug up to make houses bandit-proof, and philosophy in Europe took refuge in monasteries, in the sense that it was only monks who still read books and exchanged theories. And naturally the monks' concerns centred on God. Religious thinkers steered philosophy along certain tramlines, a situation that had begun to frustrate philosophers by the 17th century, as it seemed to them that new inventions and practical ideas – like how to govern countries – were more interesting than ever. Between the 17th and 19th centuries, the focus of philosophical debates shifted down from heaven and back very much to Earth, with thinkers like David Hume dismissing the old ways of thinking entirely.

But even as philosophy cut itself loose again from religious guidance, it tried to find for itself another kind of certainty – the certainty of maths and logic.

Proving God's Existence in Medieval Europe

To look at most philosophy histories, it seems that after the golden age of the Greeks, the flame of philosophical thought, so to speak, was extinguished for 1,000 years, as the barbarian hordes swept around Europe. But that, of course, isn't quite right. Philosophy continued, but under new management – the religious orders of the Christian Church. And these new philosophers, being religious folk, had priorities that were slightly different. In particular, they wanted to prove that God really did exist, and to show how to get to heaven.

Table 5-1 presents some of the hole-y if not holy arguments put forth by philosophers for supposing that there really must be some kind of God up there.

Table 5-1	Well, Does God Exist?	
Argument	*Who Started It*	*What It Says*
Argument from existence	Augustine	The way things are is not determined by us – but someone else. And that must be God.
Ontological argument	Anselm	Perfect beings always exist – they have to, in order to be perfect!
Cosmological argument	Maybe Aristotle	Something outside space and time must have created space and time.
First mover	Aristotle and Aquinas	Someone must have started the universe.
Argument from degree	Maybe Plato, Augustine uses a similar line	You can only conceive of goodness because pure goodness exists somewhere.
Argument from design	The ancient stoics	The universe is too complicated to have happened just by chance.

Getting to grips with Saint Augustine

Augustine of Hippo (354–430 AD) was a very odd philosopher, and a very influential one. He is remembered for his very frank account of his own personal habits which included things like having too much sex and stealing pears. How much sex is too much, then? Any. At least if you want to become a saint, which he eventually did become, but only after he died, of course. He was born in North Africa, then part of the Roman Empire and for his first proper job taught philosophy in Rome and Milan. He only became a Christian (like his Mum) when he converted to Christianity in 387. He then returned to North Africa to spearhead the assault on rival religious views, which people considered dangerous heresies. For his sterling work at this he was made bishop of the city of Hippo in 395, and it was here, while the city was surrounded by the Vandals (the German tribe, that is, not just local graffiti artists) that he died.

Augustine's zeal in fighting heresy is partly explained by the fact that as a young man he himself had been tempted by one radical sect known as Manichaeism, which offered its followers convenient explanations for doctrinal problems, like that Jesus's human body was only an illusion, as if God was merely wearing a human body like a cloak. But it was their explanation for the problem of evil, a life-long preoccupation of Augustine's, that most appealed to him.

For believers in God, the biggest problem with the world is that it looks to be pretty rotten. If, as the Bible says, God is completely good, knows everything there is to be known and can do anything at all He wants (benevolent, omniscient and omnipotent), then why do bad things happen to anyone? For example, why do newborn babies, who can't possibly have offended God, get ill and maybe even die?

For the Christian radicals like the Manichaeists, the explanation is that good and evil are two opposing forces, and human souls are their battleground. That was actually a bit like Plato's view too, although they added to this the rather poetic idea that souls are particles of light that have become trapped in the darkness of the material world. Augustine liked that stuff, as he explains in his most influential work, the *Confessions* (see the nearby sidebar for more on this text).

 Augustine's idea that bad things happen to apparently normal people because God is cross with them has been influential. And so has another part of his search for a solution to the problem of evil. In Book VII of the *Confessions* Augustine says:

> *I knew myself to have a will in the same way and as much as I knew myself to be alive. Therefore when I willed or did not will something, I was utterly certain that none other than myself was willing or not willing.*

Sex and religion don't go

The *Confessions* starts by Augustine explaining how he discovered his evil nature in his 16th year, while away from school and 'a season of idleness being interposed through the narrowness of my parents' fortunes', the 'briers of unclean desires grew rank over my head, and there was no hand to root them out'. (Think about it. He's 16 and his parents are away . . .)

He then delicately introduces the unwholesome topic of unwanted erections:

> When that my father saw me at the baths, now growing towards manhood, and endued with a restless youthfulness, he, as already hence anticipating his descendants, gladly told it to my mother; rejoicing in that tumult of the senses wherein the world forgetteth Thee its Creator, and becometh enamoured of Thy creature, instead of Thyself, through the fumes of that invisible wine of its self-will, turning aside and bowing down to the very basest things.

Fortunately, his mother, Monica, a devout Catholic unlike the rest of the sinful family, was less content. Saint Monica (as she would later become):

> . . . was startled with a holy fear and trembling; and though I was not as yet baptised, feared for me those crooked ways in which they walk who turn their back to Thee, and not their face. Woe is me! and dare I say that Thou heldest Thy peace, O my God, while I wandered further from Thee? Didst Thou then indeed hold Thy peace to me? And whose but Thine were these words which by my mother, Thy faithful one, Thou sangest in my ears? Nothing whereof sunk into my heart, so as to do it. For she wished, and I remember in private with great anxiety warned me, not to commit fornication; but especially never to defile another man's wife.

Alas, as many commentators have noted, disapprovingly, at the age of 16, he failed to contain his lust and sinned. However, later on Augustine changed his view because he decided he didn't like the idea that God wasn't omnipotent, and so his preferred solution became instead . . . guess what! To abolish evil. From then on all the bad things that happen to people, even babies, are in reality just punishments for their own sins – either in the present life or in a past one. The world is still rotten (full of evil things), but God wants it that way! No wonder Augustine says that God wants only a few people in the next life, in heaven.

Descartes' famous philosophical dictum 'I think, therefore I am', actually comes from . . . Saint Augustine. No great coincidence there, either, because Descartes was educated by Augustinian monks.

The main argument for the existence of God that Augustine offers starts by asking if we know that we exist, pointing out that you need to exist in order to argue that you do not exist. He then moves on to say that if you agree with that, then you must be able to reason, that is to tell a good argument from a bad one. Good arguments and bad arguments are different. But who makes them that way? Not us. Just as 12 and 12 make 24 whether we can add up or not, what is true is not decided by people, but is determined by God. Or so he says. God in this way becomes a kind of cosmic referee, calling all the judgements.

Wicked, greedy baby!

In the Middle Ages, saintly experts such as Augustine saw human life as essentially a rather unpleasant sort of moral trial, with the unpleasantness a necessary part of achieving saintliness. Augustine believed (rather negatively for modern taste, as Bertrand Russell once put it) that mankind was a mass of corruption and sin proceeding inevitably towards hell. In Book I of the *Confessions* he describes the evil already there in the newborn baby, before going on to show how the adult is no better.

I have personally watched and studied a jealous baby. He could not yet speak and, pale with jealousy and bitterness, glared at his brother sharing his mother's milk . . . it can hardly be innocence, when the source of milk is flowing richly and abundantly, not to endure a share going to one's blood brother, who is in profound need, dependent for life exclusively on that one food.

With writing like that, no wonder that Augustine was the top philosopher in Europe for eight centuries – until another saint, Aquinas, toppled him from the number one spot by replacing his reheated versions of Plato (what philosophers call *neo-Platonism*) with the much more exciting new theories of Aristotle, manuscripts of which had just been freshly rediscovered.

Augustine is also rated very highly for another book called *The City of God*. This has been particularly praised by philosophers for supposing that history has a pattern to it – despite the fact that *historicism* (as it is known) has encouraged political dictators ever since, and the fact that history has no pattern to it. He was also intriguing with his discussion of time, where he concludes famously that only the present moment exists. The worrying thing about this is that the present moment is always vanishing into the past – literally, it's vanishingly small!

Understanding God: the ontological argument

It was Saint Anselm (1033–1109), an Italian priest, who eventually ended up as Archbishop of Canterbury in the 11th century, who came up with the ontological argument. The argument, which Anselm presented very devoutly in the form of a prayer to God, begins with a description of Him as 'something than which nothing greater can be thought'.

The logic of the argument is that because everyone accepts that – by definition – God is the greatest possible being, and secondly that God does at least exist in people having this concept of Him (that is, He exists 'in the understanding'), you only need a small step farther to realise that God exists in reality as well. So what's the small step? Well, the third, clever, bit of the argument provides this. It states that 'something that exists in reality, as well as in theory, is greater than something that exists in just the understanding'.

In one sentence: because God is the greatest, and because not existing isn't as great as existing, God must exist in reality as well as in the understanding.

That's it. The monks considered this demonstration of God's existence a triumph. But the weakness with the argument is that God still exists only by definition.

Examining the evidence with Thomas Aquinas

One problem with the old ontological argument (see the preceding section) is that it may well be more perfect to exist as an abstract idea than to exist in grubby reality. In fact, it seems quite likely that it would be more perfect to exist like that.

Because of that weakness, and other lingering doubts, Thomas Aquinas (1225–1274) decided people needed a whole lot of new reasons to believe in God. He summarised several other philosophical arguments to that end:

- **Cosmological argument:** Really a 'kind' of way of looking at the issue rather than any particular case. As usual, Plato had already given his own version in one of his little playlets. But the Cosmological Argument was spring-cleaned by Aquinas. His version can be summed up as saying that there must have been a time before the universe existed, and because physical things exist now, there must have been something non-physical to bring them into existence. This thing has to be non-physical, because you're talking about before physical things existed. Some people call this an *infinite regress*.

An *infinite regress* is an argument that goes round and round feeding on itself. And, oh yes, it's bad for arguments to do this.

- **First mover:** This idea rests on the assumption that you can see that movement exists in the universe and that everyone knows nothing moves unless something else moves it. This argument also looks like an infinite regress. It's particularly unconvincing as an argument because everyone accepts nowadays that things in fact continue to move unless stopped (for example, by friction). The question of why things in the universe move disappears without needing to prove the existence of God.

This argument was developed by Aquinas from the dodgy science of Aristotle, who wasn't a religious believer, but a biologist with philosophical leanings. He thought that because stones stayed quietly on the ground unless kicked, so must everything in the universe want to be at rest too unless something was kicking them.

✔ **Argument from degree:** Another of Aquinas's arguments for God, which the contemporary philosopher of science Richard Dawkins (but hardly anyone else these days) calls the *argument from degree*, is that humans can be both good and bad so you can't ever find the purest form of goodness in people. Therefore, something else that's pure goodness must exist, and people call that maximum good thing *God*.

However, again, this argument only seems to deal with ideas and ideals: the ideal of goodness, yes, but also the idea of being a table, or being a chair, or maybe even of being a number like 2. God ends up existing in the alternative mental world of Plato's theory of the forms (see Chapter 2) – not in the universe!

✔ **Argument from design:** This argument says that the world is so complicated, someone must have designed it – it couldn't have come about by chance, could it? Which is where Charles Darwin comes in, with his subversive explanation of how complex life-forms *can* develop simply by trial and error. (More on that in Chapter 18.)

The problem for theologians, such as Aquinas, was to get God from existing only in the mental world to also existing in the physical world.

Trying to Do Without God

At some point, people decided it might be better to leave God out of their philosophies, because it was so hard to prove the existence of God. This shift is much praised these days as the Enlightenment – but precious little about the movement was enlightened really. Rather, it was a practical response to the very impressive new inventions of the Age of Science; things like the first mechanical clocks on church steeples, telescopes capable of showing the mountains on the moon and, of course, guns. All these made scientific and mathematical thinking much more prestigious than poring over dusty old religious texts for clues as to fundamental reality.

Several philosophers, starting with Descartes, attempted to produce arguments for believing in the universe, that required, logically, that God also existed.

Dealing with doubting Descartes

Enter René Descartes **(1596–1650)**, with whom, philosophy books and courses say, real philosophy came into being. 'Here we finally reach home', wrote Hegel, the famous German philosopher a few centuries later (the style reminds you he wasn't only a philosopher but a school teacher) in his heavyweight *History of Philosophy*, 'like a mariner after a long voyage in a tempestuous sea, we can shout "Land ho!", for with Descartes the culture and thought of modern times really begin.'

Descartes' late mornings

Like Socrates, Descartes is a philosophical legend. And you can also understand the work of the military gentleman who wrote the *Meditations* and *the Discourse on Method* as the product of an egotist, as well as the work of a genius. So it was that at the sprightly age of 23 Descartes confidently predicted that he'd discovered an 'entirely new science', and announced his intention to reveal all in a book. But then, ever worried about being ridiculed, he couldn't bear to commit himself, and this book, after years of revisions, fell by the wayside. The same fate awaited his next project, 'Rules for the Direction of the Mind', and indeed the one after that, 'Elements of Metaphysics'. Perhaps his inability to finish a project was because he had the habit of not getting out of bed before 11 o' clock (he said he was spending the time there reading). But the fact was that by the middle of his life Descartes had published nothing and the whispers said that he was as a celebris promissor – a great promiser who boasted everything but produced nothing.

However, Descartes wasn't finished yet. In a letter to his monkish friend Marin Mersenne, he wrote that although out of necessity he had to modify, abandon and restart previous works as he gained new knowledge, he now had a new work that would at last be beyond modification, 'whatever new knowledge that I may acquire in the future'. Ironically, this was the book entitled *A Discourse on Method* that would in due course be heralded as introducing the method of doubt.

Descartes died only a few years after publication of his masterpiece the Meditations, in Sweden, that 'land of bears between rocks and ice', as he describes it unfondly. He was intent on his writings to the last – but not (as those reared on the Descartes' legend may assume) great philosophical treatises, but rather on finishing a comedy and a ballet for the queen of Sweden and her courtiers' amusement. In fact, it seems that what finished him off was having to get up very early each morning to give the queen her philosophy lesson. In this way, Descartes at last demonstrated an important truth: getting up early is bad for some people!

So what's so good about Descartes – so often at the heart of philosophy courses? Philosophers praise Descartes for two things:

- The method of doubt
- Dualism

Method of doubt

Descartes says that in order to separate out real knowledge from unreliable hearsay, optical illusions and tricks by other people (including evil demons), you have to suspect everything you think you know, not trust anything you see or hear and even assume that everything is either a dream or a wicked trick.

The Cogito

Philosophers like Descartes' 'I think, therefore I am'. The funny thing is, that's not exactly what Descartes said. *'Ego sum, ego existo, quoties a me profertur, vel mente concipitur, necessario esse verum'* is the original Latin text of 1641, for those wishing to impress people. Descartes wrote in Latin to do just that. But, being French, he also wrote a version in French and here his famous phrase was 'Je pense, donc je suis' (still good for those wishing to impress French people). That looks, superficially, nearer to the English version, but an accurate translation of it isn't 'I think, therefore I am', but 'I am thinking, therefore I exist'. You see, French doesn't have a special way to distinguish the two senses. If that seems confusing to you, it is because it is confusing, and indeed much misunderstood in philosophy ever since.

As noted in Chapter 2, Descartes was far from being the first to wonder about all this. The Ancient Greek sceptics had, and their conclusion was that you can't be sure of anything at all. But Descartes is famous because, at the moment when all human knowledge seemed to have been reduced to mere optimistic guesses and convention, he brings forward dramatically something that he says is absolutely reliable and certain – something you can really be sure of. This is probably the most famous quote in philosophy: 'I think, therefore I am.' No one, he says, can doubt the truth of that.

Dualism

The second thing Descartes is remembered for is dualism. Descartes split thoughts and experiences apart.

Dualism is the philosophical jargon for viewing the world as being made up of two things: mind and matter. Descartes thought everyone had both a mind and a body. However, he thought animals had only bodies – and he even dissected a few to test his theory out. Sure enough, he found no minds inside. The Church liked his approach because it fitted in well with the idea of souls. Descartes even found a small gland (the *pineal* gland, not that this is worth knowing) in human beings that didn't seem to do anything, so he suggested this was where the human soul resided, directing the body.

This is lousy philosophy, and not very good science, either. The pineal gland is just a gland. But even if it were true, a very practical problem still existed with the theory. If minds and souls have no physical parts, how can they have any physical effects – how can my pure soul (wherever it is) tell my flesh-and-blood arm to turn the page?

Seeking out Spinoza

Spinoza was a Dutch lens-grinder, not exactly a 'spectacle maker' as some books try to tell you, who turned down a chair in philosophy at the posh university of Heidelberg to continue his polishing and grinding.

Spinoza thought Descartes (see the preceding section) was wrong to split the world into two types of thing, and instead put it back together again, saying that everything is fundamentally made of the same thing. He says mind and body are just two aspects of something else, which has many aspects including that of being God.

The heart of Spinoza's ideas comes from the Eastern philosophical tradition, especially Taoism (see Chapter 6). Philosophers today very much admire Spinoza's writings, supposedly a series of proofs in the Euclidean or mathematical style (and he was Einstein's favourite philosopher), but he's not had as much influence as either of them.

Spinoza disagreed with other key Cartesian (meaning to do with Descartes) ideas. He didn't believe in either minds or souls, nor even in brute matter. He decided that the impression you have that you choose to do things is an illusion. Put another way, Spinoza didn't believe in free will. In his *Theological-Political Treatise* (1670) he subversively examines the Bible, treating it as a text that scholars should analyse rather than treat as divine revelation. He believed scholars should examine and analyse the Bible without necessarily assuming it's the truth.

In 1656, when Spinoza was just 24 years old, the elders of his synagogue had had enough. They excommunicated him from the Jewish community. The official decree speaks of 'evil opinions and acts', 'abominable heresies' and 'monstrous deeds'. It sounds pretty exciting! But alas, however, the decree doesn't record specific deeds and so philosophers have had to be content with speculating about it ever since.

Looking at Locke

John Locke (1632–1704) was born in a quiet Somerset village into a rather less quiet period of Civil War between Parliament and Royalists.

As a bright young hound, his interests ranged widely, with his 1689 *Essay in Human Understanding* reflecting an interest in new machines and other scientific inventions of the time by detailing how the mind might take in 'simple or complex ideas', via the senses, to assemble knowledge. He believed that the complex world is built out of little simple sense impressions. Babies playing with shapes and colours become aware of space and time, the problem of evil, induction and causation – the whole lot!

Locke limits liberty

In the *Two Treatises* John Locke says that 'initially the earth, and all inferior creatures on it' belong to everyone in common – with one important exception. Individuals do own one thing; they have property in their own person. In the 'original state' (which is how people he thinks lived before there were governments) nobody has any right to anyone else's body Locke adds: 'It is only this property that gives individuals freedom'.

But crucially, Locke adds a new requirement to being able to be free. The freedom of someone to follow their own will is now 'grounded on his having reason which is able to instruct him in that law he is to govern himself by . . .'. This additional requirement allowed Locke to justify the ownership of slaves, and indeed to invest in a slave trading company himself.

This was radical, because Plato had said that people are born with lots of innate knowledge, ready to do complex things like mathematics and indeed talk, as the contemporary American sort-of-philosopher Noam Chomsky has argued.

However, it's John Locke's political theory, set out in the *Two Treatises on Government* (1690), that has been over time the more influential. Like Plato's, this theory starts with a search for moral authority. And like Plato, Locke says the human conscience must account only to God for judgement on all matters, placing individual judgement firmly above that of both Church and state, and limiting the latter's role to protecting property. 'All being equal and independent, no one ought to harm another in his life, health, liberty, or possessions', Locke proclaims. Does that ring a bell? It ought to – it's the basis of the political system of the United States.

John Locke fitted the times so well (Bertrand Russell even described him as the 'apostle of the Revolution of 1688') that contemporary politicians and thinkers actively adopted his philosophy. The 18th-century French philosopher Voltaire used Locke's ideas in his writings to inspire the principles of the French revolution. From there, Americans were encouraged by Locke's thinking to declare that they had 'fundamental rights' too. (Or at least, that some Americans had . . .).

In his writings, Locke creates a picture of the world in which rationality is the ultimate authority, *not God*, and certainly not, as the English philosopher Thomas Hobbes had insisted, brute force. He argues that people all have certain fundamental rights and also attempts to return the other half of the human race, the female part, to their proper, equal, place in history, the family and in government.

Just a pity then, that his day-job for the government was organising the slave trade. No rights for slaves!

Introducing a great British triple

Locke–Berkeley–Hume are the three Brits who had an enormous influence over British philosophy. Philosophers love them! But they do also make a good theoretical triple. Locke said knowledge comes from things out there via the senses; Berkeley said it all comes from ideas in the mind, because all you ever really know about is what you *think* you sense; and Hume said in fact you know nothing at all.

Barking at Berkeley

George Berkeley was an Irish bishop who lived in the 18th century.

He had a very strange view of the world – namely that material objects like stones, or even pet dogs, exist only as complexes of ideas through being perceived. To the objection that if this really were the case, a tree, for instance, in a forest would cease to exist when no one was around, he replied that God always perceives everything. In his opinion, this was a weighty argument.

Philosophers often express this theory, like Descartes' little *cogito ergo sum*, in Latin: *esse est percipi*. (Better make a note of that one, otherwise it might cease to exist.)

Bishop Berkeley's conclusion is that he has excellent, thoroughly logical grounds for holding the view that only minds and mental events exist. This still wasn't enough for many of his parishioners, with clothes to wash and meals to cook – but it was good enough to be adopted by Hegel and other subsequent philosophers. (The section 'Marching alongside Hegel to the beat of dialectical reason', covers this later in this chapter.)

Being woken up by Hume

The Scotsman David Hume (1711–76) and Bishop Berkeley wouldn't have got on, even though Hume was born into a devoutly observant Presbyterian family. But from the age of 17, he instead began work on a great philosophical project that would in due course challenge all the old ideas in both science and religion, and 'wake the philosophical world from its dogmatic slumber', as the celebrated German contemporary Kant later aptly put it. (More on him in the upcoming section 'Waking up Kant from his dogmatic slumbers'.)

Mind over matter

Berkeley wrote his main works while in his 20s: *A New Theory of Vision* in 1709, *The Principles of Human Knowledg*e a year later and the *Dialogues Between Hylas and Philonous* in 1713. In this last, he best sets out his argument that minds are real and matter is imaginary. Hylas (the names all have particular meanings too) stands for scientific common sense, and Philonous for Berkeley's own view. After some amiable remarks, in the manner of Plato and Socrates, Hylas says he has heard that his friend holds the view that there's no such thing as matter. Can anything be more fantastical, more repugnant to common sense or a more manifest piece of scepticism than this, he exclaims!

Philonous tries to explain that sense data is in fact mental, as you can see by considering lukewarm water. Put a cold hand in the water and it appears warm; put a hot hand in and it appears cold. Hylas accepts this point, but clings to other sensible qualities. Philonous then says that tastes are either pleasant or unpleasant, and are therefore mental, and you can say the same of smells. Hylas valiantly rallies at this point, and says that sounds are known to not travel through a vacuum. From this, he concludes, they must be motions of air molecules, not mental entities. Philonous responds that if this is indeed real sound, it bears no resemblance to what people know as sound, so in that case sound may as well be considered the mental phenomenon after all. The same argument fells Hylas when it comes to a discussion of colours, which he realises disappear under certain conditions, such as when a golden cloud at sunset is seen close up to be just a grey mist.

Likewise, size varies depending on the observer's position. Here Hylas suggests that you should distinguish the object from the perception – the act of perceiving is after all mental – but a material object still exists. Philonous replies, 'Whatever is immediately perceived is an idea: and can any idea exist out of the mind?' In other words, for something to be perceived, there must be a mind somewhere perceiving it.

At 23 Hume left his native Scotland for La Flèche, a small town in France, home to the Jesuit college attended by Descartes a century before, and set out the bulk of his *Treatise on Human Nature* on paper. Some philosophers start young.

In his introduction to the *Treatise*, David Hume advises the reader to be wary of philosophers who 'insinuate the praise of their own systems, by decrying all those, which have been advanced before them'. Then he proceeds to denounce the weak foundations of everyone else's philosophical systems, replete with 'incoherencies' which are 'a disgrace upon philosophy itself', and instead to propose a complete system of the sciences of his own.

For Hume is a profoundly modern thinker. He bases his arguments solely on abstract or experimental reasoning:

> *If we take in our hand any volume of divinity or school metaphysics, for instance; let us ask, Does it contain any abstract reasoning concerning quantity or number? No. Does it contain any experimental reasoning concerning matter of fact and existence? No. Commit it then to the flames: for it can contain nothing but sophistry and illusion.*

Religion has no place and no role in his philosophy. Knowledge, ethics and God are all obliged to return to Earth for Hume's scrutiny.

Hume sees people as essentially animals, with the additional facility of a sophisticated language. Reason is merely a product of people's use of language, and animals too can reason, albeit in simpler ways. He offers accounts of both emotions and ideas as if people were essentially machines, motivated by pleasure and pain; or, as the British subversive philosopher Thomas Hobbes had put it earlier, by 'appetites and aversions'. Hume's observation that 'an *is* does not imply an *ought*' also stresses that, sooner or later, people fall back on their feelings in order to make any choices.

In his later life, Hume accepted the label *sceptic*, and certainly that's how his contemporaries saw him. The first victim of his approach was consciousness, or the self, that feeling you have that you exist. Hume says you can't be sure you exist. This is because consciousness is always of something, of an impression of some sort – being hot, cold or whatever – and so you (and I) are really just a bundle of these feelings or perceptions. No one can perceive the self, as such, certainly not in anyone else. Hume thus went one step further than Bishop Berkeley, who'd demonstrated that no matter existed by proving that no mind existed either.

No causes, no effects

Hume rejected the notion of cause and effect, which is pretty drastic, saying for example that when you see an event constantly followed by another, you only infer that the first event caused the second. However, 'we cannot penetrate into the reason of the conjunction'. For instance, if you eat apples, you expect them to taste a certain way. If you take a bite and it tastes, say, of banana, you'd consider it very odd. But Hume says that this assumption that apples will taste like apples is lazy thinking. It is, in fact, another aspect of the problem of induction. 'The supposition that the future resembles the past is not founded on arguments of any kind, but is derived entirely from habit.'

Given all that uncertainty, it looks like you ought to conclude that all knowledge is flawed and that we have no reason to believe in anything that is beyond our sensory impressions and the the simple ideas in our memory derived from these impressions. Hume sees this, but, in the manner of the gentleman philosopher he was, suggests that 'carelessness and inattention' offer a remedy – you should neglect the flaws in your arguments and continue to use reason whenever you find it suits you. Philosophy remains, then, only an agreeable way to pass the time (he found, anyway), not a reason to change your views.

Hume might have found philosophy an agreeable career had it not been for the controversy raised by his critique of religion. Instead his great friend Adam Smith (at that time a much more famous philosopher) responded to a request for a reference for Hume's application for the post of Professor of Ethics and Pneumatic Philosophy (don't ask me why it was pneumatic) in Edinburgh, advising against his friend's appointment! That's the price you pay for saying philosophy is all bunk.

David Hume brings us to a sort of theoretical stop – he drives philosophy into a swamp. That didn't put the philosophers off, though. In fact, it just caused them to redouble their efforts; particularly, to think and behave like machines.

Thinking Like Machines

During the 18th century, a number of thinkers addressed the problem of developing a mechanised way of thinking, formalising human reasoning into a series of logical calculations. These philosophers, whose interests also included mathematics and the first calculating machines, included Leibniz, Pascal, Hegel and Kant.

Learning to love Leibniz

Gottfried Leibniz (1646–1716) was born in Berlin and soon became one of the 17th century's great intellectuals and a famous logician. When he was just a tiny tot, he taught himself Latin from an illustrated book, and at just 15 years old he came out with the first of what would be many grand schemes, 'On the Art of Combination' – a system by which you reduce all reasoning to a complicated grid of numbers, sounds and colours. This was the start of his quest for the 'universal language', for which he later tried to build what would have been the first computer.

In fact, Leibniz, like many philosophers before and since, was really in love with numbers. The affair had become serious when, waiting to start university, he found out about the mathematical philosophy of the Pythagoreans, and in particular their view that numbers are the ultimate reality. What a great idea, he thought! Pythagoras revealed to him that the universe as a whole was harmonious, based upon simple mathematical ratios, like those of the basic intervals in music (the 'harmony of the spheres'). Leibniz's philosophy reflects both these perspectives.

Because the fundamental structure of reality seemed to be mathematical, as a logician Leibniz thought that it was possible and desirable to construct an artificial language to investigate tricky philosophical issues. The first step was to make the world itself more rational by suggesting a way to rearrange the universe (or rather, the way people think about it) into fundamental and eternal simple facts – or *logical atoms*, to use the term Bertrand Russell later coined. These logical atoms became for Leibniz the ultimate building blocks of reality, and he gave them a special name: the *monads*. Knowledge of the universe was for him essentially a matter of analysing these building blocks of reality.

Because of this kind of belief in the power of the human mind to solve the great issues simply by the power of reason, Leibniz is remembered today as a key *rationalist* philosopher – along with Descartes and Spinoza. (For more on those two, see the section 'Trying to Do Without God', earlier in this chapter.)

As an individual, though, Leibniz lived a fairly modest, bachelor existence working as the personal secretary to the Archbishop of Mainz and later at the court of the elector of Hannover. However, he was a great social climber – 'an elegant man in a powdered wig', as one contemporary summed him up – and he used his positions as a base to energetically correspond by letter with most of the other thinkers in Europe at the time, as well as with many of the names in high society. 'I love Leibniz,' said one such, the French writer and philosopher Voltaire. 'He is surely a great genius, even if he is also a bit of a charlatan . . . add to that, his ideas are always a bit confused.' But not everyone loved him; he famously fell out with the most famous scientist of the time, Isaac Newton in England, over the question of which of them had been the first to invent calculus.

The only book that Leibniz published in his entire lifetime was nothing to do with maths but was the Theodicy (in 1710), which was concerned with the problem of evil. This is the work that advances his view, parodied by Voltaire in his novel *Candide*, that everything that happens in this world happens because it's for the best – because people live in 'the best of all possible worlds'. But how can that be so when so much pain and suffering exists in the world? In an essay 'The Principles of Nature and Grace, Based on Reason' Leibniz explains away the apparent contradiction:

It follows from the supreme perfection of God that he chose the best possible plan in producing the universe, a plan in which there is the greatest variety together with the greatest order . . . The most carefully used plot of ground, place and time, the greatest effect produced by the simplest means; the most power, knowledge, happiness, and goodness in created things that the universe could allow.

From a divine perspective, things that appear rotten aren't bad at all, as they're necessary in order to create more happiness somewhere else. The present world is the best possible one. His argument, of course, has political implications, and Leibniz was counted both as an aristocrat and a snob.

But what of his thinking machine? Actually, Leibniz was quite a skilled inventor. He made a watch with two symmetrically balanced wheels working in tandem. He devised a gadget for calculating a ship's position without using a compass or observing the stars. He designed an aneroid barometer and came up with various improvements to the design of lenses, not to mention a compressed-air engine for propelling vehicles and projectiles, or plans for a ship that could go under water to escape enemy detection. In his way, Leibniz was a little Leonardo da Vinci, interested not only in all the arts and sciences but practical enough to want to implement his ideas too.

Pascal applies some mathematics

Blaise Pascal (1623–62) was born in Clermont-Ferrand in France and soon became a celebrated philosopher whose *Pensées* (that's French for thoughts) were collected together and published shortly after his death. Despite – or perhaps because of – being a mathematician, his philosophical essays are models of elegance and precision. (He once wrote apologetically to a friend to explain that his letter was so long 'because he didn't have the time to write a short one'.)

The central theme of his writings is the wretched and sinful nature of human life. If that was how he saw his own time on Earth, he certainly also left behind important contributions to geometry, number theory and probability, as well as devising an early kind of computer.

Another way in which he applied mathematics to the philosophical questions of human life concerned that old issue of whether or not God exists. Some people count 'Pascal's Wager' as an argument for God's existence, but it's not that, merely an argument for believing in God; or put another way, advice to selfish people as to how to best guard their interests. Mind you, maybe God wouldn't want people like that in heaven!

Pascal thought that the foundations of knowledge rested on faith rather than reason. This renders all knowledge uncertain, the obvious example being knowledge of God. His wager is that because you can't be sure God really exists, you should assume God does, because the consequences of error in this case are none, but if you assume God doesn't exist and are wrong, the consequence is eternal damnation!

Perhaps of all his inventions it was the computer that was the most characteristic (and most impressive) achievement. In 1673 Leibniz demonstrated his 'calculating machine' to the Royal Society in London, which promptly elected him to membership, thereby infuriating Newton. Writing in 1685, Leibniz gives the following account of his moment of inspiration for this invention:

> When, several years ago, I saw for the first time an instrument which, when carried, automatically records the number of steps taken by a pedestrian, it occurred to me at once that the entire arithmetic could be subjected to a similar kind of machinery so that not only counting, but also addition and subtraction, multiplication and division could be accomplished by a suitably arranged machine easily, promptly, and with sure results.

However, as with his wrangle with Dr Newton over which of them had invented calculus, Leibniz was not the first to think of the computer. The French philosopher-mathematician Pascal had made a calculating machine a generation earlier to help his father – a tax inspector – with his tedious sums. Although Pascal's machine could add five-figure numbers, it couldn't do any other calculations. It was very expensive to manufacture and jammed easily. Probably only a few more than a dozen machines were ever made. (The nearby sidebar 'Pascal applies some mathematics' has more on Pascal.)

Leibniz and the first computer language

As part of his original quest for a 'universal language' ready for the computation of thinking, Leibniz realised that existing languages are poorly structured, illogical and hence quite unsuitable for deep thought. For this reason, he set about creating a new, logical language (based on Latin), an enterprise in the spirit of Aristotle himself. Indeed, Leibniz is sometimes called the 'Aristotle of the Modern Era'.

So, how did it work? A phrase like 'Leibniz invented calculus', for example, he would have preferred to see expressed as 'Leibniz is the inventor of calculus'. In fact, Leibniz had decided, you should jettison all verbs with the exception of one – *is*. More importantly (for Leibniz anyway) you should rewrite expressions like 'All A are B', such as, for example 'all Leibnizes are great inventors' as (A is not B) is not possible, or, for the example:

'(Leibniz is NOT a great inventor) IS (not possible).

Experts say all this is a forerunner of the system finally produced by George Boole (1815–64) that's central to today's computer science. Boole manipulates statements that are given truth values, but Leibniz tries to go one step further and turn concepts into numbers, the better to manipulate them mechanically. Intriguingly, like later logicians, he considered that all concepts are made up of simpler ones that you can't break down further, similar to the way all numbers are made up of factors, except the prime numbers themselves (8 is also 2×4, but poor old 13 is stuck for ever being just 13, for example).

Leibniz's father wasn't a tax collector like Pascal's, but a moral philosopher, and fittingly Leibniz's machine was designed instead to automate the (equally dreary) task of solving moral problems. It utilised:

> *. . . a general method in which all truths of reason would be reduced to a kind of calculation. At the same time, this would be a sort of universal language or script, but infinitely different from all those imagined previously, because its symbols and words would direct the reason, and errors – except those of fact – would be mere mistakes in calculation.*

Leibniz lived in an age before electricity, let alone electronics. Inevitably, his machine proved a vain dream. However, he might have had more success if he'd continued to study the binary system, and indeed he'd been one of the first mathematicians to do so. He was fascinated by the way that you could express derive the whole of arithmetic with just two numbers (or symbols) 1 and 0, and considered that likewise the whole universe was generated out of pure being and nothingness. 'God is pure being: matter is a compound of being and nothingness', he wrote rather impressively.

Marching alongside Hegel to the beat of dialectical reason

Although communism and fascism are seemingly very different, indeed they both owe their origins to Georg Hegel (1770–1831), former schoolmaster and philosophy professor. Hegel's ideas not only sent Marx padding off to the British Library every day in search of the footprints of dialectical material-ism, but inspired Nietzsche, Gentile and many others with his talk of a new era to be ushered in through war and destruction. According to Hegel, and thus the Marxists and the Fascists, the new era was inevitable – it was noth-ing less than the goal of history.

Dialectical materialism is the Marxist version of Hegel's *dialectical reason*. It sounds complicated but it isn't really. The idea in both cases is that two opposed forces – ideas or arguments for Hegel, social classes or even nations for Marx – come into conflict, and in the process destroy each other resulting in a new, higher idea or stage.

Hegel sees human beings as cogs in an impersonal and irresistible cosmic machine, grinding through societies in order to eventually produce . . . guess what! Pure rationality. Human beings aren't able to be entirely rational, being mere creatures of flesh and blood, but governments or states can be. In the *Philosophy of Right*, Hegel explains in his excellent, headmasterly way that individuals must understand that the state doesn't exist for them, but rather that the individual exists for the state. He writes: 'On the Stage of Universal History, on which we can observe and grasp it, Spirit displays itself in its most concrete reality.' Conveniently, the concrete reality was also Hegel's employer – the king of Prussia! Hegel finishes with this grand promise:

> *The German Spirit is the Spirit of the new World. Its aim is the realisation of absolute Truth as the unlimited self-determination of Freedom.*

Hegel warns against allowing any restraints on this rising German spirit, such as those of international organisations with the task of preventing conflict, explaining (again in the Philosophy of Right) that war is crucial:

> *Just as the blowing of the winds preserves the sea from the foulness which would be the result of a prolonged calm, so also corruption in nations would be the product of prolonged, let alone 'perpetual' peace.*

Experts like to say that Hegel's thought represents the summit of Germany's 19th-century philosophical idealism. Afterwards came the descent. First came the historical materialism of the Young Hegelian, Karl Marx – that is, the view that history is the story of people fighting one another for food, land and money. Then came the new philosophy of fascism in Italy, Spain, Austria and Germany. Fascism is based on the idea that people fight for abstract ideals, such as the nation and greatness.

In 1831 cholera was endemic in Berlin (Hegel's colleague and intellectual enemy Schopenhauer, despite or perhaps because of being famously pessimistic, quickly left the city for the healthier climes of Italy) but Hegel stayed, perhaps out of his preference for his own nation, contracted the disease and died.

Waking up Kant from his dogmatic slumbers

Immanuel Kant (1724–1804), or the Chinaman of Königsburg as Nietzsche rather obscurely dubbed him, spent his career devising rules as a university professor (making him one of the first great philosophers to be paid to philosophise). Aristotle had written out the laws of thought already, but Kant now added a few of his own (see Chapter 13). It's these rules, rigid and inflexible but supposedly also the manifestation of reason itself, that make Kant's thinking so distinctive. Of these perhaps the best known is what he calls the categorical imperative. This says:

> *Act only according to a maxim by which you can at the same time will that it shall become a general law.*

This is a bit like the old Christian maxim 'Do unto others only what you would have them do unto you', which runs through the New Testament like mould through blue cheese. And when Kant's version appears in the Metaphysic of Morals (1785) he offers it to decide all moral issues. Curiously, though, the rule seems to collapse at the most easy tests. For example, it allows things that surely should be banned, but outlaws things that don't seem to matter very much. A rule, for instance, that anyone who spills tea on a *For Dummies* book should be beaten with a stick and have their tongues cut out is approved by the rule because it's universalisable (that is, it's logically possible to apply this rule in all cases), but borrowing is forbidden because if everyone borrowed it would lead to a run on the bank. Kant would have to condemn the charities that make micro-loans to Third World farmers for seeds and shovels, for example, as being wicked.

Kant argued that you have to follow moral principles unconditionally and without regard for the consequences. That's what makes his imperative so categorical. So, for example, it's certainly always necessary to tell the truth, even to a madman hunting your grandma to kill her. When he asks you 'Which way did your grandma run?', you better be sure to say honestly which way it was! (Kant says that if the madman then kills her that's *his* responsibility, whereas lying would be *yours*.) On the other hand, someone who never does anything to hurt anyone else isn't a good person if their action is prompted merely by fear of going to prison. In a way, this is both ancient ethics and a more modern effort to construct a moral code or even machine to deal with all those tricky questions concerning right and wrong. (I look at how successful the imperative is in more detail in Chapter 13.)

Despite his scientific interests, Kant criticises knowledge obtained by the senses and suggests that it's better derived by 'transcendental deduction' instead. Unfortunately, no one's ever been able to find out what this is. But certainly mind is better than matter, which in any case only takes on the form it does thanks to you looking at it. Although this is an old philosophical story, Kant had the boldness to describe his idea in the preface to the second edition of the *Critique of Pure Reason* as 'a Copernican revolution' in philosophy. And in case it wasn't clear, he added, 'I venture to say that there is not a single metaphysical problem that has not been solved, or for the solution for which the key at least has not been supplied.'

Certainly, Kant made a valiant and important attempt to show the respective contributions of two human faculties – sense perception and reason – to the creation of human knowledge. He thought like Locke that all knowledge of the world derives from sensory impressions (which however he calls confusingly, intuitions') and cannot reach beyond these; but he insisted that such impressions, if they are going to yield knowledge of stable objects must be organised in conformity with concepts supplied by the understanding. The Transcendental Deduction was that part of a project to identify which particular concepts were *necessary* for the organisation of our impressions into knowledge of objects.

A large part of the *Critique of Pure Reason* is devoted to exposing the errors that follow from failing to understand the true nature of space and time. This is a bit like Zeno with his paradoxes, and indeed the most effective part of the 700 odd pages of the *Critique* is the short section of 'Antinomies' that seeks to demonstrate four examples of paradoxical reasoning:

- The world must have had a beginning in both time and space, and it can't have done.

- Everything must be made up of smaller parts, and everything must be all part of the same thing.

- Cause and effect are entirely mechanical – and they're not.

- God exists necessarily – and God doesn't necessarily exist.

However much Kant borrowed from the debates of Zeno and the ancients, he certainly impressed Georg Hegel, who conducted his entire philosophy using the same style of thesis followed by antithesis. (For more on Hegel, see the section 'Marching alongside Hegel to the beat of dialectical reason', earlier in this chapter.) Hegel, however, solves the riddles by adding a supposed *synthesis* (an answer obtained by combining the two opposed views), whereas Kant, like Zeno, was content to merely discredit certain ways of thinking. So perhaps Kant's most important philosophical influence wasn't one of his rules, but one of his methods – a kind of automated reasoning system of its own.

Kant proceeds further in *Religion Within the Limits of Reason Alone* (1793) to roundly demolish all the popular theories of God's existence, and was forbidden, for his trouble, to do so again by Frederick William III, the then ruler of Prussia. This time Kant very evidently broke the rules!

Pushing Aside Philosophy with Mathematics

The philosophers' dream of creating a logical language to make solving philosophy problems a matter of calculation and not endless debate took another giant step forward (well, that's what they thought) in 1890 when the British philosopher Bertrand Russell met the famous Italian logician Guiseppe Peano at a philosophy conference in Paris.

Peano inspired the young Russell to undertake the task of putting mathematics on a logical foundation. Like Gottlob Frege, his German contemporary, Russell's aim was to demonstrate that you could reduce mathematics to logic, and that it depended on nothing but pure reason. And at first things went very well. From 1907 to 1910, Russell worked in his study at Cambridge from 10 to 12 hours a day, writing out logical theorems under the benevolent supervision of Alfred North Whitehead, of whom history has recorded that he hosted 'legendary afternoon teas'. These would eventually become the magisterial (read complicated and very technical) *Principia Mathematica*. (Russell's notes, that is, not Whitehead's teas.)

The Maths of counting dogs

The *Principia* is very long and very boring and not much read nowadays. But you can sum up its point in just one sentence: logic is more important than mathematics, which in fact you reduce to just a few logical principles.

For example, Russell reveals numbers, so dear to mathematicians, to be merely adjectives. Three dogs, for example, is just another way of saying of some dogs that they have the quality of 'threeness'. See that group of dogs over there? It belongs in the class of 'threeness', along with the number of leaves clover has, the number of chances you get to hit the white thing in baseball, Russell's first three wives – in fact, every other group of things that has this ephemeral quality. But what about that pack of six dogs? Does it too belong in the group of three things? For it contains *two* collections of *three* dogs.

But this is already getting complicated. It already looks like you have to leave this question to the experts. So how is Russell's approach an improvement? Yet for many modern philosophers, it is. They think that ordinary language is much better expressed formally using logic. (For more on this, see chapter 11.) You should strip sentences of their 'cannibal superstitions' to reveal their logical essence, to recall the rather non-politically-correct phrase Russell uses in his book, Mind and Matter.

Russell worries that people should do away with words that precede nouns such as *some*, *no*, *a* and *every* – or *quantifiers*, as he calls them. This is because, like *unicorns* and *the king of France*, they don't really stand for anything. *Socrates* stands for Socrates, and the word *philosopher* stands for certain scholarly attributes in a person, but in the phrase 'Socrates is a philosopher', what does the *a* stand for? A quantity, yes, but that complicates things. Because to say a unicorn has one horn doesn't really mean that there really is a unicorn that has one and only one horn. You even need to clarify simple sentences like 'Snow is frozen water', for what kind of verb is *is*?

(That's two uses of the little word in a row.) Is this *is* an *is* as in something exists? Or is *is* is (that's three) as in *equals*? Or is it *is* as in describing a property of snow? Which *is* is it?

Another nasty problem was that of negatives. To say that 'Socrates is a man' is complicated, but to say that 'Socrates is not a woman' is much, much worse. Russell wanted to outlaw such negative assertions too. He wanted to make all statements simple ones directly relating to either logical or empirical truths. And how can you directly refer to something that doesn't exist? Clearly negatives won't do. Or perhaps I should say, clearly only positives will do.

Anyway, these are the sorts of questions analytic philosophers like Russell debated in the 20th century. Russell decided that everything you say must consist only of statements (perhaps combined) about things you have immediate direct knowledge of – knowledge, quintessentially, by sense perception.

Because even after all this tightening up of the rules for thought and language, Russell found himself confronted with a problem, and a bitter problem it turned out to be too. In fact, in due course it would become his philosophical monument – known for ever after in philosophy as *Russell's paradox*. It is expressed in mathematical parlance as 'the problem of the set of all sets that are not members of themselves' and the problem is simply whether it's a member of itself or not. But you can do better than that if you remember the case of the hairdresser of Hindu Kush.

Once upon a time, in far away Hindu Kush, there was a hairdresser who was supposed to cut the hair of everyone in the town who didn't normally cut their own hair. For the hairdresser, the range of possible clients for haircuts is simple enough: either people normally cut their own hair or they don't. But what about his own hair? If the hairdresser doesn't normally cut it, he can certainly cut his hair this time. But if that's so, he'd appear to be cutting the hair of someone who normally cuts his own hair – which he's not supposed to do. So the hairdresser shouldn't cut his own hair. But if he doesn't cut his hair, then clearly he fits the category of people whose hair he can cut.

It all goes round and round in an ultimately rather futile self-referential fizzle. So Russell decided to save his excellent theory by outlawing all statements that are self-referential (not just ones about hairdressers). This is his *theory of types*. For this great work Russell naturally expected equally great public acclaim. But he was disappointed.

However, at least he wasn't put into prison, as happened twice later in his life because the aristocratic 'Earl Russell' was also something of a social misfit and political radical. Perhaps this was the inevitable consequence of applying logic to everyday life.

Analytic philosophy

Bertrand Russell was writing during the first part of the 20th century, a time when some of the most eminent philosophers, such as Ludwig Wittgenstein (Russell's sometime student), Gottlob Frege and G.E. Moore, also reacted against the metaphysical speculations and grand theories of the previous century. They all believed that scholars needed to promote the breaking down or analysis of statements into a more philosophically rigorous method. All of its practitioners were too busy crunching maths and logic to be minded to trace their approach back, but they all shared a similarity of approach to Leibniz with his search for a way of computing the answers to philosophical questions, and indeed the Ancient Greeks with their attempts to apply the techniques that worked so well in geometry for solving maths problems to philosophical questions and debates.

By the end of the Second World War philosophy had moved on slightly and Wittgenstein drolly parodied his own position on the nature of language as over-simplistic. Gilbert Ryle disputed the idea that the so-called simple 'atomic propositions' (like 'Snow is white' or 'Philosophy is complicated') that philosophers sought in language could reflect facts, when reality itself isn't composed of bits like this. According to such as the US philosopher Willard Quine, the attempt was doomed from the start because language has no defining structure.

Doomed or not, though, philosophy has always sought to analyse claims and often the method adopted has been to translate them into several simpler, smaller, ones. Plato in the *Republic* seeks to analyse the meaning of justice in terms of harmony in an ideal state; Locke, Berkeley and Hume seek to analyse the meaning of physical objects in terms of ideas in the mind. As Fred Holman put it recently in his article 'Analysis' in the *Essentials of Philosophy and Ethics*, '. . . analytic philosophy was really more a new name than a new idea, and a new way of phrasing very old debates'.

Leaving aside the name of the movement itself, analytic philosophy's practitioners liked to grab terms from chemistry – such as *atomic* and *molecular* – suggesting an analogy with laboratory science where chemists analyse or break down ordinary, everyday substances into their basic constituents, atoms and molecules.

What Russell and others of that ilk conceived themselves as doing was replacing vague, clumsy, imprecise, insufficiently discriminating, descriptive claims of ordinary speech and writing with logically equivalent but far more basic *atomic propositions*. These are very precise statements of fact that you can't express any more simply. Ironically, their rejection of the grand claims made by past philosophers concealed a new, equally grand claim – that reality itself consisted of simple, basic entities with simple attributes or in simple relations. Their project only made sense because they thought that their atomic propositions better pictured and helped people to understand that reality, but the ambiguities and contradictions of language were hiding that reality from people and rendering all claims to knowledge dubious.

As the 20th century progressed, a new and different purpose seized those engaged in analytical philosophy. They adopted what was also in its way a grand, metaphysical position by claiming that only empirical statements (based on physical measurements and such like), notably scientific ones, and *tautological* statements (truisms) were meaningful. All other claims, including ethical, theological and aesthetic ones lacking a truth value, were strictly speaking 'non-sense'. Mere grunts!

That was to be the end of philosophy, although professional philosophers would now help people to express themselves properly. The trouble was that at this point, for everyone else, it seemed that the philosophers had ceased to talk about the things people cared about. And, as for the logic, in the second half of the 20th century computers arrived that were capable of performing the propositional manipulations favoured by the new analytic philosophers in milliseconds! At least Leibniz would have been pleased . . .

Chapter 6

Looking at Eastern Philosophy

. . . .

In This Chapter

▶ Popping over to China to find Confucius preoccupied with how to run society

▶ Exploring Lao-Tzu's fascination with the notion of change

▶ Pestering Buddha about the problem of human suffering

▶ Pondering the perplexing and alarming possibilities of reincarnation

. . . .

> *By three methods we may learn wisdom: first, by reflection, which is noblest; second, by imitation, which is easiest; and third, by experience, which is the bitterest.*
>
> – Confucius

Almost all the guides to philosophy (the ones that are written in English anyway) are actually guides to Western philosophy. A century ago, people like Bertrand Russell used to put that fact upfront in the title, so that his much read *History of Western Philosophy* doesn't pretend to be anything more comprehensive. Nowadays, though, most philosophers either don't realise a difference between Eastern and Western philosophy exists, or they don't bother to acknowledge it. Western philosophy has become for them the whole of philosophy. But that need not be the case for us! You can gain a much deeper understanding of not only the history of philosophy but of the issues and ideas if you allow traditions – Indian, Japanese, Korean, African, Native American and above all Chinese philosophy – at the philosophical table.

Now a *For Dummies* book, like a harassed waiter, can't cover *everything*, but if you don't have a good serving of Eastern philosophy at least, then it's a bit like afternoon tea with no biscuits or like riding a bicycle without first fitting the wheels. Eastern philosophy is holistic. Its sages don't divide everything up like many Western philosophers in the long tradition of Aristotle (who liked to put everything into neat boxes of mutually exclusive categories), but like to keep everything joined up. And so should we.

This chapter helps correct the balance between the dominant, Western kind of philosophy – and everyone else's. In particular, it tells you what you need to know about Eastern philosophy.

Contemplating the Mysterious Tao

Western philosophy started with Descartes splitting the world into two parts – mind and matter. But Eastern philosophies regard thinking and acting as two aspects of one activity – two sides of the same coin. Chinese philosophy, in particular, says ultimate reality (*T'ai Chi*) is a combination of mind (*li*) and matter (*chi*). The aim, both for the philosopher and for everyone else, is to align yourself with the *Tao*. (People often translate *Tao* as 'The Way', and you pronounce the 't' as a 'd' as in *dow*). But what is the *Tao*?

Lao Tzu (*Lowl-zoo*, but sometimes alternatively pronounced *Lousy*, which at least is easy to remember) wrote in the fourth chapter of the *Tao Te Ching* that *Tao* is empty:

> . . . *like a bowl, it may be used, but is never emptied, it is bottomless, the ancestor of all things, it blunts sharpness, it unties knots, it softens the light, it becomes one with the dusty world – deep and still, it exists for ever.*

In Hergé's classic *Tintin* book, *The Blue Lotus*, the madman tries to reunite people with the *Tao* by cutting their heads off with a scimitar. But you can do better than that if you go back to its origins in one of the Ancient Chinese texts of philosophy.

Tao Te Ching

The story goes that one day Lao Tzu was unhappy with China and decided to leave it to travel the world. To his annoyance (like many celebrities since) a guard recognised him at the frontier as 'the great sage' and refused to allow him to pass – unless he first recorded all his wisdom on parchment.

Despite, or more likely because of, being so very wise, Lao Tzu managed to do this in just a few weeks. The result was a slim volume of a little over 5,000 Chinese characters. It's the classic work of Chinese philosophy. At its heart, for example, one of Lao Tzu's philosophical reflections runs:

> *Something amorphous and consummate existed before Heaven and Earth.*
>
> *Solitude! Vast! Standing alone, unaltering. Going everywhere, yet unthreatened.*
>
> *It can be considered the Mother of the World.*
>
> *I don't know its name, so I designate it, 'Tao'.*
>
> *Compelled to consider it, name it 'the Great'.*

Anyway, handing the complete text to the guard, Lao Tzu then climbed back on his bull and disappeared off, heading (perhaps significantly?) westward. Images of the sage riding his bull are popular in China to this day.

This text is known today as the *Tao Te Ching* (the *Classic of the Way and Its Power*). The earliest manuscript copies found date back to the second century BC. Because this is a few centuries later than Lao Tzu lived, some Western experts dispute that Lao Tzu's text ever really existed (yet no one disputes Socrates' existence and he's left no written records at all!). Meanwhile, at the other extreme, devout followers of Lao Tzu's teachings consider the text to have a divine origin and revere its author not merely as a prophet but as an immortal. Yet for those who wish to accord Lao Tzu only the same level of historical proof as, say, Plato, he was born in the sixth century BC at Juren in the State of Chu, and was the original author of the *Tao Te Ching*.

But whoever wrote it, the *Tao Te Ching* is clearly a storehouse of big ideas. Just one of them is the notion of yin and yang. These are the two aspects of everything in reality. *Yin*, the feminine aspect, is dark, soft and yielding. *Yang*, the masculine aspect, is bright, hard and inflexible. Everything in the world consists of both elements, and everything's in a state of flux, changing to become more yin, or more yang.

> *Human beings are born soft and flexible; yet when they die are stiff and hard . . .*
>
> *Plants sprout soft and delicate, yet when they die they are withered and dry . . .*
>
> *Thus the hard and stiff are disciples of death, the soft and flexible are disciples of life.*
>
> *Thus an inflexible army is not victorious, an unbending tree will break.*
>
> *The stiff and massive will be lessened, the soft and fluid will increase.*

This idea of the cyclical nature of reality reappeared in Ancient Greece in the philosophy of Heraclitus, where it influenced Plato.

Doing the I Ching

Another message of the *Tao Te Ching* is that everything follows certain patterns – 'the way'. Human beings should also follow the way, and yield to the times and influences. Judging and yielding to the times is also the theme of the even more ancient text the *I Ching*, or *Book of Changes*. The *I Ching* is often pronounced just as it looks, a bit like an old-fashioned cash register, but to be correct you should pronounce it *E Jing*. It was written in stages and originated in fortune-telling traditions. The *I Ching* includes philosophical commentaries written about 5,000 years ago, which makes it probably the oldest book in the world. What were the Ancient Greeks doing then? Archaeologists think that farming had just arrived on the North European plain – complete with wooden saws fitted with chipped flint teeth – and yet most books will tell you that the Greeks were the first philosophers!

The *I Ching* is a guide to action, to achieving the best outcome in the circumstances. The great 20th-century psychologist and philosopher C. G. Jung wrote of the *I Ching*, 'this is a book for lovers of wisdom', and so it is. But it's foremost a practical guide to action, consulted, over the last 3,000 years, first of all by emperors and sages, but later on by farmers and generals as well. Because, after all, it's part of the philosophy that 'the way' applies to very small as much as to the great things.

Texts like the *I Ching* and the *Tao Te Ching* contain many of the key ideas of Western philosophy. Although you can't say that one led to the other, it's certainly noteworthy that the Chinese wrote on these matters, and with greater sophistication, first. It could just be that Europeans have preferred to downplay their intellectual debt to the East in the same way that the history of technical innovation and invention was rewritten to give the West the leading role.

You might not get the impression sometimes, but it was the Eastern thinkers (especially the Chinese) who were the pathfinders in the development of astronomy, medicine, printing and mathematics, so it would be remarkable if they hadn't also produced the key works of philosophy. The recent writing out of the Ancient Chinese philosophers from the story of philosophy has more to do with political and social prejudices than it has with intellectual let alone philosophical ones.

The *I Ching* is a book like no other philosophy book. It consists of 64 strange diagrams made up of six lines each – called *hexagrams*. Each line is either solid or broken in two – dashed. They represent thus either yin or yang. By creating one of the 64 hexagrams randomly, by the wonders of coincidence (or what the psychologist C.G. Jung called *synchronicity* – he was a fan of the *I Ching*) you can place your tiny self and your tiny concerns in the context of the whole of the ongoing tendencies of the universe! Not bad!

Of course, interpretation is the key. And the hexagrams are, well, inscrutable. Take Hexagram 64, for example, shown in Figure 6-1. To you or I, it's a block of six alternating solid and dashed lines, but to the sages of Ancient China it resembles a tree with doubled branches at the top indicating that the tree is barren of flowers or leaves and means 'not yet' or 'incomplete', in the sense of continuing the eternal cycle.

This hexagram is called *Wei Chi* which means 'Before the End' (all the hexagrams have a name). The sages believed it symbolises the purity of order and harmony.

Figure 6-1:
Before the End.

For the Ancient Chinese at least, this symbol has a deep significance, expressed in words as:

> *Bare trees before the leaves come.*
>
> *Crossing over to order and harmony.*
>
> *The past is gone, the future yet to be.*

Honouring Confucius

If Lao Tzu is scarcely known in the West (see the section earlier in this chapter), at least philosophers recognise his contemporary Confucius (551–479 BC) as an important thinker. Confucius was the essence of the Ancient Chinese sage: a social philosopher, an educator and the star of a highly influential text, the *Analects*.

Confucius always presented himself as a transmitter who invented nothing and emphasised instead learning from the ancient sages. In this way, he's similar to Socrates, who also denied any special knowledge or expertise. Nonetheless, sources indicate that altogether he had 3,000 disciples and that '72 of them were influential'. What of the other 2,928? His teachings, preserved in the *Analects*, form the foundation of much of subsequent Chinese thinking about education, government and human conduct. In this way too, Confucius's influence can be compared with that of Socrates in the West.

Often people reduce the philosophical ideas of Confucius to being a collection of aphorisms or moral maxims, which hardly suffices to explain the depth of the influence of Confucianism. If his philosophy was merely aphorisms and maxims, Confucius's influence would have been far less. The *Analects*, like all Chinese philosophy, requires a lot of decoding.

At the heart of Confucius's philosophy are the twin concepts of rites or ritual rules (which he calls *li*) and the correct way for people to live (which he calls *ren*).

Life of the master

Confucius was born in Qufu in State Lu (now part of present-day Shandong province) and died at the age of 72. As a child, Confucius is said to have enjoyed putting ritual vases on the sacrifice table. His first role was as a minor administrative manager in the state of Lu but he soon rose to the position of justice minister where he earned a reputation for fairness, politeness and love of learning.

However, at about the age of 50, seeing no way to improve the government he gave up his political career. He began a 12-year journey around China, seeking the way and trying unsuccessfully to convince many different rulers of his political beliefs and to push them into reality.

Confucius returned home around his 60th year, and spent the rest of his life teaching and editing the ancient classics. He became what the Chinese call a 'throneless king', seeking to share his experiences with his disciples and to transmit the old wisdom to the later generations.

The whole notion of 'rites' may seem odd these days, but think of the importance of religious traditions and social institutions like marriage, birthdays – and funerals!

In his emphasis on rules, Confucius is opposed to the spirit of *Taoism* (the school of thought that follows Lao Tzu), which fundamentally seeks a kind of freedom that, while integrated with the world, is unfettered and dependent on nothing. Taoists consider the traditional rites to be artificial and false, an external constraint on people's lives. Lao Tzu even stated that trying to be proper was 'a superficial expression of loyalty and faithfulness, and the beginning of disorder'. For Confucius, the rites were the key to virtue, but for Lao Tzu they were an obstacle to finding the way.

Another school, called *Legalism*, also opposed Confucian traditions and the social codes built around special rites – this time from a very practical point of view. The goal of the Legalists was a wealthy and powerful state; a very different vision from the Confucian ideal of an ordered world of peace, harmony and simple contentment. In a world where huge armies were girding themselves for terrible battles, the Legalists offered themselves as experts in the arts of enriching and strengthening the state. And a key element of their approach was to advocate the destruction of ancient hierarchical distinctions including the ethics of Confucius, which they saw as perpetuating old feudal values and practices.

Confucius and his followers insisted, however, that the problem wasn't in the rites or traditions themselves, but in the way that the rites were carried out and the fact that people no longer followed them properly. To regain the validity of the rites, the Confucians said people needed to be able to practise them meaningfully in their daily life. In this way Confucius changed the moral emphasis away from actions and towards motivations – away from objective morality and towards the moral subject.

For Confucius, what must be emphasised in performing a ritual is having the correct attitude. For example, when performing a sacrifice, he said, you have to feel reverence for the spirits; when carrying out the rites of mourning, you have to feel grief for the decreased. Without this emotional component, ritual becomes a hollow performance. Confucius once remarked: 'A man who does not have humanity, what can he have to do with ritual?' It's not enough to do the right thing – you must also have the correct attitude. This important ethical concept reappears in the Western philosophical debates between the Utilitarians, who emphasise outcomes irrespective of motives, and the followers of Aristotle and Kant with their emphasis on personal virtue and duties.

Yet for Confucius it's unimaginable that you can understand moral rules and virtues separately. He argued (as have some Western moral philosophers) that you must see the ethics of virtue and the ethics of rule as adding up, rather than as cancelling each other out.

And Confucianism was also opposed to Legalism over the question of whether or not to try to force the masses to be good by a severe system of penal law. As Confucius said:

> *Lead the people with governmental measures and regulate them by law and punishment, and they will avoid wrongdoing but will have no sense of honour and shame. Lead them with virtue and regulate them by the rules of propriety, and they will have a sense of shame and, moreover, set themselves right and arrive at goodness.*

Confucian Music

Confucius not only said interesting things, he sang them and accompanied himself on a *qin* (a kind of zither; a useful word for Scrabble players!) while singing classic poetry. In China the image of the philosopher–musician is firmly established.

And Confucius had clear ideas about the importance of music. He said: 'Let a man be stimulated by poetry, established by the rules of propriety and made perfect by music.' Confucius considered that music didn't just reflect the feelings of people but it shaped them too, and so could mould people's characters. He hoped that the harmony (at least in traditional Chinese music) that is the essence of music could then find its way into the depths of the human heart.

This is all a great contrast with Plato, who was suspicious of the influence of music, worrying that it beguiled simple folk, leading them into bad habits. But for Confucius, musical training is the most effective method for changing the moral character of man and keeping society in order.

Meeting up with Mencius

Mencius (371–289 BC) was born in the State of Zou, located in what's now the Shandong province, only 30 kilometres (18 miles) south of Qufu, the hometown of Confucius. As Confucius in the Eastern tradition might be to Socrates in the Western philosophical tradition, so Mencius is to Plato. Plato's writings are all about Socrates' view of 'the good', and so are Mencius's books all about Confucius's wisdom. For Mencius, known as 'the Second Sage', is the communicator of Confucian philosophy known for his insistence that human nature is basically good. His views, set out in the *Book of Mencius* or *Mengzi*, were adopted as the basis for the Chinese civil service exams in the 14th century, and remained the core texts for the next 600 years.

Mencius declared that human nature is fundamentally good. For example, he argues that if a person sees a child about to fall into a well, invariably she'll feel a sense of alarm and compassion and will rush to save the child. What's more, this action isn't for the purpose of gaining the favour of the child's parents, or seeking the approbation of her neighbours and friends, or for fear of blame should she fail to rescue the child. It's rather a selfless and spontaneous response from their shared human nature. From this it follows that the sense of sympathy, the sense of repentance, the sense of courtesy and the sense of judgement on what's right and wrong are the four beginnings of humanity, righteousness, propriety and wisdom. Nothing drills these virtues into you from outside. They're an integral part of universal nature.

Unfortunately, many people have lost track of their moral inheritance. That's why Mencius once sighed: 'When a person's fowls and dogs are lost, they know enough to seek them again; but if they lose their human heart/mind, they do not know to seek for it.' According to Mencius, the goal of moral cultivation is to return to your innate nature. This is also the aim of the ideal state that Plato attempted to build in his *Republic*.

Fluttering with Chuang Tzu

Another of the great sages of Chinese philosophy, Chuang Tzu (369–286 BCE), stresses the unity of all things, and dynamic interplay of opposites. Good and bad, he points out, are like everything else: interrelated and interchangeable. What's good for the rabbit – lots of nice, juicy grain to nibble – is bad indeed for the farmer, to offer a rather weak example of my own. A book called the *Chuang Tzu* – of which historians believe about a quarter is Chuang's work – is lively and playful, a mixture of stories and poetry as well as philosophical arguments, and has always been highly popular in China.

Mencius against utilitarianism

Once, when challenged to justify elaborate funeral traditions, Mencius replied:

> In ancient times there was no burial of one's parents. When a man's parent died, he simply threw the body into a ditch. When he later passed by, what he saw was that the body was being eaten by the foxes or bitten by the gnats or flies . . . He could not bear the sight. The feeling of the heart flew out to his face. He then hurried home and came back with baskets and a spade for covering up the body. If the covering up of a human body was the right thing for primitive man, it is quite right today for a filial son or man to prepare the funeral for his parents.

Funeral traditions rate large in Chinese philosophy – and not at all in Western debates! But if it seems an odd choice of philosophical example, it's not necessarily a bad one. For here's something people may feel strongly about, yet which has, it seems, no practical, utilitarian purpose. The efficient way to arrange society, even the way that maximises happiness, may yet not be the right way to do it.

Chuang Tzu's influence throughout the East, ranging from Buddhism (which draws on his teaching that suffering is mainly a result of refusing to accept what is) to Zen philosophy (which reflects his love of paradoxes or *koans*) has been profound. And his message of nonconformity and freedom unshackled the Chinese mind from some of the effects of over-rigid Confucianism.

An example of his simple but elegant style of argumentation is a passage in which he describes the way language works. Language, Chuang says, is a fishing net cast into the waters of reality, useful for catching meanings. Thoughts and concepts are slippery fish, and you need the net of language to capture them. But the net itself is just a means to an end.

Another simple example attempts to show the relativity of moral judgements. Chuang asks whether if, as some sages said, killing is wrong, then would it also be wrong to kill a hare when it was the only way to save yourself from starving? Surely not. Perhaps then it's always wrong to kill another human being? But what if that human being is a robber intent on killing and robbing a family? Surely it's then not wrong to kill the robber, if that's the only way to stop this human?

All moral knowledge depends in this way on context and situations: it's relative. Chuang goes on to prove that in fact all knowledge – not just moral or aesthetic judgements – is equally rooted in context, and equally relative. He puts it in this perfectly inscrutable way:

Once I, Chuang Chou, dreamed I was a butterfly and was happy as a butterfly. I was conscious that I was quite pleased with myself, but I did not know that I was Chou. Suddenly I awoke, and there I was, visibly Chou. I do not know whether it was Chou dreaming he was a butterfly, or the butterfly dreaming it was Chou.

Western philosophy is rooted in a search for definitions – of justice, truth or of knowledge. Chuang Tzu's conclusion instead was that you should strive to transcend the world of distinctions.

Debating with Buddha

Buddhism describes a kind of educational approach developed by the Buddha, one Siddhartha Gautama (see sidebar 'The original Buddha'). Buddhism isn't a religion in the normal, Western sense. It's a philosophical education leading to insights about the true nature of life. Originating in India, Buddhism gradually spread throughout Asia to Central Asia, Tibet, Sri Lanka and Southeast Asia, as well as the East Asian countries of China, Mongolia, Korea and Japan.

Today, there are around 350 million Buddhists, and a growing number of them are Westerners. They may follow many different forms of Buddhism, but all traditions are characterised by non-violence, lack of dogma or official rulebook, tolerance of differences and, usually, by the practice of meditation. The aim of Buddhist practices is to become free of suffering and to develop the qualities of awareness, kindness and wisdom.

The original Buddha

Siddhartha Gautama was a prince born some 2,500 years ago in a small Indian kingdom in what is today southern Nepal. He renounced his royal heritage in order to escape the human cycle of birth, death and rebirth that he saw as inevitably leading to suffering, loss and pain. After six years searching, putting his body through various extreme practices, he finally gained enlightenment in his 30s. Motivated by a sense of profound compassion for suffering beings, Buddha shared his wisdom with them, and so embarked on a teaching career that would last for nearly 50 years. He travelled around India, teaching all who wished to listen, responding to the needs and mindsets of his listeners, and skilfully adapting his teachings for each. Of his 79 years, he dedicated 49 to teaching.

Yet if Buddhism is essentially education, this form is rarely seen today. Over the centuries Buddhism has assumed the form of an organised religion. After all, Albert Einstein considered it to have all

> *. . . the characteristics of what would be expected in a cosmic religion for the future: it transcends a personal God, avoids dogmas and theology; it covers both the natural and spiritual, and it is based on a religious sense aspiring from the experience of all things, natural and spiritual, as a meaningful unity.*

Accepting suffering: Hinduism

One of the key messages of Buddhism, with all its social implications, is to persuade people to accept their place in society, be it low or high, without complaint. In this way a political arrangement becomes embedded as a religious duty. You can lay similar philosophical effects at the door of another quasi-philosophy – Hinduism.

Hinduism, like Buddhism, isn't quite a philosophy nor yet a religion. Rather, it combines them both, becoming a complex and multifaceted phenomenon with social, cultural and religious manifestations. Its teachings, as much as its rituals, reflect the myriad geographical, social, racial and linguistic perspectives of the vast Indian subcontinent. There are highly intellectual varieties of Hinduism, just one part of the deep pool of Indian philosophy with its investigations of the nature of perception, of space and time, and of the correct way to live. Alongside the intellectual versions exist the simple, even naive practices of millions of villagers, and it's these together that form Hinduism.

Hinduism is full of contradictions but seems to thrive on this creative antagonism. Several key texts are associated with Hinduism, such as the *Vedas*, ancient and anonymous texts that originated as part of an oral tradition of knowledge between 1500 and 500 BC. The oldest parts are in the form of hymns or prayers, and the more recent writings, including the *Upanishads* (which particularly impressed Spinoza (discussed in Chapter 5) in 17th-century Holland), were written between 400 and 200 BC and are more philosophical in nature and content.

Getting born again: Reincarnation

Another key Eastern idea that reappears in Greek philosophy, where Western philosophers largely pass over it with shrugs, is that of *reincarnation*. This is the theory that people have some sort of personal identity over and above their physical one, and what's more that this identity (religious people call it the *soul*) can survive the destruction of the physical body (death). Having survived, the soul either goes to heaven or is reincarnated and reappears on Earth in a new form – for the Buddhists, as animals or, if you've been very good, as men (not women; traditional Buddhism is totally sexist). Actually, for Buddhists and philosophers like Plato, the ultimate aim for a lucky few is being released from the body to become pure spirit.

Everyone knows (well, quite a few people know) that belief in reincarnation is part of many Eastern religions. What fewer people remember is that the idea seems to have been with mankind from earliest times and in many different and apparently unconnected cultures.

Indeed, belief in personal reincarnation is part of the traditional understandings of the universe of the Australian Aborigines and other Pacific islanders, as well as many of the peoples in the Arctic circle: Finns, Lapps, Danes and Norse as well as the Inuit (or Eskimos). Closer to home, the ancient Celts of Gaul, Wales, England and Ireland assumed people were reborn, which is why they buried important ones with all their hunting gear and weapons.

Hinduism and social life

Hinduism is integral to the life of its followers, not just a weekly church ceremony but a guide to everyday actions that covers everything and everyone from the cradle to the grave. In Hindu thought, as in Eastern philosophy generally, reflection detached from practice has no meaning. Hinduism isn't organised or taught but the daily custom and practice that surrounds everyone from the cradle to the grave – social rules and structures, in effect. And many of these are totally opposed to Western values. Hinduism allows customs such as child marriage, polygamy, idolatry, animal sacrifices and the pernicious caste system.

Despite its many restrictions on women, Hinduism offers a great contrast to Western notions of propriety in its celebration of sex. (Actually, Plato too occasionally praises sex – but only between men!) Refreshingly, and in contrast to Christianity and Islamic traditional teachings, sexuality is considered an essential part of being human, and the medieval branch of *Tantrism* specifically celebrates the enlightenment brought about through imaginative sexual union. Hindu goddesses, depicted in temple carvings that Western explorers were later shocked by, are erotic beings of great sexual power.

Two hundred years ago, the Raja Ram Mohan Roy (1774–1833), who was familiar with Western as well as Eastern philosophy, attempted to reform Hinduism. He hoped that liberal and enlightened philosophies would serve reforms needed in India. And indeed, the government abolished many practices as a result – at least on paper.

But traditional religious systems are highly resistant to reform. In India, the caste system, like discrimination against women in many Islamic states, or the Japanese castes, or even the class system in England, all of which have appealed to religion for justification, linger on despite having little support in any religious texts.

But going back to Ancient Greece, here the philosophers known as Stoics held that the soul is immortal and periodically reincarnates. Pythagoras taught that people and animals shared the same souls. On one occasion he claimed to hear a friend's voice in the howls of a puppy being beaten, and on another occasion he burst into tears on seeing an ancient battle-scarred shield, saying that it had been his shield during the Battle of Troy!

Pythagoras may not make a terribly convincing case for the theory (but then this is the man who claimed that a river, repeat, a *river*, had recognised him and called him by name!), but Socrates and Plato also seem to have been committed to the idea of reincarnation and their views have been very influential.

Plato used the example of instinctive or built-in knowledge to argue that people inherit the minds of previous generations, whereas, in his dialogues with Plato, Socrates wrote of his last days awaiting execution and was so sure of his rebirth that he devoted 'his last morning to reasoning on the real distinction of the soul from the body, and the grounds for believing that it is neither born with the body nor dies with it'. These philosophical debates have had an enormous influence on Western literature and religions – and partly explain why Plato's works have often been on the Catholic Church's list of banned books.

The Renaissance throughout Europe meant new interest in the ideas of people like Plato and Pythagoras, and even very scientifically minded folk like Leonardo da Vinci in Italy and Paracelsus (who pioneered medical vaccinations) discussed the idea at length in their notes. As Paracelsus put it:

> *Some children are born from heaven and others are born from hell, because each human being has his inherent tendencies, and these tendencies belong to his spirit, and indicate the state in which he existed before he was born.*

A few centuries later Spinoza and Leibniz (who were contemporaries) also wrote about human immortality and reincarnation, and in France Voltaire declared: 'It is not more surprising to be born twice than once; everything in nature is resurrection.'

Of all philosophical interest in the theory it's Immanuel Kant's little book on reincarnation that's most unexpected. Kant offers a new idea too: that people aren't only reborn on this planet but on others too. Well, why not! It certainly brings *Star Trek* to life . . .

It was Schopenhauer, however, who was the first to collect and publish references to the theory of reincarnation from early to contemporary times, adding a short introduction in which he says of the idea that it 'springs from the earliest and noblest ages of the human race, always spread abroad on the Earth as the belief of the great majority of mankind'. Or, as his friend, the celebrated writer Johann Goethe expressed it:

I am certain that I have been here as I am now a thousand times before, and I hope to return a thousand times . . . Man is a dialogue between nature and God. On other planets this dialogue will doubtless be of a higher and profounder character. What is lacking is Self-Knowledge. After that the rest will follow.

The Ancient Greek Oracle at Delphi couldn't have put it any better.

Chapter 7

Understanding the 'Isms'

> *. . . in spite of itself any movement that thinks and acts in terms of an 'ism' becomes so involved in reaction against other 'isms' that it is unwittingly controlled by them. For it then forms its principles by reaction against them instead of by a comprehensive, constructive survey of actual needs, problems, and possibilities.*
>
> – John Dewey

This chapter looks at what an 'ism' is, and at what some of the key philosophical isms in particular are about. Many of the debates in philosophy are represented by two opposed sides, each operating under their own 'ism' – for example, the great debates between empiricism and idealism or between fascism and socialism. Yet often the differences are not as clear-cut as they seem, and although it is easy to label a view by creating or using an ism, doing so often confuses rather than enlightens. And abstract though isms are, such confusions can have real practical consequences and dangers.

What's an Ism?

For example, what are imperialism, vegetarianism, monetarism, Platonism, surrealism, post-rationalism, utilitarianism, Nazism and neo-conservatism, fundamentalism, Islamism, consumerism, freeganism, communism, libertarianism, post-modernism, modernism, authoritarianism, romanticism, environmentalism . . . the list of isms goes on and on! Alarmingly!

But, in fact, an *ism* is basically just a word that has had the letters '*ism*' added on to it.

Originally, this was quite a practical idea. People added the suffix *ism* to verbs (describing actions) to form nouns, describing things. For example, vicars in church baptise babies, and this leads to the need for a new noun to describe the occasion – *baptism*. Or take the activity of book reviewers criticising books; what better than to call that thing the *criticism*. Actually, several quite different kinds of isms exist that people use to express different kinds of concepts. Table 7-1 lists the ones that particularly interest philosophers.

Table 7-1	Different Kinds of Ism
Conceptual Category	*Example*
Doctrine or philosophy	Empiricism, relativism, hedonism, existentialism
Theory developed by an individual	Platonism, Hegelianism, Marxism
Political movement	Fascism, socialism, feminism
Prejudice or bias	Sexism, ageism, racism, speciesism
Artistic movement	Surrealism, expressionism, impressionism

Isms only really became something in their own right in the late 17th century (the dictionaries record the first known use of the term in 1680), but once identified, the word soon caught on, particularly as a way of being rude about certain groups of people. By the middle of the 19th century, lots of new derogatory uses had become popular in the United States, with the isms being a convenient way of summing up supposedly 'do-gooder movements' such as feminism, prohibitionism (those trying to prohibit things, especially alcohol) and above all, socialism. Most Americans hate socialism, and the word lends itself very well to a long drawn out snarl of disapproval when you add the letters *ism*. In 1856 one newspaper, the *Richmond Examiner*, summed it all up by running a series of fiery editorials headed 'Our Enemies, the *Isms* and Their Purposes'.

A dictionary may tell you that isms are words that describe things: *suffixes that have come to represent a way of categorising, classifying and amalgamating areas of knowledge. But actually isms* are things themselves. For example, feminism is now also a philosophy, as well as a political movement, with distinct philosophical beliefs and values. Creating a new ism isn't merely creating a new word, but a new way of thinking about the world, even to reveal a hitherto obscured Platonic form. 'Socialism' may not exist on Earth, but it certainly does in Plato's alternative universe. Put another way, a successful new ism becomes a permanent ideal of some sort, with a kind of eternal status in the world of knowledge. It's no wonder then that isms have become so integral to people's way of thinking. In the mysterious world of isms exist not only giant political ones, like socialism and fascism, but also key social and economic ones, like capitalism and monetarism, alongside more traditional philosophical isms, like relativism and existentialism. Not to forget cultural and artistic isms like . . . well, I've forgotten already.

If at one time it was enough to create an ism for it to be much admired, nowadays only some isms are worth attention. Fascism is interesting, for example, with a long history, contemporary relevance and much confusion about its significance and fundamental nature. It deserves its own word, even if no one really uses it correctly. But many other isms, like Platonism, for instance, let alone neo-Platonism, seem to confuse rather than enlighten. The world could do without them!

Unfortunately, confusing isms exist. But at least you can decide whether or not to use them. Neo-Platonism, for example, describes the efforts of later philosophers to reconcile the works of the two great masters, Plato and Aristotle, generally by seeing Aristotle's practical approach as a way into the 'higher wisdom' of Plato. Can you do without it? You bet! Like Platonism and Aristotleianism, it's more to do with impressing people through jargon than conveying a particular idea. But other isms, intimidating though they certainly seem at first, are harder to do without. Take two of the central concepts in the philosophical search for knowledge, empiricism and idealism, which the following sections discuss.

Social-ism

It was in the 19th century that critics of the emerging industrial societies, such as Robert Owen, Henri de Saint Simon and Pierre Proudhon, first used the term *socialism*. All three of these critics shared common concern about the excesses of capitalism as seen in the grim conditions of workers in the new factories, perhaps lit by gaslight and full of poisonous chemicals, and wanted to replace production for profit by social production, for need. In their optimistic vision communities of workers would organise this social production on a small scale.

Although people often link Marxism with socialism, Marx himself sneered at such aspirations, seeing them as mere reforms, *reformism* indeed, incapable of addressing the fundamental problems of capitalism. Instead, he proposed to attain true socialism through *communism*, a movement that has a number of essential characteristics that Marx and his lifelong collaborator Engels set out in their *Communist Manifesto*. The most important element is state ownership of the means of production. Contrary to the reformists, this implies the state controls and owns the labour of the people too.

Choosing between Empiricism and Idealism

Empiricism and idealism are two of the key concepts in the history of philosophy.

Empiricism, in philosophy anyway, is the theory that you have direct access to reality through your senses, and indeed build up all your grand theories out of ordinary sensory interaction with the world. It says that nothing is in the intellect unless it was previously in the senses.

Idealism, by contrast, maintains that reality is ultimately based in the mind, in that all we can really know or be certain of is our thoughts.

This section explains each concept in turn, and shows their chief differences.

Begging for a more practical approach

Empiricism contrasts with theories like that put forward in the *Meno* by Plato (see Chapter 3) where a slave boy is 'brought to remember' how to work out the area of a triangle, supposedly demonstrating Plato's view that people are born ready equipped with lots of important concepts. Plato says this is because the soul exists prior to the body and is in 'a state of communion' with all the important ideas in a kind of parallel abstract universe. Unfortunately (Plato explains), being born *is* rather traumatic for the soul, and so it temporarily forgets much that it previously knew when it joins the body at birth. If people are lucky, as they grow up they recollect (re-collect) their lost ideas and develop a progressively clearer understanding of the things that they (or their soul) once knew.

It all sounds rather theoretical, not to say implausible or even airy-fairy, and so no wonder other people immediately argued instead for a return to a more practical approach. A long series of thinkers, from Plato's student Aristotle, to today's neuroscientists, suppose instead that you can trace all the subtleties and complexities of knowledge back to plain sense-experience of the external world, coupled with later mental reflection on what you've experienced or observed.

This approach is empiricism, and one of the great pushers of the theory was John Locke who (writing in the 17th century) flatly rejected any theory of innate ideas (like Plato's) and offered instead the analogy that the mind at birth is like a blank piece of paper waiting for sense experience to write information on it. For him, and other empiricists, the mental world is a by-product of the physical one.

If Plato sounds rather old-fashioned and Locke much more scientific, that's not to say the issue is settled. Indeed, in the 20th century the influential philosopher Noam Chomsky proposed that the human mind does have an innate structure, in the manner supposed by Plato. However, Chomsky prefers to characterise it as a kind of universal grammar that reveals itself in the way that young children quickly learn to speak, even before they've learnt to do practical things like kick footballs or put boxes on top of each other (let alone eat properly) and all this despite limited exposure to their native language.

Stuffing chickens with Francis Bacon

Francis Bacon (1561–1626) was a lawyer, philosopher and politician at the court of Queen Elizabeth (and later King James) in Tudor England. As if this wasn't honour enough, he's also traditionally counted as the first British empiricist.

Bacon epitomised the renaissance faith in scientific method, and devoted himself to developing a system combining data drawn from experience with a splendid new ism and form of negative reasoning these days called eliminative inductionism. (But splendid or not, don't bother to make a note of it – it's jargon.) His aim was to provide a solid base for certain knowledge while allowing the widest possible range to ideas and research. For example, scientists looking into the relationship between heat and light should concern themselves with cases where heat is present, such as in the Sun's rays, and where it's absent, such as in phosphorescence. The approach reflected Bacon's legal training, in that English common law develops inductively (by looking backwards at decisions taken in previous cases), before being applied as established law to new cases.

Bacon's practical investigations also included an interest in the theory of natural resemblances, the ancient preoccupation of herbalists and healers (and witch doctors). They thought, for instance, that flowers with blobs on them that looked like blood might be good for the blood or that eating walnuts (which look like little brains) might be good for the brain. Bacon noticed that snow and salt were both white crystals and hypothesised that stuffing chickens with snow might preserve the meat in a similar way that salt did. In fact he not only hypothesised it, but one cold winter tried it out in practice, which is what empiricism is all about. Unfortunately, in his case, he caught pneumonia and died soon after, which is what idealists (see the following section), not empiricists, should do. To make matters worse, he left his most important book, *Novum organum* (1620), unfinished.

Trying to Pinpoint Idealism

It's easier to pick out empiricist philosophers than idealist ones because idealism is an ill-defined doctrine. On the one hand, *idealism* is the view that ideas are the proper study of philosophy, because it's only ideas that you're aware of and, indeed, ideas are quite possibly all that exist. Pure idealism in particular is opposed to what you might consider the common-sense view that a real world exists out there and that, however imprecisely, you create the ideas out of it. But, on the other hand, idealism is also the view that ideas do in some way relate to the world of things. Figure 7-1 summarises the idealist position.

Well then, which philosophers are idealists? Alas, even this isn't clear. Since Plato argued that the fundamental aspects of reality were the ideas, and sense perceptions mere shadows, he might be a good candidate, but most philosophers insist that his approach isn't strictly idealism because he seems to think the ideas do exist – outside of your mind in a parallel mental universe he calls the world of the forms.

Different kinds of innate ideas

For René Descartes there are three types of ideas – a term he uses to cover both philosophical concepts and truths:

- *Adventitious* ideas (entering the mind from some outside source) include ideas of particular things, pains, sounds, colours and other sensible (*able* to be *sensed*) qualities that are ultimately acquired by the use of the senses. Such ideas couldn't be the material of certain knowledge because the senses are fallible and potentially deceptive.

- *Fictitious* ideas (created or invented by the mind) are products of fancy and play no part in scientific knowledge.

- *Innate* ideas are different to the other two types in that they're both very general and very clear and distinct. This enables them to provide the foundations of certain knowledge – or so argues Descartes. Ideas in this category include God, freedom, immortality, substance, mind and matter, and other mathematical concepts such as circles and triangles, as well as a series of other (allegedly) self-evident truths (that Descartes never sets out precisely).

The ideal idealist

Most philosophers seize upon Descartes (1596–1650) as their example of an idealist, with his tidy distinction between the world out there of *extension* (objects capable of being measured because they're 'extended' in space) and the world of minds, populated solely by ideas.

Identifying Idealism

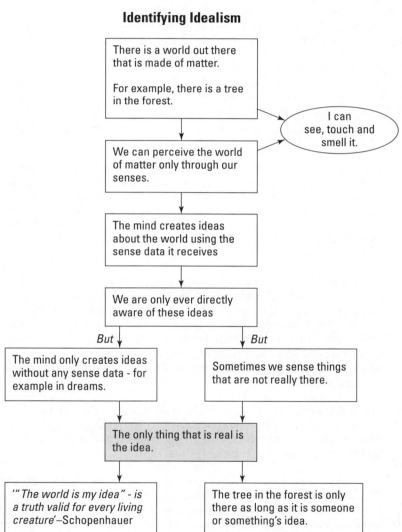

There is a world out there that is made of matter.

For example, there is a tree in the forest.

I can see, touch and smell it.

We can perceive the world of matter only through our senses.

The mind creates ideas about the world using the sense data it receives

We are only ever directly aware of these ideas

But The mind only creates ideas without any sense data - for example in dreams.

But Sometimes we sense things that are not really there.

The only thing that is real is the idea.

'"*The world is my idea" - is a truth valid for every living creature*'–Schopenhauer

The tree in the forest is only there as long as it is someone or something's idea.

Figure 7-1: Understanding Idealism

Critical idealism

Immanuel Kant tried, but failed, to impose some structure on the idealists (hence his school is sometimes called *critical idealism*), objecting to philosophers using the word *ideas* to cover both physical things like being red as well as theoretical things like justice. Kant also thought that certain concepts, such as space and time, structure ideas and so must be prior to them. Indeed, he wrote that all other ideas are based on something else – but this something, he thought, must always remain unreachable to us.

Kant lived in Königsberg in what's now Russia but wrote in German, and it was particularly obscure German philosophers (notably Fichte, Schelling and Hegel) who took this last element of his philosophy forward, producing increasingly metaphysical theories of fundamental reality and the paramount importance of the human mind within it.

Even then, as a term *idealism* doesn't appear until after Descartes. However, whether the ism existed or not, Descartes' view did help to motivate Leibniz (1646–1716) to come up with his own very idealistic and grand theory of a universe made up of mysterious monads (which are themselves pure thought). This was because Descartes' world of three-dimensional matter seemed to him to be too lifeless, passive and inert, and thus in need of some spiritual element to bring it into actuality.

Writing at the same time as Leibniz, Bishop Berkeley (1685–1710) seems to represent a pretty pure form of idealism because he firmly asserted that all people are aware of is ideas, and he considered you can't say anything that's not an idea to have any existence; assertions to the contrary being just that – assertions. Other British philosophers (notably Hume and Bradley) took the opposite view and attempted to resurrect sense perception as producing the true ideas, with the other abstract ones being manufactured later from out of this raw material.

The celebrated English author and writer of one of the first ever dictionaries, Dr Johnson, is supposed to have known Berkeley personally, and to have dealt briskly with his theory about the non-existence of matter by kicking a large rock and saying, 'I refute it thus.'

And the view that your everyday perception of the world is direct (rather than subject to some mental intermediaries, let alone the kind of random jiggery-pokery that some philosophers entertain!), is called *naive realism*. It says, reassuringly, that what people think before they study philosophy is generally, in fact, correct. The chair really is there, the snow really does look white and the stone really does hurt when you kick it.

Making magic potions with George Berkeley

Bishop George Berkeley is usually placed at the other philosophical extreme from Francis Bacon. In Chapter 5 I look at the theory that material objects exist only through you perceiving them, which makes ideas real and sense experiences imaginary and illusory. This makes him seem very unpractical – hence an 'idealist', as the philosophical isms go. Yet curiously, like Francis Bacon, Berkeley also had a practical side. Berkeley was the first major European philosopher to live in the Americas, and while he was there he took a good look around and discovered what he called *tar water*. This is a concoction based on the sap of pine trees added to water, and Berkeley believed that it had extraordinary medicinal properties. So, when on his return he found the people of his native Ireland suffering from two years of famine and plague, he tried to treat them with this 'cure-all' – and what's more, it seemed to help!

Sense, sense data and sensation

Philosophers like to invent new concepts to explain old ones. What exactly is it that the senses sense? Why not *sense data*? A similar kind of trick is at work with that rather alarming ism called *epiphenomenalism*. This grand-sounding doctrine actually propounds a very down-to-earth theory, namely that states of consciousness, including feelings and emotions, are just byproducts of various brain states. Or, as T.H. Huxley once elegantly put it, feelings are as completely without any power of modifying the working of senses as 'the steam-whistle which accompanies the workings of a locomotive engine is without influence upon its machinery'.

But back to sense data. The new concept was introduced in English language philosophy in the 20th century, through the writings of philosophers like G.E. Moore and Bertrand Russell, but long before that other (largely Anglophone) philosophers had hinted at the need for such a new entity. Locke had his 'ideas of sense' and Berkeley had his 'sensible qualities', and Hume too conjured with 'impressions'.

In the 19th century, in the United States, William James and others thought that psychology required such a distinction too. In fact, many philosophers have argued since that it's only these sense data that you perceive, and hence that you perceive both the sense data very well and the real world very badly.

As discussed in Chapter 5, Berkeley in particular dismissed the idea that you feel, say, a warm stone, because it would ascribe a quality to an inanimate object that rightly doesn't belong there – the warmth is simply a feeling you have in your mind. Similarly, Berkeley complained that when you approach a tree it becomes bigger, but in reality it doesn't – it merely appears to change. The Scottish Presbyterian and very down-to-earth philosopher Thomas Reid (1710–1796) roundly dismissed such changes in appearance as being exactly what you should expect, because if you're looking at a real object it should change as your position in relation to it changes.

Berkeley demonstrated that even idealists can be very practical when they want to be, preparing his tar-water for the ill and starving alike by carefully mixing pine tar (sap) with water, allowing it to settle and then draining off the fluid and bottling it. Mind you, he also found time to write a philosophical guide, *Siris*, subtitled 'Philosophical reflexions and inquiries concerning the virtues of tar-water, and divers other subjects connected together and arising from one another', which detailed the virtues of tar-water for curing most diseases. His own earlier invented ism – the theory of *immaterialism* – reappeared here, now woven into an account of how tar-water medicine works. And it's here, in *Siris*, that the ism really made its mark. No longer just a dusty philosophical theory, the book became a best-seller in Europe as well as back in America!

Berkeley was so encouraged by the success of his book that he even wrote a poem, entitled simply On Tar, which makes a connection between his earthly cure and the heavenly truth, and in this way is also useful for distinguishing between empiricism and idealism. However, most of the purchasers of *Siris* read it for its medical advice and missed the significance of the philosophical and ecclesiastical reflections. Berkeley's account of tar-water's universal curative powers by reference to Plato's theory of forms, as well as the Trinity and other ancient doctrines, was probably too rich a brew for the simple folk, especially when they were hungry and feeling sick.

Applying Utilitarianism

Sharing Berkeley's *paternalism* (the desire to act in the best interests of others, as a good father does for his child) the British philosopher Jeremy Bentham (1748–1832) saw the world as torn between two great forces: the quest for pleasure and the avoidance of pain. From this, he intuited that it would be better to maximise the former and minimise the latter, and that all other considerations are irrelevant. This became known as the *principle of utility*, and Bentham's writings are a pure form of utilitarianism.

The doctrine allows no space for individual taste, just as it allows no room for rights or duties, although Bentham allows that these may have socially desirable roles as convenient fictions. Instead, as he puts it in the opening sentence of his introduction to *The Principles of Morals and Legislation* (1789):

The principle of utility judges any action to be right by the tendency it appears to have to augment or diminish the happiness of the party whose interests are in question . . . if that party be the community, the happiness of the community, if a particular individual, the happiness of that individual.

Building prisons to keep everyone in with Bentham

Bentham's work ranged widely and it might seem erratically at times. He spent much time and energy attempting to advance surveillance as the tool for a well-run society, even drawing up detailed plans for the construction of circular buildings where just one person – an inspector – could watch and control the actions of many. He considered his invention to be particularly suitable for prisoners, but the *Panopticons* or inspection houses are also, Bentham makes clear, applicable to any sort of establishment where people need to be kept under inspection, such as hospitals, factories, 'mad-houses' – and schools and colleges!

In a letter to a philosophical friend, Bentham described it all in enthusiastic detail.

> *To save the troublesome exertion of voice that might otherwise be necessary, and to prevent one prisoner from knowing that the inspector was occupied by another prisoner at a distance, a small tin tube might reach from each cell to the inspector's lodge, passing across the area, and so in at the side of the correspondent window of the lodge. By means of this implement, the slightest whisper of the one might be heard by the other, especially if he had proper notice to apply his ear to the tube.*

As for the inspection:

> *. . . it may be confined to the hours of study; or it may be made to fill the whole circle of time, including the hours of repose, and refreshment, and recreation. To the first of these applications the most captious timidity, I think, could hardly fancy an objection: concerning the hours of study, there can, I think, be but one wish, that they should he employed in study. It is scarce necessary to observe that gratings, bars, and bolts, and every circumstance from which an Inspection House can derive a terrific character, have nothing to do here. All play, all chattering – in short, all distraction of every kind, is effectually banished . . .*

This is the basic principle of utilitarianism. However, it's in a less formal book by Bentham, *The Commonplace Book*, that you find the phrase 'the happiness of the greatest number', which really sums up the philosophy. ('Commonplace Books' being a kind of posh scrapbook popular at the time with intellectuals to copy out their favourite poems and so on.) Actually, that phrase originated slightly earlier with Frances Hutcheson (1694–1746) who said 'That action is best, which procures the greatest happiness for the greatest numbers'.

What sort of person was Jeremy Bentham? In some ways he was a radical, an iconoclast and progressive; in others, he was a reactionary, a die-hard and a killjoy. People often use his system, utilitarianism, to justify acts that, individually, are repugnant. Take, for example, using animals in experiments. It may seem cruel to make dogs smoke cigarettes or to put shampoo in cats' eyes, but the end justifies the means, the end being the protection of human health. And although most of the philosophical arguments for experiments on animals are utilitarian – justified by saying that the benefits to humans outweigh the costs to animals – the 'father' of that school was firmly against such arguments. In *The Principles of Morals and Legislation* Bentham says firmly:

> *The day may come, when the rest of the animal creation may acquire those rights which never could have been withholden from them but by the hand of tyranny. The French have already discovered that the blackness of the skin is no reason why a human being should be abandoned without redress to the caprice of a tormentor. It may come one day to be recognised, that the number of the legs, the villosity of the skin, or the termination of the os sacrum, are reasons equally insufficient for abandoning a sensitive being to the same fate. What else is there that should trace the insuperable line? Is it the faculty of reason, or, perhaps the faculty of discourse? But a full-grown horse or dog is beyond comparison a more rational, as well as a more conversible animal than an infant of a day, or a week, or even a month old? But suppose the case were otherwise, what would it avail? The question is not, Can they reason?, nor Can they talk? but Can they suffer?*

Rationalism or irrationalism? That is the question . . .

Rationalism comes from the Latin for *reason*, and being rational is, supposedly, the highest goal of philosophy. Yet built into the search for rationality are value judgements and prejudices. Why, after all, is the world obliged to be rational just because people want to be? The *rationalist* seeks to apply his or her powers of reason, logic and analytical skills to attaining complete understanding. Empiricism, on the other hand, unlike rationalism, claims to not prejudge issues but merely to take notes, to observe and deduce.

Nowadays, not merely psychologists but economists too have made great play of how in fact the human animal is anything but rational, and a branch of philosophy known as *game theory* attempts to explore situations where deciding what's rational in various cases depends on what other people decide, with all the confusing problems of feedback that implies.

Since Aristotle declared that 'Man is a rational animal', irrationality has been thought of as the mode of operation solely of deranged and deficient people. Yet humans aren't rational animals at all; if anything, they're quintessentially an irrational animal. Animals marshal the information at their noses to find food, shelter and reproduce; human beings do a little more than this. That's why the Chinese sages called the human a 'moral animal'. Plato certainly thought that the highest processes of thought weren't simply a mundane business of processing information, even if only a few (philosophers) could achieve these processes and in a rather mystical (irrational) way. Saint Thomas Aquinas too was sure that some important conclusions relied not on reason but on 'faith alone'. As noted elsewhere, Aristotle distinguished between men and women saying only the former was rational.

But come the 18th century and the Enlightenment, rationality was back in favour, and thinkers such as Locke, Leibniz, Bentham and Spinoza all set about trying to achieve well-ordered systems for processing information and obtaining sound conclusions.

Like Francis Bacon, Jeremy Bentham was a lawyer (descended from two generations of lawyers), English and very practical in his approach. As for legal debates, he thought that what his contemporaries were celebrating as natural rights were little more than imaginary rights, and actual law created the only actual rights. The French *Declaration of the Rights of Man* he described as 'nonsense on stilts', warning that to want something isn't to supply it, just as hunger isn't the same thing as bread.

However, he still set about his own rather idealistic schemes, such as his *Plan for Universal and Perpetual Peace* (1789) too. Undeterred by the lukewarm reception to his Panopticon (see the sidebar 'Building prisons to keep everyone in with Bentham'), this plan is the same principle writ large, essentially relying on a supranational 'eye' to police the world – not by force, of course, but by the free exchange of information, shaming any transgressor nations into line. Still, doubtless mindful of the political non-response to his Panopticon, Bentham became an active campaigner for the reform of the British political system, arguing the then radical case of 'one man, one vote'.

Bentham saw himself in the role of spiritual leader of a kind of utilitarian movement, and donated his body (after his death) to University College London (which he helped found), where it remains to today, preserved in a glass case.

Letting Everything Hang Out with Relativism

If you think the ends justifies the means principle dear to utilitarianism sounds like a trampling of civil liberties, that's right, it is. But the philosophical principle so dear to utilitarians is in many ways itself an *anti-morality*: it throws out all notions of right and wrong, replacing them instead with just the measure of what's useful. In this way utilitarianism isn't totally opposed to that other great ism, *relativism*.

JARGON BUSTER

Relativism

Relativism is the idea that judgements, positions and conclusions are relative to individual cultures, to divergent situations and to differing perceptions. It denies the existence of universal or absolute criteria, holding instead that what you know and what there is to know are relative: to your own tastes, experiences, culture and attitudes. Relativism substitutes the variability of vantage points and perceptual mechanisms for universals when considering moral questions as well as more general claims for knowledge, including science.

'Man is the measure of all things', said Protagoras, back in Ancient Greece, and that's the heart of philosophical relativism. What's good for you may not be good for me if you're a cannibal and I'm a vegetarian. What's big to you may not be big for me, if you're an ant and I'm an elephant. In fact, Protagoras was particularly concerned with this latter kind of *perceptual relativism*.

Many kinds of relativism exist. They range from strong versions that maintain all truths are relative, to more limited versions that merely highlight the great number of divergent standards, values and social customs.

It's easy to see why relativism often goes hand in hand with scepticism. But relativism has more than a sceptical eye; it holds that better and worse – in testing procedures or in ethical resolutions – are without grounding beyond the box of perception, extending no further than a particular individual or culture. Plato quotes the sophist Protagoras as saying, 'The way things appear to me, in that way they exist for me; and the way things appear to you, in that way they exist for you' (*Theaetetus,* 152a). Yet this also highlights a problem for relativism: that there can't be such a thing as falsehood.

The ancients were well aware of cultural relativism. Herodotus's famous *Histories* described the range of customs he encountered on his travels. One of his best-known stories concerns the strange practices of the Callations, a society that considered it essential for people, out of sincere moral sentiment, to eat their fathers after they died. This contrasts, rather with the view in our own culture that eating people is totally gruesome. The moral is, if you *really* want to be a relativist, you better be willing to eat your parents too!

But relativism has grown alongside a historical trend. The main tenor of the modern and post-modern eras has challenged and in large measure ousted ideas such as the animism of nature and the ultimate authority of God, just as a common awareness of the diversity of cultures and angles of perception came to light. (*Animism*, by the way, is the idea that matter, from rocks to humans via animals, contains an *animating* breath of spirit.) Just as it did for Herodotus, knowledge of other perspectives has undermined certainties that one universal or unconditional truth exists.

Even with regard to ethical judgements, relativists hold that moral positions don't reflect absolute truths. Instead, they stress that these judgements unfold from social customs, cultural tendencies or personal preferences.

Rejecting Emotion with Stoicism

Stoicism is the Ancient Greek school of philosophy founded by Zeno of Citium around 300 BC that acknowledged the senses could be deceived, but thought that calm reflection could get around this problem. As a doctrine, it proved especially popular with the Romans, and famous Italian stoics included Seneca (a kind of philosophical playwright who was especially good at depicting evil) and even an emperor – Marcus Aurelius.

All the stoics were materialists, but they also identified God with nature. They held only virtue to be properly good, but acknowledged that it's always better to be rich than poor, even though neither state should alter your happiness. They argued that emotions are unhelpful because they're based on mistaken judgements, and that you should overcome emotions via an analysis of judgements. In their strict rationalism they followed Socrates, and in fact some of the stoics wished also to be called Socratics.

These days philosophers remember the stoics most for their rejection of emotion. (Hence, people use the word *stoical* for that reason.) The stoics said emotional responses are the product of judgements that something bad has happened. But because external things have no intrinsic value, such judgements are a mistake. If a thief takes your possessions then all you've lost are what they called *preferred indifferents* that are of no consequence. So long as your virtue is intact, nothing bad has really happened, for only this has intrinsic value.

Seneca retells the story of Stilbo, a stoic whose town was captured by invaders, resulting in his wife's disappearance, his children's deaths and all his worldly possessions being destroyed. But when Stilbo was asked by another philosopher whether he'd lost anything, he replied, 'Why no, I have all my valuables with me.'

Doubting with the Sceptics

Although *scepticism* derives from the Greek word *skepsis* meaning consideration, nowadays scepticism implies doubting various things. The evidence of the senses is suspect, given the (occasional) inability to distinguish between true perception and false perception. Ancient Greek sceptics like Arcesilaus of Pitane (circa. 315–240 BC) and Carneades of Cyrene (circa. 210–130) BC insisted that no one could ever justify claiming knowledge about anything in the world; instead they could only make naive and optimistic assertions.

Other stoics later on insisted that there were ways of dividing knowledge and sense data up and distinguishing arrant nonsense from well-founded evidence. However, this was never the view of the true sceptics. During the Renaissance, 1,800 years later, the internal disputes resurfaced with renewed interest in the writings of Sextus Empiricus (circa. 150–210) who'd discussed the possible reasons for such stoic distinctions.

Relativism and physics

Those who teach philosophy rather frowned upon relativism, seeing it as something to drum out of students. Not so in physics. Ever since Einstein, relativism has been central to trying to make sense of the universe. In a paper entitled 'Geometry and Experience', Einstein wrote: 'As far as the propositions of mathematics refer to reality, they are not certain; and as far as they are certain, they do not refer to reality.' In fact, he said, mathematics and physics operate with different rules, and should be kept apart to some extent. Physics is empirical, based on measurement, but mathematics is based on axioms that you assume at the outset.

Einstein's *Special Theory* replaced Newton's pet concepts of what he called absolute space and absolute time, both of which were eternal and unchanging, for more complex, fundamentally relational systems. The surprising consequences of the *Special Theory* are that bodies have different lengths, clocks run at different speeds and the same event can occur at several different times – depending on the relative motion of the observer.

'The Special Theory of Relativity' (which he published in 1905) was initially entitled 'The Electrodynamics of Moving Bodies' and was intended to tackle apparent inconsistencies in another great physicist's, James Clarke Maxwell's, electromagnetic theory.

It makes two sweeping claims. The first is that the speed of light is the same for all observers, regardless of their motion relative to the source of the light. The second is that all observers moving at constant speed should observe the same physical laws. But Einstein showed mathematically that the only way you can combine these two assumptions is to make time and space (how large something is) *relative*. This flies against our everyday experience where we assume that time flows at the same speed everywhere, and objects have just one 'size', but the theory has since been demonstrated to hold in a number of very solid experiments.

Einstein's discovery of the relativity of space and time led to another insight – that matter and energy are fundamentally connected – indeed that they are the same thing. This is summed up in the famous equation:

$E = mc^2$, where m = mass and c = the speed of light, squared.

Fine stuff though this is, the theory is only called 'special' because it is not quite complete. It does not include the effects of gravity. To include those took Einstein 11 more years. The end result: Einstein's drab-sounding but more important theory of General Relativity.

This ancient Stoic debate is still central to philosophy today. The conventional position is that knowledge is justified true belief.

Descartes offers a (useless) criterion in his writings of knowledge as anything that's perceived 'clearly and distinctly', this in turn resting on the claim that God wouldn't play tricks. The shrewder response of Bishop Berkeley to sceptical claims about what people think they perceive was to say that what you think you perceive is exactly what you perceive, because nothing higher or more real than thoughts exists anyway. (You can find lots more ideas about what makes something 'knowledge' in Chapters 9 and 10.)

Avoiding Dangerous 'Isms'

Many dangerous isms exist – especially when you start to get into the area of political theory. Fascism is perhaps the most famous one. The political doctrine combines three other isms: nationalism with militarism and totalitarianism added on. The *fascist* state suppresses individual rights in the interests not so much of the majority as of the nation encapsulated by its leader. The high water mark of the doctrine came before the Second World War, when Mussolini in Italy, Hitler in Germany, Franco in Spain and the Emperor of Japan all proudly counted themselves as fascists.

As a political shorthand, *fascism* has come to have a much wider usage, however, signifying a political approach that glorifies the nation, celebrates military power and oppresses individual rights – individualism. Indeed, the original doctrine of fascism did all these things, but then so does socialism. In fact, fascism is one of the least understood terms of the political vocabulary.

This is less surprising when you find out that Mussolini was aided in his writing by an eminent advocate of neo-Hegelianism (a philosophy professor called Giovanni Gentile, who was hanged by the Allies following the end of the Second World War for his trouble. Whether that makes neo-Hegelianism a dangerous ism or only fascism isn't quite clear. But the 20th-century philosopher Karl Popper thought that the problem was neither of these two isms, but rather the view that history had a pattern, which is called *historicism*. For Gentile, as for Hegel and for so many other political theorists (of both left and right), the world was following through an inexorable march of progress that was essentially benign, even if accompanied by much blood, destruction and slaughter.

Indeed, one aspect of fascism is that it celebrates the blood, destruction and slaughter because it's considered to be the mark of just this sort of useful social Darwinism. *Social Darwinism* is another dangerous ism that teaches that it's nature's way to promote the strong over the weak. People have used this theory to justify programmes of sterilisation of supposedly inferior races, and the killing of 'defective' children in many countries including the United States.

The Italian fascists specifically compared their approach to classical *liberalism* (with its emphasis on individual rights and freedoms) and interpreted it in dialectical fashion as a reaction to *absolutism* (that is, societies run by all powerful absolute monarchs, for example). This kind of society with all the power invested in the monarchy had exhausted its historical function, and so liberalism had appeared, trying to give all the power to the people. Fascists believed that society's problems could best be resolved by the new fascist state in which the state is the expression of the conscience and will of the people.

This is exactly the same thinking that lies behind two great left-wing isms – *Marxism* and *communism* – which is less surprising when you remember that Marx and Engels, like the fascists, were also influenced by neo-Hegelianism!

But if you think the isms are beginning to make sense, along comes *Nazism*, which added onto the grand theatre of fascism (and don't forget it also called itself a brand of socialism – national socialism) a sinister layer of not only social Darwinism but also rampant racism. And that's where the dangerous side of isms ended up: in the mass killings in the name of an ideology carried out by the Nazi regime.

Part III
The Nuts and Bolts of Philosophy

'I'm sure Aristotle would have been more philosophical over a burst tyre, dear.'

In this part . . .

*N*uts are good, but bolts are better, and in this part you get both of them. The nuts are all in logic, of course, and if you want to find out about knowledge, you'll have to bolt yourself down. What kind of talk is this, though? It's an attempt to use metaphor and analogy, and by the time you've read the chapter on the philosophy of language you'll know it's harder to get away from this sort of stuff then you might have previously imagined. When you call a spade a spade, you're actually involved in a rather complicated social and linguistic exercise. That's why philosophers *never* call spades spades: they'd much rather call them 'implements useful for digging', and that's also, metaphorically speaking, what philosophy is.

Confused? Don't be. This part not only separates out the fancy stuff of *epistemology* and *linguistics* but it also shrinks it all down to size.

Chapter 8

Seeing the Limits of Logic

In This Chapter

▶ Seeing what a bit of logic can do when you apply it

▶ Getting under the bonnet on reasoning

▶ Testing out some new ways of thinking

> *Poets do not go mad; but chess-players do. Mathematicians go mad, and cashiers; but creative artists very seldom. I am not, as will be seen, in any sense attacking logic: I only say that this danger does lie in logic, not in imagination.*
>
> – G. K. Chesterton

This chapter looks at what logic is, and why the Ancient Greeks plunged deeply into it. And this is where Aristotle's work comes into its own. Aristotle saw that some of the ways people reason in everyday life were both unreliable and misleading, and so attempted to set out once and for all the correct ways to reason. His promise is that, if followed, the rules always lead to true conclusions, and he also tries to indicate arguments to avoid because they lead to errors and false conclusions.

Understanding What Logic Really Is

Philosophical logic is the study of the structure of arguments. It doesn't necessarily help you with any particular argument, concerned with particular facts and personal values, but gives a general guide to your reasoning, warning you against ways of thinking about issues that can lead to mistakes. That's the idea anyway.

And certainly logic is big in philosophy departments these days, which is rather odd, really, because it's not really a branch of philosophy at all. It is, in fact, a kind of mathematics, bearing only the same sort of connection to philosophical debates as, say, studying geometry does. The idea that when you argue you're really manipulating facts in the same kind of way that mathematicians manipulate numbers in their equations is more a dream than a reality. But the nice thing about maths is that after you've proved something, everyone's satisfied and admires the elegance of your work.

So, everyone wants to be logical, even more than they want to be philosophical. In fact, if you want to insult someone, you can always say that they're being illogical, that they've contradicted themselves, or that their point isn't valid. All of these appeal to logic as a kind of umpire in the great game of truth and falsehood. But how impartial is logic anyway? Should you always trust its judgements?

Philosophers have always wanted to impose order on concepts, language and ideas; particularly after Euclid produced his elegant geometrical proofs that are certainly so much better – so much more authoritative! – than ordinary arguments using ordinary language. Aristotle helpfully provided philosophy with a mathematical way of looking at the world, albeit one that bears only a rather flimsy resemblance to it, entirely based on the assumptions you start with.

Despite this problem, most philosophical logic proceeds in a very black-and-white way, quite content to tackle all kinds of issues. Many of its proponents see only the excellence of their proofs and not the limits of the overall strategy. Leibniz, in particular, thought that logic would enable humankind to construct a machine to solve all its problems ('Come, let us calculate'), a delusion all the more popular since the invention of the computer.

Appreciating the Things Aristotle Got Right

Aristotle wasn't the first philosopher to try to be logical, but philosophers generally take Aristotle's writings, especially the *Prior and Posterior Analytics*, as the first serious attempt to build up a system of logic. In fairness, however, Aristotle was building upon the work of other Greek thinkers, such as Zeno of Elea and Parmenides. In his writings he introduces key concepts in logic such as that of *propositions*, which are basically sentences that have a *truth value*, which means they make a claim about reality that's either true or false. 'Maths is fun', or 'All dogs like bones', or 'My hair's a mess', for example, are propositions, but 'Look at that!' and 'Let's go for a swim' are not.

Notice that the verb *is* has a special role in both language and logic. It acts just like the equals sign in mathematics, the stuff on one side of it equals the words on the other side. Other words, too, have special roles:

> ✔ *All* as in 'All people are mortal'.

> ✔ *No* as in 'No people can live for ever'.

> ✔ *Some* as in 'Some people live to be 100'.

> ✔ *Some . . . not* as in 'Some people do not live to be 100'.

Now, take a deep breath as I get a bit more formal about this. These four special kinds of sentences are called respectively:

> ✔ The universal affirmative ('All S is P')

> ✔ The universal negative ('No S is P')

> ✔ The particular affirmative ('Some S is P')

> ✔ The particular negative ('Some S are not P')

You see how the jargon quickly piles up! Quite marvellous, really. And all thanks to Aristotle. But not content with that, Aristotle identifies *propositions* as a special kind of sentence having two parts (which he calls *terms*). In language nouns represent both these parts. 'My hair', for example, and 'a mess' are both nouns. One of the terms is the subject and the other is the predicate. That's why logicians use the letters S and P here: the S is standing for the subject and the P is standing for the predicate. In this case, the subject is 'my hair' and the predicate (loosely speaking, the thing predicted, which would be the word again, predicated, only this time without the *a*), is that it's 'a mess'. Add to which there are *copulas* (words like *is* that join up the Ss and the Ps) and *operators* like *all* and *not*, which, well, operate on them.

Drawing inferences

Aristotle pointed out that in reasoning and in arguing people draw inferences from facts. For example, if your bike tyre has a puncture in it, you say you won't be able to get home on time. That is, you infer a new proposition (you won't be able to get home on time) from the first one. The fact that you have a puncture has implications (late home, no tea, miss second episode of *Zambo versus the Inter-Galaxian Dwarves*) and indeed philosophers like to talk of things being *implied* by other things. However, when a logician says something's *implied*, they don't mean it like you do in everyday language (which allows an element of doubt about the matter); they mean it absolutely does follow. 'If my bike has a puncture then I'll get home late' becomes, in logic, a certainty. This is a problem with logic, because in reality very few things are so simple, and even if you have a puncture, you may get home on time – someone might give you a lift, or you just might be very good at mending punctures.

Secret codes of the logicians

Although logicians behave as though everything's very black and white, in fact they can't even agree among themselves on very much. For example, logicians can't agree on how to represent the 'operators' in logic, things like *and*, *not* and *or*. Just some of the symbols they use are shown in this table.

Not P	~P	−P	¬ P	P̄
P and Q	P.Q	PQ	P∧Q	P & Q
P or Q	PvQ	P∨Q	PQ	
If P then Q	P⊃Q	P→Q		
P iff Q	P≡Q	P↔Q	P~Q	
(P if, and only if, Q)				

However good the logic is, a gap exists between the certainty of the logical representation of the facts – and the world itself.

Aristotle, however, like most logicians after him, was less interested in how well logic fits the world and more interested in logic as a theoretical abstraction.

Surveying Syllogisms

Aristotle invented a simple form of argument called the *syllogism*, which consists of just three *propositions* (sentences with a truth value). The first two are called the *premises* and are things that you assert to be true. The important thing about the two premises is that they must share one term (called the *middle term*), and this is the key to arriving at the conclusion and knowing that you've validly deduced it from the first two.

Deducing things logically with Sherlock Holmes

A *deductive logic* is one that permits you to deduce things, like author Sir Arthur Conan Doyle's fictional detective Sherlock Holmes used to do. Like Holmes, you put the things you know in a long list, and then you deduce some interesting and significant new finding from your list. Holmes used to say things like 'Mr Wilson used to be a manual labourer' (concluded from the observation that his right hand was larger than his left hand) and that he'd been recently writing something (deduced from the observation that he had a shiny spot on his jacket's right cuff). That's classic Holmes. But take a few of the real-life observations you may make:

✔ There's a pool of water on the carpet along with shards of glass.

✔ The window's open and the curtain's blowing.

✔ Felix the pet fish has disappeared.

These are what logicians would call premises (statements with a truth value) – they're either true or false, not both and certainly not neither. So, what can you deduce?

Having given his premises, Holmes would typically solve a ghastly crime. In the example, you have to be content with deducing that Moppet the cat has climbed in the window and knocked over the fishbowl in order to eat poor Felix the fish.

Even so, this is an example of how you use a kind of informal logic to solve everyday problems. But it's not quite how you use logic in philosophy. Because, ingenious though your deductions may be, they're not quite reliable. Any number of alternative explanations exist to explain the disappearance of Felix the fish. Philosophers want *certainty*.

Here's an example:

Apples are fruits

All fruits are edible

——————— *(Therefore; the all-important conclusion marker)*

Apples are edible

It's not very impressive, is it? But the method is the thing. Here, the shared middle term is being a fruit, and hence apples also share the property of being edible. Are all fruits edible? Actually, I don't think they are. But this is logic, and it's not really about facts.

Using this basic idea, Aristotle drew up a list of all the ways people could conceivably argue, coming up with no less than 256 different possible types of syllogisms of which only a few, given that they start off with true assumptions, will always produce true conclusions. These are just three line arguments: two premises (sentences saying something that's capable of being either true or false) followed by a conclusion.

Silly whats?

Syllogisms are arguments with two premises followed by a conclusion. In medieval times they had names like *barbara*, *festino* and *baroco*. That's pretty silly! An example of one is:

> *All apples grow on trees*
>
> *All Golden Delicious are apples*
>
> ------------------------
>
> *All Golden Delicious grow on trees*

It's not a great piece of deduction, this one, but it illustrates the process of inference and qualifies as an argument in philosophical terms. It uses a very common kind of argumentative structure too – All S is P, as logicians put it. In fact, Aristotle identified and defined four types of 'claim':

- ✔ All S are P
- ✔ No S is P
- ✔ Some S is P
- ✔ Some S is not P

These can be arranged in various ways in a syllogism, leading altogether to the 256 different possible syllogistic arguments. The great majority are invalid, and Aristotle concentrates on the valid forms. But how does he *prove* that the valid forms are valid? After all, the original idea was that he was going to show that arguments are valid because they're one of the valid forms. It doesn't seem to be possible to apply this to the argument form itself. However, Aristotle argues that there are inevitably starting points to any chain of reasoning that are themselves left unproven. Such starting points are acceptable, he thinks, as long as they're self-evident. This notion of being self-evident is central to his approach, but the question always lurks: self-evident to whom? In fact, saying something is self-evident is more of a psychological statement than a logical one.

Aristotle invented a whole new notation for his reasoning, pioneering the use of letters to stand for the terms, thereby demonstrating an easy way for philosophers to give the impression of saying great things, which philosophers have always been indebted to him for.

Syllogisms are impressive, especially when given Latin names and arranged in 256 different ways! So no wonder for the next 2,000 years learning philosophy involved doing just that – fiddling with silly syllogisms. But none of this would have been possible without Aristotle's other achievement – setting out the laws of thought – which was a necessary first stage in his effort to put everyday language on a logical footing (see Chapter 2).

As I say, Aristotle needed syllogisms to create and guide his logic. But don't think just because logic requires certain assumptions that they really are the case. After all, those other Ancient Greeks, the Stoic philosophers, came up with a rather different logic based on the idea that there aren't two kinds of statements (true ones and false ones), but three! In Stoic logic there also exist statements that are in between true and false, a new category that fits very well with reality (is this a lake, or a pond, or in between? Is this essay a pass or a fail, or an in between?). Naturally, three truth values are harder to manipulate logically.

Out with informality – in with formal systems!

Aristotle developed his ideas in a book called the *Prior Analytics*, which was the first attempt to create a system of formal deductive logic, and followed this great work up with another called the Posterior Analytics, which despite its slightly rude-sounding name is actually about ways to use logical methods to make scientific knowledge more systematic.

So what is a formal deductive system of logic anyway? Let's take this step by step. Why? Because that's the key to logic: you always take things step by step. If that sounds a bit like maths, that's because logic is a kind of maths. Anyway, formal (as opposed to informal) means following rules. A formal system is one that has rules, and an informal system doesn't. A formal requirement for working in Australia, for example, is that you must have either an Australian passport or a special visa. An informal requirement is that you must not be afraid of spiders.

When is an argument valid?

What makes an argument convincing? It's not just that the evidence advanced for a claim is correct, some reason must exist to accept that the conclusion follows from the evidence.

Take this bad argument, for example:

All dogs have four legs

My table has four legs

My table is a dog

The premises (the first two lines of the argument) are true (or near enough for these purposes). However, the conclusion isn't very convincing. Why is that? You can answer that in two ways. One is to just look at Aristotle's list of different kinds of arguments – he calls them different argument forms.

The most important distinction is between the argument forms that are 'valid' and those that are 'invalid'. And look it up, and sure enough, you'll see this is an invalid argument. The conclusion does not follow from the assumptions.

To understand why, you need to strip down the particular argument to its basic structure, ignoring the particular details. Stripped down the argument goes something like this. (I use the letter D to stand for the property of being a dog, and the letter L for the property of being four-legged and the letter T for the property of being a table.)

All D are L

All T are L

———

All T are D

The problem isn't that the premises (that dogs have four legs and that my table has four legs) are false, because they are true (as far as this example is concerned anyway). And what looks like (but it isn't) a very properly shared middle term exists – that property of having four legs. But the conclusion is certainly false. My dog isn't a table, let alone all dogs being tables. In logic, an argument with true premises that ends with a false conclusion is invalid. That's because, in logic, true premises don't ensure a conclusion is true unless the reasoning (the argument) is valid. In this case the argument isn't valid.

Rules and Tools

The same things crop up in philosophy again and again, and nowhere is that more true than in logic. Indeed, the whole idea of setting out arguments in their general 'forms' is to show how many debates share the same logical structure - and so share the same answer. What a great idea! But by the time you have 'stripped the arguments down', they look rather plain. Here's a few of the best-known 'off-the-peg' arguments and associated deductions, together known as 'rules of inference'.

Perhaps surprisingly, when combined with a few simple 'rules of replacement', such as 'simplification' (which says that if you have P and Q, you can also just say you have P), these rules entitle logicians to say that propositional calculus (another name for formal logic) is "complete". That means, the axioms used are sufficient to demonstrate any true proposition or to justify any valid argument. Just fancy that! Table 8-1 shows some philosophical rules and their meanings.

Table 8-1		Philosophical rules	
Name of Rule	**Logical form of the Rule**	**Example in plain English**	**Comment**
Modus Ponens	If P then Q P --- Q	If it is raining, then I will get wet. It is raining. Therefore, I will get wet	Yup, you're right. The 'argument' is basically repeating the original claim.
Modus Tollens	If P then Q Not Q --- Not P	If I had read my Philosophy for Dummies book, I would have passed the exam I did not read my Philosophy for Dummies book Therefore, I did not pass the exam	There's a useful life lesson!
Hypothetical Syllogism	If P then Q If Q then R --- If P then R	If my dog wakes up, I will have to give him his dinner If I give my dog his dinner, I will have to boil the kettle Therefore, if my dog wakes up, I will have to boil the kettle	Conclusions can look odd, but still be logical…
Disjunctive Syllogism	Either P or Q Not P --- Q	Either its fish for tea or it's boiled eggs It's not fish Therefore, its boiled eggs	Useful, but not terribly impressive reasoning
Constructive Dilemma	If (P then Q) and (if R then S) Either P or R ---- Therefore, either Q or S	If I'm late again to work then I will be made to make the coffee, and if the boss is in a bad mood then I'll get given the stock cupboard to clean For sure, either I'm going to be late again to work, or the boss is going to be in a bad mood Therefore, I'll either be made to make the coffee or I'll get given the stock cupboard to clean	There's a dilemma!

Biggles uses logic

In one of Captain W.E. Johns' famous stories, the heroic fighter ace Biggles uses cool logic to explain his indifference to risk:

> When you're flying, everything is all right or it is not all right. If it is all right there is no need to worry. If it is not all right one of two things will happen. Either you will crash or you will not crash. If you do not crash there is no need to worry. If you do crash one of two things is certain. Either you will be injured or you will not be injured. If you are not injured there is no need to worry. If you are injured one of two things is certain. Either you will recover or you will not recover. If you recover there is no need to worry. If you don't recover you can't worry.

From W.E. Johns' Spitfire Parade (1941)

Aristotle's contribution was to see that arguments have different structures or forms and only some of them always reliably produce true conclusions. Formal logic then is very simple: it's the study of the forms of arguments.

In everyday language people call points valid, or conclusions to arguments valid, quite freely, essentially to mean they agree with the point or conclusion because they think the point is correct or the conclusion is justified (that is, supported by evidence). But in philosophical logic, validity is quite different. It applies only to whole arguments (not to individual claims or conclusions) and simply means that the argument follows the rules of logic. Does this matter? Why yes, because it means an argument can be philosophically valid but have a conclusion that's false.

Telling the Truth via Tables

One way logicians and others (Truth Tables are very popular nowadays with electronic engineers) can examine an argument is by listing all the possible values the argument can have. Confused? Don't be. Truth Tables are very easy. That's why they are popular with electronic engineers. A table typically contains several rows and columns, with the top row representing the logical variables and combinations, in increasing complexity leading up to the final function. Our table is not going to get very complex, don't worry. We're just going to consider the argument:

If it is raining, then the grass will be wet

It is raining

———

The grass is wet

Why use symbols?

For most of logic (like maths) you use symbols rather than words. This obviously simplifies and so helps reveal the structure of the arguments – but it also makes it impossible to apply common sense to what someone's saying or presenting. The suspicion raises that those who like putting philosophical arguments into symbols also enjoy having their own private language to impress or even baffle people!

But to be generous, here's an example of a rather confusing attempt to use words to explain the definition of *validity*: if an argument is valid then the compound proposition that consists of the conjunction of all its premises linked to its conclusion by a further implication is a tautology.

Oh dear! So sometimes symbols are better. At the very least, using words is no guarantee of clarity.

The thing about this argument there are in fact just four possibilities. Table 8-2 gives them all. It's just automatic, every possibility.

Table 8-2		How to find the truth
It is raining	*The grass is wet*	*If it is raining, then the grass will be wet*
true	true	
true	false	
false	true	
false	false	

The third column is filled out by applying the rule and looking at each line, each 'possible world' in turn to see if it works. Table 8-3 shows the completed table.

Table 8-3		How to tell the complete truth
It is raining	*The grass is wet*	*If it is raining, then the grass will be wet*
true	true	TRUE
true	false	FALSE
false	true	FALSE
false	false	FALSE

How did I fill out the third column? In the third and fourth lines, the argument, or 'function', demands that it be raining before it can be true. But it is not raining so the function returns 'false', whatever the state of the lawn! Put another way, if it is not raining, but the grass is wet, it does not prove that when it does rain, the grass will become wet. All seems a lot of trouble to state the obvious? That's logic!

Fixing the Things Aristotle Got Wrong

People used Aristotle's logic (known as *classical logic*) without much modification for nearly 2,000 years. But in the late 19th and early 20th century philosophers challenged the logic because it has two big faults:

- ✔ It's incomplete – it covers only a few of all the possible kinds of deductive arguments.
- ✔ It's not absolutely reliable about the deductive arguments it does cover.

A third objection to classical logic is that Aristotle assumed that the subject of a premise, as in all cats have whiskers, existed. Later logicians have wanted to avoid this, and have changed the sense to: for any *x*, if that *x* is a cat, then that *x* has whiskers. This in itself produces a gap between ordinary language and logic.

Another debate exists over whether subjects can ever be predicates. For example, take the assertion 'My hair is a mess': my hair equals a mess. In this case, the subject is my hair and the property, 'being a mess', is the predicate. But sometimes being a mess could be the subject of a sentence too, as in 'Your room is a mess'. The subject–predicate distinction collapses! You might say hooray! Let everything be equal and relative and why not put a flower in your hair too! But Frege and Russell and others thought instead they needed to try to fix the problem, and so along comes modern logic.

Developing modern logic

Modern logic is of course much better than the old stuff. Aristotle's system allows you to deal with only two premises (consisting of three terms) at a time. Modern logic allows you to stack up any number of premises into a great big monster of an argument, and indeed to join together any number of terms into a long slithery snake of a proposition.

The new kind of logic, modern logic, consists of various new nasty sounding things such as propositional calculus and predicate calculus. *Propositional calculus* is concerned with how propositions relate to each other, and *predicate*

calculus is concerned with the internal structure of propositions. But that's not all! There's now also *modal logic*, which is concerned with necessity, probability and possibility (something is necessary, probable or merely possible) and *tense logic*, which is to do with time – the past, the future and the present.

Philosophers often say modern logic began in 1879, credited to Gottlob Frege (1846–1925) with additional work by Bertrand Russell (1872–1970) in the 20th century. Aristotle was interested in the structure of sentences, but much of modern logic tries to treat sentences as propositions and units that you then manipulate, usually via symbols and notation.

The main symbols and notation you need are:

- And: or to give it the 'posh name', conjunction
- Or: disjunction
- Not: negation
- If . . . then: conditional
- Iff: bi-conditional

All sorts of funny symbols to represent these exist, depending on philosophers' fancies. The *or* in logic is inclusive – both possibilities are allowed to be true. If a logician asks you if you'd like a drink of orange juice or tea, and you reply, 'Yes, thank you,' don't be surprised to get an unappetising mixture. And another confusing thing is that the *conditional*, the 'if . . . then', doesn't imply any sort of relationship, causal or otherwise . . .

The question to what extent logic really is the way people reason is at the heart of much of contemporary Western philosophy. For example, the definition of *validity* used in a standard formal logic is that it must not be possible for the premises of an argument to be true and yet the conclusion to be false.

You have to swallow two strange and slightly ridiculous consequences even with this fairly modest assumption. The first is that any argument with inconsistent premises is valid, irrespective of what the conclusions of that argument are. For example, if 'snow is always white' is the first premise, and the second is that 'snow is sometimes not white', it follows logically that the moon is a balloon, because *anything at all* follows from inconsistent premises.

Another wondrous thing is that if a conclusion is necessarily true, then the argument is valid irrespective of what the premises were. This is because no circumstances exist in which the conclusion can be false and the premises true, because the conclusion itself can't be false. Likewise, 'if cats can fly on broomsticks then dogs can drive buses' is a perfectly *valid* inference, because a false statement implies any statement whatsoever. (Because the only way you can falsify 'If P then Q' is by finding a situation where P is true and Q is false, which can't ever happen here.)

Good Gottlob! Frege (1848–1935)

The German logician Gottlob Frege's goal was to demonstrate that you could reduce mathematics to logic, and that it depended on nothing but pure reason. It's claimed that this is the first formal system, distinguishing between axioms and rules of inference. In order to define numbers, he produced some complicated logical statements such as this one for cardinal numbers: 'the class of all classes that can be mapped one-to-one on to a given class', and many others I need not go into here, other than to say that in the process he made a considerable contribution to the study of the fundamentals of arithmetic. That definition of cardinal numbers, incidentally, merely says that if, for example, you have as many knives on a table as you have forks, you know you have the same number of them even without counting them.

Logicians consider his *Foundations of Arithmetic* (1884) to be a philosophical classic. The book takes apart earlier efforts to explain numbers and mathematics. In the process of examining the nature of deductive arguments, Frege also offers a way of looking at the nature of language. He distinguishes between the sense of a word (which is objective and determines its truth value) and its *colouring*, which is subjective and to do with the context in which the word appears. On top of that, he explores the word's *reference*. The evergreen example is the planet Venus, which typically appears in the night sky twice, both at dawn and dusk, and was at one time called both the Morning Star and the Evening Star. Thus, the word *Venus* has two *senses* but only one *referent*.

Proving your arguments and arranging your terms

In common parlance an argument is a quarrel or acrimonious dispute, but even so, there's much in everyday argumentation that you can express philosophically.

Most disagreements centre upon a fact or claim, and the argument proceeds by working backwards, as it were, by offering reasons why the statement is either true or false, depending on the point of view of the speaker. Philosophers typically present arguments as a series of statements (propositions) that are themselves either true or false, coupled with a conclusion. The philosopher then judges whether the statements entail or logically necessitate the conclusion. This depends not only on the truth of the propositions themselves, but on the structure of the argument. A favourite example shows that Socrates is mortal. This runs:

Socrates is a man. (first proposition)

All men are mortal. (second proposition)

———

Socrates is mortal.

Aristotle examined the structure of arguments such as this, and decided whether they were sound or not (a *sound* argument is truth preserving; that is, if the assumptions made are all true, so will the conclusion be) starting the philosophical fascination with the structure of arguments.

Oh dear! I feel a Venn diagram coming on! Take a look at Figure 8-1:

The Universe

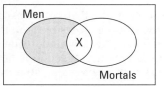

This just says the same thing in diagrammatic form. A circle represents a set, for example the set of 'mortals', and you can use shading to indicate (as here) that the category of men who are not mortal is empty; that is, it has no members. (Being left unshaded doesn't say anything, by contrast.) Socrates provides all the members I need to populate my diagram very nicely. He belongs bang in the middle because he's a member of both the set of men and the set of mortals. (I've plotted him with a little *x*.) Maybe the diagram doesn't do much here, although they can brighten up logic books, and hey, you might be surprised: Venn diagrams can also be a powerful tool for cutting through the complexities of certain kinds of arguments, especially silly syllogistic ones.

Spotting Fallacies

In logic, a fallacy is an *invalid argument* – one in which it's possible for all the premises to be true and yet the conclusion is false. As such you should clearly avoid the invalid argument. People often use the term colloquially to include arguments they consider false because they disagree with one or other of the premises. 'It's a fallacy that paying people the dole encourages laziness' is probably a critique of the following informal argument:

If people can get money without having to work for it first, then they'll become lazy.

The dole is a form of getting money without having to work for it.

––––––––––

The dole encourages laziness.

Here, the argument hinges on 'if people can get money without working then they'll become lazy', which looks plausible, when understood as 'sometimes, if people can get money without working then they'll become lazy' but less so when understood as 'in all cases'.

But in logic, 'if X then Y' is an absolute and automatic function, just as it is for those designing electronic circuits or some such (when programmers write 'If x=2 then day=Tuesday', they aren't planning to leave open the possibility that x becomes equal to 2 but the day can stay Monday).

Incidentally, while I'm on (or near) the subject, the British philosopher, John Stuart Mill, famed as an expert in both logic and matters of right and wrong, considered that this particular argument was indeed sound, using it to warn against the dangers of the state attempting to help out sections of the citizenry. Whole series of fallacies and dodgy arguments exist, so now take a look at some of them.

Fallacies of material implication

What a grand-sounding phrase! But it's all really rather mundane. *Material implication* is just the logical claim that you can't have P and yet not have Q. That means whenever P is true, then Q is true too. P implies Q. Bertrand Russell invented the term but logicians hate him for it, because logically speaking nothing's implied, materially or otherwise. Anyway, that's not your problem.

Here are two valid forms of material implication to train your symbolic skills on:	If P then Q	If P then Q
	If Q then R	If P then R
	--------	--------
	If P then R	If P then (Q and R)
And here are two 'invalid' forms of material implication to never again trip over . . .	If P then Q	If P then Q
	Q	Not P
	--------	--------
	P	Not Q

What's invalid about the last two? Well, the first one, 'If P then Q', followed by Q, is flawed because Q could be true for a different reason than that P is true. Think 'if it's raining then the grass is wet', plus the fact that the grass is wet. Yes, it is true that if it is raining the grass is going to get wet, and yes, the grass may be wet. But actually the reason for that is the neighbours have put their turbo-sprinkler on again The second invalid argument is saying that because 'it's not raining', then we know that 'the grass isn't going to be wet' too, but of course it could be – for a different reason (like that turbo-charged sprinkler).

Fallacious fallacies and tactics in informal argumentation

Argumentation is the process of providing reasons to support a position. Reasons are in practice often limited to producing authorities whom people claim hold the same view, perhaps important people, important books or, of course, God.

Here are half a dozen legitimate tactics:

- *Reductio ad absurdum*: From the Latin for reduce to absurdity, the process of taking the other person's argument and showing that it leads logically to absurd consequences.

- **Affirming the antecedent:** An argument of the form if P then Q (P therefore Q). If it's autumn, then the leaves will fall off the trees. It is autumn; therefore the leaves will fall off the trees. Although valid, the argument is little different from the illegitimate tactic described later in this list as 'begging the question'. Aristotle called it the *modus ponens*.

  On the other hand, denying the antecedent (for example, saying if it's autumn, then the leaves will fall off the trees, but it is not autumn, therefore the leaves will not fall off the trees) is a fallacy, because trees may lose their leaves for any number of reasons (such as a drought, for example).

- **Denying the consequent:** An argument of the form if P then Q (P therefore Q). If you eat too many cream cakes you'll get fat. You're not fat, therefore you haven't eaten too many cream cakes. Although arguments of this form are technically valid, it's clearly more a logical truth than a practical one! Aristotle called it the *modus tollens*.

- **Analogies:** Some say thought experiments are a form of analogy, and certainly you can use the term that way. An analogy is simply a comparison in which you claim one case to be 'like' another in some important respect.

- **Counter-example:** A special kind of analogy that challenges or even demonstrates the falsity of what someone has claimed.

- **Enthymeme or suppressed premises:** These are arguments to which you have to add extra premises to make them valid, such as 'Smoking in bars affects people whether they're smoking or not; therefore it should be banned'. Here the extra premises are that 'The effect of smoking on people is bad' and 'bad things should be banned'.

And here are 12 illegitimate tactics people often seem to use in arguments:

- **Affirming the consequent:** A surprisingly common error of the form if P then Q (P therefore Q). If it's autumn, the leaves will fall off the trees. The leaves are falling off the trees; therefore it's autumn. This is a fallacy because the leaves could be falling off the trees for some other reason, such as during a drought. A related common fallacy in argument sometimes called *correlation confusion* consists of assuming because two things often go together a link must exist.

- **Begging the question:** The fallacy of assuming the very point at issue. In effect, the conclusion is one of the premises in an argument supposedly intended to prove it. It's a form of circular argument.

- **The false dichotomy:** You give two choices when actually other alternatives are possible.

- **Equivocation and ambiguity:** You use a word or phrase that has two or more meanings as though it has just one. Various types of ambiguity exist: *lexical* refers to individual words, *referential ambiguity* occurs when the context is unclear and *syntactical ambiguity* results from grammatical confusions.

- **Non sequiturs and genetic fallacies:** From the Latin meaning 'that which does not follow'. You offer statements in a way that suggests they follow logically one from the other, when in fact no such link exists. The important genetic fallacy is both a kind of non sequitur and a product of ambiguity; this is where you draw assumptions about something by tracing its origins back, although in fact you can't make a necessary link between the present situation and the claimed original one.

- **Special pleading:** Employing values or standards against opponents' positions but not applying them to your own position.

- **Wishful thinking:** Assuming conclusions because you wish them to be so. An appeal to majority opinion to back up a factual claim is a particular kind of wishful thinking.

- **Red herrings:** Irrelevant topics or arguments brought into a discussion with the effect of allowing the real issue to go unexamined. Apparently, in days gone by huntsmen used herrings sometimes to confuse dogs chasing after foxes.

- **Straw man arguments:** Introducing and attributing a weak or absurd position to an opponent, and proceeding to demolish it.

- ***Ad hominem* attacks:** From the Latin meaning 'towards the man'. These are comments directed not at the issue at hand but at the individual opponent. (People occasionally use the term to refer to the legitimate tactic of exposing an inconsistency in a person's argument too.)

Another variety of *ad hominem* attack that takes place before you introduce the main argument is known as *poisoning the well*. There is also the
so-called *bad company tactic*, where you criticise the opponent's position for its supposed association with some other view. The Nazis often
appear in arguments for this purpose.

✔ **Humpty-Dumptying:** After Lewis Carroll's egg-shaped character who sits
on a wall (but not, it seems, a fence) and insists:

*'When I use a word,' Humpty Dumpty said, in rather a scornful tone, `it
means just what I choose it to mean – neither more nor less.'*

✔ **Self-contradiction:** And finally, the unfortunate tendency of a poor argument to inadvertently shoot itself in the foot.

Examining Meaningless Statements

Lots of meaningless statements are possible, although for some reason philosophers struggle to come up with many examples. They often fall back on
a famous example created by the contemporary US philosopher of language,
Noam Chomsky, which is: 'Colourless green ideas sleep furiously'. This is
supposed to illustrate that even when following the rules of ordinary, everyday language (grammar) words can cease to be meaningful.

However, logicians aren't very interested in meaningless statements like this;
instead we're interested in ruling in and ruling out certain kinds of topics as
being suitable for us to treat them as logical arguments. For example:

✔ Do people have free will or are humans really programmed like biological machines?

✔ Are people anything more than bodies – do humans have minds or souls?

✔ Do gods exist? What, not even one little one?

✔ Is there life after death, as the religious folk like to believe?

These questions certainly haven't been answered yet. And maybe you can't
answer them, which is enough for some people to say it makes them pretty
pointless to ask – meaningless even. A group of philosophers known as the
Logical Positivists centred in Vienna in Austria just before the Second World
War (hence they're sometimes also known as the Vienna Circle) insisted
that these questions weren't suitable for study. They thought philosophers
should only look into matters that either logic or empirical science could
settle. Of course, this reduced the workload for philosophers enormously.
But it also left out most of the questions people cared about.

Chapter 9

Understanding Knowledge

> *The totality of our so-called knowledge or beliefs, from the most causal matters of geography and history to the profoundest laws of atomic physics or even of pure mathematics and logic, is a manmade fabric which impinges on experience only along the edges.*
>
> – Willard Quine, Two Dogmas of Empiricism

This chapter looks in detail at what philosophers mean by 'knowledge', a study they call grandly 'epistemology', and the debate between those who think it can be found by looking around, and carefully examining the world, and those who think knowledge comes from equally careful reflection upon ideas. The great champion of that point of view is Descartes, whose views are set out in detail later in the chapter.

Laying the Foundations of Knowledge

Beliefs are very important. As one contemporary philosopher, Tom Morris, puts it, they're the map by which you steer through life. As such it's important that the map is accurate or you may end up getting hopelessly lost. Working out whether your map through life is accurate or not is the same problem as laying the foundations of knowledge.

Most of the philosophical theories of knowledge have three essential components. Before you can say you know something

🖛 You must believe it is the case.

🖛 You must have good, relevant reasons for your belief.

🖛 What you believe must in fact be true.

If you do all that, then you can say you know something. Sounds pretty water-tight, doesn't it? Only it's not quite.

Thousands of years ago the most famous philosopher of them all, Plato, neatly spelt out the problem of knowledge in his little playlet, the *Theaetetus* (lines 201c⊘210d, if you're looking and, believe it or not, lots of people still do). The problem has stumped philosophers ever since. If anything, it's been getting more bothersome to them since the 20th-century interest in analytic philosophy. (Analytic is the name for people who like taking things apart; in this case, philosophers who take sentences apart to look at the exact meaning of each of the words. There's more on this at the end of Chapter 5). What problem cases like the 'Cow in the Field' all suggest is that philosophers need a different definition of knowledge. Although all knowledge may have to be true, justified beliefs, not all true, seem to be knowledge. So, many philosophers say what you need is a more complicated account!

The Cow in the Field

Imagine a farmer, Farmer Field, who's concerned about his prize cow, Daisy. In fact, imagine he's so concerned that when his dairyman tells him that Daisy is in the field happily grazing, he says he needs to know for certain. He doesn't want to just have a 99 per cent certainty that Daisy is safe, he wants to be able to say that he knows Daisy is okay.

Farmer Field goes out to the field and standing by the gate sees in the distance behind some trees a white and black shape that he recognises as his favourite cow. He goes back to the dairy and tells his friend that he knows Daisy is in the field.

Here comes the philosophical doubt. At this point, does Farmer Field really know the shape he saw is his cow? Well maybe, maybe not.

But then the dairyman says he'll check too, and goes to the field. There he finds Daisy having a nap in a hollow, behind a bush, well out of sight of the gate. He also spots a large piece of black and white paper that's got caught in a tree. Now it gets a bit strange. Daisy is in the field, as Farmer Field thought. *But was he right to say that he knew she was?*

You might think that the answer is no because the farmer's belief was based on a misapprehension so it can't count as true knowledge. Yet, in this example

- ✔ Farmer Field believed the cow was safe.

- ✔ Farmer Field had evidence that this was so (his belief was justified).

- ✔ It was true that his cow was safe.

And all this is normally good enough to count. However, you might still feel Farmer Field didn't really know his cow was in the field.

Source: Adapted from 101 Philosophy Problems, *Martin Cohen (Routledge, 1999).*

One tactic philosophers have used is to try to add an extra rule such as that no view (even if in fact it's right) counts as knowledge when it's based on a false belief. But then, how do you know which beliefs are false? And anyway, this approach seems to sweep away too many things that you're happy to count as knowledge, because they work for you in practice. Other philosophers have gone in the opposite direction and tried to dispense with the first requirement (that you must believe something is the case), allowing people to know things without necessarily believing them. And yet others have wanted to make the criterion for knowing to be something more than just belief, suggesting instead that what's required is acceptance, whatever that is . . .

The riddle of how to find rock-bottom certainty is one of the great underlying themes of philosophy, as practised by the Ancient Greeks and summed up by Plato in the *Theaetetus*, where he spelt out the three conditions but left it to subsequent philosophers to solve the problem. Alas, no one has done! Instead, you still have to wonder whether people (or chickens) really know something when they tell you they do.

So philosophers continue to worry about what counts for knowledge, and have had to settle instead for establishing a few rules:

✔ Setting the limits of knowledge – which questions philosophers should ask, and which they should recognise as being impossible to answer.

✔ Appreciating the proper role of science. Because limits exist here too. For instance, to what extent should common sense yield to scientific theories when the scientists say that the world of solid objects and a myriad of colours is actually almost completely empty space full of colourless particles?

As Willard Quine said in *The Ways of Paradox and Other Essays*:

> *I am a physical object sitting in a physical world. Some of the forces of this physical world impinge upon my surface. Light rays strike my retinas; molecules bombard my eardrums and fingertips. I strike back, emanating concentric air waves. These waves take the form of a torrent of discourse about tables, people, molecules, light rays, retinas, air waves, prime ministers, infinite classes, joy and sorrow, good and evil.*

Getting your tongue around epistemology

You sometimes hear it said (at philosophy conferences anyway, less so down the pub) that the 17th and 18th centuries were the age of epistemology. This was the time of Descartes ruminating in his nice warm oven room on the question of what knowledge is really certain, and also a renewed interest in scepticism, the philosophy of the sceptics like Pyrrho in Ancient Greece. These philosophers argued that people knew very little, and most of that what they thought they knew was really mistaken. Plato was influenced by their views, and came up with a distinction between the kinds of things he thought you could be certain about and the things that you merely believe to be the case (a kind of knowledge he called *doxa*).

Aristotle considered the matter to be simpler, saying that when you have good, relevant reasons for your beliefs, then you do indeed have reliable knowledge (which he called *episteme*). His only concession to the doubters, from the sceptics to Plato, was that the reasons have to be really good. Quintessentially, in fact, knowing something means believing the conclusion of an argument that's logically valid.

This is all very well, but as arguments are no better than the assumptions fed in at the beginning of them, it ends up with you knowing not much more than before you started – things like snow is white and 2 + 2 = 4, which Plato had already offered (especially in the dialogue the *Republic*) as knowledge. So some agreement exists, which is always reassuring in questions about knowledge.

Knowing things instinctively

You come into this world equipped with instinctive knowledge. You know how to breathe, how to sleep, to digest. Later on you know how to smile, talk, laugh, do up shoelaces, wink and prove complex logical theorems (well, some people do, anyway). But that shouldn't distract you from the important feature of this kind of knowledge: it's a physical kind of knowledge, sometimes seen as genetic, and it's certainly a kind of knowledge that animals share.

Pyrrho and the philosophical pig

The first great sceptic of the Ancient World was Pyrrho (two Rs) who travelled around Europe in the company of Alexander the Great in the third century BCE. When he popped back to Greece, he gave lectures on his personal philosophy, which essentially was that the wise person is indifferent to the world around them. A famous story told of him says he was once on a ship caught in a violent storm. All around him people were rushing around and panicking, while he sat and looked on impassably. When someone asked him how he could remain so calm, he's supposed to have simply pointed to a little pig also travelling on the boat, which was contentedly crunching through its food even as the storm raged. Pyrrho's advice thus was for humans to seek to emulate the calm practicality of the little pig.

Anyway, here are some of the different ways of 'knowing' I know about:

- **Knowing how:** Knowing how or *know-how* is practical knowledge about practical matters. Several levels of practical knowledge exist. First you have physical (bodily) skills, such as all those instinctual things like eating or running away from wolves. Then you have skills you have to learn, such as how to ski or cycle, and also technological things like how to program a video recorder or telephone New York. Know-how thus includes things that you don't consciously think about at all, and things that you do think about, perhaps repeating rules to yourself (such as 'press the green button twice').

- **Knowing facts, friends and how to do up your shoelace:** Do you know what a headache is like? Yes? But probably not because someone told you what it's like or gave you a book on it. Similarly, you know that you don't like yellow jumpers, but you do like green ones. Perhaps you know that green colours suit you better, in general. Whatever, this is the second type of knowledge – by acquaintance.

- **Knowing by experience:** In fact, we build up most of our knowledge through experience (acquaintance and experience are closely linked; perhaps the main difference worth making is that the first is more practical and the second is more theoretical) – as a baby we soon found out that floors are hard by falling on them, or that grass isn't tasty by trying it out. After we find out something like this, we may generalise it, and it may become theoretical, conceptual knowledge. But the knowledge started through experience.

- **Knowing that:** This is the kind of knowledge that interests the philosophers. It involves language and concepts, and pretty much excludes the rest of the animal kingdom. Your dog may know that he'll get his supper in a special bowl marked 'Gnasher' every evening, but this is still only that knowledge by acquaintance kind of thing. Dogs (as far as philosophy is concerned) know nothing.

Admiring intuition

Intuition is a funny sort of thing. By intuition people mean the ability to obtain knowledge without actually being able to produce any evidence or reasoning to back it up. 'I knew intuitively that writing a *Dummies* book would be a bad career move,' for example! Some people say women have more of it than men; some people say it helps them to win the lottery or avoid car accidents. Lots of people say intuition isn't a respectable kind of thing to claim to have anyway – better by far to stick to facts. But you could also say intuition is a kind of subconscious processing of the information and data you have, noticing details and minimal cues in the environment. It would be rash to rely only on what you consciously know or remember when you either half-forget or don't notice the vast majority of information you have.

And another kind of important use for intuition is in ethics. Philosophers even give it a special term: *moral intuitions*. People may feel something is wrong (or maybe right) without being able to explain why they think that way. Many times people think that something is right, but hang back, feeling a doubt, a contrary intuition. Again, it would be a rash philosopher who would override all such moral intuitions.

Decoding Empiricism and Rationalism

I devote all of Chapter 7 to the different isms. But here, to understand empiricism and rationalism, you need to appreciate that a great rift exists amongst philosophers between:

- ✔ *Empiricists*, who think you obtain knowledge via the senses.

- ✔ *Rationalists* (sometimes known as *Idealists*), who think knowledge comes from reflection upon ideas.

Don't say maybe it comes from both, or you'll have created a third category and thus a lot more bother. In fact, the divide makes sense only in the same sort of way that splitting people up into physical beings directed by minds does.

The philosophical issue had religious and political undertones. For some reason, most of the empiricists were British, and most of the rationalists were from mainland Europe, thereby giving another rather political aspect to this supposedly abstract philosophical debate.

Let's give the empiricists the first turn in the debate. Step forward, then, John Locke to set out the British position – without any concessions. John Locke is supposed to have decided to write his 'Essay Concerning Human Understanding' in 1689 after a fierce debate amongst his friends over the issue when they couldn't satisfactorily resolve it. This partly explains the very firm language of his essay. He starts by advising people to stop 'meddling with things' that are beyond their natural abilities to know. He then asks us to 'suppose the mind to be a white paper, void of all characters' and then asks, 'Whence has it all the materials of reason and knowledge?' His answer sums up the empiricist view: 'All that we know comes from sense experience, and from reflection upon experience.' He goes on to say:

> It is an established opinion among some men, that there are in the understanding certain innate principles; some primarily notions, characters, as it were, stamped upon the mind of man, which the soul receives in its very first being and brings into the world with it. It would be sufficient to convince unprejudiced readers of the falseness of this supposition, if I should only show (as I hope I shall in the following parts of this discourse) how men, barely by the use of their natural faculties, may attain to all the knowledge they have, without the help of any innate impressions, and may arrive at certainty without any such original notions or principles.

JARGON BUSTER

Continental rationalism and continental rationalists

Rationalism is an umbrella term that covers a variety of philosophical positions. The only thing that they share in common is a confidence that human reason can find the answers to all the big philosophical questions and is the route to true knowledge.

Because most of the British philosophers thought otherwise, the term *continental rationalism* evolved, meaning the continent of Europe, thereby excluding the British Isles. Under this heading comes a very weighty group of philosophers, including René Descartes from France, Baruch Spinoza from Holland, Immanuel Kant from Poland (although he's usually called a German philosopher) and Gottfried Leibniz and G.W.F. Hegel from Germany.

But straight away came a continental riposte. 'Is the soul empty, like a tablet upon which nothing has been written?' responded Leibniz, in what he pointedly called his 'New Essay on Human Understanding'. He said:

> *Our differences are about subjects of some importance. There is the question about whether the soul in itself is completely empty like tablets upon which nothing has been written [tabula rasa], as Aristotle and the author [John Locke] maintain, and whether everything inscribed on it comes solely from the senses and from experience, or whether the soul contains from the beginning the source of several notions and doctrines, which external objects awaken only on certain occasions, as I believe with Plato and even with the Schoolmen, and with all those who find this meaning in the passage of Saint Paul where he states that the law of God is written in our hearts.*

Leibniz (and the others) worried that if all knowledge came originally from the physical senses, then people were little different from animals! As Leibniz put it, in the same essay:

> *. . . it is in this respect that human knowledge differs from that of beasts. Beasts are purely empirical and are guided solely by instances, for, as far as we are able to judge, they never manage to form necessary propositions, whereas man is capable of demonstrative knowledge. In this, the faculty beasts have for drawing consequences is inferior to the reason humans have.*

That's true: animals are bad at philosophy.

Deducing Impressive Truths with Descartes

René Descartes (pronounced Ren-ay Day-carts) was born in Poitiers, France, in the dying years of the 16th century and although most of his contemporaries had practical hobbies like digging allotments or fiddling with chemicals, Descartes was much more high-minded (although he did join the army), and preferred to pursue his knowledge investigations using mathematics and rigorous logical reasoning. For this reason he's sometimes dubbed the father of modern philosophy. His most influential book, the *Meditations*, describes his questions to himself while meditating in a nice, warm oven room. Eventually, he thought he'd found the answer to the question 'What do I know for sure?' in the certainty of his awareness of his own thoughts, famously encapsulated as Cogito ergo sum ('I think, therefore I am'). But he doesn't state this in the *Meditations*, although in the 'Replies to the Second Set of Objections' he does offer *Ego cogito, ergo sum, sive existo* ('I am thinking, therefore I exist'), which says much the same sort of thing, but in a hopelessly and deservedly forgotten form.

This simple claim was, René believed, something that he definitely did *know* – not just believed to be the case. It's been very influential, having a profound effect on how people see the world, mostly for the worse but that's a different story, part ethics, part politics and, for the moment, we'd do better to stick to just what Descartes' reasoning was . . .

Descartes' second meditation

Descartes begins his second meditation (not exactly a meditation in the strict mystic sense, more like extended periods of philosophical reflection) by drawing conclusions from his first meditation, the one in which he tries to separate out in his mind the things he really knows from the things he merely believes, and ends up throwing away everything.

> I suppose that everything I see is false. I believe that none of what my deceitful memory represents ever existed. I have no senses whatsoever. Body, shape, extension, movement, and place are all chimeras.

Chimeras, by the way, are a kind of imaginary animal made up of the body of a lioness with a goat's head and a snake for a tail. You don't want any of those following you around! Descartes then argues that even if all of his previously held beliefs are false (not just doubtful), at least one of his old beliefs *must* be true.

> *Is it then the case that I too do not exist? . . . there is some deceiver or other who is supremely powerful and supremely sly and who is always deliberately deceiving me. Then too there is no doubt that I exist, if he is deceiving me. And let him do his best at deception, he will never bring it about that I am nothing so long as I shall think that I am something. Thus, after everything has been most carefully weighed, it must finally be established that this pronouncement that 'I am, I exist' is necessarily true every time I utter it or conceive it in my mind.*

Descartes isn't just idly day-dreaming in that cosy oven room. No way! This is a philosophical deduction. And the formal argument (not that he expresses it formally) is something like this:

> *If I'm not being deceived, then I exist.*
>
> *If I'm being deceived, then I exist.*
>
> *I'm either being deceived or not being deceived.*
>
> ——————— *(Therefore)*
>
> *I exist*

This is a *syllogism* (see Chapter 8 for more about these). The argument is certainly pretty persuasive. It's certainly valid as you see if you use the same structure for something less dramatic.

> *If it's Monday, then the canteen will serve vegetable surprise for lunch.*
>
> *If it's not Monday, then the canteen will serve vegetable surprise for lunch.*
>
> *It's either Monday or it's not Monday.*
>
> ———————
>
> *The canteen will serve vegetable surprise for lunch.*

The crucial assumption is the second one, 'If I'm being deceived, then I exist' (but not quite so crucially, 'If it's not Monday, then the canteen will serve vegetable surprise for lunch'). This is the interesting assumption, but it wasn't actually original to Descartes. It was suggested by the much earlier philosopher Saint Augustine (354–430) who said, *Fallor, ergo sum,* for those who like collecting bits of Latin to impress people. Actually this means not 'I think, therefore I am' but 'If I'm mistaken, at least I am', which is a much more useful phrase. For example, when you've just failed an exam with a mark of 17 per cent (as I seem to remember failing logic with once), you can write at the bottom *Fallor, ergo sum,* and surely feel a bit better.

It's important to see that the crux of both Descartes' and Augustine's arguments is that as long as they're thinking (being deceived or being absolutely spot on in their ideas, no matter) then they exist.

This idea is a bit ambiguous, because you could read the argument to mean that in order to exist you have to be thinking, which is obviously not true (for example, you might be asleep). But if you give Descartes the benefit of the doubt on that, one ambiguity remains that you really can't brush away.

Descartes' great idea, the foundation stone for constructing a reliable system of all knowledge, is that he's at the very least aware of his existence as long as he's aware of his thoughts. But put that way, it's obvious that he can't really be confident that those thoughts belong to him at all. He'd have done better to have supposed:

> *If there's a thought, then there's a thinker.*
>
> *A thought does exist.*
>
> ─────────
>
> *There is a thinker*

Alas, arguing this way doesn't prove that Descartes exists, only that there is a thinker, who could be someone else. Sounds crazy? But you can think of a unicorn, and that does not make the unicorn exist – at least not in the normal sense. Perhaps though (as Descartes hoped) his reasoning could serve as proof of God, if all that is required of God is to be pure thought.

Spending a lazy week with Descartes dreaming in the oven room

Descartes' *Meditations* was very much about Descartes the individual. When it was first printed, it was presented as a collection of famous people talking about a new essay – the *Meditations de Prima Philosophia* by Renatus Des Cartes (as Descartes, who was French, decided he now wanted to sign himself, using a kind of Latin flourish). Among the famous people invited to comment on Descartes' philosophical efforts is Thomas Hobbes, the English philosopher, who accuses the Frenchman of not really 'doubting everything' at all, despite his pretensions. Descartes lightly brushes off this objection, saying briskly that he'd only mentioned the disease of doubt in the spirit of a medical writer intending a moment later to demonstrate how to cure it, and thus had no intention of doubting everything. (And, perhaps mindful of the comments received, Descartes adds in the preface to the *Meditations* that his book isn't intended to be suitable for 'weaker intellects'.)

So what does Descartes come up with after all his meditations? Basically, the idea that your senses are reliable after all, as long as you draw any conclusions from them carefully. Of course, Descartes' ideas weren't really dreamt up in a few days in a warm room; they seem to have dawned on him rather slowly over as many years as the six days that, in his book, he describes the process of reasoning as taking. The appealing notion of the oven room and the week of reflection is a literary device – and a very successful one at that. Add to which, the whole enlightenment process has religious (Jesuit) undertones and so, very particularly, does the choice of *six* days. God created the universe in that; Descartes modestly aims at something similar!

Here's how the book goes, in my own potted version:

✔ On the first day, Descartes enters the terrifying world of nothingness by allowing everything to be unknown and uncertain.

✔ On the second day, he calms his fears by reflecting that at least he knows one thing, that he's at least a doubting, fearing, thinking thing: 'What am I? A thing that thinks, what is that? A thing that doubts, understands, affirms, denies, is willing, is unwilling and also imagines and has sensory perceptions . . .'

✔ On the third day, he proves to himself that the existence of God is certain.

✔ On the fourth day, he teaches himself some ways to avoid error.

✔ On the fifth day, he furnishes himself with a superior proof of God's existence.

✔ On the sixth and final (working) day, he throws aside any doubts and prepares to re-enter the world equipped with a new science for understanding it, a science that applies more carefully the very tools of sense perception originally jettisoned on day one.

Descartes' findings are one of the crown jewels of Western philosophy – but there's not really much there when you look into it. Don't let that put you off, though. The search for knowledge within philosophy isn't even expected to produce very much.

As Bertrand Russell said in *The Value of Philosophy*:

> *Philosophy, like all other studies, aims primarily at knowledge . . . But it cannot be maintained that philosophy has had any very great measure of success in its attempts to provide definite answers to its questions. If you ask a mathematician, a mineralogist, a historian, or any other man of learning, what definite body of truths has been ascertained by his science, the answer will last as long as you are willing to listen. But if you put the same question to a philosopher, he will, if he is candid, have to confess that his study has not achieved positive results such as have been achieved by other sciences . . .*

But, as Russell goes on to add:

> . . . to a great extent, the uncertainty of philosophy is more apparent than real: those questions which are already capable of definite answers are placed in the sciences, while those only to which, at present, no definite answer can be given, remain to from the residue which is called philosophy.

Chapter 10

Separating Fact from Fiction

. . . .

. . . .

Reality is merely an illusion, albeit a very persistent one.

– Albert Einstein

Most philosophy books talk about just one thing: how you can tell the right answer from all the wrong ones. Because, for most people, this seems to be the important thing to be able to do. Take crossing the road, for example. Get it right and you reach the other side. Get it wrong and you may get run over. Simple! Or consider buying a cold remedy. You want to get one that will cure you, not do nothing except taste nasty, or worse still, give you some awful side-effects. The point is that you're used to thinking of things in terms of factual answers and demonstrable proofs. People are brought up these days on the whole with a very tidy, logical worldview of facts and evidence and regularity.

Yet in many, many ways, the gap between fact and fiction isn't just narrow – it isn't there at all. Doctors prescribing cold remedies, for example, know that people can often get better given placebos (drugs with no active ingredients that nonetheless patients imagine have some special powers because they believe in the cures). Equally, people who are depressed may get ill. In both cases, the physical effects of illness are responses to a purely mental – imaginary – state.

Some may say, okay, but illness is a bit of a special case. But then, what about things you remember happening? Are these facts or fictions? That great expert on the workings of the human mind Sigmund Freud found that many of his patients had problems that related to things they remembered happening; things that (wait for it) he strongly suspected had never happened. These people were trapped in an unsatisfactory world – of horrible parents or traumatic incidents or whatever – and were released from it not by investigating reality but by investigating unreality – their hopes, their fears, their dreams.

As psychologists put it, what you are is ultimately a kind of narrative – a fictional story that's made up both by yourself and those around you. Reality hardly comes into it. Investigating the way the mind works is what this chapter's about.

How Do You Know You're Not Dreaming Right Now?

Philosophers have always been very interested in what people are able to do when they're asleep. This is less because most people nod off during philosophical arguments, but because they think that in sleep the soul becomes free from the chains of earthly sense experience to attain philosophical truths. (Well, that's what to say anyway if you're caught dozing off while on the job!)

According to Plato, all knowledge consists of recollecting pre-birth experience of the ideal forms. That great German philosopher Immanuel Kant put it optimistically in the *Critique of Practical Reason* that in 'deepest sleep, perhaps the greatest perfection of the mind might be exercised in rational thought'. Mind you, Kant also thought that each human being had only a certain amount of this invaluable sleepy time in them, and warned against using it all up too soon – for example, by lying in bed in the mornings.

On the other hand, as the medieval pessimist philosopher Saint Thomas noted, if a man devises logical arguments while asleep, when he wakes up 'he invariably recognises a flaw in some respect'. And Plato himself records that Socrates asked Glaucon, 'Does not dreaming consist in mistaking the semblance of reality for reality itself?'

But it's Descartes who took the issue most seriously. Descartes wrote in the *Discourse on Method* that 'all the same thoughts and conceptions which we have while awake may also come to us in sleep,' adding later in a letter: 'I had good reason to assert that the human soul is always conscious in any circumstances, even in the mother's womb.'

Fiction and the philosophers

Fiction raises some puzzling questions for philosophers – how can something not real be important? What's going on when you react emotionally to fiction? Aristotle thought that dramas must always create the two feelings of pity and fear in the audience. Plato thought that fiction was in principle objectionable, but if people must have it (for example as poetry) then it should be wholesome and uplifting. But it's Augustine who writes most eloquently in *The Confessions, Book III*:

> Stage-plays also carried me away, full of images of my miseries, and of fuel to my fire. Why is it that man desires to be made sad, beholding doleful and tragical things, which yet himself would by no means suffer? Yet he desires as a spectator to feel sorrow at them, and this very sorrow is his pleasure. What is this but a miserable madness? For a man is the more affected with these actions, the less free he is from such affections. Howsoever, when he suffers in his own person, it used to be styled misery; when he compassionates others, then it is mercy. But what sort of compassion is this for feigned and scenical passions? For the auditor is not called on to relieve, but only to grieve: and he applauds the actor of these fictions the more, the more he grieves. And if the calamities of those persons (whether of old times, or mere fiction) be so acted, that the spectator is not moved to tears, he goes away disgusted and criticising; but if he be moved to passion, he stays intent, and weeps for joy.

Philosophers have also batted to and forth the question of truth; in fiction 'King Lear has ungrateful daughters' looks like it's the same kind of statement as 'Queen Elizabeth II has several grandchildren', yet in the first one King Lear doesn't seem to really exist, or as philosophers put it (in the language of Meinong and Frege) no *referent* (no 'thing' out there in the world)) out there to which you can finally tie the truth or falsity of the claim.

Funnily enough, as Jeremy Bentham pointed out, much of what passes as reality is actually fiction. Motion, power, even matter are all made up by people; they aren't there in the world. David Hume joined in too, denouncing substance, the self and space and time as all fictions. (That's not even to start to consider the status of things like rights, values, duties and obligations . . .) In *A Treatise of Human Nature* Hume adds that personal identity is nothing more nor less than a complex construction made up of your lifetime activities and experiences, taken altogether, not separately.

Doubting Everything with Descartes

Descartes ultimately decided in the *Meditations* that because God was 'supremely good and cannot err', a rational person must still be able to distinguish any false information presented to the soul in the dreamy lands from the (supposedly) tidy, coherent knowledge of the world. This confidence neither Leibniz nor Bertrand Russell shared, Leibniz saying that 'it is not impossible, metaphysically speaking, that there may be a dream as continuous and as lasting as the life of a man' – or indeed, as the life of a butterfly, as described in a few lines of verse by the great exponent of life as a (butterfly) dream – the Ancient Chinese sage, Chuang Tzu (as described in Chapter 6 for example).

Descartes says that to separate out real knowledge from unreliable hearsay, optical illusions and tricks by other people (including evil demons) you have to assume everything you're told, everything you see or hear and everything you can't be absolutely sure of is a trick. He asks:

> *How do I know I'm not in the middle of some awful, philosophical nightmare? A nightmare of unusual proportions, certainly, that goes on and on with remarkable consistency and detail – but a miasma nonetheless, completely detached from reality? Or then again, how do I know I haven't fallen into the clutches of a malignant demon, intent on deceiving me?*
>
> *Or perhaps even a malignant doctor. One who has recovered my brain after some nasty accident and is now keeping it suspended in a vat of chemicals as part of a ghastly medical experiment? How do I know that everything I think I'm experiencing isn't really made-up 'sense-data' being fed to my poor old brain-in-a-vat, along coloured wires: purple for hearing, black for touch, yellow for taste, blue for vision . . .?*

Rather alarmingly, no one knows but instead assumes these things. But Descartes sums up the philosophical search for something better than that – the search for real knowledge.

Descartes was far from being the first to try doubting everything. The Ancient Greek Sceptics, who so annoyed Plato, specialised in doubting, and their conclusion was that you can't be sure of anything at all. That's why they're called *sceptics*.

You might think you'd never be fooled by either a malignant demon or doctor. But it's a very short step from experiencing something directly to experiencing something indirectly. Take remembered experiences, for example. How real are those old experiences?

I think, therefore I am

Descartes is famous because, at the moment when he seems to have reduced all human knowledge to mere optimistic guesses and convention, he brings forward dramatically something that he says is absolutely reliable and certain – something you can really be sure of. This is the most famous quote in philosophy, probably:

> *I think, therefore I am.*

Dualism

The second thing Descartes is remembered for is *dualism*: viewing the world as being made up of two things – mind and matter.

Dualism is the philosophical jargon for viewing the world as made up of two things: Mind and Matter.

Descartes thought everyone had both a mind and a body. However, he thought animals had only bodies – and he even dissected a few to test his theory out. Sure enough, he found no minds inside. The Church liked his approach, as it fitted in well with the idea of souls. There was, however, one practical problem with the theory. If minds have no physical parts, how can they have any physical effects – how can my pure mind tell my arm to turn the page?

You might think you would never be fooled by either a malicious demon or a malicious doctor. But it is a very short step from 'experiencing' something directly to experiencing something indirectly. Take remembered experiences, for example. How 'real' are those old experiences?

Remembering the Role of Memory

Everyone has souvenirs – sticks of rock or thermometers made out of shells from seaside resorts like Blackpool and Bognor Regis, or more personal ones like pieces of Bob Dylan's broken guitar string. But most of all, souvenirs are in the form of memories in your head.

Yet how can something from the past that's no longer in existence remain present in your memory? Right at the dawn of philosophy, scholars debated this issue. Plato described memory as a storage system fashioned out of wax. Expanding on his metaphor, Aristotle claimed that memory was made up of physical traces of experiences, which in some way record and represent them. Similarly, British empiricist philosophers (see Chapter 7) such as John Locke and David Hume thought of memory as a storehouse of ideas copied from previous impressions. Hume insisted that memories differed from both perceptual impressions and purely imaginary ideas only in their degree of vivacity. And it's Hume's view that remains dominant to this day.

Using the mind as a storehouse

Although the exact details of this traditional storage view of memory are constantly being modified to meet the results of neuro-scientific research, the majority of philosophers and cognitive scientists have shared the general approach. For example, according to the Gestalt-psychologist Wolfgang Köhler (1887–1967) and the renowned neuroscientist Antonio Damasio (1944–) your experiences are stored inside the brain as codified physiological traces. That is, our memories are physically stored and indexed as 'neural representations' somewhere at the back of the brain. When you remember something, your brain looks it up in the index and then decodes and recovers the relevant memory-data stored.

In the 19th and 20th centuries, Bertrand Russell (1872–1970) and William James (1842–1910) tried to expand on Aristotle and Hume's theory by suggesting that imagery is a necessary but not sufficient condition for memory – leaving just what the extra bit might be still as a mystery. Russell's student Wittgenstein and other Wittgensteinians later disputed the assumptions lying behind the whole approach. They argued instead that it was an illusion to think that such a thing as a picture that contained its interpretation in itself could exist. To do this is like suggesting that an arrow points only because you connect it mentally to a picture of an arrow.

Wittgenstein always disagreed with his sometime supervisor Bertrand Russell, but in this case he's surely right. Take the souvenirs of Bognor Regis and of the Bob Dylan concert, for example. Sticks of rock don't look like seaside towns, nor yet broken guitar strings make any sound let alone that like a musician. Yet in your mind the one points quite happily to the other.

Nothing about a complex image (or state) could make it refer to one and only one state of affairs. Even if a mental image does accompany say, a cup of coffee, it can't explain it, because you'd in turn have to recognise that the two really are connected.

Examining questions of identity

What makes something, something? What makes me, me, or the ship of Theseus, the ship of Theseus – as opposed to any other? Questions of identity, especially personal identity, have preoccupied philosophers over the centuries and continue to raise new problems today as advances in medicine create ever more possibilities and with them questions.

In Plato's dialogues the *Republic* and the *Symposium* only the immaterial, divine forms never change in themselves, because they're complete and perfect. Everything else, including people, is constantly changing, both in time or space.

Despite this physical reality, the idea that each person has a fixed identity is central to systems of ethics, law, medicine and indeed everyday personal, social interactions. But what is it about a person, exactly, that stays the same?

Over the centuries philosophers have returned again and again to the problem, focusing on different aspects. Some have found identity in the nature of names; others in spatial identity; still others have discerned it in souls. Some have wondered about the essential elements of the body; after all, scientists say that our genetic code, or DNA, always stays the same. Many have pondered in one way or another the nature of the brain, the mind, consciousness, memory and experience.

Classic thought experiments used to explore the issue include

- ✔ The Ship of Theseus (in which a ship is gradually replaced plank by plank until not a single physical part of it remains the same)

- ✔ The medieval debate over survival of the soul that led to Thomas Aquinas's thought experiment of the family of cannibals who appear to consist of the atoms of people who need them in order to enter heaven.

John Locke's (1690) *Essay Concerning Human Understanding* includes an early kind of body exchange, in this case between a prince and a cobbler, but you can do better than that if you imagine a fully-fledged body-and-mind transfer machine.

But the issues aren't just theoretical. Today, genetic manipulation, biotechnology, surgery or drugs subtly affect personal identity. People sometimes undergo dramatic alterations, including sex changes and adding bionic or transplanted body parts (including animal parts). Mad scientists happily mix up different species of animals in *chimerical* experiments (that is ones created by or as if by a wildly fanciful imagination), creating pathetic and desperate monstrosities.

Using mind-transfer machines

Stories of body (mind) transference abound – it's a staple of folk tales and science fiction, not just philosophy. Even Aristotle pondered the essence of Socrates and Plato, wondering if in fact it might ultimately be the same thing, and John Locke used that pioneering tale of the prince and the cobbler who wake up to find they've swapped bodies to show that identity is really more to do with mental characteristics than with the physical ones.

But take a more recent case, from my own book, *Wittgenstein's Beetle and Other Classic Thought Experiments* (Blackwell, 2004), of Dr Gibb – a dull, ugly, tweedy academic who's discovered a 'body-exchange machine' exists in the university science park. After some soul searching, he decides to give it a go.

He enters one booth and transfers various elements of his mental capacities to Steve – a young, handsome and, frankly, not too bright, postgraduate student of his – in the second booth.

Steve thinks he's going to benefit by having some of his tutor's skills and knowledge implanted in him and is very excited. But in fact, Gibb has more sinister intentions. He wants to take over his young student's body entirely by reprogramming it with all his mental attributes, and at the same time transferring poor Steve's mind to his own clapped-out body. Amongst the options flashing on the control panel are ones to transfer all his skills, all his memories and even all his personal preferences and idiosyncrasies.

In a fiendish touch, to make matters worse, Gibb types in details setting out who the bill for the process should be sent to afterwards. As the bill is several millions, this is no laughing matter, either. Of course, poor Steve can't afford it – he might even end up in prison for not being able to pay.

Now Gibb is an utter rotter: he wants to do the selfish thing. He immediately starts typing in Steve's name and college address. But then he pauses. If he's transferring *himself* to Steve's body, shouldn't he send the bill to the old Gibb, soon to have Steve's thoughts, rather than the new one in Steve's body?

This being only a thought experiment, in order to decide who's who you can imagine various possibilities. Suppose, for example, that Gibb chose to transfer all of his memories, skills and character. In this case, the thought experiment may make you think it shrewd, if unethical, of him to send the bill (and consequent prison sentence) to the old decrepit 'Gibb' who has poor Steve's skills and memories. Meanwhile the real Gibb would sneak off scott-free in Steve's body. Such an approach fits the intuition that personal identity is really to do with mental attributes, not the physical ones. So that's clear.

Yet what would you think if the booth *malfunctioned* after sending Gibb's mental attributes to Steve, leaving them still intact in the original Gibb? Or (worse still) if it simply *erased* all Gibb's mental attributes, leaving Steve disappointed at not getting any of his tutor's skills but otherwise intact? Then you might feel sure a real Gibb still existed, one who was now defined just by his physical husk and one who would now be doubly unfortunate in ending up being bankrupted by the process.

Listening to the stories of the subconscious mind

In the late 19th century people generally understood mental disorder in *positivist* terms as something rooted in a disorder of the body. Positivism means looking at the world for measurable causes and effects, and disregarding intangible things like what people were thinking. Treatment typically included being put in an asylum and injected with various chemicals. One Austrian doctor called Sigmund Freud, however, was interested instead in treating the mind and understanding its role.

Sigmund Freud (1856–1939) was born in Moravia, then part of the Austro-Hungarian Empire, into a very respectable, non-practising but ethnically Jewish family. (This made his later forays into sexual fantasy all the more remarkable, not to say *disgraceful*, of course.)

When Freud was four, the family moved to Vienna and there he trained as a doctor and remained for most of his life. In fact, Freud always saw his theories as part of a scientific, empirical tradition, but then so did Aristotle and many others who scholars now recognise as essentially philosophers. Freud saw himself as extending the understanding of the human being, both normal and pathological (or *sick*, as people now avoid calling it).

Phantasies and the Oedipus Complex

In a famous series of case-histories, Freud presents various patients and their symptoms and describes the process of talking through the associated memories, which typically are rooted in the years of early infancy.

The strange case of Anna O

In the 1880s Freud and his medical colleague Josef Breuer treated a number of wealthy Viennese women using hypnosis. The most well-known of these cases is that of Anna O, a young woman who was suffering from a series of incapacitating physical complaints that appeared to have no cause. Anna O complained of paralyses that at times were so severe that she couldn't walk. At other times she was unable to speak in her native German, but only in a variety of foreign languages. Freud and Breuer treated her by inducing a hypnotic state and then delving into her deepest memories (not for the last time, Anna O's treatment had to be abruptly broken off when it turned out that she'd fallen in love with her analyst!).

But before that disgraceful outcome, Anna O's case led Freud to develop the idea that you could treat physical and mental symptoms alike by talking about them – what psychoanalysts call the concept of the talking cure (and what the rest of us call lots of money!). But the philosophical significance is there in the idea that the self is split between a conscious, rational and social self and a hidden self that inhabits a parallel inner world outside reason or social control, and that the 'everyday', conscious self is in a constant battle to repress.

Freud's explanation for all this was that human beings were driven by the *libido*, a powerful sexual impulse. He observed in his patients that they could direct the libido towards many objects, which sometimes led to internal conflict. The attempt to repress what patients felt to be forbidden desires could produce symptoms.

One thing that quickly struck Freud was how many of his women patients remembered being seduced by their fathers, or other male family figures. By 1897 Freud had come to the view that these were in fact early childhood phantasies. They were false memories in that the remembered experiences were imaginary not real ones. Freud described these phantasies as *the Oedipus Complex*, after the Greek myth in which a son kills his father and marries his mother, and argued that this was a phase that everyone has to go through. Not literally, you understand! Strictly speaking, theOedipus Complex is a syndrome which infant boys have when they get very attached to their mothers and hate their fathers while girls have their own complesx - the Electra Complex when they fall in love with Dad and hate Mum. To some extent, every child falls in love with the parent of the opposite sex and becomes a rival of the same-sex parent. When all goes well, this is just a stage and the child works through these feelings satisfactorily, emerging with a balanced approach to both parents and indeed both genders.

The id, ego and superego

Later on, Freud decided that it was in fact more complicated than he'd first imagined, and that in fact three elements drive people:

- ✔ **The id:** The irrational and primitive part of emotions and the libido.

- ✔ **The ego:** The part attempting to regulate and control the id, which is the rational self.

- ✔ **The superego:** Created out of the individual's sense of social and ethical norms. Like a strict headteacher, the superego is fixated on stopping and punishing misbehaviour.

Going ego, egoism, egoistic

For Sigmund Freud, the mind has three parts; the *id*, the *ego* and the *superego*. The id has appetites but is not rational; it's what Freud originally called *the unconscious*. The superego, on the other hand, is the body's moral faculty; it's the conscience and is quite capable of acting not in the individual's interests but with regard to an idealised or general interest. But it's the ego that speaks for the real you; it has to try to decide between the opposed promptings of the id and the superego. It's a bit like a cartoon of a drunkard looking at a bottle of whisky while two thought balloons pop up, one with a forked-tail devil saying 'Go on – a little bit won't harm!', and the other saying 'Remember your vow never to drink again while on duty!'. Anyway, in all this, the ego represents the compromise position dictated by prudence and responsibility.

In ethics *egoism* (sometimes called *normative egoism* or *rational egoism*, albeit to no particular advantage) is the view that satisfying yourself is a sufficient justification for choosing one action over another. In Plato's *Republic* Thrasymachus strongly makes the case for egoism, and similarly, egoism is the founding principle of government for Thomas Hobbes in the *Leviathan*.

Freud decided that the strange symptoms of his patients were in fact the result of an over powerful and intolerant superego attempting to repress the id and the ego.

In *The Interpretation of Dreams* (1900) Freud described the unconscious world of the id. In the unconscious no logic exists, but everything can co-exist and your most forbidden desires rule unchecked. The unconscious reveals itself in your dreams and through slips of the tongue. The conscious mind attempts to repress desires that the superego deems morally or socially impermissible, but the unconscious reveals itself in distorted form: in symbols that you have to decode and interpret.

Freud's ideas and the future

Freud's ideas have been very influential on the modern concept of the human self and how the human mind works. His theories have entered into the common language, and his concepts – the different parts of the mind, and the conflicting worlds of desire and social and moral demands – shape the modern concept of the self. But of course every action has its opposite reaction, and in the tradition of empirical science Freud's fellow Viennoise, Karl Popper, gave a devastating critique of psychoanalysis. Popper, a philosopher with a particular interest in the workings of science, complained that the ideas of Freud and of psychoanalysis didn't meet any of the usual scientific criteria and had no objective basis, but were merely assertions that you couldn't prove.

Understanding the unconscious

Carl Jung (1875–1961) was born in Kesswil, Switzerland, and died in Zurich. He was the founding father of analytical psychology. He met Freud in Vienna in 1907 and initially collaborated with him. Jung was president of the International Psychoanalytical Society from 1911 to 1914 but became increasingly critical of Freud's methods. They parted completely in 1913 after publication of Jung's *The Psychology of the Unconscious*.

Jung takes a very positive view of the mind, and he sees the psyche as a self-regulating, creative system striving for individual identity, which he termed *individuation*. Dreams convey practical advice from the unconscious to the conscious, assisting achievement of individuation. In *Modern Man in Search of a Soul* Jung suggests that the modern world causes alienation by severing humanity from its roots, which are essential to psychological growth and hence satisfaction. This has resulted in unprecedented levels of depression, despair and suffering. Humanity must understand its symbols and allow them to inform the creative development of the conscious mind. For this reason Jung placed great emphasis on dreaming to allow the unconscious to communicate with the conscious mind. This is a natural process.

The division between objective, measurable reality and the shifting, subjective world of the self, noted by Plato so long ago, remains. And if neuroscience, with its fancy machines capable of showing the brain's electrical activity, is currently hailed by some as a new way of finally pinning down what determines personality and behaviour, Freud's work reminds you that the human mind is full of contradictions.

William James and consciousness

Another philosopher with a deep interest in how the mind works is William James (1842–1910) who has an interesting (and possibly confusing) family tree, being the son of Henry James, the religious philosopher, and brother of another Henry James, the novelist. He himself was a philosopher and psychologist who taught at Harvard, publishing *The Principles of Psychology* (1890), an account of how the brain relates to the mind, or rather consciousness.

James took Darwin's view that consciousness has an evolutionary origin and purpose; he developed the notion that consciousness is a transient state of the brain that the brain continually destroys and refreshes. This is what has become famous as the *stream of consciousness*.

Another of William James's influential ideas is the distinction between the *I* and the *me*. James says that the *I* is the thinker and the *me* is made up of the *material me*, which is essentially preoccupied with bodily concerns, and the *social me*, which is preoccupied with how others perceive it in social situations. Personal identity consists of the *I* remembering the demands of the various *mes*. In this sense, James is a *phenomenologist*: he believes mental states are based on physical processes. However, he makes one exception. James hopes that free will is indeed free, arguing that the *I* is able to choose freely the thoughts it wants to think about.

What Happens When the Brain Goes Wrong?

The neurologist and writer Oliver Sacks has described how certain kinds of brain damage result in enhanced memory, indeed the extraordinary ability apparently to recall, day by day, every event the individual's experienced. He surmises from this that the brain of the healthy individual contains a complete record of everything it's experienced since birth, but mercifully, most of this is inaccessible to our conscious mind.

But if you can't remember anything beyond the last few minutes, then it may be more serious. Because to the extent that you've lost your grip on the past, you may be unable to function in the present.

A personal experience of memory loss

I once had an accident while cycling. I hit my head and was knocked unconscious for about half an hour – along with getting a lot of quite nasty other injuries. It took about a month before I was well enough to stagger around the house again – but that was just recovering from the visible, physical injuries. It turned out the invisible, mental effects lasted a lot longer. In fact, it turned out that I'd lost the ability to remember new things that happened. I could remember my childhood, but not what had happened yesterday. In fact, I couldn't remember why I was injured and so each day my family had to explain the same things to me. The experience backed up the theory that the mind is a kind of storehouse, one which is divided into two parts – a short-term memory part and a permanent, organised, long-term storage part. In my case my brain was holding events in the short-term memory and then filing them away incorrectly and thus losing them.

After about six weeks, my filing system somehow corrected itself and I was able to remember again. I was lucky. But others are not so.

Dr Sacks and his curious tales

In *The Man Who Mistook his Wife for a Hat* (Picador, 1985), a gripping account of the various kinds of disasters that can affect the brain, Dr Sacks describes the case of a memory-challenged person, Jimmie 'the Lost Mariner', a man in his 60s whose memory has erased any recollections of events that had occurred after his 30th year. Jimmie is continually shocked at the changes all around him both in the physical world, and most horrifyingly to the people he knew (if he recognises them). 'Guess some people age fast,' he says in an attempt at explanation.

Dr Sacks tries to substitute for the failure of Jimmie's memory by providing him with a simple backup system – a notepad. Jimmie writes down events in his diary and then Dr Sacks can ask Jimmie to refer back to them. How well does that work? Not so well. For a start, such tricks serve to 'jog' memory. But Jimmie simply doesn't recognise the entries as his own. 'Did I write that?' he asks, let alone 'Did I do that?'. When Dr Sacks asks Jimmie how he's feeling, the answer is rather sad. He says, 'How do I feel? I cannot say I feel ill. But I cannot say I feel well. I cannot say I feel anything at all.' And he scratches his head in bewilderment.

Dr Sacks's patient is in rather a bad way; lost in a ten-minute world, he feels scarcely alive! But in this case a glimmer of hope exists. Sacks refers to a passage from his professional Bible, *The Neuropsychology of Memory* by A.R. Luria, which says:

> But a man does not consist of memory alone. He has feeling, will, sensibilities, moral being – matters on which neuropsychology cannot speak. And it is here, beyond the realm of an impersonal psychology, that you may find ways to touch him, and change him.

The smell of coffee – again!

Dr Sacks also describes the case of a man who's sense of smell is irretrievably destroyed. Smell is a subtle sense that affects everyday life far more than you may realise. The interesting thing about the case is, however, not how much he suffers and how he comes to terms with the loss, but that one day he finds a drink yield up that rich aroma of coffee again. The same miracle happens when he takes out his pipe and fills it with tobacco.

But the medical facts remain unchanged. His nose could no more detect smells than his ears could. The scents he was savouring were entirely in his mind, but not imagined, exactly. They were previous experiences that his subconscious mind was faithfully replaying at the correct moment.

And indeed, Dr Sacks finds that when Jimmie is in chapel singing or praying, or when he's playing certain games or solving tricky puzzles, he does become a different, more complete person. As long as he's fully occupied with the present, his loss of memory ceases to trouble him. But of course he can't spend all this time praying or solving puzzles . . .

Dr Sacks's excellent 'cure' is to give Jimmie the hospital garden to look after. Once there, Jimmie begins to make good progress. At first, every day the garden is new to him and he has to rediscover it afresh, but after a while he begins to remember it and is able to build upon his plans and strategies for tending it. As Sacks puts it, Jimmie is lost in space-time but located in what he calls *intentional time*. Although Jimmie's unable to organise memories in time and in space, he can create a new kind of memory world based upon aesthetic, religious, moral and dramatic feelings.

Philosophy meets neuroscience

Many young children genuinely can't tell the difference between something they've invented and something that really exists or happened. (Teachers know this also makes children unreliable witnesses, not least as regards their own activities.) This enables them to have imaginary friends, imaginary feasts and, of course, imaginary lives. Yet the child's charming characteristic has an unfortunate shadow companion in the grown-up world of brain disorders.

Paul Broks, a neuroscientist based in the rather chilly city of Plymouth in the UK, describes in his philosophical-psychological book *Into the Silent Land* (Atlantic Books, 2004) a female patient. When he asks the lady, 'Do you know where you are?' she answers that she's in exotic Majorca and loosens the button on her blouse on account of the heat. 'I should leave that on if I were you,' Broks says to his patient rather drily. He realises that his patient's brain has registered the image of the postcard from the little tropical island on his desk, and is now busily creating a network of entirely false connections with the information, confusing events in the private, mental world with events in the public, external one.

Life in the real world

Only in the real world do actions have demonstrable effects and tangible consequences, as Bishop Berkeley's friend supposedly tried to demonstrate by kicking a real stone. Yet *real* is a problematic word. Bishop Berkeley was insistent that what's real in the world isn't stones, but thoughts. The material world, he says, exists only in our minds. You suppose the images you have in your mind, like the apparently involuntary sensations that assail you (for example if the rock is too big or your shoes are too thin), to have been caused by a mechanical chain of events that starts with physical matter, is conveyed by electrochemical means via the various senses and finishes up as a tidily organised mental representation in your head. But, says Berkeley, why suppose this? Wouldn't it be much simpler to say that what you have in your mental world is real and what you think it must correspond to out there is imaginary?

A big part of the answer to this mystery of 'who you are' is that you create in your head a life-story, an inner narrative whose continuity or sense is your life. You may say that this narrative is you; it's your identity. (The existentialists talk a lot about this – see chapter 12).

Biologically speaking, people aren't so very different. It's personal narratives that really give distinct identities. Some people's life stories are full of tales of misfortune and repression, burdens imposed and opportunities lost. Others are full of special opportunities, exceptional abilities and good fortune. Whether the 'real' histories were really so far apart – or even reversed – is of no matter. Such narratives have their own logic. The individual plays out a role determined by their life-story, not by any crude physical or historical fact.

Romanticism

Romanticism is notoriously difficult to define, both as an historical movement and a school of thought. It has no definitive beginning or end point, but its influence is wide. Writers, painters, musicians and philosophers have all been influenced by romantic ideals.

During the 18th century Europe experienced an Age of Enlightenment in which many intellectuals began to feel that humans were growing close to knowing all there is to know in the scientific world. However, this intense focus on objective, scientific discovery also made people feel small and unimportant, left without purpose or design. This latter sentiment led a small, underground group of anti-rationalists to create what's since become known as the Romantic Movement.

Romanticism, in the most general sense, takes the emphasis away from objective reason and places it with the emotions, intuition, nature, faith or other 'irrational' concepts. Even the Ancient Greeks did this. Aristotle, for example, dedicates Book VIII of the *Nicomachean Ethics* to a discussion of friendship, and Plato devotes the entirety of his *Symposium* to a long discussion of the nature of love. However, the 18th-century Romantic Movement is radical in its rejection of rationality. Although Plato and Aristotle argue that the proper role of reason is in control of the irrational passions, real romantics reverse these roles.

One of the great Romantic philosophers was the French/Swiss eccentric Jean-Jacques Rousseau, who wrote in praise of the glory of 'natural man', of the superiority of the 'noble savage' and against the corruption of modernity and science. John Stuart Mill, too, is often considered a romantic philosopher due to the central role of happiness within his ethics. Mill, who was brought up to be drily logical, later was greatly influenced by romantic poets like Wordsworth and Coleridge. But the most romantic philosopher of them all is probably Søren Kierkegaard. In his book *Fear and Trembling*, Kierkegaard argues that there are three basic ways of existing, the highest of which you can achieve only through a wholly irrational leap of faith.

However, as Travis Rieder recently put it, philosophical romanticism never became more than a hiccup in the history of Western philosophy. Gritty reality has a way of taking over.

Chapter 11

Interpreting Language

> *I really believe that languages are the best mirror of the human mind, and that a precise analysis of the significations of words would tell us more than anything else about the operations of the understanding.*
>
> – Leibniz

All philosophers sooner or later have to address two questions. The first is, what's the relationship of thoughts in the mind to the words people use to express those thoughts? And the second is, what's the relationship of words as people express them to things out there in the world?

In all philosophical systems, save perhaps those slightly dodgy ones based on meditation, words and language are either the link between mind and matter or the barrier separating the two.

This chapter is an attempt to show how philosophers have investigated the enigma of words and language over the centuries, and a summary of the latest thinking in the area, as it relates to many aspects of modern life from computing to animal rights.

The 20th-century British writer George Orwell (the one who invented Big Brother and warns about government newspeak) was perplexed and shocked by the abuse of language he saw around him. Writing in his popular 1946 book *Politics and the English Language*, he says:

> *When one watches some tired hack on the platform mechanically repeating the familiar phrases – bestial atrocities, iron heel, bloodstained tyranny, free peoples of the world, stand shoulder to shoulder – one often has a curious feeling that one is not watching a live human being but some kind of dummy: a feeling which suddenly becomes stronger at moments when the*

light catches the speaker's spectacles and turns them into blank discs which seem to have no eyes behind them. And this is not altogether fanciful. A speaker who uses that kind of phraseology has gone some distance toward turning himself into a machine. The appropriate noises are coming out of his larynx, but his brain is not involved, as it would be if he were choosing his words for himself.

Deconstructing Language

Language is philosophy. It is both the medium we must use to carry out the study, and the subject of that study.

And just as some philosophers have sought to make the world only what you sense, some have tried to reduce ideas to being only the words you use. But for many other philosophers, the problem of language is that it's imprecise, and so a perennial theme of philosophy has been the quest for better, usually more logical ways of expressing findings. This was the mission of Leibniz, Russell, Frege, the logical positivists and Wittgenstein, to mention just a few.

Many 20th-century philosophers, such as G.E. Moore and J.L. Austin (who wrote a book called *How to Do Things with Words*, which took a lot of words to do very little . . .), investigated the play of words, contrasting everyday usage with the supposedly more rigorous philosophical one. Others (such as Suzanne Langer or Paul Ricoeur) explored the use of metaphor, which in many ways is the essence of language, conveying meaning through the use of symbols. In fact, many words, even the most abstract ones, derive originally from ones designating very tangible, common or garden things.

In recent years people have also been very interested in the way words can convey prejudices, such as racism, gender and sexism, and even speciesism. *Speciesism* in language involves using words or phrases that make acceptable animal exploitation. Not so many people are bothered about it, but once you start looking, there are lots of cases. For example, people often use the term *animals* to mean *non-human animals*, although literally humans are animals. In this way, people distance themselves from their animal brethren – at the animal's expense!

Propagandists can twist language both by stoking up prejudices or by minimising the significance of actions through euphemism, the results of which have been seen time and again in the worst atrocities of human history. Hitler and his propaganda chief Goebbels provide a dark example of this. In his autobiography *Mein Kampf*, which is full of long, rambling and hate-filled tirades, there's also a sophisticated analysis of the use of propaganda in which Hitler says, 'Words build bridges into unexplored regions' and goes on to explain how he used his skill with words to build up and inflame public opinion against those he terms Jews and Social Democrats.

How to make words out of things

The study of word origins sheds light on how people both use and develop language. Many words seem to start off being quite literal, and then become increasingly abstract. *Religion*, for example, derives from the Latin term for tying people up with rope (*ligature*).

Another curious case is that of the word *assassin*, which you may use to describe a certain kind of politically motivated killer. The word derives from the historical case of a certain religious sect that used to murder people while under the influence of hashis. The word for someone who smokes hashish is *hashashin*.

Then there's the word *hazard*, which signifies something dangerous. It comes from the Arabic term *al zahar*, which simply means *dice*. Equally, the word *dice* in English has acquired the extra use as a verb: *dicing with death* means to do something risky.

Finally, the word *important* derives straightforwardly from the practical activity of trade, and *emportas* and *exports*. The implication is that something imported is noteworthy and interesting.

In *Politics and the English Language* Orwell says the following on the use of euphemism by politicians:

> *In our time, political speech and writing are largely the defense of the indefensible. Things like the continuance of British rule in India, the Russian purges and deportations, the dropping of the atom bombs on Japan, can indeed be defended, but only by arguments which are too brutal for most people to face, and which do not square with the professed aims of the political parties. Thus political language has to consist largely of euphemism, question-begging and sheer cloudy vagueness. Defenseless villages are bombarded from the air, the inhabitants driven out into the countryside, the cattle machine-gunned, the huts set on fire with incendiary bullets: this is called pacification. Millions of peasants are robbed of their farms and sent trudging along the roads with no more than they can carry: this is called transfer of population or rectification of frontiers.*

But these concerns about language aren't the most philosophical ones.

Chatting with the Ancient Greeks

The Ancient Greeks were preoccupied with the particular problem of what they called *universals*, or working out how exactly a word can describe a whole group of things. The Greeks also inquired into how people come to join words together in phrases and sentences, and most importantly, how you could use words correctly to make claims about the world.

Universals are terms like *golden* or *warm*. The word *Socrates* can be a universal too, if you want to use it as such. For example, you could say that Zenon Stavrinides, the contemporary philosopher, is the Socrates of the North.

Plato describes the Sophist philosopher Gorgias as having raised the very important philosophical doubt about the gap between words and ideas. Gorgias says that asking someone to think about, say, a fluffy dog (and that's *not* his example, by the way) doesn't mean that he'll really think about either a fluffy thing or a doggy thing – let alone something that's both fluffy and doggy. For example, he may think the word fluffy means overweight, and think about a fat dog, or worse still he may consider dogs to be kinds of wolves and actually visualise a fluffy wolf. Not to forget, you – the questioner – may have used the wrong word in the first place. You may have meant not *fluffy* but *fussy*, and mixed the words up. Everyone does that. It shows how the word and the idea in your head aren't one and the same thing. Or does it? Some psychologists say that an apparently erroneous choice of word reveals what's really going on in your head. If someone in the DIY shop says, 'Have you got any posh books?' when they meant to say, 'Have you got any posh *hooks*?', some experts say this means that they were really thinking (and wanting) more (philosophy?) books . . .

In another of Plato's dialogues Cratylus discusses with Socrates what's become known as *correspondence theory* – the idea that although originally any word is arbitrary, just as choosing names for new babies, new planets or new species is (all right, I know in many cases the choice isn't arbitrary, but carefully thought about), certainly use of the label after it becomes established is anything but arbitrary. If you call your baby John, then next time you take John to the doctor you want to be sure that it's your baby, that the John baby comes back, not some other baby that used to be called Samantha or Eustace or Jessie. Or again, the label *Scottie dog* applies to only certain animals. If you want to adopt a Scottie dog at the local animal shelter, you don't want them handing over a Doberman or a Pit Bull and saying that it's just arbitrary and conventional what you happen to call different kinds of dogs. Arbitrary it may be, but it also matters.

Plato thought that words were in fact signs or symbols for *the Forms* – ideal objects or examples of everything. (We look at this strange but important theory in Chapter 2). But Aristotle straight away complained that if the heavenly Forms were supposed to embody the essence of the worldly objects – that is, all dogs, from Scotties to Doberman Pinschers, participate in the Form of the Dog (as Plato puts it), then all Plato has done is create a new thing with certain properties that in turn have to be explained. What does the Form of the Dog and any earthly dog have in common, he wonders? Yet surely this is to miss the subtlety of Plato's theory, because the Forms aren't really things, but essences. The idea is that all the dogs in the world share the property dogness, or are dogs, to put it more simply. End of problem, thanks to the use of words. Well, maybe . . .

Supposition theory

William of Ockham (1285–1347), nicknamed the More than Subtle Doctor, was a Franciscan monk who was born near Guildford in England but who worked mainly near Oxford. He has been immortalised through the power of language: the Ockham's Razor is named after him. This isn't a hair-cutting razor but rather the rule of reasoning also known as the *technique of parsimony*. Simply put, the rule says that, given a range of possible explanations, you should prefer the most simple explanation. More people should listen to that!

The approach makes a contrast with those from Aristotle onwards who like to generate new categories and distinctions. But the aspect of the razor that concerns us here is Ockham's approach to *nominalism*, or questions about the appropriateness of use of language. (A *nominalist* is someone who thinks that the thing dogs have in common is just the use of the word – that is, that they're all called dogs.)

Ockham's contribution was to come up with a distinction between words about words and words that point at words. Ockham's conclusion is that many philosophical errors arise due to the misunderstanding of language. Grand philosophical terms are the worst culprits, in his view. For example, attempting to think about human beings in general leads people to use the word *humanity*, and then philosophers suppose *humanity* is a real quality that all people possess.

Stop right there! says Ockham, brandishing his razor. Instead, for Ockham, the word *humanity* is merely a kind of mental marker standing for all the people you know or have heard about, minus all their other (specific, individual, collective) characteristics. In this way, Ockham's theory is supposed to explain how words you use in sentences, which Ockham calls *terms*, refer to things. Alas, that's not why the theory is also sometimes called *supposition theory*. Instead, that label is attached, so to speak, because originally, in the Latin, the word *supposition* means *standing for* and approximates to the idea of bearing reference in English. (Think supporting theory.)

Ockham had a great influence on the theorising of other English philosophers – such as Thomas Hobbes and John Locke – on language. For all his hard work on this (and other matters) he was summoned by the Pope in 1324, not for a nice chat, but to face charges of heresy! Further differences with the Church shortly after led to the Church excommunicating him.

Dog-ness, in this way, although useful is still clearly very abstract. Plato's Forms don't exist in the normal sense. And so philosophers from the Ancient Greek sceptics on have sought to throw out these invented entities – metaphysical creations – and stick to a simpler universe made up of just words and things. Words are labels stuck on things, and ideas don't enter into it. Tidy. But does that trick solve the problem? Not really, because the trouble with the approach is that words lose their meanings. So in the 17th century philosophers returned to Aristotle's notion of *signs*: making words the signs for ideas and ideas themselves the signs for things.

It all goes round and round (as philosophy ever does) in an ultimately rather futile circle.

Building up structuralism

The systematic study of language and its role in societies flowered into a separate quasi-scientific discipline in the 19th century. The discipline's founding figure was the Swiss linguist Ferdinand de Saussure (1857–1913). Saussure said that language was a system of signs that were in themselves entirely arbitrary.

However, the work of Ferdinand de Saussure only really became trendy in the second half of the 20th century (those crazy 1960s!), when a fine new 'ism', structuralism, really took off. (Confusingly, a lot of people call the study of the structure of language *semiotics* rather than structuralism! This was the term preferred by the American philosopher Charles Pierce.)

Saussure's original idea was that it's the structure of language, rather than the rules of logic, that explain how you think and speak. His notion of the *sign* and of language as a system, called *semiology*, resurrected an older distinction between the structure of language, which he now called *langue*, and manifestations of langue, called *parole*. The game of chess is one way to illustrate this: the rules exist only in abstract, but their embodiment is a particular game. In the same way, language is a system of signs people use to express ideas – comparable to writing, to sign-language for deaf people and to symbolic rituals. The sign, of course, is arbitrary. It's only the system that gives signs their meaning.

In the 20th century, the French philosopher and anthropologist, Claude Levi-Strauss, rediscovered structural linguistics and applied it to culture as a whole, as an anthropologist. He believed that because language was humanity's distinctive feature, it also defined cultural phenomena. If you speak of humanity you speak of language, and if you speak of language you speak of society. Structuralists looked below the surface of words to discover the hidden signifying system – the *langue*. All philosophical problems became problems of analysing systems of signs that structured the world.

A system of signs

The central idea of Ferdinand de Saussure's theory is that the meaning of words and phrases has more to do with their relationship to other words and phrases than it does to anything outside the *system* – say objects or happenings in the world. He insists instead on the arbitrariness of the sign. Words are symbols, like traffic signs are symbols. Their meaning comes from their role in the system or language game. (Mind you, you mustn't take this simile too far; traffic signs aren't entirely arbitrary, or even if they are, it's still best not to treat them that way.) Saussure argues that a language exists in the minds of its users, but that it is, in turn, 'quite independent of the individual, it is essentially social; it presupposes the collectivity'.

The structuralists explained the world around us by saying that people cut up the continuum of space and time with which they're surrounded into segments so that they're predisposed to think of the environment in certain ways. For example, people are boxed in to seeing the world as consisting of lots of separate things belonging to named classes, and to make sense of change by seeing a mono-directional flow of time carrying them (and events) smoothly and inexorably along from the past to the future.

Another 20th-century French philosopher Michel Foucault developed the approach by arguing that power operates through complex social structures, incorporating the view that far from knowledge and truth being fixed, they were constantly changing. He was in some respects the first poststructuralist.

Later on, Foucault's slightly younger French contemporary, Jacques Derrida, attempted to pull down the structuralist edifice when he wrote that their creations were merely metaphysical imaginings. To look for a science of signs, to attempt to make sense of the relationship of words to things, was as irrelevant, he said, as Descartes' suggestion (made to explain how mind can influence matter, when the two things have supposedly nothing at all in common) that the body and soul ran together like two synchronised clocks. Derrida goes on to complain that the way philosophers have used concepts historically, and philosophy's claims to grapple with truth, are pretence. The whole exercise, he said, was nothing but *jiggery pokery* – which is the ancient nomadic term for doing things with words.

Relying on grammar

Philosophy of language conventionally starts with the discussion of the Ancient Greeks (I just did too!), yet probably the first philosophical treatment of the issue comes not from the Western tradition but from the East. As early as 380 BC a whole school of early logicians had an interest in the relationship of language and reality, which was known as the Chinese School of Names. And (as I mention in Chapter 6) the celebrated thinker Chuang Tzu once compared language to a fishing net that tries to capture meanings (because individual words are useless, they acquire meaning only in context and in combination with others) and asked whether any difference exists between 'the tiny tweets of baby birds' and people's words.

And yet another Chinese philosopher, Kung-Sun Lung (circa. 320–250 BC) argued that a white horse was not a horse, saying that as the word 'horse' denotes the form and 'white' denotes the colour:

> *What denotes the colour does not denote the form. Therefore, a white horse is not a horse.*

What's he on about? Well, Kung-Sun Lung then goes on to explain that he means that if a knight asks for a horse, his squire will bring him either a white one or a yellow one or a black one. However, if he asks for a white horse, then his squire won't bring either the yellow horses or the black one. This proves, Kung-Sun Lung says, that a white horse isn't a horse, because if it were then what the squire brought in both cases would have to be the same.

Ancient Indian philosophers too were puzzled by the role of words. Panini's *Sanskrit Grammar* (circa. 350 BC) and the *Great Commentary of the Patanjali* 200 years later were especially early attempts to set out rules for using language. But it is with the Buddhist philosopher Nagarjuna (who lived around 150–250 AD) that the Indian debate becomes more truly philosophical. One of Nagarjuna's ideas was that language doesn't refer to things but is self-referential. For example, to say that 'Philosophy is difficult' is *tautological* (that is, something that says the same thing twice) because without the referring to philosophy this activity of being difficult doesn't occur, and similarly if you strip the property of being difficult from philosophy, it's no longer the same sort of subject!

Playing games with words

Philosophers have long played with language, hoping to make sense of it or even to remodel it into something better. Two of the most diligent attempts at this were made respectively by Gottfried Leibniz and (some centuries later)

Russell' and artificial language

Bertrand Russell, who both thought that it was possible and desirable to construct an artificial language to better exhibit the logical form of arguments.

JARGON BUSTER

Semantics and semiotics

Semantics is the study of linguistic signs, particularly the interpretation of the sentences and words of languages. In *Foundations of the Theory of Signs* (1938) the American philosopher Charles Morris divided the general study of signs into three parts: the study of the relation of signs to other signs, which is to do with *syntax*; communication or the relation of signs to their users, which is *pragmatics*; and the relation of signs to the things they represent, which is semantics.

Semiotics is the general theory concerned with signs, in this case distinguishing between icons, such as pictures that look like what they're supposed to represent (typical of traffic signs for falling rocks and so on), natural signs (such as grey clouds signifying rain) and conventional signs (such as a four-leaf clover, signifying good fortune).

At a time when scientists were grandly talking about creating new kinds of compounds (plastics mainly, unfortunately) out of chemical elements, Russell's talk was of creating molecular propositions out of logical atoms, and Leibniz had already passed several happy decades describing possible complex arrangements of his monads. As part of doing this, Leibniz explained that the monads, like 'atoms' don't *really* exist, but you must postulate them, you must make them up, at least in logic in order to explain reality and understand the meaningfulness of language.

Russell, however, warned against such grand 'system building' and emphasised instead the need to identify the logical structure of language and the confusing ways in which it could differ from the grammatical one. For example, how many ways can an *is* be used? Russell declared it was a disgrace if you used *is* in more than one way. Much better, he thought, to split up all the different ways of using the most important verb. He tidily lists various different uses (albeit his list is slightly different from all the earlier philosophical experts' ones, such as Aristotle's, or Aquinas's one, or Duns Scotus's one . . .). How many lists of the way people use *is* can you make?! Anyway, having firmly announced the need to sort out the strange ways people actually use words and language, Russell never followed the idea up. But the idea did, later on, become the project of his one-time doctoral student, Wittgenstein (see the following section).

Wittgenstein and language games

In fact, it was Wittgenstein, in his lectures at Cambridge in the mid-20th century, who first apparently employed the term *language games*. Naturally, then, these were not real games, but merely philosophically curious ways that people use language. Wittgenstein's own favourite examples were things like 'giving orders' and 'asking, thanking, cursing, greeting, praying' (as he puts it in his book *Philosophical Investigations*, 1953). Why call these *language games* then? Ah, but the term is supposed 'to bring into prominence that the *speaking* of language is part of an activity', Wittgenstein explains. The words don't always do the same thing, or have the same purpose. Nor are they just passively conveying thoughts from one mind to the next, such as thoughts about the weather, the time or the latest cricket scores.

One small example of how words don't really stand for one thing was proposed by another British philosophy professor, highly influenced by Wittgenstein, called Peter Geach (born 1916). Geach was actually one half of a rare philosophical couple, with Elizabeth Anscombe (1919–2001; also known as G.E.M. Anscombe) whose philosophical work (on her own initiative) included destroying Wittgenstein's papers in order to conceal his homosexuality. Geach, however, has a more direct influence on British philosophy in the sense that he produced dreary books and articles dressed up in technical language, such as *Reference and Generality* (1962), in which he sought to demonstrate that the word *every* in statements like 'every dog has four legs' doesn't refer to a special dog after all. Which dog? you may wonder. Why, the *every dog*, which some might otherwise have supposed to have this interesting feature.

Linguistic frameworks

Rudolf Carnap (1891–1970) was a student of Frege's, the logician preoccupied with issues of sense and reference, and an influential member of the so-called Vienna Circle in the 1930s. His particular theme was that philosophical disagreements were really produced by differences between linguistic frameworks. His approach is sometimes called *logical empiricism*, and his ideas appeared in *Der logische Aufbau der Welt* (*The Logical Structure of the World,* 1928).

Rudolf firmly believed people could rationally discuss questions in mathematics and logic and get objectively true answers, but outside these areas only the methods of scientific observation were useful. However, he recognised that even logics and mathematics are based on assumptions that can't be justified by anything more rigorous than a judgement of practicality or expediency, and that science too has its assumptions. In *The Logical Syntax of Language* (1934) he explains that 'It is not our business to set up prohibitions, but to arrive at conventions'.

Conducting Philosophical Investigations with Wittgenstein

Wittgenstein's position in the philosophy of language is rather grand; at least it is if you read books written by his fellow Oxbridge types in the UK. This is probably because his position is actually rather unclear, or to be more precise, is totally incoherent and self-contradictory.

In principle, as his PhD-cum-book the *Tractatus* says, it should be possible to construct a new logically rigorous language. Of course, this new language won't deal with a lot of topics for as he (famously) says in the book 'wherefore one cannot speak, thereof one must be silent' and

> *Most propositions and questions; that have been written about philosophical matters, are not false, but senseless. We cannot, therefore, answer questions of this kind at all, but only state their senselessness. Most questions and propositions of the philosophers result from the fact that we don't understand the logic of our language.*

This is the sort of language that has meant later scholars credited Wittgenstein as being the inspiration and one of the leading lights of the Vienna Circle – the informal group of inter-war philosophers who were devoted to making philosophical reasoning as logical and scientific as they could. But that's a myth. Wittgenstein was a young nobody at the time, and in any case he firmly believed a higher, mystical reality existed that neither language nor logic could reach.

Partly because of these beliefs, after publishing the *Tractatus*, his youthful recipe for putting the world into a nice logical structure, Wittgenstein attempted to exit philosophy. But sure enough, after some years he was back, taking up a chair at Cambridge. And although he never committed himself again to print, many of his notes, comments and lectures were later collected up and published. It is in these that Wittgenstein describes language as a series of inter-linked language games, in which words and sentences can function in many different and subtle ways: as deeds, as symbols and as commands. Words, he says (borrowing, without acknowledgement, as was his style, from the great Swiss structuralist Ferdinand de Saussure), are like pieces in a game of chess, taking on their meaning only in the context of the game.

That's quite a turnaround. Indeed, in one aside in *Philosophical Investigations*, Wittgenstein ruefully acknowledges:

> It is interesting to compare the multiplicity of tools in language and of the ways they're used, the multiplicity of kinds of word and sentence with what logicians have said about the structure of language (including the author of the Tractatus Logico-Philosophicus).

Poking at Colour Terms with Pinker

In all this, philosophers like Ferdinand de Saussure and Wittgenstein were trying to break free from the ancient assumption that language merely followed thinking, which in turn depended on laws of logic or reason that were supposed to be the same for everyone, no matter what language they used. It was this conviction that had kept Bertrand Russell wrestling with the task of producing what he called a logical foundation.

But you can look at things another way and make language really rather unimportant, and instead try to connect thoughts to reality – direct.

Step forward, then, Steven Pinker, a contemporary philosopher who normally describes himself more imposingly as a cognitive scientist (well aware of the power of language!). He explains in his book, *The Language Instinct*, that the idea that thought is the same thing as language is an example of what you can call a conventional absurdity. Pinker helpfully sketches out the science (neglecting the role of consciousness, which Cognitive Scientists don't believe in):

> . . . the cells of the eye are wired to neurones in a way that makes neurones respond [to certain colours]. No matter how influential language might be, it would seem preposterous to a physiologist that it could reach down into the retina and rewire the ganglion cells.

And Pinker again:

> *The idea that language shapes thinking was plausible when scientists were in the dark about how thinking works or even how to study it. Now that cognitive scientists know how to think about thinking . . .*

Professor Pinker's hypothesis is that the human brain works as a kind of computer, a symbol-processing machine that converts data, be it linguistic or sensory, according to predetermined, biologically hardwired rules.

> *In the brain, there might be three groups of neurones, one used to represent the individual that the proposition is about (Socrates, Rod Stewart, and so on), one to represent the logical relationship in the proposition (is a, is not, is like, and so on), and one to represent the class or type that the individual is being characterised as (men, dogs, chickens, and so on). Each concept would correspond to the firing of a particular neurone; for example, in the first group of neurones, the fifth neurone might fire to represent Socrates and the seventeenth might fire to represent Aristotle; in the third group the eight neurone might fire to represent men, the twelfth neurone might fire to represent dogs. The processor might be a network of other neurones feeding into these groups, connected together in such a way that it reproduces the firing pattern in one group of neurones in some other group . . . With many thousands of representations and a set of somewhat more sophisticated processors . . . you might have a genuinely intelligent brain or computer.*

This, says Pinker, is the

> *. . . 'computational' theory of mind. In this view, there really is a colour red coded into the brain (in 'mentalese') even when the language people use does not have it.*

And now Pinker plays his trump card against all those rival theories, which try to place a linguistic barrier between thoughts in the head and sense data coming in. His secret weapon against all these is what he calls 'The clinching experiment carried out in the New Guinea Highlands by Eleanor Rosch', in 1972.

Playing with colours

So off to the New Guinea Highlands we must go. And there, the Dani people, as Eleanor Rosch discovered, have only two colour terms. There is *mola* for bright warm colours and *mili* for dark cold colours. Since the tribespeople only recognise the two colours, some people are tempted to refer to them crudely as 'black and white', as Professor Pinker indeed terms them. Yet Professor Rosch found that the Dani were just as good at discriminating the colour spectrum in tests and so it seemed that their lack of words for colours was irrelevant to their perception. End of story, as far as Rosch was concerned. But not so fast! For Rosch's research has itself been found wanting. Methodologically, her tests, involving pairing colours on charts, seem to have been inadvertently biased towards precisely the colours typical of an English speaker's language categories – blue, red, green and so on – over the shades distributed around them. And then the test was so complicated that a mere 20 per cent of the Dani were able to complete them.

In fact, it seemed rather the reverse. People's perceptions are influenced by their vocabularies – and their linguistic structure.

Investigating the Causes of Fires with Benjamin Whorf

Benjamin Lee Whorf was born in Winthrop, Massachusetts, on 24 April 1897, the eldest of three boys. His father, Harry Whorf, was evidently something of a cultural polymath, earning his living as a commercial artist, author, photographer, stage designer and playwright. His mother, Sarah, encouraged Benjamin in 'a great sense of wonder' at the universe, as his biographer Trager puts it. Young Benjamin was fascinated by ciphers and puzzles, and read widely on botany, astrology, Mexican history, Mayan archaeology and photography. In adult life he came to anthropology via the unusual route of physics, and lots of complicated-sounding things like Jungian synchronicity, systems theory and Gestalt psychology (with its foregrounding and backgrounding) and above all linguistics.

But Whorf was only able to pursue his studies in his spare hours and on business trips. For his day-job was rather mundane – investigator and engineer for the Hartford Fire Insurance Company. Yet the time at work was by no means wasted. Within his work he came across many examples that he would later see as language influencing thought patterns, and his linguistic theory appeared in several influential articles set around the topic of fire prevention. People, he observed in the first of these, tended to be careless around empty drums of gasoline, drums empty of petrol but equally full of vapours more explosive than the liquid. He noticed how people were complacent towards industrial waste water and spun limestone, both again flammable and dangerous despite the innocuousness that the words *water* and *stone* convey.

His book *Language, Thought and Reality* doesn't have a very interesting title, and in many ways Benjamin Whorf's subject isn't very promising, being about the structure and nature of language. But in a few words, here's the essence of philosophy, the strange, imprecise, but absolutely crucial way that the three things relate to one another. Recall that the great Chinese philosopher Chuang Tzu put it very nicely in one of his metaphorical asides – language he said, is like a fishing net cast into the waters of reality, useful for catching 'meanings'. Thoughts, concepts are slippery fish, and we need the net of language to capture them. But the net itself is just a means to an end.

Ancient Chinese philosophy doesn't rate very highly in academic philosophy; many times I've been outvoted on its relevance and importance in discussions with philosophers. And nor does the work of Benjamin Whorf, who was never a real academic, merely an investigator for a fire insurance company. Such people, of course, don't produce important theories, and so people don't take Benjamin Whorf's ideas very seriously. His big idea, indeed, which he named the Principle of Linguistic Relativity, only lives on because it was renamed (and re-credited) to his academic supervisor Edward Sapir as the Sapir-Whorf Hypothesis. How many graduate students have had their ideas grabbed by professors? But actually, I don't think Sapir particularly wanted to do so; it was more likely a kind of institutional prejudice that assumes a certain kind of person will come up with all-important ideas and twist the world to fit that assumption. Benjamin Whorf didn't fit the image of a philosophy professor, so his work couldn't have been very important. His idea was, however, of some interest; therefore it must have been due to someone else. And so you must rename the idea. Out goes the Principle of Linguistic Relativity and in its stead comes the Sapir-Whorf Hypothesis.

Now the nice (if slightly ironical) thing about all this is that it exactly illustrates what Whorf wanted to show – that the world is reconstructed around the terms people use. People do this all the time – when you say 'Allied forces minimised collateral damage' or 'The Prime Minister unveiled his reforms of the City of London', you don't describe anything objectively but rather convey a whole series of psychological and cultural assumptions. This is the message Whorf conveyed very elegantly.

Finding Linguistic Relativity Amongst the Hopi Indians

In his book (well, not strictly speaking his book but merely a later collection of his essays made on his behalf), Whorf examines the linguistic structures of the American Indians. He uses their structures to illustrate his idea (which originates not with the Indian languages but with his work investigating the causes of fires) that people dissect nature along lines laid down by their native languages. He says:

> *The categories and types that we isolate from the world of phenomena we do not find there because they stare every observer in the face; on the contrary, the world is presented in a kaleidoscopic flux of impressions which has to be organised by our minds – and this means largely by the linguistic systems in our minds. We cut nature up, organise it into concepts, and ascribe significances as we do, largely because we are parties to an agreement that holds throughout our speech community and is codified in the patterns of our language.*

Making sure all words are relative

Benjamin Whorf did not invent the idea of linguistic relativity, which, in itself, is not a particularly new idea. Indeed, it's rather an old one, older than the physics variety, going back at least to the 19th-century founder of linguistics, Baron Wilhelm von Humboldt in Germany. The baron himself viewed thought as being entirely impossible without language, and that language completely determined thought (not Whorf's position at all). Von Humboldt's theory took on new life after Einstein's demonstration of the relativity of space and time. Einstein himself cited von Humboldt's theory in a radio programme.

The agreement is, of course, 'an implicit and unstated one', Whorf continues, but 'its terms are absolutely obligatory; we cannot talk at all except by subscribing to the organisation and classification of data which the agreement decrees'.

This then is the theory, and it's backed up by a wealth of fascinating examples and scrupulous research. It's curious, then, that Whorf's work is almost universally dismissed. In philosophy, as I noted in the previous section, he's excluded from the pantheon; within Whorf's nominal discipline of linguistics, Noam Chomsky describes his work as 'entirely premature' and 'lacking in precision and 'popularisers', and Stephen Pinker explains that Whorf's idea that thought is the same thing as language (not, of course, that this is what Whorf does say) is an example of 'what can be called a conventional absurdity'.

In another of his essays, Whorf adds:

> In [the] Hopi view, time disappears and space is altered, so that it is no longer the homogeneous and instantaneous timeless space of our supposed intuition or of classical Newtonian mechanics. At the same time, new concepts and abstractions flow into the picture, taking up the task of describing the universe without reference to such time or space – abstractions for which our language lacks adequate terms. These abstractions . . . will undoubtedly appear to us as psychological or even mystical in character . . .

Having Another Go at Deconstructing Language with Derrida

Jacques Derrida was born in Algiers, and after some bumpy educational transitions ended up at the elite École Normal Supérieure in Paris, where he also taught. His book on the German existentialist philosopher, Edmund Husserl,

Voice and Phenomenon (1967), sets out most of his ideas, including his notion of deconstruction. The 1960s (think flower power and hippies) was of course a very good time for academics to join in the upturning of conventional structures, if such radicalism was not perhaps already a bit passé. Anyway, *deconstructionists* are intellectual radicals who say they must throw away all the fruits of philosophy: epistemology, metaphysics, ethics – the whole apple cart. After all, these are products of a view of the world rooted in 'false oppositions' like the is/is not scientific one, the past/future chronological time one and the good/bad ethics one. Derrida explains that all the other thinkers' and philosophers' claims and counterclaims, theories and findings are no more than an elaborate word game. They've been playing, as he puts it, *jiggery pokery* with us. Jiggery pokery, hey! That's messing around with words . . . Not allowed.

Instead, deconstruction is concerned with the category they call the *wholly other* and preventing the *violent exclusion of otherness*.

Derrida takes on Ferdinand de Saussure's project to describe the workings of language, and deconstructs it to show that in seeking to provide a list of distinctions between writing and speech, the father of structuralism has inadvertently produced some – it's arbitrary in form, material and relative – that apply as much to speech as to writing. The difference between speech and writing is thus revealed as nothing more than a philosophical illusion. (You see how deconstruction cunningly takes the hidden assumptions buried in a text and turns them upon themselves.)

Derrida then tries to develop a supposedly radically different conception of language that starts from the 'irreducibility of difference to identity', thereby bringing about a correspondingly different conception of ethical and political responsibility.

Following his successful deconstruction of the speech/writing distinction he looks to destroy Descartes' soul/body one (see Chapter 5); to collapse the difference between things the mind knows and the things the senses know; and to reject distinctions between literal and metaphorical, natural and cultural creations, masculine and feminine and more.

Another of the 20th-century philosophers who wrestled painfully with existentialism was Martin Heidegger, who as well as being one of Husserl's protegés, was a big influence on many French intellectuals including Derrida. In particular, from Heidegger, Derrida also takes the notion of presence. He says philosophy's central task is to destroy this notion. Heidegger's footprints are there too in the concept of being, and the difference between beings and being, which he calls the *ontico*-ontological difference and describes at heroic length in a book called *Identity and Difference*.

What's the difference between *différance* and *différence*?

There's plenty of competition between philosophers for creating complicated-sounding new terms. But it was Edmund Husserl, however, who created *one of the 'biggies' – the alarming-sounding term transcendental phenomenology*, noting that

> Reason is the logos which is produced in history. It traverses Being with itself in sight, in order to appear to itself, that is, to state itself and hear itself as logos . . . In emerging from itself, hearing oneself speak constitutes itself as the history of reason

> through the detour of writing. Thus it differs from itself in order to reappropriate itself.

And you thought language was about communication! It's about bewitchment. Anyway, this is the origin of *différance*, Derrida's favourite punning term, playing on the two senses of to *differ* in position (in space) and to *defer* or delay in time – that is, *defer*-ence. (What is the difference between difference and différence, as in the heading of this sidebar, by the way? There isn't one! Just playing 'jiggery-pokery' . . .)

Derrida's not really a great philosopher; in fact, he's a lousy one. But hey, lots of people study him, so let's get a flavour of his kind of philosophy.

In *Of Grammatology* he says

> All dualisms, all theories of the immortality of the soul or of the spirit, as well as all monisms, spiritualist or materialist, dialectical or vulgar, are the unique theme of metaphysics whose entire history was compelled to strive towards the reduction of the trace. The subordination of the trace to the full presence summed up in the logos, the humbling of writing beneath a speech dreaming as pleniture, such are the gestures required by an onto-theology determining the archaeological and eschatological meaning of being as presence, as parousia, as life without différance: another name for death, historical metonymy where God's name holds death in check.

It's a great game for Derrida, and he makes no bones about it, admitting to not only making up new words when he wants but using existing ones in ways that no one else does. That's what's called 'Humpty-Dumptying' sometimes – after the large egg that sits on the wall in *Alice in Wonderland* and says firmly that words mean whatever he wants them to mean. Mind you, Derrida doesn't see himself as doing quite that. In *Semiology and Grammatology* he even harks back to his old structuralist roots by admitting that words are an interconnected web, or tapestry – or as he puts it (punning again!) textile.

> *The play of differences supposes in effect, syntheses and referrals which forbid, at any moment, or in any sense, that a simple element be present in and of itself, referring only to itself. Whether in the order of spoken or written discourse, no element can function as a sign without referring to another element which itself is not simply present. . . . This interweaving, this textile, is the text produced only in the transformation of another text. Nothing neither among the elements nor within the system, is anywhere ever simply present or absent. There are everywhere, differences and traces of traces.*

In fact, Derrida argues that there can be no meaning as nothing is fixed within the great web of language, or indeed life and perception. Everything is a mirage, or what's worse, a kind of 'fine powder' residue left behind by boiling off politico-sexual assumptions – loaded terms like *is* that discriminates against *is not*, or *me* that's set against *you*. We must destroy the web of words!

Confused? What exactly is Derrida saying? No one knows, not even Derrida himself. Indeed, he once declared, in his 'Letter to a Japanese Friend', that it's never possible to say either that 'deconstruction is such and such' or 'deconstruction is not such and such', for the construction of the sentence would be false already.

One translator, Alan Bass, who may be taken as something of an enthusiast, says that Derrida is 'difficult to read'. It's not only by virtue of his style, but also because 'he seriously wishes to challenge the ideas that govern the way we read . . . Some of the difficulties can be resolved by warning the reader.'

Part IV
Exploring the Mind, Consciousness and Morality

'People are always asking Darren why
he decided to become a Buddhist.'

In this part . . .

Now we're really getting down to it. What exactly does go in our heads? How do medical theories about human brains fit in with philosophical theories about disembodied minds? What on earth could this force be that we now find out is manipulating people all around us like so many puppets on strings? Add to which, who would have thought of arranging the world like that, for goodness sake! All of these great issues, from personal values to political judgements and the hidden mechanisms of economics and social life are exposed, revealed, and explained here.

Well, maybe that's going a bit far, but we make a start on it anyway.

Chapter 12

Exploring the Strange Notion of Mind

Mind is the attribute of the gods and of very few men.

– Plato

*M*ind is an odd thing when you think about it. You're pretty sure you have a mind, and can use it, but what about other people around us? What about animals, what about plants and rocks? If you believe that rocks and plants don't have minds, then at what point in the evolutionary scale did humans start to think? If human beings evolved from simpler life forms, did those simpler forms have minds, too?

In this chapter, we look at perplexing questions like just what do we mean by 'thinking' anyway? Is it something computers do? And what about that general sense of existing that we all seem to have – the thing called 'consciousness'? You can be conscious without exactly thinking, but can you be alive without being conscious? These are the sorts of issues that this chapter will delve into.

Getting to Grips with Philosophy of Mind

According to a strange school of philosophers known as *panpsychists*, even stones have minds, and the only thing different about humans is that over the years people have become more and more complex, and once simple minds have developed into the present slightly more impressive ones.

Consciousness

Descartes left a legacy of consciousness as the crucial feature of knowledge, but also the problem of whether this crucial thing was a mental or a physical phenomenon. Certainly consciousness is something hard to define. There seems to be some sense to the notion, but is it a form of inner speech or merely a series of automated reactions to stimuli? Descartes himself made all the processes of the human mind activities of the soul, and hence part of being conscious, and all the activities of animals into the unconscious pre-programmed reactions of machines. But he offered no good reasons for this split, and nowadays such analyses (although widely adopted) look superficial.

The key question for philosophy of mind (as it's called) isn't the practical study of how the mind works (which scholars now separate off as *psychology*) but whether anything is worthy of the name anyway? If there's a sense to the term, then when I say, 'I think I can see the sun coming out,' I report not merely some sensation of photons or whatever's hitting me in the eye, but a mental event. Yet the two things are linked. Quite how has caused philosophers much anguish over the centuries.

Looking at the issue from the other end, as it were, philosophers have considered what's left once you separate the mind from all its sources of sensory information. If you're merely processing sense information in your mind, and you reach a point when this stops (perhaps after a nasty accident, and let's throw in too, we have lost our memories) it would appear that there's not much left for the mind to carry on with in any sense. Rather grimly, doctors may have to actually make the judgement of whether or not there's anything left worth calling *mind* or *being alive* with coma victims in deciding when to switch off life-support machines.

Philosophers of mind today also look at issues raised by the different kinds of content that mental phenomena may include, such as pains and itches; or seeing colours and smelling flowers; or the impressions left after images and dreams; and so on. And they also wonder about the very different kinds of thought involved in mental processes like believing or hoping or (most important of all, for many people!) wanting. These mental processes are much more subtle than most of the sensory ones. As psychologists know, people's actions are propelled by a mixture of motivations and people aren't always fully conscious of those motivations. The political philosopher (and agitator) Friedrich Engels noted this in a letter to one of his friends, writing that 'ideology is a process accomplished by the so-called thinker, but with a false consciousness. The real motive forces impelling him remain unknown to him; otherwise it simply would not be an ideological process'. In a sense, all consciousnesses are false ones.

Probing the Pesky Problem of Other Minds

That quote from Plato is just one of two quite different views the Ancient Master had of 'mind'. We might quip he must have changed his mind! But actually, Plato is full of very profound statements which contradict each other. Maybe that's why they're profound. In the dialogue called the *Timaeus*, Plato seems to think that the characteristic of minds is that they contain knowledge. That's why it's the gods that are the true possessors of mind.

The other way to think of minds, though, is as things that merely receive sense impressions, which 'set everything in order and arrange things in the way that are best', as Plato puts it in another dialogue called the *Phaedo*. It's this view that Plato's younger contemporary and sort-of-student (he tries to disagree with Plato on everything, remember) Aristotle latches onto. In fact, Aristotle makes the mind into a kind of sense organ: like the ear is the bit of the body that hears, the mind is the bit of the body that receives 'essences'. For example, when you look at a red tomato, your eye sees the colour and your fingers sense the shape, but it's your mind that sees the true tomato.

In the last book of *De Anima,* which doesn't mean 'about the animals' but 'about the animating force' (or something like that), Aristotle writes:

> *Mind as we have described it is what it is by virtue of becoming all things, while there is another which is what it is by virtue of making all things: this is a sort of positive state like light; for in a sense light makes potential colours into actual colours. Mind in this sense of it is separable, impassable, unmixed . . . When mind is set free from its present conditions it appears as just what it is and nothing more; this alone is immortal and eternal (we do not however remember its former activity, because while mind in this sense is impassable, mind as passive is destructible) and without it nothing thinks.*

This passage has caused subsequent translators and commentators many problems. Dan O'Connor, one of the latter, says that it's fair to say no one knows what it means. But Saint Thomas Aquinas identified mind, as described by Aristotle, with the Christian immortal soul, and others have said Aristotle's notion of mind is God. Naturally, no one agrees on any of this, but the theme sounds good when dropped into conversations.

Examining mind in more comfort, some time later

The next great step in the philosophy of mind was taken by René Descartes. So jump to almost 2,000 years later and his lonely meditations in a small French oven room. Unfortunately, the end result of Descartes' pondering was to make mind and body completely separate, which created two awful problems for subsequent philosophers:

✔ How do you know that other people – let alone animals, let alone plants, let alone everything else – have thoughts or feelings? This is usually called the problem of other minds.

✔ How can one possibly be affected by the other? How can my mind tell my mouth to say 'Please pass the mustard' without having some physical mechanism – say little electrical signals – to do so?

But Descartes doesn't allow the mind to make little electrical signals or anything else physical. It has to be, of course, pure mind, pure thought. One good thing about this, for Descartes and many religious types, is that the mind can survive the death of the body. Indeed, being entirely nonphysical it can hardly do otherwise.

Descartes' idea, after all, was that the one thing you can be sure of is that 'there are thoughts', and these thoughts appear in a mind, which he presumed (incorrectly, most philosophers think) was his mind. So here's the other mind problem. If all that you can ever really know is the thoughts in your own head (as it seems) then how do you know that the person who responds to that request just made above ('Please pass the mustard') also has a mind and has decoded the sound waves into thoughts and then opted (freely, as well) to pass the mustard? How do you know that the other person isn't in fact just a machine that responds passively, chemically or whatever to physical stimuli?

In Descartes' day he offered the example of a complicated clockwork mechanism masquerading as a computer, but nowadays you can use a much more plausible example – a computer in a room (see the later section 'Making computers take tests in the Chinese Room). How do you know that everyone around you isn't a complicated computer? Actually, you don't know, and indeed a lot of scientists now think that we are all just complicated machines. Out goes mind, through the window!

But that's not how it seems. You really do think you think, and if you do, why not other people too? That's why other philosophers, such as Spinoza, instead decided that the best way to resolve the contradictions in all this was to make everything mind, and everything eternal. Rocks and your Aunt Sally are both aspects of mind, and so is God: all made up of exactly the same stuff.

Actually, Spinoza argued that mind and matter (or in his terminology, thought and extension) were aspects of Substance, which he also calls 'God' or 'Nature'. This theory has been given its own name - the Double Aspect Theory. Out with Dualism, in with Double Aspects!

Meeting the mysterious other

One reason philosophers have come up with for thinking that other people are like you, and have minds and thoughts just like you do, is simply that other people behave like you. Put a chocolate on your friend's tea saucer and she'll gobble it up. Poke her in the back and she'll complain. Other people act like you; therefore they're likely the same kind of thing as you. This is usually called the *argument from analogy.* Most people are content to let that argument settle the problem of 'other minds'. Mind you, my dog acts like this too. Put a chocolate in his bowl and he'll gobble it up. Poke him in the back and he'll whine! But rather fewer people are sure that dogs and people think in quite the same way. Descartes certainly didn't, insisting that the correct analogy to make for dogs was with clockwork machines – not people!

This brings me to one of the very few jokes that exist in philosophy, which is the behaviourist argument for the existence of other minds. *Behaviourism* is a psychological theory that says the only, or shall we say only meaningful measure of what's going on in someone's mind is to see what that person does. So a guest coming for dinner may say that she likes your cauliflower surprise, in conventional terms reporting her mind's view – but if she's in fact leaving it uneaten on the side of her plate you might prefer to take a behaviourist stance and say that she doesn't like your special dish. Behaviourists were always keen to try out cruel experiments, especially on animals, so you could also follow up that style of philosophical investigation by force-feeding your guest the cauliflower surprise. If the guest is then sick, you could say that this confirmed that she didn't in fact like it, despite her having said otherwise (doubtless in a foolish effort to be polite).

But that's not the joke; here it is: two behaviourists have sex together. (Of course behaviourists don't 'make love'.) Afterwards the first behaviourist says, 'That was great for you – how was it for me?!' Get it? (The behaviourist tries to find out what people think by observing reactions/behaviour.)

Many people criticise behaviourism. Surely these people realise that being in pain involves well, feeling pain, and that there's a difference between having toothache and merely wanting to have the day off work. This is what the

British philosopher John Stuart Mill wrote on the matter in *An Examination of Sir William Hamilton's Philosophy* (1889):

> *I conclude that other human beings have feelings like me, because, first, they have bodies like me, which I know in my own case to be the antecedent condition of feelings; and because, secondly, they exhibit the acts, and other outward signs, which in my own case I know by experience to be caused by feelings.*

> *I am conscious in myself of a series of facts connected by a uniform sequence, of which the beginning is modifications of my body, the middle is feelings, the end is outward demeanour. In the case of other human beings I have the evidence of my senses for the first and last links of the series, but not for the intermediate link. I find, however, that the sequence between the first and last is as regular and constant in those other cases as it is in mine. In my own case I know that the first link produces the last through the intermediate link, and could not produce it without.*

> *Experience, therefore, obliges me to conclude that there must be an intermediate link; which must either be the same in others as in myself, or a different one: I must either believe them to be alive, or to be automatons: and by believing them to be alive, that is, by supposing the link to be of the same nature as in the case of which I have experience, and which is in all other respects similar, I bring other human beings, as phenomena, under the same generalisations which I know by experience to be the true theory of my own existence.*

Mill was both a logician and an economist, so his account is rather dry. On the continent of Europe, people took a more nuanced view of just what might be going on in other people's minds.

In modern European philosophy (a term which has no particular content, but certainly includes baffling and obscure ideas like this one of baffling and obscure Edmund Husserl) the *other* is everyone except yourself, the *ego*. The 20th-century French philosopher, Emmanuel Levinas argues that the whole of ethics rests on respecting the absolute 'otherness of the other'. He writes in *Totality and Infinity* (1961):

> *The absolute other is the Other. He and I do not form a number. The collectivity in which I say 'you' or 'we' is not a plural of 'I' .*

Making computers take tests in the Chinese Room

One of the best philosophical thought experiments is that of the Chinese Room posed by the contemporary American philosopher John Searle. In fact, though, the idea behind the experiment isn't really Searle's, but that of the celebrated British Second World War code breaker Alan Turing, who'd pioneered the development of the first true comparers, and who suggested that when you're unable to tell the difference, after prolonged questioning, between talking to a machine or to a human being, you ought to consider such a machine to have intelligence.

The original, so-called 'Turing test', where computers are in one room, people in another and a third group of human testers are in another, is regularly carried out today. The testers can communicate with the other people and the computers only by typing questions on keyboards. Because, after a period of thinking up questions and discussing points of view, the testers are now unable to tell the computer from the human, you should, on the face of it, concede that the computer has intelligence.

Searle, however, didn't want to concede anything to computers at all, and so added in the Chinese aspect, which is actually very unhelpful because *Chinese walls* signify imaginary barriers to communication for the purposes of privacy. For example, you might pretend a Chinese Wall exists in a bank between the desks of the share dealers and the desks of the regulators.

Anyway, the Chinese Room experiment is still basically about computers – not Chinese, not walls, not rooms. That said, John Searle's version starts with him offering to be locked up in the imaginary room with a pile of Chinese hieroglyphs. Searle then asks you to consider what would appear to happen if, from time to time, someone outside the room were to post Chinese questions through the letterbox for him to sort out and post back answers to.

Searle starts his account by saying that he 'knows no Chinese, either written or spoken', and that for him, 'Chinese writing is just so many meaningless squiggles'. So you might expect his responses to the Chinese questions to be rather hit and miss. But now suppose that, as it happens, inside the room some instructions are taped on the wall, written in English, which explain precisely which hieroglyph to post back, no matter which one is posted in. Now, when someone pops a question through the letterbox into the room, a moment later Searle can return the correct response. And for the person outside the room, it must surely appear that the person inside the room both understands Chinese and understands the questions.

Yet appearances in this case can be misleading, or so Searle wants you to conclude. His aim is to prove that such a person in such a room doesn't understand Chinese. That's why he started the experiment by stating he 'knew no Chinese, either written or spoken'. Looks like a good way to win your argument!

And because computers operate in an analogous way, Searle then went on to say that it's not really accurate to say computers are intelligent or understand things, even if they produce intelligent-looking responses.

So does the experiment show that computers aren't thinking – that they're not part of the mysterious other? The experiment is fairly convincing at showing that the person in the room doesn't understand Chinese. Nonetheless, as Searle puts it: 'from the external point of view – that is, from the point of view of somebody outside the room in which I am locked, – my answers to the questions are absolutely indistinguishable from those of native Chinese speakers'.

But what Professor Searle seems to have missed is that it's not so much that the person in the room appears to understand Chinese, but that the whole system – person in the room, sets of symbols on cards, plus instructions taped to the wall – gives the appearance of understanding Chinese. And this is much more plausible. After all, whoever wrote the instructions did understand Chinese.

What seems more likely to have happened in his example is that the expertise of the instructions' author has been transferred, via the written rules, to the person in the room. If the set-up is then replaced by a computer, programmed with the rules, then the expertise of the Chinese speaker has, at least in some cases, been transferred to the machine. Seen this way, it's much more difficult for Searle, or anyone else, to deny the computer any expertise or even understanding. Just as well because these days you may be treated in hospitals, given career advice or told where to dig for gold, who to drop bombs on or whatever by computers running 'expert systems' of rules and procedures drawn from human expertise.

Highly artificial intelligence

In the 60s Joseph Weizenbaum, a researcher in Artificial Intelligence at the Massachusetts Institute of Technology, developed a number of programs that accepted natural language from a user typing on a typewriter, and responded with what appeared to be natural language via a printer. The most celebrated of these programs was Eliza, a program that was modelled on psychotherapy. Eliza generally returned whatever people typed in a slightly different order, perhaps having picked out a keyword. Simple though the program was, it became very popular. Psychiatrists adopted it as the basis for actual therapy sessions. Users became attached and dependent on Eliza, and computer pundits cited it as an example of how computers could learn to 'talk'.

After this experience, Weizenbaum decided that computers should not be allowed to give responses that appear human. 'What I had not realised is that extremely short exposure to a relatively simple computer program could induce powerful delusional thinking in quite normal people,' he noted sadly. This warning, which is more about human psychology than anything else, nonetheless has had little effect.

Weizenbaum describes all this in a 1964 paper called 'Against the Imperialism of Instrumental Reason'. The purely random yes and no responses to a fully aware patient, Weizenbaum says, is interpreted as deep thought, reflecting the aura that computers have for many. Weizenbaum hoped to demonstrate that computers could appear to talk without understanding the content of what they were saying. This was a debate carried on from Alan Turing's Second World War challenge to researchers that when you're unable to tell the difference, after prolonged questioning, between whether you're talking to a machine or to a human being, you ought to consider the machine to have intelligence.

Philosophers like John Searle (see the preceding section) have sought to provide reasons not to give mere machines such fine things, but the computer's victory in the public mind is reflected by the habit (noted by the educationalist and psychologist Jerome Bruner) of people increasingly to compare themselves to information processing machines. People imagine data entering their central processing unit, the brain, which sorts it in various parts of the memory and manipulates it following internal rules – just like computers do! As long ago as the early 1980s, a UK government poster depicted a human being as a 2,048,000 kilobyte memory. (That's only two megabytes – about one song on an iPod – but at the time it sounded a lot!)

Attempts to develop true 'thinking machines' originally followed a 'top-down' approach, using complex programmed rules, largely as a result of the influence of Marvin Minsky and Seymour Papert in the US. Their influence in the late 60s, ridiculing the attempts to model biological systems to make the computer mimic the physical and biological architecture of the brain, together with the actual hardware available, resulted in the new science of *Artificial Intelligence* attempting the emulation of the characteristics of human reasoning.

Neural networks

Not long afterwards, though, Artificial Intelligence (see the preceding section) abandoned the tidy rules-based approach for a more irrational, organic one.

Neural networks instead became much more fashionable, with their advocates making magnificent claims for their powers. A neural network is a series of simple processing elements based on memory chips, connected together and to various 'inputs' and 'outputs'. Information is fed into these inputs and the resultant activity is monitored. The relationships between the parts is 'tweaked' until certain inputs always produce a desired output. In this way, the neural network is said to 'learn'. The first commercial neural network, built by Igor Aleskander and others in London, was successfully employed picking out defective components on production lines and distinguishing between bank notes in banks. Rules-based Artificial Intelligence systems have, by contrast, been very poor at recognising shapes and patterns.

It certainly seems that computers may now be intelligent after all, if by *intelligent* you mean being able to answer tricky questions, but the contemporary philosopher (or 'cognitive scientist' if you prefer) Marvin Minsky has claimed instead, on the humans' behalf, that the element computers lack now is common sense. Or put another way, computers are good at thinking precisely, but only humans are good at thinking fuzzily.

Exploring Existentialism with Ryle's Ghost in the Machine

Gilbert Ryle used the expression 'ghost in the machine' in his book *The Concept of Mind* (1949) as part of his attack on what he called Descartes' 'myth' – that is, the view that mind is a kind of ghost mysteriously entombed in a machine – the physical body – with all the logical and existential problems that view brings along with it (existential in the sense that Descartes' ghost in the machine must inhabit a different universe from the bodily one). This, Professor Ryle soberly warned, is a *category mistake*; that is, the error of treating something as if it belongs in one category when really it belongs in another. Asking how the mind can influence the body is like asking what colour the number 5 is. The question results from an earlier misunderstanding and confusion of the issue. We can sympathise with Ryle on that!

Ryle argued that traditional notions of will, imagination, perception, thought and so on are all contaminated by *Cartesianism* (in particular, the view that there are two different kinds of thing in the universe – mind and matter) and you need to jettison this 'ghost in the machine' for a kind of behaviourist model of how the mind works. It is, he explains, a kind of category mistake to treat mental phenomena in the same way as you treat physical phenomena – actions aren't made up of the two parts Descartes proposes, the mental idea and the physical action, but are just one part: behaviour.

Ryle like many of his contemporaries saw himself as wielding the tools of logical analysis to solve and clarify all other philosophical questions, in the manner of Cambridge University's celebrated iconoclast and philosophical rebel Wittgenstein.

Clinging to your sense of personal identity

So who are you? Is your mind your mind or someone else's? Maybe everyone else in fact has minds and people are just a kind of automaton – like Searle in his sealed-up Chinese Room (see the earlier section 'Making computers take tests in the Chinese Room') – responding to their requests? Ridiculous? Yes, but as an idea, it has had a considerable attraction on the Continent (particularly in France and Germany).

Feeling existential again

One of the most flamboyant schools of recent philosophy, the *Existentialists*, accuse those not in their camp of acting out roles, of failing to be true to their real selves and of exhibiting bad faith. Fashion-conscious Frenchman, Jean Paul Sartre (1905–80) mocks the bourgeoisie with their comfortable sense of duty; homosexuals who pretend to be heterosexuals; and, most famously of all, waiters who rush about. All these people, he says, are slaves to other people's perceptions – in fear of the regard of the other and thus exhibiting *bad faith* – not being true to themselves but letting other people decide for them what they should be like.

Mind you, Sartre, like his mentor, Karl Marx, was always a man of letters, not a man of action. Brought up in rural France, Jean Paul describes spending most of his childhood in his grandfather's library and his adolescence in France's elite colleges, emerging only to become a school teacher.

When the Second World War arrived and interrupted his intellectualising, Sartre became a meteorologist in the army, and when the French surrendered to the victorious Nazis, he found himself a prisoner of war, albeit on a long leash that allowed him parole to organise his first play and indeed to return to philosophy. When the war ended he decided against life as a professor, instead choosing that of a writer and intellectual.

Sartre's philosophy is characteristic of all the existentialists in that it emphasises the use of the imagination. Sartre says it's only in the process of exercising your imagination – imagining what might be – that you're truly free.

He emphasises what *is not* over what *is*, the latter being a rather humdrum sort of affair consisting of the kind of facts that scientists examine, while the *what is not* is really much more interesting. In *Being and Nothingness* (1943) he sums up his view (if *sums up* is ever an appropriate term in existentialist writing) thus:

> *The Nature of consciousness simultaneously is to be what is not and not to be what it is. And this is where our search for identity, personal identity, comes to an end. We exist, yes, but the important thing is how do we 'define ourselves'?*

And to illustrate the significance of this question, Sartre gives his famous example of the waiter:

> *His movement is quick and forward, a little too precise, a little too rapid. He comes toward the patrons with a step a little too quick. He bends forward a little too eagerly; his voice, his eyes express an interest a little too solicitous for the order of the customer. Finally there he returns, trying to imitate in his walk the inflexible stiffness of some kind of automaton while carrying his tray with the recklessness of a tight-rope walker by putting it in a perpetually unstable, perpetually broken equilibrium which he perpetually re-establishes by a light movement of the hand and arm.*

This a passage that's to my taste rather snooty (sneering at the workers?) but people often hail it as offering a spotlight on consciousness, and it's certainly part of what made Sartre's name as an original thinker. But some people think he was showing a little bit of bad faith himself in claiming to have thought up the idea.

Borrowing from Simone de Beauvoir

Curiously enough, another book that came out in 1943, *She Came to Stay*, was by Sartre's lifelong intellectual confidant and companion Simone de Beauvoir, and this book also describes various kinds of consciousness, in terms very similar to Sartre's.

Simone de Beauvoir's much-less-well-known book offers classic existentialist descriptions of what it feels like wandering through an empty theatre (the stage, the walls, the chairs, unable to come alive until there's an audience) or watching a woman in a restaurant ignore the fact that her male companion has begun stroking her arm ('it lay there, forgotten, ignored, the man's hand was stroking a piece of flesh that no longer belonged to anyone') – as well as this one:

> *'It's almost impossible to believe that other people are conscious beings, aware of their own inward feelings, as we ourselves are aware of our own,' said Francoise. 'To me, it's terrifying when we grasp that. We get the impression of no longer being anything but a figment of someone else's mind.'*

Someone seems to have been copying someone! And Simone de Beauvoir wrote her book years before her partner's (even if it wasn't published then). Just fancy that! (Actually, Sartre even records in his diary how de Beauvoir had to correct him several times for his clumsy misunderstanding of the philosophy.) If you've ever wondered why all the 'famous philosophers' are men, this is one example of how that strange fact might come about. Sartre simply borrowed all de Beauvoir's ideas and used them unacknowledged in his own work. (If you're interested in the philosophical relationship see Kate and Howard Fullbrook's 1994 page-turning account, *Simone de Beauvoir and Jean-Paul Sartre*.)

Another explanation for Simone de Beauvoir's generous lending of all her ideas to her partner may be that de Beauvoir, unlike Sartre, acknowledged her sources. She was aware that many of existentialism's elements weren't new at all, but instead had come from the Eastern philosophy tradition. Most importantly, that key existentialist notion of the other.

Take Buddhism, for example. When it comes to thinking about 'the other', the Buddhist viewpoint tends, as commentator James Whitehill has put it, in matters of self and community, to be 'biocentric and ecological'. Bio-what? Tree-hugging, greenie, lovey-dovey. Or as he goes on, Buddhism doesn't begin with the 'substantial, separable and distinctive self' of both Western philosophy and religion. That said, de Beauvoir's later development of the notion to class all women as 'the other' in male-dominated society was, and remained, her own.

Discovering the Will to Philosophise

Traditionally, as philosophy professors like to say (to reassure the natives) *the will* is a kind of mental faculty, or attribute of mind, with the useful ability to take decisions, to choose, to decide and to invent. What's more (traditionally) philosophers saw this faculty as being peculiarly human – as if animals can't take decisions or have ideas!

The reason why philosophers thought will must be peculiar to humans, was that activities like deciding and having an idea seem to involve creating something new and escaping from the restrictions of both what's been and what currently is. No wonder then that Immanuel Kant (see Chapter 5) emphasised the importance of the will in his writings on right and wrong, saying that it's what your actions say about your intentions that matters, not the consequences of your actions. Tell that to the person you run over in your car while rushing to help out at the church jumble sale! Anyway, fortunately, the philosophy of the will was helped along shortly after Kant had made his small contribution by that other German philosopher Schopenhauer, who had the good timing to be born right in the middle of a peculiarly fruitful era for German philosophy. (Schopenhauer's enemies were his elder and betters: Immanuel Kant who lived from 1724–1804, Georg Hegel, 1770–1831 and Johann Fichte 1762–1814; Schopenhauer himself lived 1788–1860.)

So what is this thing we call the *will*? It's volition, instinct, desire – call it what you, er, will – the basic force that drives life. There's nothing behind it – no strategy, no reason, no purpose. Will is outside space and time; after all, it creates them, creates regularities, appearances. Will is primary, it sweeps perception before it, it dictates all actions. It even drives evolution, not the other way around, as Darwin supposed. Schopenhauer even says that animals reflect their wills in their forms – the timidity of the rabbit is made physical through those large ears, always ready to detect the faintest whiff of threat. Similarly, the hawk's cruel beak and talons reflect its constant desire to rip other creatures apart.

Will is also irrational; it can create reason but is by no means bound by it. Both the will to live and the will to have offspring are irrational, a point he illustrates with reference to a particularly nasty kind of ant that lives in Australia, that goes in for a lot of cannibalism, especially after sex. Australian ant's – and Schopenhauer's – message is that life is meaningless: instead the reality is that birth must lead rapidly to death and the only useful activity in between seems to be to produce children who can then repeat the cycle – not that that gives the cycle itself much purpose.

Anyway, for Schopenhauer only will exists. It precedes and succeeds the individual – it's indestructible. Actually, an element of free will exists too, which emerges in the acts you freely choose, in between eating other ants or having sex. But what choices you make you have to discover, a point the French and German existentialists later repeated. (Schopenhauer complains that Kant's worthy attempt to demonstrate that people are ends in themselves is mere egotism.) Humans, Schopenhauer woefully concludes, are like so many May flies – created one day and dead the next, leaving only their eggs. Nature has use only for species, not for individuals, and, actually (ask the dinosaurs!) often not even for the species.

On a more positive note, even death is an illusion. Schopenhauer also writes of the need to penetrate the 'veil of Maya' in order to see the common reality of will, which is *Maharakya* or 'Great World', Hindu wisdom. (Schopenhauer is one of very few philosophers to relate his work equally to Eastern as well as Western works). That's why pain is the norm and happiness the exception. From Buddhism too comes his solution: nothingness. Nothingness is exactly the best you can obtain. *Nothingness*, after all, is the literal meaning of *nirvana*, which is what Buddhists say everyone seeks.

In his book *On the Vanity of Existence* Schopenhauer explains:

> *The vanity of existence is revealed in the whole form existence assumes: in the infiniteness of time and space contrasted with the finiteness of the individual in both; in the fleeting present as the sole form to which actuality exists; in the contingency and relativity of all things in continual becoming without being; in continual desire without satisfaction; in the continual frustration of striving in which life consists. Time and that probability of all things existing in time that time itself brings about is simply the form under which the will-to-live, which as thing-in-itself is imperishable, reveals to itself the vanity of its striving. Time is that by virtue of which everything becomes nothingness in our hands and loses all real value.*

It's not hard to see that this kind of will that seeks to preserve itself through reproduction is very akin to the ideas of modern biology about how genetics drive behaviour. Yet Schopenhauer's originality is lost and forgotten. Instead, nowadays people attribute the idea of a selfish gene to the brilliance of scientists such as Richard Dawkins and the idea of 'will to power' to the ravings of Nietzsche; and the notion encapsulated in the title of Schopenhauer's book of a world created by will is carted off and transplanted in the ornamental pot of existentialist philosophy.

As to that intellectual theft, Schopenhauer does try to offer a more philosophical perspective. In his book *The World as Will and Representation* he writes:

> *The earth rolls on from day into night; the individual dies; but the sun itself burns without intermission, an eternal noon. Life is certain to the will-to-live; the form of life is endless present; it matters not how individuals, the phenomenal of the Idea, arise and pass away in time, like fleeting dreams.*

Finding the will to live in French philosophy

The 20th-century French philosopher Levinas offers a warmer, more personal, indeed purposeful picture of human spirit and motivation than Schopenhauer. Levinas points at a more subtle sense of the other, the 'irreducible strangeness of the Other'. Human beings spend a large part of their lives looking for another person – behaviourists say people are looking for someone to have sex with, but others say people are searching for their lost other half in order to become whole. (The bond between two people is more complex and longer lasting than that sexual one . . .) 'Even before I notice the colour of her eyes, the Other silently commands me not to harm her, nor to force her to conform to my image of her,' Levinas says.

In describing the 'encounter with the Other', Levinas employs the word *transcendence* – but not in the classical sense of this term. Levinas doesn't mean transcending the everyday world to some supposed separate, more perfect, reality, but intends rather to highlight the transformative force that the other can have on you. Your partner helps you rise above what you might be otherwise.

Ethics as the encounter with the other

According to Descartes everyone has the idea of the infinite within them. Descartes makes this a proof for the existence of God, saying that as finite creatures humans can't possibly conceive of the infinite on their own. Only some entity that's equally infinite could account for that idea. (Therefore, God exists.) In Levinas's version of this argument, the divine comes to mind whenever you're confronted by the disquieting presence of the other. In all your encounters with the other is the awkward sense that something, an infinite presence not of your own making nor of this world (as the contemporary British philosopher John Caruana has put it) effectively displaces your centre of attention. 'In this way the Other's inexorable capacity to call me into question insinuates the divine without ever positing it as such,' says Caruna. Of course, coming down to earth for a moment in the style of Schopenhauer, other people may have the reverse effect and drag otherwise nice people down to their own miserable, misbegotten level.

But this thought doesn't seem to have occurred to Levinas. Instead, he spent the better part of his career describing ethics as the 'provocation of the Other', meaning that it's concern for others that inspires people eventually to develop and conceive of customs, laws and moral theories. By the *Other*, Levinas means, again in Caruana's phrase, 'the singularly unique person who stands before me in the guise of a disappointed friend or lover, a dependent child, a stranger in my midst who seeks orientation', or even the homeless person you pass by lying on the side of the road. Only the other, Levinas contends, has the power to personally obligate you.

Levinas says that conventional accounts of ethics give the power of obligation to an impersonal force – Plato makes it the *Good*, the *Form of Forms*, and Kant makes it the *Categorical Imperative*. But Levinas argues that ideas and principles, however sublime or noble, lack the force imagined for them by philosophers. Principles are simply too abstract and general to change human behaviour. Instead it takes the presence of the other, that strange sense of being observed or thought about. What goes on in our minds depends on what goes on in other people's minds!

Chapter 13

Looking at Ethics and Morality

. . . .

In This Chapter

▶ Looking at right and wrong

▶ Jargon-busting those flowery ethical terms

▶ Deconstructing a few of those who say they know better than the rest

. . . .

To say that happiness is the chief good seems a platitude.

– Aristotle

T he study of good and evil, as Plato had no doubt and as political philosophers like Marx insist it should be, is essentially a practical study. *Ethics*
is about regulating behaviour, both individual actions and more general
activity too, all of which means entering the political realm. Many people
think politicians should steer well clear of ethics, but this view is naive. Laws
are essentially based on perceptions of right and wrong, and it's politicians
who ultimately make laws. Mind you, how they arrive at laws is often rather
complicated, and certainly both philosophers and religious experts (as well
as the usual economic interests) all play a role.

Most of the time for most people it's might, in the form of the law, that
makes right. Take intimate sexual relations, for example. Her Majesty's (the
United Kingdom) government has very clear views on these matters. No one
should have more than one spouse, and strict age limits exist – at the lower
age range, that is! – not to forget no sex with animals, or in public places, let
alone with a sum of money being exchanged. Couldn't be clearer, could it?
And just following the law saves people a lot of trouble because they don't
have to go back to first principles. That's what upright German (and French,
and others too!) citizens thought when the law told them that they should
hand over any Jewish neighbours they knew were hiding in the attic to the
Gestapo for transportation to a concentration camp for 'processing' . . .

But in fact the law isn't much of a guide to sorting out right from wrong for
several very good reasons. One is that the law varies. In some countries, for
example, you can have several spouses, and men can have child wives. In the

United Kingdom homosexual relations are a human right, but in other countries you can be executed for having a same-sex partnership. In some countries the state organises sex-for-money as a public service, like dental care or bingo evenings; in others prostitution is considered unspeakably wicked and punished with prison. What's more, what's wrong in one place at one time often changes with fashion or circumstance, as (for example) the laws on homosexuality have changed in the United Kingdom. In many areas of human life, the law is less the thing that decides what's right or wrong and more a reflection of prevailing attitudes. In Nazi Germany, the law reflected widespread prejudice against Jewish people, homosexuals and gypsies, not to mention the particularly 'Nazi' views of the new (but democratically elected, don't forget!) German leadership. So, in ethics, reference to legal codes is generally not very enlightening.

So instead, in this chapter I start with the claims of religious types to have found a shortcut to knowing right from wrong – because they have books based on the word of God. Next, I look at some 'radical' perspectives on morality, like Nietzsche's view that everyone has got it back to front (except him) because what they call right is 'wrong' and what they call 'bad' is 'good'! Then we take to pieces some of the attempts to make ethics scientific, and finally we try to make ethics modern – by applying it to trees and animals. Well, why not?

What Would God Do?

The former United States Vice President Al Gore is rumoured to have a block of wood on his White House desk inscribed with the letters *WWGD* for *What Would God Do?*. That's despite the fact that in the US, religion and politics are supposed – it's written there in the US Constitution – to be kept completely apart. Some hope!

The reality is all those ancient religious texts – the Jewish Torah, the Christian Bible and the Muslim Koran – not only talk about heaven and the afterlife, but also all attempt to stipulate the correct mode of behaviour for all the essential stages of life, and, like a totalitarian state, couple this 'advice' with threats of dire punishments. Unfortunately, two important logical weaknesses exist in all attempts to base morality on a religious text:

 ✔ **One of them is that the texts don't agree:** Either between themselves or within themselves. The Bible, for example, contains many instructions to believers to ruthlessly exterminate rivals – men, women and children included – alongside equally firm rules to forgive and love your enemies!

 ✔ **What philosophers call the *Euthyphro problem*:** This problem appears in one of Plato's little playlets in which a chap called Euthyphro is considering suing his dad in order, as he puts it (to Socrates' dismay), to please the gods. This prompts Socrates to ask the simple but profound question: is something good because the gods say it's good (in which case the gods can say anything at all is good and people must accept it), or is it rather that the gods say things are good because they see that they're good? Gods, you might suppose, would be good judges of such things, but if this is still what makes things right as opposed to wrong, having the gods' approval doesn't offer any explanation of *why* a thing is good or not.

In fact, religious texts are no better than legal codes in providing a proper explanation of why something is right or wrong. You have, of course, to take their accounts on faith. So for actual reasons, the world needs philosophers. But they can't agree on the possibility of a deeper insight. Indeed, some philosophers still think God ultimately decides right and wrong – indeed, religious types offer optimistically that the human political need for there to be a difference between right and wrong, coupled with the philosophical failure to provide one, gives us a reason to suppose God exists. Others, however, (doubtless spotting the weakness in the last argument!) try to base their ethical systems on logic, and still others on a kind of maths that's based on calculating the consequences of any action. And of course other philosophers say that the notion of right and wrong is either a fiction or just a matter of applying personal taste.

Islamic ethics

Islam is an all-embracing comprehensive approach to living, covering all aspects of both individual and social life. A text known as the Koran (which originated around 700 BC) is revered by Muslims as the literal word of God, superseding all previous revelations such as the Bible. It forbids gambling, the consumption of animal blood, foods offered to pagan gods and idols, pork and alcohol and the eating of carrion. It describes at length punishment in hell and reward in paradise. The *Sharia*, or Islamic law, is cruel and seems barbaric. The penalty for habitual thievery may be loss of a hand, for premarital sex may be 100 lashes in public, for adultery may be death.

In traditional Islamic society no distinction exists between material and spiritual, or religious and political, and some Muslims see the most minute act as being subject to guidance by ethical experts who are, by definition, religious leaders. The only flexibility in the system is the fact that it subdivides good (*Hasan*) and bad (*Qibih*) into several categories: imperative, recommended, allowed and forbidden. The Koran says the purpose of all this is to enable people to better themselves. Humans are seen as 'a source of potentiality', not sufficient as they are but at least not 'fallen', as in the Christian stories of the Garden of Eden, of Cain and Abel and of Noah and the flood.

Many 'moderate' forms of Islam exist, and many Muslims restrict their religious beliefs to their personal, spiritual life – not allowing them to dictate their relations with others in their family let alone society. However Islamic fundamentalists claim religious authority for things that otherwise appear quite wrong, such as stoning people to death for holding hands in public, or listening to pop music, as has happened in countries like Afghanistan and Somalia in recent years under fundamentalist governments.

Among the philosophers' best efforts have been famous rules such as

- ✔ **The utilitarians' one:** This says that the correct thing to do is whatever policy (or action) brings about the greatest happiness of the greatest number of people. That's often what you hear politicians say today, but it's in fact a very old philosophical story, and not a particularly persuasive one.

- ✔ **The Hobbesian one:** From Thomas Hobbes. It says that right is whatever the most powerful individuals say is right.

- ✔ **The Kantian one:** From Kant. This is the philosophers' favourite. It says that you must always act as though your actions could be following a universal law. This, the *categorical imperative*, rules out borrowing money without paying it back, but still allows people to commit suicide.

I look at all these – in suitably jargon-free detail – in the later section 'Understanding Key Ethical Theories'.

A similar ideal lurks behind the 20th-century philosopher John Rawls' work, putting forward the merits for policy-making to take place behind a *veil of ignorance* (that is, ensuring that people take decisions in ignorance of how the decisions will affect them personally, or their mates), thus ensuring that they act in the interests of everyone and not in the interests of just a few). Like Kant, John Rawls seeks to remove the distorting effects of self-interest from decision-making. Sounds sensible? Yet, funnily enough, an alternate theory, advanced by the 18th-century Scotch philosopher Adam Smith, makes selfishness the key to society. Smith, who's what you'd nowadays call an economist, says selfishness is good! He points out that it's the mechanism that allows complex societies to arrange their affairs in the way that both generates the most wealth and creates, therefore, the most opportunities for its citizens. Sounds complicated? Contradictory? That's ethics.

Pinning Down the Difference Between Right and Wrong

No wonder some philosophers say that no right thing to do exists, and one or two, such as the iconoclastic German philosopher Friedrich Nietzsche (1844–1900) even went so far as to say that what you ought to do is whatever everyone else thinks is the wrong thing. In fact, Nietzsche declared himself to be the world's first immoralist, and tried to revalue all values starting with the unmasking of Christianity as a plot to disempower great men like himself. (Well, it was his theory so he could make of it what he wanted.) His aim, he wrote, was literally to make good, bad. Unfortunately for him, if not the rest of the world, he was unable to complete this task. In 1889, aged just 45 (which is about the same age as me, although age and philosophical leanings are the only things we have in common, I hope) he descended into a twilight world of his own, never emerging from madness.

Thus spake Nietzsche

The German philosopher Nietzsche is the *enfant terrible* of philosophy. Here's what he has to say on God:

In his book *Thus Spoke Zarathustra*, a madman carrying a lantern announces that 'God is dead'. 'Where has God gone?' he cries. 'I shall tell you. We have killed him – you and I. We are all his murderers.'

And in another book, *The Anti-Christ*, Nietzsche asks 'What is good?' before replying: 'All that heightens the feeling of power, the will to power, power itself in man. What is bad? All that proceeds from weakness.'

As for Nietzsche's view of himself, in the concluding chapter to his book called *Ecce Homo*, in a section called modestly 'Why I Am Destiny', Nietzsche writes:

> I know my fate. One day, there will be associated with my name the recollection of something frightful – of a crisis like no other before on earth, of the profoundest collision of conscience, of a decision evoked against everything that until then had been believed in, demanded, sanctified. I am not a man, I am dynamite.

Friedrich Nietzsche was against morality, considering it to be a rather nasty tendency – a sort of form of weakness. Instead, he favoured what he called *anti-morality*, where a great man (and it had to be a man) enjoyed his power to the full, untrammelled by dreary notions of responsibility, duty and pity let alone (of all things) being 'good'. After all, as Nietzsche once put it:

> . . . *in the concept of the good man common cause [is] made with everything weak, sick, ill constituted, suffering from itself, all that which ought to perish – the law of selection crossed, an ideal made of opposition to the proud and well-constituted, to the affirmative man, to the man certain of the future and guaranteeing the future.*

That's rather a simplistic reading of Darwin's theory about evolution where poorly designed species are supposed to sort themselves out by being eaten by well-designed ones. And in many ways, for all his philosophical fans, Nietzsche isn't really so original. His theory is really just an attack on Christian morality, and many others prior to him (not least Thomas Hobbes) had observed that might is in some sense right. Nietzsche's bizarre prose trumpeting that he at least had transcended all other values overstates his radicalism because he'd only reversed the conventional ones.

Nietzsche wrote that you don't find the goal of humanity in some supposed general strategy or process, such as maximising happiness, but in the activities of its 'highest specimens'. These men (and it is only men) transcend history and are bound to no laws other than that of their own pleasure. He says, 'The man who would not belong in the mass needs only to cease being comfortable with himself; he should follow his conscience which shouts at him:

"Be yourself!" You are not really all you do, think and desire now.' This sort of stuff has been very popular in French and German philosophy ever since.

Nietzsche's writing is part prose, part poetry, with a sprinkling of philosophy. Always egocentric, he went clinically insane in 1889. His is not terribly good literature – even if many philosophers think it is. Nor is his thinking (others disagree, of course) terribly good philosophy – even if so many outside philosophy assume it is so. Nonetheless, Nietzsche is important within ethics for providing an alternative position to the usual, rather sanctimonious one.

Rubbing Gyges' ring

Most philosophers see their task as being to lead people to virtue and goodness. Most of them, like both Plato and Aristotle, assume that this is also in everyone's long-term interest. Even so, Plato wonders whether if you could get away with doing wrong, wouldn't most people soon lose their interest in doing the right thing and prefer instead greed and selfishness? In his book the *Republic*, Plato's character Glaucon tells the story of Gyges, the shepherd who discovers a magic ring that makes the owner invisible when he rubs it. The story, which is part of a wider discussion of society, is a way of exploring this issue of whether the concept of right and wrong is about more than just a sense of self-preservation and fear of the consequences of being caught out.

Glaucon uses the story as a way of illustrating his view that the origins of right and wrong have more to do with plain self-interest than anything greater. Glaucon says virtue is simply a compromise between doing what's most desirable, which is doing wrong and getting no punishment, and what's most undesirable, which is suffering wrong and being unable to do anything about it. In this sense, the story of Gyges' ring is also the story of the *social contract*, the imaginary agreement citizens sign where they exchange liberty for security.

Is Glaucon right? Certainly, Plato has Socrates argue vigorously against Glaucon's view, saying that any individual who allows himself to misbehave will suffer a heavy penalty in terms of loss of his own internal harmony and balance. Plato's key idea, in fact, is that doing wrong as an individual is similar to allowing a state to become badly managed – both the individual and the society fall apart in the same way. Someone like Gyges, he warns (hopes?!), will soon become debauched by his excesses and lose the spiritual benefits of the moral way he (presumably) used to follow when he was but a simple shepherd.

Mind you, I've certainly come across plenty of selfish, greedy and plain nasty people who don't seem to mind losing those spiritual benefits, so Socrates' response is rather unconvincing. But that's looking at it as advice to an individual. Because the Greeks considered the community to be more important than the individual, Plato's argument about maintaining a balance and internal harmony may have been more persuasive. Societies that rely on cheating, plundering and general short-term methods to achieve happiness do seem to eventually pay a price. Er . . . don't they?

Achieving balance in Ancient China

Most philosophers see the ethical life as the balanced life, and offer some sort of internal harmony as a clinching argument to those tempted by the apparent attractions of the unethical path. It's not just New Age hippies who think that everything's interconnected and the health of a person is much more than a biological machine.

Plato's warnings in his books about the dangers of excess and greed echo the Ancient Chinese Yellow Emperor's approach too. Eastern philosophies are generally clear in their emphasis on achieving balance. The Emperor emphasised the need for moderation and balance and took the view that if people were behaving badly, it was because they'd become ill or, more precisely, unbalanced. Of course, this point of view is very much in vogue nowadays. For example, people speak of a person who's particularly evil as having a 'sick mind'.

Acquiring just a bit of justice

Justice sits traditionally at the heart of ethics, but it can be displaced from its throne there, as the utilitarians decided to do in the 19th century. Indeed, for many practical ethicists today justice must defer to *utility* (a calculation of what's most useful) in working out policies. Doctors make decisions about organ donations, for example, on the basis of how many years they expect each potential recipient to live, rather than on the basis of how socially worthy or noble they may expect that person's life to be. Often the pursuit of justice these days tends to be in the law courts; indeed, they have in a sense usurped the term. But legal justice is only the application of the law, and the laws have to be written by human beings operating with a sense of . . . justice.

Philosophically speaking, you can easily sum up *justice* as 'to each his own' – you get what you deserve. But how do you decide what someone deserves? Everyone seems to think they deserve better than they have, and at least some of them must be wrong! Lawyers are concerned with *corrective justice*, which is punishment, but moral philosophers are usually more concerned with *distributive justice*, which is that complicated calculation of laws, rights and happiness.

Plato's most influential book, the Republic, is primarily concerned with the nature of justice because Plato sees justice as very much a matter for states, or republics. Add to which, Plato says that you can see justice more easily when considering the larger organism (a community or city) than the smaller (the lone individual). And Plato argues that as justice is essentially that which follows from having everything well organised and harmonious, so it's best to let the philosophers rule the city and take charge of the 'spirited ones' (the police and army), who in turn must stop the masses from indulging their natural tendency towards squabbling over material goods.

Making life-and-death decisions

Ethics isn't just about running the town's garbage system. It's about whether or not to kill people, and whether or not to save lives. In recent years, politicians acting on their sense of what's right (or at the very least, what's not clearly wrong) have set about killing tens if not hundreds of thousands of entirely innocent civilians – people like you and me – in countries such as Rwanda (where the government set about trying to eliminate a rival ethnic group); in the Lebanon (where the Israelis wanted to make an example of what happens to countries that allow terrorists to operate); and in Iraq and Afghanistan (where the United States and Britain said they were 'introducing democracy'!).

And an old theme in philosophy is that of the *just war*, not so much the nearly war as the justified one. The principle seems to be that you should only fight a war when you have a good reason. Thanks, philosophers! Effectively what the Germans call real politik (practical politics) rules in international relations. But within countries too, people have to make many unavoidable 'life and death' decisions, like those surrounding euthanasia, a word from the Greek for 'good death' that's usually translated as 'mercy killing'. Three sorts of euthanasia exist:

- **Voluntary:** Where someone, perhaps a chronically ill person, asks for drugs to help him to die.

- **Non-voluntary:** For example, where doctors switch off a life-support machine.

- **Involuntary:** Where the subject doesn't agree it's time for him to die and can say so! People usually describe this as murder.

Related considerations for euthanasia are

- The individual's well-being (*beneficence*).

- The social interest. Utilitarian calculations routinely, if still not easily, made in modern hospital intensive care units – an old geezer no one will miss may not get the same treatment as a dashing young TV personality!

- The principle of respect for autonomy.

- The need for informed consent (if only of relatives).

- The principle of the 'inviolability' of life.

Nowadays, some countries offer euthanasia (under carefully controlled circumstances) to their citizens – notably the government in the Netherlands.

Looking at business practices

Business ethics is big business, and that justifies the subject's inclusion here.

To borrow some jargon from economics, micro-*business ethics* looks at the correct (the just) management and organisation of commercial enterprises: working practices, recruitment issues, management styles, financial accounting and so on, as well as the effects of these enterprises' individual decisions on suppliers and the environment.

Macro-business ethics considers notions of free will and of rationality as well as the dictates of human rights, in contrast to the form of utilitarianism known within economics by the imposing term *pareto optimality*, which is simply the attempt to arrange the world so that as many people as possible are satisfied.

Adam Smith (1723–1790) is a much more radical philosopher than he's usually given credit for. Earlier philosophers, such as Plato and John Locke, thought people should base society on altruism, or at least the suppression of selfishness. Thomas Hobbes, writing in 17th-century England, saw selfishness as the great problem the state must combat. Not so Adam Smith. He thought society was determined by an entirely greater, non-human force – economics. His two great works are the Wealth of Nations (published in the same year as the American Declaration of Independence – 1776) and the *Moral Sentiments*. The works say that all moral behaviour depends on social interaction and starts from the observation of each person by another. Upholding justice becomes the key task of governments, even as they allow economic forces to let rip.

Large enterprises today often have codes of ethics, which contain things such as 'It's wrong to tell the public that the olive oil is being made with anti-freeze' or 'It's right to report your colleague if he's looking at saucy videos on the Internet in his lunch break'. For managers and bosses, these additional ethical rules for employees can be a powerful control tool, because unlike ordinary rules and procedures for running a business the rules are grey – they're up for debate and affected by context and detail. Employees may not be quite sure what they're supposed to do, and the code may actually undermine their autonomy and confidence as individual judges of their actions. Sanctions and punishments may then follow supposed breaches of the ethics guidelines.

However, the codes don't seem to be good at stopping dodgy business practice at high levels. For example, when the third largest corporation in the US, Enron, imploded in 2001, amid much shredding of internal memos, a later official inquiry found that a culture of systematic deceit and fraud had coexisted quite happily with some of the most sanctimonious and puritanical moralising. The contemporary Australian ethicist Trevor Jordan says that people put too much emphasis on rules in business and professional ethics, and talk too much of setting up ethics regimes and giving ethics codes 'teeth'. Instead, he says, what the business world needs is more people who'll do the right thing even without a rule book or manual.

Sorting out torture

Torture is one of the few things that the world's governments have managed to agree on outlawing. Ever since the Hague Conventions of the 20th century, the practice has been both outlawed. Not that governments have really stuck to the new policy of not using torture, of course!

People have generally favoured the use of torture over the ages, devising new and more horrible forms of it. Dungeons have often been part of the process too, ingeniously constructed to destroy the will of the prisoner. Consider this account from a notorious British prison called Newgate (London) in which a pair of suspected highway robbers were refusing to answer questions:

> . . . *they were ordered back to Newgate, there to be pressed to death; but, when they came to the press-room, Phillips begged to be taken back to plead; a favour that was granted, though it might have been denied to him: but Spiggot was put under the press, where he continued half an hour, with three hundred and fifty pounds' weight on his body; but on the addition of fifty pounds more, he likewise begged to plead.*

Spiggot pleaded not guilty, but that was enough for those in charge to promptly convict the men, sentence them to death and then execute them on 8 February 1720. The account records a curious thing about all this:

> *While under sentence of death Phillips behaved in the most hardened and abandoned manner; he paid no regard to anything that the minister said to him, and swore or sung songs while the other prisoners were engaged in acts of devotion; and, towards the close of his life, when his companions became more serious, he grew still more wicked; and yet, when at the place of execution he said he did not fear to die, for he was in no doubt of going to heaven.*

Today for 'highway robbers', read 'terrorists'. Anyway, after people obtained confessions of misdeeds through torture, a painful death was the historical norm, with burning probably the most cruel and yet the most easily arranged.

Today, torture is still alive and well in many countries. During the 'Troubles' in Ireland at the end of the last century, The British were in the habit of torturing suspects in Ulster. And as part of what he called the War on Terror following attacks on New York in 2001 , the US president signed a special memo authorising the use of torture as long as it didn't (normally) cause major organ failure or death, and the US authorities fine-tuned methods such as sleep-deprivation, beatings and sexual humiliation for use in special camps scattered around the world. Philosophically, the issue is one of utilitarian arguments against rival approaches, notably those formulated in terms of human rights.

Looking at the three Rs of the law

In law enforcement, the philosophy of punishment is quite straightforward. Basically, only three ethical justifications for harming people who have to be punished exist – the three Rs plus the element of deterrence:

- ✔ **Reform** is things like making a car thief do a course on car mechanics – the justification is to help the offender to become a better person.

- ✔ **Restitution** involves forcing the criminal to make amends for the harm he's caused; to try to undo the damage and put things right again. It's not a very practical response to many crimes, even those involving damage to property or theft of goods or money, but it's certainly a minimal sort of justification for fines and community work orders or such like.

- ✔ **Retribution** recognises the desire of law-abiding citizens to get their own back on the criminals. More serious crimes tend to be impossible to undo, just in terms of the emotional and psychological harm to the victims. However, a punishment that makes other people think twice before repeating the crime is also justified under certain utilitarian measures. In 19th-century England, the principle of retribution allowed the public to sit in judgement on their fellows, ultimately with the power of life or death over them, and also to witness the public executions.

Today, many countries have rejected the use of the death penalty as a violation of more fundamental human rights that even, say, highway robbers have, but equally countries like China and the United States continue to apply the penalty – even for children.

Understanding Key Ethical Theories

Much of ethics revolves around three theories:

- ✔ **Utilitarianism** is the easiest to get the hang of – and the most popular with democratic politicians. Utilitarianism is where people evaluate various policies on the basis that the right policy will be the one that results in the most votes or the greatest happiness (delete as applicable).

- ✔ **Theories of ethics** are based on rules, which can themselves either come from heaven via human messengers or come from philosophy heaven via logicians. The most important philosophical theory like this is Immanuel Kant's Categorical Imperative, which basically says the opposite of the utilitarians and insists that people have an obligation to perform the right action, *regardless* of actual consequences.

- ✔ **Virtue ethics** assert that the right action is what a virtuous person naturally does, and that people can become virtuous through making sure they always do the right thing. With the preceding two theories cancelling each other out, no wonder recent professional philosophers have favoured the ancient theory of virtue ethics, derived from Aristotle's and Confucius's notions.

Attentive readers will have spotted that all these theories are a bit circular – they kind of assume what's right before saying how the theory will help establish it. No wonder, then, that philosophers also spend a lot of time examining their theories – and this is the practice known as *metaethics*.

Separating ethics and metaethics

One of the things people find most confusing about philosophical ethics is how exactly ethics is different from plain old everyday morality. And notwithstanding numerous offers to specify ethics, the answer is that there really isn't one.

Ethics and *morality* are both words people use to describe the study of right and wrong. Sometimes people like to say that ethics deals with systems and morality with individual actions – but equally sometimes people talk of systems of morality and of particular kinds of ethics – personal ethics, work ethics, ethics of duty and so on. So save yourself some bother and just use the two terms interchangeably. If anyone complains, point out that the word ethics comes from the Greek *ethikos* and the word morality comes from the Latin *moralis* and that originally Cicero picked *moralis* to be the Latin equivalent of *ethikos*.

Ethics is concerned with finding the right policy. But *metaethics* is concerned with ethical theories themselves – examining them critically and looking at key concepts with them, like what do people mean by *good* anyway? Another topic philosophers discuss often is the notion of free will – that is, the idea that people really are responsible for their actions.

Free will is a fiction, and a very useful one at that. It says that when you think you make a choice, you really have made one. Did you choose to just stand there watching someone drown in the pond – or were you unable to help because of your timid nature? Of course, no one can ever know whether that freedom is real or just an illusion. Some people – *determinists* – say that every decision is, well, determined by circumstances, genes, chemicals, even

Nietzsche books or whatever. Some people say that as you're free to do otherwise, you should be held responsible for your decisions and behaviour, and that even if you're not really free at all, say, just born bad tempered! – you must still be treated as though you were.

Why is free will definitely a fiction then? Because to be responsible for your behaviour, you have to be not only taking a decision freely, but you have to be held responsible for being the sort of person who, given all the circumstances, will take that sort of decision. You are held responsible, thus for being born cowardly, or lazy, or selfish. To make free will possible, you have to be held accountable for being what you are. In a sort of logical sense, the responsibility is infinite. Kant says that although no one can understand how human freedom is possible, you must accept that it exists, and that the freedom belongs to the *noumenal* self (not the everyday physical one), the noumenal world being outside the usual rules of cause and effect.

Weighing up utilitarianism and consequentialism

The most useful ethical principle for considering the consequence of actions is that of utilitarianism – although in a very real sense it's not an ethical principle at all. Utilitarianism is an old idea. It's there in one of Plato's dialogues – the one in which Protagoras suggests that to sort out right and wrong you need to weigh up the pleasures against the pains likely to result from a policy. His idea is to turn ethics into a kind of maths, which philosophers sometimes call *hedonic calculus* (*hedone* is Greek for pleasure; the word *hedonist* is still in common use).

Making the right thing equal the most pleasurable thing was a controversial approach even then. On the one hand, the respected astronomer Eudoxus went so far as to say that pleasure was the sole good and that all other things that people consider good were only valuable because in some way they *increase* the amount of pleasure someone experiences somewhere. On the other hand, another ancient expert, Speusippus, insisted that pleasure and pain were two sides of the same thing and that thing was not good, but evil. Think about it! In fact, his idea (like other Stoics) was that being indifferent was good.

The naturalistic fallacy

G.E. Moore (1873–1958) (George to his friends) accused other philosophers of committing something he called the *naturalistic fallacy*, which is supposing that right and wrong exist in nature. Instead, Moore thought you had to derive moral values either by logic or by intuition. In nature, no right or wrong exists. He sets out this view in his 1903 magnum opus *Principia Ethica*, where he also declares that art and love must be the defining values of the non-natural world.

But philosophers usually trace the utilitarian principle back to the 18th-century (and the early 19th century) thinker Jeremy Bentham, and his saying that the right action is the one that brings about the greatest happiness of the greatest number. Bentham acted as a tutor to another highly influential moral philosopher, John Stuart Mill (1806–1873), who indeed adopted this theory for his own philosophy, and specifically rejected alternative moral theories for representing the interests of the ruling class, not justice. Those who taught the virtue of a life of sacrifice, Mill wrote, wanted others to sacrifice their lives to them. Mill and Bentham say that people desire to be happy, and that this is actually the only thing they desire. When desires conflict, the utilitarians simply weigh up the consequences and decide which action produces the greater happiness.

> *On the contrary, Speusippus might say that because pleasure (and pain) are equally bad, utilitarianism is a way of maximising the amount of evil in the world.*

Mind you, most people do seem to like their pleasure. That's why philosophers so often use utilitarianism to justify practical decisions. But Speusippus and the Stoics were perhaps also wrong to try to put people off feeling pain. Because the idea that pain is always bad and pleasure is always good breaks down from an ecological perspective. Pain is nature's way of telling you to see the dentist, after all. As one environmental philosopher, J. Baird Callicott, recently put it:

> *A living mammal which experienced no pain would be one that had a lethal dysfunction of the nervous system . . . the idea that pain is evil and ought to be minimised or eliminated is as primitive a notion as that of a tyrant who puts to death messengers bearing bad news on the supposition that thus his well-being and security is improved.*

Another contemporary philosopher, Joel Feinberg, has argued in the same spirit:

> *The question 'What's wrong with pain anyway?' is never allowed to arise. I shall raise it. I herewith declare in all soberness that I see nothing wrong with pain. It is a marvellous method, honed by the evolutionary process, of conveying important organic information.*

Who's right? Everyone or those philosophical cranks? Yet these views appealed to that biological expert Darwin, who pointed out that pain and anxiety are part of life and can't be removed, any more than death can, without destroying the whole natural system. If nature as a whole is good, then death and pain are good too.

Making sure to do your duty

If some philosophers think pain is good, others think that happiness is bad; or at least that increasing happiness is a form of selfishness, and thus a bad motivation. Instead, for some philosophers, sometimes called *deontologists*, good intentions are enough. Their leader is the jargon-wielding German philosophy professor Immanuel Kant. This is how he sets out the stall for doing something *despite* the consequences:

> *Even if, by some especially unfortunate fate or by the niggardly provision of step-motherly nature, this will should be wholly lacking in the power to accomplish its purpose, if with the greatest effort it should yet achieve nothing, and only the good will should remain (not to be sure, as a mere wish, but as the summoning of all the means in our power), yet would it, like a jewel, still shine by its own light, as something which has full value in itself. Its usefulness or fruitfulness augment nor diminish this value.*

So Kant thought while writing a much respected work called the *Groundwork of the Metaphysics of Morals* (1785). He extends his theory in a book called the *Critique of Practical Reason* (1786) further into the practical realm. Morality, says Kant, is not connected with the inclinations that you're subjected to as a result of your material, physical nature. Rather, your duty is to reflect upon what could stand as universal duty for any rational agent – God included.

Kant derives the famous formula of the categorical imperative. This is one (like Descartes' *cogito*) of those dodgy one-liners in philosophy that everyone repeats respectfully but that really says nothing new. Anyhow, here it is. Make a note.

> *Act only on a maxim that you can at the same time will to be a universal law.*

In this formula, what's crucial isn't the success of the outcome of an action, but the intention. This doesn't mean that consequences are irrelevant, because they identify which actions are (theoretically) *universalisable* (could be carried out by everyone), but consequences in the sense of asking what's useful are most certainly not wanted. One example Kant gives is of a world in which the practice of making false promises when convenient has become a universal law. But, Kant points out, in such a world, the institution of promise-making would soon collapse because no one would trust anyone else's word. This contradiction means that it's not possible to *universalise* the action in question, so that the maxim of not making false promises is 'demonstrated' to be morally binding.

The categorical imperative

Kant illustrates his fine imperative with a few examples. One is of the act of borrowing money, without intending to pay it back on time. If everyone did this, Kant argues, then no one would trust anyone else, and the institution of promising would collapse.

Being illogical is what people really mean when they say something is wrong. Kant was wholly opposed to any attempt to introduce some consideration of the effects of actions. For him,

the rightness of an action depended not on its results, but only on the principle that justified it. Theft, murder and being unhelpful to others are likewise ruled out as illogical and self-contradictory. This last, the 'everyone looks after number one' philosophy of living, Kant concedes is strictly speaking *universalisable*, but he maintains that it still involves a contradiction because everyone at some time or other needs help.

'The moral law,' wrote Kant, is 'a law of duty, or moral constraint'. In a general sense, duties are obligations that come with a role. In ethics duties are those obligations that a person of good will would feel. Kant attempted to show that they were all in some sense logically demonstrable. He thought this logical process started by dividing duty up between things dictated by law and duties dictated by virtue, as well as distinguishing between actions carried out for a positive reason, and 'negative duties' – actions dictated by a desire to avoid doing something wrong.

More precisely, a *duty* is an action that you're under an obligation to perform, and to have an *obligation* is to be under a special kind of necessity (moral necessity) to perform a certain action. So the word *duty* stands for an action, and the word *obligation* similarly represents the fact of the moral necessity to perform an action.

Deontological ethics (from the Greek deon for duty or dei for 'you must') is concerned with duties and considers certain acts to be right or wrong in themselves, not by consideration of their consequences.

Another example Kant offers (he's not very good at thinking them up, but at least he tried) is of the dilemma faced by a loyal servant who opens the door to a mad knifeman looking for the servant's master in order to kill him. The dilemma (Kant thinks, anyway) is that if the knifeman asks a question, the servant can't lie to protect his master, because lying, like murdering people, is always a bad thing. Lying to a murderer at the door about the master being at home is morally forbidden – even though telling the truth would put the master in mortal danger. That's where morality gets you: when you're stiffly logical. Kant seems to realise the implausibility of his guidance here. So he offers some rather unconvincing further arguments to justify telling the truth to the knifeman, such as that if the master got killed because, unbeknownst to the servant, he'd actually slipped out the back door and then bumped into the murderer going home disappointed at the news that his intended victim wasn't in, the servant could rightly be accused of being responsible!

Kant is resolutely opposed to any consideration of consequences because he thinks this makes every person a selfish calculator, rather than truly virtuous.

Quite where Kant got his categorical imperative from (logically speaking – socially speaking it's there in the Bible) isn't clear: he merely asserts it in the *Metaphysics of Morals*. Here he explains that every 'rational being' considers their own existence to be an end in itself. On the other hand, the things these rational folk want (like meat pies) are means to satisfying the desire, but the desires themselves are a nuisance and

> . . . *the inclinations, themselves being sources of want, are so far from having an absolute worth for which they should be desired that on the contrary it must be the universal wish of every rational being to be wholly free from them.*

So, Kant continues ponderously,'if all worth were conditioned and therefore contingent, then there would be no supreme practical principle of reason whatever'. Better than that is to assume that

> . . . *there is a supreme practical principle . . . being drawn from the conception of that which is necessarily an end for everyone because it is an end in itself, constitutes an objective principle of will, and can therefore serve as a universal practical law. The foundation of this principle is: rational nature exists as an end in itself.*

The universal practical moral law, the practical imperative, then is as follows:

> *So act as to treat humanity, whether in thine own person or in that of any other, in every case as an end withal, never as means only.*

JARGON BUSTER

Life, liberty and the pursuit of eudaimonia

Eudaimonia? Happiness, surely? That's what it says in the preamble to the American Declaration of Independence, anyway. But the Founding Fathers got the idea that happiness was something people had a right to from the philosophers, who had in mind a rather special kind of happiness, which is specified in the Greek word *eudaimonia*. This comes from the Greek, *eu* for good and *daimon* for demon (albeit the nice kind of demon that has the job of looking after people; Westerners would say guardian angel, perhaps). People sometimes use the word *happiness* as a shorthand for *eudaimonia*, but this loses its particular significance, which is that the happiness here is of the whole and not merely that transient, illusory happiness you get, for example, through the senses. For Plato, Aristotle and Epicurus, *eudaimonia* was the state you achieve only by living virtuously, which sounds bleak and indeed is.

Being virtuous with Aristotle

One important difference between Aristotle and Plato is there in the *Nicomachean Ethics*, where Aristotle starts with a survey of popular opinions on the subject of right and wrong to find out how people use the terms. Plato makes very clear his contempt for such an approach. Thomas Hobbes later on said the method had immediately led Aristotle astray, because by seeking to ground ethics in the 'appetites of men', he'd chosen a measure by which, for Hobbes, correctly no law and no distinction between right and wrong exist. Societies, like businesses, create these distinctions and people sign up to them.

In Plato's dialogues the source of goodness is wisdom, and he describes good like a light that reveals truth. No one does evil, says Plato reassuringly, except out of ignorance. After all, doing something wrong makes the wrongdoer themselves less perfect and less harmonious, and who'd do that knowingly to themselves? Aristotle adds that the path to ethical health is a series of assessments of the middle option: not too much wine, not too many slave boys, nor yet too few canapés for the dinner guests – as he describes in his portrait of the truly virtuous man (Aristotle despises women and calls them a kind of domestic cattle!) in his celebrated work on ethics called the *Nicomachean Ethics*:

> *Such, then, is the magnanimous man; the man who goes to excess and is vulgar exceeds, as has been said, by spending beyond what is right. For on small objects of expenditure he spends much and displays a tasteless showiness; for example, he gives a club dinner on the scale of a wedding banquet, and when he provides the chorus for a comedy he brings them on to the stage in purple, as they do at Megara. And all such things he will do not for honour's sake but to show off his wealth, and because he thinks he is admired for these things, and where he ought to spend much he spends little and where little, much. The niggardly man on the other hand will fall short in everything, and after spending the greatest sums will spoil the beauty of the result for a trifle, and whatever he is doing he will hesitate and consider how he may spend least, and lament even that, and think he is doing everything on a bigger scale than he ought.*

Recently Aristotle has had something of a revival, and this theory is called on ethics courses *virtue ethics*. Essentially, the idea is that it's through the healthy practice of virtuous behaviour that people become virtuous. The lesson from that is (as parents know) forcing people to be virtuous makes them better people . . . sooner or later. Philosophers like to treat this as a great insight quite different from other theories, but in fact this notion is a pretty ancient one, and even appears in Plato's dialogues. He was robbed!

Spreading the happiness

One of the big ideas in philosophy is that the right action is what increases the amount of happiness. But what do they mean by 'happiness' exactly? In the *Nicomachean Ethics*, Aristotle describes his special idea of 'happiness':

> *To judge from the lives that men lead, most men, and men of the most vulgar type, seem (not without some ground) to identify the good, or happiness, with pleasure; which is the reason why they love the life of enjoyment. Happiness, above all else, is held to be; for this we choose always for self and never for the sake of something else, but honour, pleasure, reason, and every virtue we choose indeed for themselves (for if nothing resulted from them we should still choose each of them), but we choose them also for the sake of happiness, judging that by means of them we shall be happy. Happiness, on the other hand, no one chooses for the sake of these, nor, in general, for anything other than itself.*

> *Happiness, therefore, does not lie in amusement; it would, indeed, be strange if the end were amusement, and one were to take trouble and suffer hardship all one's life in order to amuse oneself. And any chance a person – even a slave – can enjoy the bodily pleasures no less than the best man; but no one assigns to a slave a share in happiness – unless he assigns to him also a share in human life. For happiness does not lie in such occupations, but, as we have said before, in virtuous activities. We think happiness has pleasure mingled with it, but the activity of philosophic wisdom is admittedly the pleasantest of virtuous activities; at all events the pursuit of it is thought to offer pleasures marvellous for their purity and their enduringness, and it is to be expected that those who know will pass their time more pleasantly than those who inquire.*

The Stoic and Eastern traditions offer a slightly different perspective (as explored, for instance, by Spinoza) of the good life being a case of adapting and harmonising with nature and the times, and indeed both approaches try to avoid the right/wrong duality of standard Western ethics, recognising that everything contains elements of both good and bad. Which is why sorting out what is right from wrong can be so hard to do!

All the virtues

What is a virtue? Literally, a *virtue* is a property, but one that's not so much actual as potential. Opium, famously, has the dormitive virtue. And a good person has the virtue of being kind to animals in that when they see an animal they're kind to it. For the Ancient Greeks, a virtuous person is just like a virtuous spade, or knife or whatever. Just as the spade must be good at its function, which is digging, so the virtuous person must be good at their function, which Aristotle decided was being rational.

Alas, not everyone agrees on virtues. In the 12th century Moses Maimonides, the Spanish-North African rabbi-philosopher (1155–1204) advised in his *Guide to the Perplexed* (circa. 1190) that virtue is simply a means of becoming good at following the religious code. And virtues like those Aristotle attached so much importance to, such as being balanced, honourable, magnificent and so on, were for the Stoics only valuable in as much as they may assist someone to achieve harmony with the world as it is. Even the difference between virtue and vice isn't very important. This is because both are intellectual states. *Virtue* is the result of the appliance of the science of the good, the activity of the wise. *Vice* is the result of allowing an excessive role of the passions, leading to errors of judgement.

But later on the Christian virtues harked back to something not that unlike the Socratic ones: justice, prudence, temperance, fortitude, faith, hope and charity. Crucially, virtue, for Socrates and Christians too, is truly its own reward.

The Magnanimous Man

Aristotle's magnanimous man, sometimes called the great-souled man or the magnificent man, is virtuous in the sense of being excellent in all he does and is proud of it too. After all, as Aristotle explains in the *Nicomachean Ethics*

> . . . *greatness in every virtue would seem to be characteristic of a proud man. And it would be most unbecoming for a proud man to fly from danger, swinging his arms by his sides, or to wrong another; for to what end should he do disgraceful acts, he to whom nothing is great?*

The magnanimous man (who has all the virtues) makes better sense today if you remember that the Greek word *virtue* (*arete*) described a quality related to being good at doing things. The word wasn't just about virtuous intentions, as people nowadays understand it (although there's still a shared emphasis on 'how to be' over 'what to do'). Aristotle expected that any virtuous man would be tall, handsome and strong too. People still respect this cultural value in modern celebration of the Olympic champions. In the *Nicomachean Ethics*, Aristotle puts it like this:

> *Further, a slow step is thought proper to the proud man, a deep voice, and a level utterance; for the man who takes few things seriously is not likely to be hurried, nor the man who thinks nothing great to be excited, while a shrill voice and a rapid gait are the results of hurry and excitement.*

Just like a gold medal winner! Which reminds me, part of virtue for Aristotle is finding the *golden mean* in (nearly) all things – not too much, not too little. Actually, the Oriental philosophers put it more radically, saying that nothing is all bad and nothing is all good, but Aristotle allows that some things – justice, for example – are always good. Magnanimous man is angry 'in the right way, at the right time', and considers those who aim 'at being pleasant with no ulterior object' obsequious and the others irreconcilably 'churlish and contentious'.

A discussion of the golden mean strategy appears in the *Nicomachean Ethics*, Book II. Table 13-1 represents the discussion, (except, I admit, the last two lines, which I made up).

Table 13-1	The Goldilocks Table of Virtues and Vices		
Sphere of Applicability	*Too Much*	*Too Little*	*Just Right*
Fear	Rash	Cowardly	Courageous
Pleasure	Licentious	Cold fish	Temperate
Spending	Prodigal	Stingy	Generous
Honour	Vain	Pusillanimous	Magnanimous
Anger	Irritable	Lacking spirit	Patient
Expressiveness	Boastful	Humble	Truthful
Conversation	Buffoonery	Boorish	Witty
Social skills	Flatterer	Cantankerous	Friendly
Social conduct	Shy	Shameless	Modest
Attitude towards others	Envious	Malicious	Lofty
Porridge	Steaming hot	Stone cold	Warmed through
Philosophy book	Plato and Aristotle	Everyone else	Martin Cohen's stuff

Aristotle continues to play with words, in the way that Thomas Hobbes thousands of years later found so maddening, saying that virtue has two parts: intellectual, which is of the rational part of the soul, and moral, which is the irrational part of the soul. So wisdom and prudence are rational (intellectual) and generosity and self-control are moral (irrational). As ever with Aristotle's tireless taxonomies, he subdivides virtue further. Intellectual virtue consists of *sophia*, which is theoretical reason (and from which the word *philosophy* comes), and *phronesis*, which is practical wisdom.

Aristotle's point is that to be truly virtuous requires both types of intellect, otherwise the brave become rash, and the generous wasteful and spendthrift.

Getting emotional with relativism, emotivism and anti-morality

The word *emotion* comes from the Latin *e*, meaning out, and *movere*, to move. In moral philosophy, emotions are important because the notion of right and wrong links to the emotions of approval and disapproval in some way. The doctrine of *emotivism* in fact claims that the two things are interchangeable: that is, to say something is right is only to say that you feel positively towards it, you like it.

Aristotle thought that emotion was indeed a kind of motion. He describes embarrassment as the motion, or impulse, for revenge accompanied by pain, after you perceive an insult or slight. Both Hume and Descartes characterised emotions as feelings, not so different from the yellow feeling that comes from seeing the colour yellow, for example. But, as Descartes stressed, emotions have some sort of additional bodily response. William James and the Danish psychologist C. Lange took this idea further, to the point that the emotion sorrow becomes simply the theoretical mental parallel to exhibiting bodily behaviour like crying, and to be afraid is the theoretical mental state paralleling the state of having gone white and started to tremble. The feeling is thus secondary to the behaviour.

Relativism

'Man is the measure of all things,' said the sophist Protagoras (circa. 481–420 BC), and that is the heart of philosophical relativism. (The Sophists were Ancient Greek philosophers who wandered around Greece charging lots of money for their philosophical views, annoying Socrates who did it for nothing.) What's good for you may not be good for me if you're a cannibal and I'm a vegetarian. What's big to you may not be big for me, if you're an ant and I'm an elephant. In fact, Protagoras was particularly concerned with his latter kind of 'perceptual relativism', and Plato and many since have searched high and low for exactly those kinds of truths that are eternal and unchanging.

Philosophically speaking, *relativism* is the doctrine that holds that judgements, positions and conclusions are relative to individual cultures, to divergent situations and to differing perceptions. It denies the existence of universal or absolute criteria, holding instead that what you know and what there is to know is relative to your tastes, experiences, culture and attitudes. Relativism substitutes the variability of people's vantage points and 'perceptual mechanisms' for *universals* – perspectives and experiences that can be shared by everyone – when considering moral propositions and in the realms of human knowledge, including science. Relativism ranges from its strong version, which maintains that all truths are relative, to its more limited version, which highlights and refers to the great number of divergent standards in etiquette and custom.

As far as ethics is concerned, relativism is the view that moral claims don't reflect absolute truths. Instead, relativists insist that moral judgements are the product of social customs, cultural tendencies or personal preferences. Relativism disallows a single, objective standard by which you can evaluate an ethical claim. Thus, according to some relativists, one person's view has no more truth value and is no better than any other. Rather, you can trace moral positions or reduce them to certain cultural or individual biases.

The ancients were well aware of cultural relativism. Herodotus's *Histories* describing the range of customs he encountered in his travels still shocked them. Similarly, people today wonder whether the fact that the Cashibo tribe in South America, for example, who consider it essential, out of religious sentiment, to eat their dead, undercuts the view in our own culture that this practice seems gruesome. And even if cultures share a religious sentiment, expressions of that sentiment can differ widely.

Plato also quotes Protagoras as saying, 'The way things appear to me, in that way they exist for me; and the way things appear to you, in that way they exist for you.'

Getting emotional

David Hume (1711–1776) is a humbugger of ethics. ''Tis an object of feeling – not of reason!' he scoffs. And in his *Treatise on Human Nature* (1740) he makes the following points about what to think about the fact that 'when you pronounce any action or character to be vicious, you mean nothing, but that from the constitution of your nature you have a feeling or sentiment of blame from the contemplation of it'. Vice and virtue are merely qualities that you see in things, just as you see colours. Aren't colours real then either? Bah, just perceptions in the mind!

And in *Of Morals*, Book III, part I, Hume adds:

> *I cannot forbear adding to these reasoning an observation which may, perhaps, be found of some importance. In every system of morality, which I have hitherto met with, I have always remark'd, that the author proceeds for some time in the ordinary way of reasoning, and establishes the being of a God, or makes observations concerning human affairs; when all of a sudden I am supriz'd to find, that instead of the usual copulations of propositions, is and is not, I meet with no proposition that is not connected with an ought or an ought not. This change is imperceptible; but is however of the last consequence.*

Hume was not the first and certainly not the last to make the point. In *The Origin and Development of Moral Ideas* (1906) Edward Westermarck describes society as a kind of school in which 'men learn to distinguish between right and wrong' (the headmaster is custom, and the lessons are the same for all – watch out young Westermarck!). He warns that the presumed objectivity of moral judgements is a 'chimera' and there's no such thing as moral truth at all. He says, 'The ultimate reason for this is that the moral concepts are based upon emotions, and that the contents of an emotion fall entirely outside the category of truth.'

Similarly, A.J. Ayer, batting for the logical positivists (see chapter 8), astonished 20th-century academics with the observation that 'ethical concepts are pseudo-concepts' in *Language, Truth and Logic* (1936). Wittgenstein shared the theme:

> . . . *to write or talk Ethics or religion [is] . . . to run against the boundaries of language. This running against the walls of our cage is perfectly, absolutely hopeless. Ethics so far as it springs from the desire to say something about the ultimate meaning of life, the absolute good, the absolutely valuable, can be no science. What it says does not add to our knowledge in any sense.*

Applying Ethics to Hard Cases

Hippocrates of Cos (fifth-century BC) was a physician who maintained early on that epilepsy and other illnesses weren't the result of evil spirits or angry gods, but were due to natural causes. He's been called the father of medicine and the 'wisest and greatest practitioner of his art'. Hippocrates taught the sanctity of life and called other physicians to the highest ethical standards of conduct.

The anthropologist Margaret Mead has noted that throughout the primitive world the doctor and the sorcerer tended to be the same person, both with the power to kill or the power to cure. According to Mead, the Oath of Hippocrates marked a turning point in the history of Western civilisation because for the first time it created a complete separation between curing and killing. The Oath says:

> *I swear by Apollo Physician, by Asclepius . . . I will use treatment to help the sick according to my ability and judgement, but never with a view to injury and wrong-doing. I will neither administer a poison to anybody when asked to do so, nor will I suggest such a course.*

No support there for euthanasia. And similarly, it continues:

> *I will not give to a woman a pessary to cause abortion.*

In any case, under Hippocrates, medicine emerged as the prototype of the learned professions.

When is it okay to kill?

Killing newborn babies (infanticide) is something that people used to consider quite okay. Until very recently, only the odd country, like Egypt and Cambodia, had divergent customs that *all* children must be reared. Usually it was girl babies that were killed, but it could be, as in Madagascar, any child born on an 'unlucky day'.

The Roman philosopher Seneca writes of killing 'defective' children as a wise and prudent action suitable for use as a policy benchmark.

When the Icelanders accepted the moral guidance of Christianity they insisted on just two exceptions: they must be able to continue to eat horses and to kill children. Curiously, the notion that children not wanted at birth died unbaptised had a greater effect in changing practice than the mere fact that children so treated died.

Getting rid of old folks

Killing old people was widespread until recently, but never universal. Herodotus's story of the Massagetae, who boiled their old folk with beef and ate the mixture, is perhaps the best known on the subject, but many other equally queasy-making stories exist. One tribe along the banks of the river Niger were said to kill their old people, smoke and pulverise the bodies, and then compress the powder into little balls with corn and water. These unedifying burgers were then kept for long periods as a basic food.

Some say the killings reflected the cruel necessity of life in harsh conditions, with stories of Inuits (like the Hudson Bay Inuit who strangled the old, the Tupis of Brazil who killed any elderly person who became ill and then ate the corpse, or the Tobas of Paraguay who were reputed to bury their old folk alive) used to illustrate both the necessity and the good intentions of the tribes.

However, American Indian tribes like the Poncas and Omahas created a role for the old and infirm by leaving them at home, with supplies, while the rest of the tribe hunted or gathered. The old watched the cornfields and scared away birds, so they were of some use too, a practice also found amongst the Incas.

Eating people isn't wrong, as such. A Miranhas cannibal explained to anthropologists Spix and Martius that

> . . . *it is all a matter of habit. When I have killed an enemy, it is better to eat him than to let him go to waste. Big game is rare because it does not lay eggs like turtles. The bad thing is not being eaten, but death . . . you whites are really too dainty!*

If 'killing babies' is now not allowed, it is not thanks to philosophers but changes in society. Abortion remains a topic where views are completely polarised. That's partly because it is not clear when life starts – and that's also part of the problem with the treatment of the very, very old. At what point does someone 'cease to be a person'? Again, philosophers have not been able to provide simple answers.

Sorting out the planet

Another historical constant is the use of slaves, be they slaves from birth, from conquest or whatever. Aristotle and Plato both produced justifications for slavery centred on the lower abilities of slaves, seen as more akin to animals. Both Christianity and Islam have been willing apologists for the practice, despite Mohammed setting free his own slaves and instructing that all men should be brothers and treated as equals. (Not, of course, including women in that pronouncement.)

Today you find churches spearheading social change, calling for civil rights, the protection of unborn children, an end to human rights abuses in other countries and so on. This hasn't always been the case. Some say that on issues such as women's rights and human slavery, religion has impeded social progress. The church of the past never considered slavery to be a moral evil. The Protestant churches of Virginia, South Carolina and other southern US states actually passed resolutions in favour of the human slave traffic. People said human slavery was by divine appointment, a divine institution and was not immoral but 'founded in right'.

Many New Testament verses call for obedience and subservience on the part of slaves (Colossians 3:22–25; Ephesians 6:5–9; I Peter 2:18–25; Titus 2:9–10; I Timothy 6:1–2), and people used the verses to justify human slavery. Many of Jesus's parables refer to slaves and Paul's infamous epistle to Philemon concerns a runaway slave who he unambiguously states should be returned to his master. Other than Deuteronomy, in the Old Testament, which says 'You shall not surrender to his master a slave who has taken refuge with you', the abolitionists (people who wanted governments to abolish slavery) had to find non-Biblical sources to argue the immoral nature of slavery, a cautionary tale for those who take their lead from religion.

Examining environmental ethics

Aldo Leopold (1887–1948) was born in Iowa. He developed an interest in ornithology and natural history, and became the first graduate of forestry in the US. Today, people considered him to be the father of wildlife conservation in America. You can sum up his views as man-eating wolves are good and people are bad, although wolf-eating people are slightly less so. Appropriately or not, he died while helping his neighbours fight a grass fire.

Conventional views of environmental ethics look at changes caused by human beings to the environment, and at whether the changes are in human interests. Concerns such as climate change, depletion of the ozone layer and over-pollution of rivers, the seas and the air are all essentially human-centred. Concerns about humans' propensity for destroying habitats and with them animals and plant species are also sometimes put in terms of the loss to humans – what if such and such a plant contained a cure for cancer? How would you feel if there were no more pandas to look at – even in cages? Often the degradation of the environment is more prosaic (as it is in the bulk of areas where people actually live – no song birds, fewer green spaces, more noise and fumes from cars) and it's not concern for the environment for itself but rather concern for the ability of people to flourish in such bleak, urban conditions. Other ethicists say self-interest, when you fully understand it, leads inexorably in a sort of holistic way to respect not only for other humans but for all creation. Either way, much of environmental ethics is still the same sort of human self-interest as any other ethics.

Seen from a human perspective, then, the taming of nature is good, and the dangerous or simply inconvenient activities of wild nature are bad. This is what so-called *deep ecologists* insist that people must move away from – to accept that what's good for you isn't necessarily good for nature, and that you should instead begin to apply values such as freedom and autonomy to rivers and animals, and respect for others to trees and mountains.

The first step in moving to a wider concern for the environment is to consider the interests of animals. Pollution of habitats – perhaps rivers full of raw sewage, air full of toxic particles from industrial processes, seas dying from agricultural run off – as well as many more subtle, harder-to-spot changes, will in the first place affect animals.

Secondly, what people eat is both profound, pervasive and fundamental. People's attitudes and their whole approach to life stem from fulfilment of this basic need. 'There is nothing more intimate than eating, more symbolic of the connectedness of life, and more mysterious', as one 'Deep Green', Paul Callicott, wrote.

Giving animals rights

Many kinds of rights exist these days: human rights, women's rights, animal rights, tree rights. But none of them are really worth very much. No one seems to agree on them. Philosophers have spent millennia trying to pin down just what are the 'real' rights, but perhaps Thomas Hobbes came the nearest when he said that just one right exists – the fundamental right to self-preservation. From that, to be sure, he derived some more rights including the right to remain silent, and even the right to run away in battles, but that one on its own causes enough problems.

Against animal rights

According to the 20th-century American philosophers Donald Davidson (1917–2003) and John McDowell (b. 1942) animals don't have any thoughts, beliefs or intentions. Their reasoning is that you can't say a creature believes (or thinks, intends and so on) anything unless it has a full-blown language. John McDowell goes even further, adding that animals have no inner experience and consequently you can't say they have a fully fledged subjectivity but only a 'proto-subjective perceptual' sensitivity to the environment. A what? Call it 'automatic responses'. McDowell is saying that animals are just reacting like a complex machine might, to varying physical conditions.

Strictly speaking, having a right implies the ability to make a justifiable claim, which animals lack. Moreover, as one contemporary philosopher, Roger Scruton, has argued, if animals can have legal rights it must also make sense to ascribe legal duties to them! Roger, however, is a keen fox-hunter and you must take his argument with a pinch of snuff, and in any case, it's neither here nor there because people can make a claim on animals' behalf. The implications of formally giving animals rights are considerable. It obliges people to review their thoughts concerning commercial agriculture, animal experimentation, zoo-keeping, the management of wildlife and the use of animals in travel, entertainment, clothing and sport.

From the Genesis story of the Bible to the analytic arguments of Donald Davidson recently (see the nearby sidebar 'Against animal rights'), Western thought has allotted non-human animals a relatively low status. Some philosophers, most notably Descartes, have even insisted that animals are mere machines that are incapable of sensation and perception, let alone belief and emotion. Most, however, are happy to allow that animals feel pain, though they stop short of attributing any kind of rationality to them on the ground that they don't have language. This has potential ethical consequences, for according to many systems of ethics if a being is to be of moral concern it's necessary for it to possess rationality, in the sense of being able to use abstract reason. Against this view, utilitarians such as Jeremy Bentham and (recently) Peter Singer have argued that sentience (being able to sense and feel things) is sufficient to render animals worthy of moral consideration. This has led to the recent movement of animal liberation whose aim is to defend the interests of animals.

Another thinker whose philosophy puts the power of reason first in explaining the world, Baruch (Benedict) de Spinoza (1632–1673) allowed that animals are sentient but claimed that their lack of rationality prohibited them from qualifying as members of the moral community. This view isn't dissimilar from that of the materialist Thomas Hobbes (1588–1679), who as a materialist thought that even human beings are essentially just physical objects and machines. His bleak view of human nature (people are brutish and power-seeking) led him to believe that morality is constructed only when human beings of roughly equal strength and intelligence enter into agreements or social contracts with each other. The moral rules help of these contracts ensure mutual security, and the better life that follows. If animals lack rationality (as Hobbes and Spinoza believed), they can't enter into any mutual agreements with people (or indeed with each other), and consequently remain in a state of war with both humans and themselves.

The so-called empiricist philosophers (see chapter 7), such as John Locke (1632–1704) and David Hume (1711–1776), found it easier to endow animals with not only perception and sensation but also some degree of rationality, maintaining that no great gulf between humans and animals existed. They shared this belief with Chinese philosophers such as Chu Hsi (1130–1200), as well as Native American peoples. Hume writes that only the most stupid and ignorant don't recognise thought and reason in animals.

Bentham didn't hesitate to add that a full-grown horse or dog is beyond comparison more rational, reasonable and indeed more easier to communicate with, than an infant of a day, or a week, or even a month, old. This wasn't because he thought rationality and language play an important moral role, but on the contrary because he wanted to show that moral intuitions may be contaminated by unrelated factors.

Recent research on the question of whether or not animals possess the power of cognition has done much to combat the view that animals have no thoughts at all. Behavioural scientists such as Marc Bekoff have advanced evidence in support of animal displays of consciousness, cognition, memory, intelligence, passion, devotion, jealousy, playfulness, anger and more.

Taking up vegetarianism

Vegetarianism – that range of human diets from those who'll eat only the seeds of plants to those who allow honey, eggs, milk and cheese, and even fish and birds, but hesitate at mammals – isn't an issue accorded much space in standard encyclopaedias of philosophy, even if people recognise it to be part of debates over animal rights. Yet vegetarianism occupies a central position in early Eastern and Western philosophy, when it was often linked to the concept of reincarnation.

Plutarch, however, was one of the few writers in the Ancient World to advocate vegetarianism for other reasons, in his essay 'On Eating Flesh' a literary, if not a philosophical, classic. Warning that meat-eating corrupts morals, he challenges the flesh-eaters, who insist that nature has intended them to be predators, in that case to kill their meals for themselves and eat the raw meat uncooked with their bare hands.

> *'Oh, my fellow men!' exclaimed Pythagoras. 'Do not defile your bodies with sinful foods. We have corn. We have apples bending down the branches with their weight, and grapes swelling on the vines. There are sweet flavoured herbs and vegetables which can be cooked and softened over the fire. Nor are you denied milk or thyme-scented honey. The earth affords you a lavish supply of riches, of innocent foods, and offers you banquets that involve no bloodshed or slaughter.'*

A brief history of meat-eating

Nowadays people are used to the idea of eating meat, but that's not to say the activity is in evolutionary terms a very old one. Baron Cuvier, who established the sciences of palaeontology and comparative anatomy, wrote

> *The natural food of man, judging from his structure, appears to consist principally of fruits, roots and other succulent parts of vegetables. His hands afford every facility for gathering them; his short but moderately strong jaws on the other hand and his canines being equal only in length to the other teeth, together with his tuberculated molars would scarcely permit him either to masticate herbage, or to devour flesh, were these condiments not previously prepared for cooking.*

Yet dentition and aeons of behaviour are no barrier to a radical change of diet. Horses have been trained to eat meat and sheep have become so accustomed to it as to refuse grass.

Most of the world's religions hold killing and eating animals to be the natural state of affairs for mankind. In Genesis God gave humans absolute rights over animals. This God, it seemed, favoured the slaughter, cooking and savouring of animals, especially lambs. The Temple at Jerusalem must have been a vast slaughter house that ran with blood and molten fat at Passover. The stench of barbecued flesh would've hung over the Temple permanently, pleasing both human and divine nostrils.

Zarathrustra was the most likely initiator of vegetarianism. He lived in the early sixth century BC. He held that:

- ✔ Horticulture and the rearing and caring for animals are all that's noble in life.

- ✔ Opposing spirits of good and evil exist, and giving life or condemning to non-life is the fundamental dualism.

- ✔ Air, water, fire and earth are pure elements never to be defiled.

On these principles Zarathrustra based a vegetarian, teetotal, pacifist lifestyle using animals solely for transport and watering his sacred and wholly
horticultural state in Eastern Iran, where he settled after being driven from
his native Media.

The Bible at Genesis 1.29 has God instruct:

> *Kill neither men, nor beasts, nor yet your food which goes into your mouth.*
> *For if you eat living food, the same will quicken you, but if you kill your*
> *food, the dead food will kill you also. For life comes only from life, and*
> *death comes always from death. For everything which kills your food, kills*
> *your bodies also . . . And your bodies become what your foods are, even as*
> *your spirits, likewise, become what your thoughts are.*

But, of course, Adam and Eve were then ejected from their paradise garden a
little later in the Bible, and the thinking in Genesis 1.29 got quietly forgotten.
In practice, Judaism, Christianity and Islam have all perpetuated the notion of
meat-eating as the natural state for mankind.

You can find an economic link between flesh-eating and war in Plato's
Republic. Plato records a dialogue between Socrates and Glaucon in which
Socrates extols the peace and happiness that come to people eating a vegetarian diet. The citizens, Socrates says, will feast upon barley meal and wheat
flour, making 'noble cakes' as well as salt, olives and cheese 'for relish', all
served on a mat of reeds. For dessert, some roasted myrtle berries or acorns,
even boiled figs and roots. These are the foods of peace and good health:

> *And with such a diet they may be expected to live in peace and health to a*
> *good old age, and bequeath a similar life to their children after them.*

Plato's pupil Aristotle, however, didn't favour vegetarianism. He held that
animals exist to be useful to mankind. Because in many matters you can
square Aristotle's thinking with that of the Bible and its derivative the Koran,
his philosophy was the most influential on the development of first Islam and
then Christianity during the Middle Ages.

What's right is what's natural

Often people tend to fall back on a sense of what's natural, to back up their
views of right and wrong. They say that two men having sex together isn't
natural (actually, it turns out that homosexuality is also part of the sexual
activity of many animal species) nor that women giving philosophy papers is,
nor . . . Often the arguments are very weak. But take eating meat, which does
seem to be pretty natural.

Yet radical environmentalists immediately point out that today's meat eaters,
or more precisely meat producers, are the number one industrial polluters –
contributing to half the water pollution in the US, responsible for the poisoning

of rivers all over the world and even the slow death of the seas as wetlands disappear and poisons accumulate. The water that goes into a 1,000-pound steer could float a destroyer. It takes 25 gallons of water to produce a pound of wheat, but 2,500 gallons to produce a pound of meat. Remarkably, the livestock population of the United States alone today consumes enough grain and soybeans to feed over five times the entire human population. American cows, pigs, chicken, sheep and so on eat up to 90 per cent of the country's wheat, 80 per cent of the corn and 95 per cent of the oats. If, in the United Kingdom, much of the barley you may see in fields ends up as bread, less than half of the harvested agricultural acreage in the United States is for human consumption. People use most of it to grow livestock feed. Or recall the 2001 Foot and Mouth Disease crisis in the UK. Foot and Mouth disease is not fatal to cows – it's a bit like a bad cold – but it is to export sales of meat. And so it led to the Prime Minister cancelling his holiday, all the country's footpaths being closed, cost about £8 billion, and – last but not least! – involved the mass slaughter of over ten million animals. The army was called in to burn all the corpses in vast pits. It has had widespread adverse effects – on the farming community, the tourist industry, millions of farm animals, the environment, and citizens' quality of life. And how natural is that?

> The Green philosopher Aldo Leopold says that: 'A thing is right when it tends to preserve the integrity, stability, and beauty of the biotic community. It is wrong otherwise.'

Leopold not only ate meat, he hunted it too! Wolves and everything! But he surely wouldn't have gone along with factory farming. Perhaps somewhere in the middle, as Aristotle would say, is the right policy.

Chapter 14

Political Philosophy

In This Chapter

▶ Choosing authority over anarchy with Plato

▶ Developing totalitarianism with Hegel and the Nazis

▶ Battling against capitalism with Marxism

▶ Going back to Hobbes and Rousseau to imagine the very first human societies

The penalty that good men pay for not being interested in politics is to be governed by men worse than themselves.

– Plato

*P*olitical philosophy covers all areas of social life, from the family and the attitudes and psychological character of people, to the state and the institutions and rules that define it. Many burning issues from what's nowadays also called *applied ethics* could also fall with political philosophy, such as questions like, what are the rights of religious minorities within a secular state? Or (equally important!), what are the rights of atheists within a religious state? Should Muslim women be able to wear hoods covering their faces in court – even when they give evidence? In a Muslim state is it reasonable to punish people with different values for drinking alcohol in their homes? Or consider the many diverse opinions relating to death. Here, political debate is equally racked by the question of whether capital punishment (the death penalty) is ever justified as it is by arguments about whether states should provide facilities to help people who want to kill themselves.

However, treating hot issues in current affairs as political philosophy misses what's most important about the topic. Here is one form of philosophy that really 'does the business', that really does try – as Marx insisted philosophers should always be trying – to change the world.

So in this chapter I leave the applied ethics discussions and the technical debates about the rules and institutions of government to their own textbooks, and instead taste a bit of the rich and rather glamorous writings of the great political philosophers, setting out their theories of human society.

Meeting the Great Political Philosophers

People like Plato, Hegel, Marx and Engels, Confucius and Mao Tse Tung were enthusiastic *authoritarians*, which means they put forward political systems based on an all-knowing, powerful authority. Then you have the *pragmatists*. These are both philosophers such as Machiavelli, Hobbes and Jeremy Bentham, who argue that the end justifies the means (a form of *pragmatism*) and those who trust to human nature to see that everything works out eventually, such as Jean Jacques Rousseau, John Locke and Bentham's own protégé, John Stuart Mill.

Jeremy Bentham and John Stuart Mill created the politics of liberalism. *Liberals* are people who have certain principles, the most important of which is a commitment to protecting individual liberty. And indeed, looking at the great political philosophies of history also brings in many of those issues from social life – requiring views about citizens' rights and liberties, equality, welfare and economics, and questions about the origins of the ruler's authority and the limits of the state's power; about civil disobedience, workers' rights and revolutionary change; and about voting systems and democracy.

Choosing Between Authority and Anarchy: Plato

Plato, indisputably the most famous of all the Ancient Greek philosophers, actually started off as a member of a highly distinguished family and always had both the means and the inclination to be a member of the governing elite. His perspective on politics is both elitist and authoritarian – he thinks that people need to be organised by an expert – an authority. His message is as relevant today as it has ever been (and as problematic). As Honore de Balzac (the French playwright living in the years following the French revolution) wrote:

> *Liberty begets anarchy, anarchy leads to despotism, and despotism brings about liberty once again. Millions of human beings have perished without being able to make any of these systems triumph.*

In Plato's lifetime (427– 348 BCE) the Greek citizens (men only! no slaves!) lived in relatively small communities called *city-states*. These were small enough for every citizen to have a direct say in the way things were run – to publicly debate and then vote on big decisions like whether to wage war again on the Spartans, as well as on little decisions like how much wine to provide at the stadium, or whether to sentence poor old Socrates to death! Where citizens had this role, it was called a *democracy*.

Plato had a very dim view of such arrangements – long before his fellow Athenian citizens voted to execute his boss, Socrates, for spreading subversive ideas. As far as Plato was concerned, democracy was just a form of *anarchy* – the absence of rules. And he spent much of his life trying to promote a very different political philosophy characterised by lots of rules.

Needed: A few good Thatchers

That Plato never did govern – having to content himself with saying how he would run things in his blueprint for society, the one that we now call Plato's *Republic* – was due, he complained, to the impossibility of finding others to join with him and share the burden of government. In this he was perhaps a bit like Margaret Thatcher, the first woman prime minister in Britain in the 1980s, who's said to have once remarked that she needed just six men, good and true, to govern the United Kingdom, but that she could never find them all at the same time. Anyway, because Plato found the lack of good people to be the critical factor, he decided that education was the key to society. Rulers in particular, he thought, needed special training if there were ever to be enough of them (six at least!) starting at age zero and 'graduating' only 35 years later.

Not that Plato found himself without plenty of good advisers. In addition to Socrates himself, many other philosophers (or at least their ideas) were around to guide Plato in the design of his republic. There was Parmenides' (one of his Ancient Greek predecessors) earlier advice that 'truth must be eternal and unchanging', and Heraclitus's enigmatic observation (said after standing in a river) that 'all is flux'. Both of these views had helped create a tradition in Ancient Greece in which people saw the earthly, visible world as being illusory and impermanent, and the world of the intellect and truth as much better, being eternal and timeless. For Plato, it followed that he needed to design the ideal state not to adapt and evolve, but rather to have a fixed and unalterable structure, standing aloof (perhaps like Heraclitus in that river) from all the change and flux.

The ideas of Pythagoras had also made a strong impression on Plato. For example, at a time when such opinions were rare, Pythagoras (see Chapter 2) had made it the rule for members of his sect to treat men and women as equals, to hold property in common, and to live and dine communally. All of this reappears in Plato's *Republic* as the recommended lifestyle for the rulers of his society too, who Plato calls reassuringly 'the guardians'. And other Pythagorean flourishes exist too: Plato's guardians operate as a separate and higher class, taking their decisions in secret (public opinion neither sought nor required). After all, for Pythagoras's followers, the first rule was silence. 'He, Pythagoras, says it' was the only thing they needed to know in their search for wisdom. Similarly, the citizens of Plato's ideal state weren't to participate in important decisions, because Plato thought that the only concerns of the masses are practical things. The world of knowledge is best left for the rulers – the philosopher-guardians – to explore alone.

Plato's search for the just society

Plato's politics are based on the philosophical and ethical question, 'What should I do?' It was Plato's concern at what he saw as the deterioration of morals in Greek society that inspired his most famous book, the *Republic*, and drove his conviction that there can be no escape from injustice and the many ills of society until it's guided by those who have come to a knowledge of the 'good'.

The *Republic*, then, is a serious bid to sketch out the ideal society. Its main recommendation, not helped by coming from a philosopher, is that philosophers should be in charge of governments. Other city-states had already tried the rule of philosophers, and it was common practice to employ a sage to draw up laws.

The *Republic* makes the link, strange to modern eyes, of justice in the way large things, like cities or whole countries, operate. Justice is an ideal for individuals in deciding how to live their lives. Nevertheless, for Plato political philosophy is just another form of practical ethics. It's because Plato believes it's easier to see justice at work in the larger organism that he recommends looking at the ordering of society to find the answer to the related question of how to live as an individual. He says:

> We think of justice as a quality that may exist in a whole community as well as in an individual, and the community is the bigger of the two. Possibly, then, we may find justice there in larger proportions, easier to make out . . .

Entering Plato's Republic

Plato suggests that communities, like the city-states of Greece in his time or for whole countries later on, come into existence for practical,, economic reasons. This is because no individual is self-sufficient, and everyone has many needs – for food and shelter, for heat and tools, for roads and paths, and for protection from attack – and so it just makes sense for people to live in groups, able to call on one another's help. When people come together to live in one place, helping and supporting each other, Plato says you call that settlement a state. The starting point, then, of Plato's political philosophy is in the free exchange of goods and services between people. It's here in economic need and self-interest (as the Marxists later echoed 2,000 years later in an 'insight' that wasn't as radical as they claimed!) that you find the origin of society. Plato's *Republic* states:

> *Let us build our imaginary state from the beginning. Apparently, it will owe its existence to our needs, the first and greatest need being the provision of food to keep us alive. Next we shall want a house; and thirdly, such things as clothing.*

So if economics is the starting point for society, how else can the state help supply the things people want?

Plato suggests that it's through the division of labour – when you divide jobs out and people can concentrate on just what they're good at – that communities flourish. He says, 'We shall need at least one man to be a farmer, another a builder, and a third a weaver.' In fact, as Socrates and his audience then apparently realise in Plato's account, at least two more will be useful: namely a shoemaker and someone to provide for personal wants, the like of which he doesn't specify.

This 'minimum state' works best when each member of it is making only the things for which he or she is best suited (Plato is very egalitarian, giving women the same employment opportunities as men because, after all, the only important part of human beings is the soul, and that's neither male nor female). And that means specialisation. He says, 'The work goes easier and is better done when everyone is set free from all other occupations to do, at the right time, the one thing for which they are naturally fitted.'

In Plato's version at least, Socrates even suggests a middle class of sorts, composed of shopkeepers and bankers, managing and selling goods. This is easy to arrange because, as his companion puts it, perhaps rather unkindly: 'In well-ordered communities there are generally men not strong enough to be of use in any other occupation.'

Plato thinks that his republic will be a very happy place, unless people are greedy. After all, as Plato sums it up in another dialogue, the *Phaedo*, 'All wars are made for the sake of getting money.' Alas, he suspects most people are greedy. He gives as an example of this people wanting to eat meat instead of being content with nuts and beans (and even hints at how over-consumption can lead to environmental destruction).

Plato's disdain for 'money grubbing' and the pursuit of material things meant not only the abolition of private property for the guardians (the ruling class) but also included a general strategy for severing parental bonds with their children, as a way to reduce that perennial problem in political society of people favouring their own children. Plato says instead everyone should rear offspring collectively, using the guiding principles of eugenics (that is, breeding by selecting the best specimens) to sort the good from the not-so-promising. By destroying family ties, Plato believes it would be possible to create a more united governing class, and avoid the dangers either of rivalry between the rulers or the emergence of a governing elite. (This kind of society is what the Greeks called an *oligarchy*.)

Naturally, Plato's sure that education is too important to let parents have any say, and says the state should train and bring up all children. Plato promises that this will not be a threatening process, let alone state indoctrination, because the child is supposed to be active, not passive, in the learning process. The teacher will only try to show the 'source of the light' and he advises: 'Don't use compulsion, but let your children's lessons take the appearance of play.' (Alas, Plato's educational tips haven't generally been remembered.)

Approaching anarchism

The word *anarchism* comes from the Greek *anarkhos*, for 'without a ruler'. At its heart is the rejection of all authority. And if anarchism is constructive in intention, it must still always start with a destructive phase, and hence may be crushed before it can proceed beyond that stage. Although anarchists have often been welcome in revolutions (like the 20th-century Russian one) during this destructive stage that displaces the existing political system, when construction is required the anarchists invariably become the enemy too. Hey, guys, that's what happens when no one's in charge!

Plato disliked democracy, which he called a form of anarchy. However, anarchists themselves despise democracy, seeing it as enslavement by the majority – voting is the act of betrayal, both symbolically and practically. 'Universal suffrage is the counter-revolution,' declared the 19th-century French radical, Pierre-Joseph Proudhon in one of his less catchy rallying cries. ('Property is theft' was perhaps the most famous, adopted by Marxism, but 'God is evil' had its followers too.) As William Godwin put it more powerfully, 'There is but one power to which I can yield a heartfelt obedience, the decision of my own understanding, the dictate of my own conscience.'

Anarchists dislike totalitarianism, and certainly disliked Hitler, who himself disliked both anarchists and democrats. Actually, he didn't just dislike them, he persecuted (and in many cases killed) members of those political groups along with communists and non-political groups like Jews, gypsies and homosexuals.

You can identify class struggle (or *socialist*) anarchism through certain criteria that many contemporary anarchist groups use. They're usually vegans, they wear black clothes and they don't pay any rent. Those are the practical criteria, if you like. The theoretical criteria are more complicated:

- A complete rejection of capitalism and the market economy, which anarchists see as creating hierarchies and thus interfering in individual freedom.

- A concern for the interests and freedoms of others, based on a perception that individuals are all essentially of equal worth and personal identities aren't fixed but instead imposed by social forces.

- The great rallying point: the rejection of state power and all other 'top-down' forces.

- Methods used have to be compatible with the ends sought.

It's the final feature that sets class struggle anarchism apart from many other socialist movements that are based on the necessity of adopting unpleasant methods in order to achieve later a better society. One prominent anarchist thinker, James Guillaume, a colleague of the Russian revolutionary, Michael Bakunin, considered this to be the defining distinction between anarchism and Marxism. 'How could one want an equalitarian and free society to issue from an authoritarian organisation? It is impossible.'

Anarchism is a very old political story, albeit not a very influential one. However, since the collapse of the Berlin Wall and the end of the Soviet Union, anarchism has had a greater impact, both in radical environmental campaigns and among sections of the anti-capitalist, anti-globalisation movement.

Anyway, Plato hopes that if people follow all his instructions, the new state, his republic, will have all the important virtues. It will be

- ✔ Wise – in the manner of its ruling.

- ✔ Courageous – in the manner of its defending.

- ✔ Temperate (calm) – in the contented acceptance of all with their society and system of government.

Wisdom, as you might guess, is provided courtesy of the philosopher-guardians themselves. Plato briskly skips over courage in his account, but presumably a new, specialist, professional army provides this. Finally, temperance is a more subtle virtue, but Plato explains this is provided by ensuring that a balance exists between the various parts of the state – the governing part or rulers, the administering part or executive, and the productive part or the working classes. This idea of balancing power is a very important one in political theory.

How good a theory of politics is Plato's? Some critics have drawn parallels between Plato's political approach and that which in modern times was applied in the Soviet Union. They say that the communist system was 'neo-Platonism' in the key respects that in the USSR there was a governing elite – the Communist party – a huge military and an all-pervading state apparatus controlling all aspects of citizens' lives. What's more, the Soviet Union paid rigorous attention to education and moral influences; equality of the sexes; weakening of family ties; and, last but not least, a general disapproval of private property and wealth. The only problem was, the masses didn't like it. They wanted all the naughty things, all the practical goodies, more than they wanted to be virtuous.

But you see a worse problem with Plato's theory in recent societies where people did get enthusiastic for their leader's plans – as they did in Germany under the Nazis (see the later section 'Fearing Hitler and the Bewitching Effects of Propaganda'.

Saluting Hegel and Totalitarianism

Plato was bigger on ideas than action, and his *Republic* probably wouldn't have caused so much trouble if it had remained just a philosophical essay. The trouble is, his ideas weren't only adopted but also adapted later by others. And if lots more people have heard of Plato's political theory than know about Professor G.W.F Hegel's follow-up one, that doesn't mean Hegel

(1770–1831) isn't in fact every bit as influential. Maybe more! His theorising in Germany inspired Karl Marx's (see the later section 'Marching for Marxism') revolutionary theory called *historical materialism* as well as the ideology that led to the rise of the Fascist parties of Italy, Spain and Germany in Europe in the first half of the 20th century.

Georg Wilhelm Friedrich Hegel's writing is notorious for being hard work. His first and most celebrated major work is the *Phenomenology of Spirit* (by which he means *mind*) and is full of jargon and obscure Greek references. His philosophical contemporary Arthur Schopenhauer sneered at the work and called it jargon-ridden 'pseudo-philosophy'.

But despite that, buried in Hegel's garbled prose is the use of an ancient technique that's now associated with him and called *the dialectic*. Hegel introduces this as a system for understanding the history of the world itself. His idea is that history is a series of revolutionary moments arising inevitably out of the contradictions or (to put it rather blandly) unsatisfactory aspects of the previous system.

A bloody battle

For Hegel, the origin of society is in the first conflict between two humans, what he calls a 'bloody battle' with each seeking to make the other recognise him as master and accept the role of slave. In Hegelianism (another off-putting 'ism'; see Chapter 7!) it's the fear of death that drives society. Fear of death originally forces part of mankind to submit to the other, and society is for ever afterwards divided into the two classes: slaves and masters.

Nor is it merely practical rivalry and material need that propels one class to oppress the other – it's a conflict born solely of the peculiarly human lust for power over one another. What was the French Revolution (which took place during Hegel's student days) all about? It was simply the slaves revolting, Hegel says. And unlike, say, Thomas Hobbes over in England a century or so earlier, who rather disapproved of revolutions, Hegel approves of the protests. He sees in them the 'desire for recognition'. Being revolutionary risks death, but that, says Hegel, is the way towards freedom.

On the other hand, if people can achieve freedom from human oppressors, Hegel takes all the forces competing in a society – competing for wealth, for power, for justice – and makes them all obey the collective will, which he calls the *geist* (spirit). In Hegel's philosophy, this invisible thing has complete power and authority. Totalitarianism is about giving one person, or one group, total power. Advocating that as both desirable and inevitable is, essentially, what makes Hegel the founding father of the two totalitarian doctrines fascism and communism. Hegel writes:

> *The history of the world is the discipline of the uncontrolled natural will, bringing it into obedience to a universal principle and conferring subjective freedom . . .*

The Absolute

Hegel calls reality the Absolute. The Absolute is also rather like God (a rather austere kind of God, not big on forgiveness or Christmas presents). And it's definitely German, as Hegel goes on to say:

> *The German Spirit is the spirit of the new world. Its aim is the realisation of absolute truth as the unlimited self-determination of freedom – that freedom which has its own absolute form as its purpose.*

Perhaps paradoxically, given that the Absolute is supposed to be everything, Hegel opposes all forms of world government, explaining in the *Philosophy of Right* (the book that contains Hegel's version of the march of world history as it progresses from the Oriental via the Greek and the Roman to arrive ultimately at the 'Germanic) that war is crucial:

> *Just as the blowing of the winds preserves the sea from the foulness which would be the result of a prolonged calm, so also corruption in nations would be the product of prolonged, let alone 'perpetual' peace.*

Hegel's enthusiasm for conflict and war found support among both Karl Marx and the communists – and the fascists, including Adolf Hitler. Marx, although, like Hegel, a German, had no time for Hegel's theory about the German spirit and opposed nationalism. But Hitler (who in fact was Austrian!) enthusiastically took up Hegel's claim that the German people had a special and superior role to play in the world.

Fearing Hitler and the Bewitching Effects of Propaganda

These days people don't often discuss national socialism, or Nazism as it's known. But they ought to.

If you think of Nazism as a discredited doctrine, here's a peculiar thing. The principles of national socialism live on in many of the world's governing circles today. Patriotism, military strength, building a strong nation, suspicion and dislike of 'the other', loathing of communism, manipulation of public opinion, ruthless indifference to the effects of foreign policy – all of these are common currency in societies all over the world.

If today few countries (since the collapse of apartheid in South Africa) formally prefer one racial group over all the others, it's commonplace that countries project their national interest at the expense of everyone else. But alternative approaches do exist and people may need to return to these – particularly in the increasingly urgent politics of environmental and ecological protection.

The political pulling power of the fascist ideology

Fascist is a much-used term – and a much-abused one. The original fascists were Italian, and the political theory was presented like the Marxist one in a kind of manifesto, the *Dottrina del Facismo*, by the Italian philosopher Giovanni Gentile and the politician Benito Mussolini. Gentile, an academic like Hegel, carries the label of being a neo-Heglian (having a philosophical theory based on Hegel's), as do, from their contrary stance, Marx and Engels. Both fascism and Marxism adopt the idea of Hegel's that individual self-consciousness is best embodied in the state. Put another way, your purpose in life is to make your country great! And indeed, both manifestos led to the sufferings of millions of ordinary and extra-ordinary people.

Fascism, then, although widely bandied about as a term for any regime that people disapprove of, is more correctly identified as the ideology of the Italian fascists in the first half of the 20th century under Benito Mussolini. It's not simply a right-wing philosophy. Actually, Mussolini started his career as a socialist, keen on workers' rights. Add to which, Professor Gentile gave fascism an idealistic and spiritual aspect, arguing that where liberalism and socialism sought to benefit each individual, fascism sought to benefit the nation – and everyone!

The well-being of the nation provided a fine purpose for each individual, a purpose that took precedence over the greedy squabbles of workers and unions on the one hand, and capitalists and libertarians on the other. This kind of individualism served only to divide the nation and weaken it, the original fascists felt, so instead of trade unions and private enterprise they proposed a single, unifying force, capable of ensuring companies and workers alike worked in the interests of the state. This force was the Fascist party, united behind a charismatic leader.

Hitler – whose Nazi party, remember, was formerly called the National Socialist party – much admired the Italian fascists and adopted three of their main aims:

- Destruction of trade unions as protectors of the whole class of workers.

- Devotion of the nation's resources to the development of military power as an instrument of national policy and measure of national pride.

- Centralisation of power in one central government headed by a supposedly charismatic figure.

What was original to Nazism (if you want to use that term) was the effort to weed out all the weak elements among the people making up the state. In particular, Hitler was obsessed by ideas of racial purity. By contrast, the Italian fascists were originally anti-racist because they considered racism to divide the nation (which it does).

The fascist philosophy – Hitler, the Nazis and the Italian and Japanese Fascist parties too – was eventually only stopped with the sacrifice of many millions of lives, and so people assume that the political programme must also have ended there. But if even though racism is discredited, those three key fascist ideas have become the modern political consensus. Western democracies are essentially *fascist* states!

Most bizarrely of all, European countries and the United States have followed Hitler's strategy, which he formally proposed to the Allies during the War as a way of solving 'the Jewish problem', of moving the Jewish people out of Europe to a separate state – supposedly to make up to the Jews for the Holocaust and evidently not doing enough to stop Hitler. Yet the tragedy of the founding of a Jewish state anywhere, let alone in Palestine, is that it has – by definition – had to be built upon racial and religious discrimination.

Remember, just because Hitler supported a policy doesn't make it necessarily wrong. He was (for example) a vegetarian. But it ought to make you pause to think carefully . . .

Mein Kampf

Many subtle legacies of the Nazi philosophy abound in today's societies:

- ✔ The elevation of propaganda as a way of manipulating opinion and controlling the population.
- ✔ The calculated use of rites and the creation of traditions to create a charismatic aura around the leader of the government.
- ✔ Centralised government control of education.
- ✔ Creation of an all-powerful police and secretive security apparatus.

All that's left to bridge the contradiction between supposedly defeating Nazism in the war but adopting key ideas from it later are frequent government pronouncements on their dedication to the causes of liberty, democracy and freedom. But *Mein Kampf,* Hitler's own account of his political 'awakening' and 'struggle' to build up the Nazi party, too, is full to the brim of these great words, along with pious references to serving the will of the people or, even more ludicrously, the Lord, and is decorated with paeans to beauty, nobility and goodness.

Mein Kampf is such an obnoxious document, that perhaps the most remarkable thing about it is that people were prepared to support Hitler, the Nazi party and their programme. This surely says something profound if unwelcome about human nature. Hitler had considerable support among the general population, particularly women. Historians often neglect this last factor. Women had only gained the right to vote, along with guarantees of equality, in Germany's 'democratic revolution' of 1918. Their support handed Hitler, who declared that women were inferior human beings and certainly not fit to take political decisions, victory at the polls in 1932. Did they choose authority over anarchy?

Anyway, that was the voters' decision. But votes do go the way powerful individuals and groups want. And in 1930s Europe, not just Germany, the reality was that the establishment – the old elites and the bosses of the centre-right parties (even British Prime Minister Lloyd George) – had sided with the Nazis, despite some misgivings about the Nazi Party's violence, radicalism and even its *plebeian* (working-class) character.

In fact, the democratic parties in Germany in the 1930s were prepared to tolerate Hitler's violent coup attempt, which only failed due to the loyalty of those state bodies nowadays associated with Nazism and fascism – the army and the police – to the official government.

Unlike *Das Kapital* (Marx's long rambling account of economics), to which Hitler compares his work, *Mein Kampf* (which translates as 'My Struggle') is surprisingly readable. It opens with an engaging, even amusing, account of Hitler's arrival in Vienna, the grand capital of Austria, from the small school in the provinces, 'after two weeks' trip to Vienna', which he took aged 15.

> *The purpose of my trip was to study the picture gallery in the Court Museum, but I had eyes for scarcely anything but the Museum itself. From morning until late at night, I ran from one object of interest to another, but it was always the buildings which held my primary interest. For hours I could stand in front of the Opera, for hours I could gaze at the Parliament; the whole Ring Boulevard seemed to me like an enchantment out of the 'Thousand and One Nights'.*

This is the personable, the charming Mr Hitler that so impressed Western statesmen. Hitler is a leader who knows how to tell little personal stories. However, Hitler doesn't wish only to please.

Nazism

Nazism is a philosophy with only one plank – prejudice. It was successful because racial prejudice – however outrageous, however irrational – is never very deeply buried in the human psyche. Hitler launched his early tirades, as he would his later wars, against many other categories of 'inferior humans' too: the Slavs who'd taken the land that rightly belonged to the German people (of whom many tens of millions would perish); the 'negroes' he accuses of having begun to threaten Europe's bloodlines via France (he plays two race cards at once!); and the 'yellow races', such as the Japanese. If, a few years later, Hitler would rely on the Japanese alliance for his strategy of war, in *Mein Kampf* he calls such a tactic 'almost unpardonable' on account of his racial theories. Indeed, he even says Germans should avoid his future allies, the Italians – Hitler refers to their blood as 'hopelessly adulterated', especially in the south. Hitler explains the significance to the German public with a crude parody of Darwin's (then rather new) evolutionary theory:

> *Any crossing of two beings not at exactly the same level produces a medium between the level of the two parents. This means: the offspring will probably stand higher than the racially lower parent, but not as high as the higher one. Consequently, it will later succumb in the struggle against the higher level. Such mating is contrary to the will of Nature for a higher breeding of all life. The precondition for this does not lie in associating superior and inferior, but in the total victory of the former. The stronger must dominate and not blend with the weaker, thus sacrificing his own greatness.*

Even though Hitler's *super race* excludes most people, even most German people, this sort of philosophy was attractive to many in his audience. If that seems strange, it's only like the well-noted paradox today whereby you can advocate the channelling of wealth towards a privileged few and the working class majority will applaud enthusiastically even though they'll gain nothing and indeed may have to pay, yet they prefer to imagine themselves as one of the elite.

Certainly, the rewards Hitler dangled before the public for supporting his Nazi programme were rather meagre. Hitler is contemptuous towards 'the Germans' and regularly criticises them for their supposed weakness and failings. He warns the 'imperfect' ones that they won't even be allowed to have children, only to undertake military service and expect to die for their country. And in the meantime, of course, they must work harder.

Was it the scolding that was the secret of the success of Nazism, as evidenced by the rapid growth of the movement? Or was it, rather, the careful application of the power of hate? The Nazis offered a chance to hate the enemy within society – a dreadful enemy that was, they said, the cause of poverty, strife and sickness; the enemy that Hitler calls *social democracy*. The enemy consists of the 'reds', the trade unionists, the pornographers, the handicapped, the deviant artists and so on. It was such a long and confusing list of enemies that it's no wonder Hitler invented a simple version. All of the bad things in German society, indeed in the world, were the fault of what he called *the Jews*.

Manipulating public opinion with propaganda

In *Mein Kampf*, Hitler admits that when he started, back in 1918, 'there was nothing like an organised anti-Semitic feeling', adding:

> *I can still remember the difficulties we encountered the moment we mentioned the Jew. We were either confronted with dumbstruck faces or else a lively and hefty antagonism. The efforts we made at the time to point out the real enemy to the public seemed to be doomed to failure.*

Only very slowly did 'a kind of anti-Semitism' begin to 'slowly take root', he explains in his book, very proudly. Crucial to this, he thinks, was his theory that 'all great cultures of the past perished only because the originally creative race died out from blood poisoning'. War follows logically on from this theory:

> *Nature knows no political boundaries. First, she puts living creatures on this globe and watches the free play of forces. She then confers the master's right on her favourite child, the strongest in courage and industry.*

Like Nietzsche and Hegel (see the earlier section 'Saluting Hegel and Totalitarianism'), Hitler promises the Germans that a better world can be achieved through future conflicts.

Hitler's alternative theory of the state follows soon after. He rejects the conventional philosophical view that the state is primarily an economic institution that can be governed according to economic requirements, saying firmly that 'the state has nothing at all to do with any definite economic conception or development'. Instead, a mysterious higher purpose exists: 'the achievement of the aim which has been allotted to this species by Providence'. This is what Hegel had said too.

Hitler's big idea, however, is less mysterious than Hegel's. Hitler takes up Plato's notion of breeding better people. He explains nastily that in his 'ideal state' contraception will be made legal, and 'procreation impossible for syphilitics and those who suffer from tuberculosis or other hereditary diseases, also cripples and imbeciles'. Indeed, he rules out children for most of the citizens under one or other prejudice.

Of course, some people may not like being told they're unfit to have children. Yet Hitler is optimistic. Why shouldn't it be possible to induce people to make this sacrifice, he chunters gaily, if, instead of such a precept, 'they were simply told that they ought to put an end to this truly original sin of racial corruption which is steadily being passed on from one generation to another'? Alas, Hitler complains, some won't understand these things:

> *They will ridicule them or shrug their round shoulders and groan out their everlasting excuses: 'Of course it is a fine thing, but the pity is that it cannot be carried out.'*

Mein Kampf includes lengthy descriptions of practical policies for the new state, notably eugenics, indoctrination and propaganda. The book says that first of all, the cleansing of culture in general must be extended to all fields.

> *Theatre, art, literature, cinema, press, posters, and window displays must be cleansed of all manifestations of our rotting world and placed in the service of a moral, political, and cultural idea. Public life must be freed from the stifling perfume of our modern eroticism, just as it must be freed from all unmanly, prudish hypocrisy. In all these things the goal and the road must be determined by concern for the preservation of the health of our people in body and soul. The right of personal freedom recedes before the duty to preserve the race.*

And it's here, in the area of manipulating public opinion, that *Mein Kampf* becomes a distinctive if rather poisonous contribution to political theory. Despite having just criticised collective, social endeavours, Hitler promptly then recognises their power:

> *Mass demonstrations on the grand scale not only reinforce the will of the individual but they draw him still closer to the movement and help to create an esprit de corps. . . And only a mass demonstration can impress upon him the greatness of this community . . . if, while still seeking his way, he is gripped by the force of mass-suggestion which comes from the excitement and enthusiasm of three or four thousand other men in whose midst he finds himself; if the manifest success and the consensus of thousands confirm the truth and justice of the new teaching and for the first time raise doubt in his mind as to the truth of the opinions held by himself up to now – then he submits himself to the fascination of what we call mass-suggestion. The will, the yearning and indeed the strength of thousands of people are in each individual. A man who enters such a meeting in doubt and hesitation leaves it inwardly fortified; he has become a member of a community.*

This is Hitler's forte: propaganda and mass-suggestion. He says that:

> *The art of propaganda lies in understanding the emotional ideas of the great masses and finding, through a psychologically correct form, the way to the attention and thence to the heart of the broad masses.*

Mind you, he warns that the 'receptivity of the great masses is very limited, their intelligence is small, but their power of forgetting is enormous'. In consequence of this:

> *. . . all effective propaganda must be limited to a very few points and must harp on these in slogans until the last member of the public understands what you want him to understand by your slogan.*

Ever wondered why politicians are so dogmatic, and just repeat one point all the time? Hitler has the answer:

As soon as you sacrifice this slogan and try to be many-sided, the effect will piddle away, for the crowd can neither digest nor retain the material offered. In this way the result is weakened and in the end entirely cancelled out.

Basically, because the masses are 'slow-moving', they always require a certain amount of time before they're ready even to notice a thing, 'and only after the simplest ideas are repeated thousands of times will the masses finally remember them'.

It's no coincidence that, instead of facts, *Mein Kampf* is made up of pages upon irrelevant pages dealing with Hitler's early years, views on clothing, descriptions of the appearance of Jews and so on. This is because *Mein Kampf* is a new kind of political philosophy – it's a work not of rational argument but of irrational or emotive appeals, of propaganda.

Everyone (except maybe the British National Party) knows where Hitler's propaganda ends: in the neat, white tiled shower-rooms of the death-camps. No government since has applied that technique to dealing with unwanted populations. Even so, genocides and mass-killings have punctuated the 20th century, and look set to continue in the 21st. And in part this is because, in another sense, Hitler's experiment continues today as governments adopt the methods and tactics that the Nazis so successfully used to consolidate their power in the early 20th century.

Hitler, propaganda and the lowest common denominator

Hitler's political manifesto, *Mein Kampf,* offers many tips on how governments can manipulate public opinion.

Propaganda is not and cannot be the necessity in itself, since its function, like the poster, consists in attracting the attention of the crowd, and not in educating those who are already educated or who are striving after education and knowledge, its effect for the most part must be aimed at the emotions and only to a very limited degree at the so-called intellect . . .

All propaganda must be popular and its intellectual level must be adjusted to the most limited intelligence among those it is addressed to. Consequently, the greater the mass it is intended to reach, the lower its purely intellectual level will have to be.

Hitler says he learnt the black arts of propaganda from the English. 'Here, too, the example of enemy war propaganda was typical; limited to a few points, devised exclusively for the masses, carried on with indefatigable persistence.'

The official British view of Hitler

In the 1930s, right up to the outbreak of war, the British government wasn't unduly concerned that in *Mein Kampf* Hitler had suggested killing ethnic minorities, 'reds' and the handicapped. Quite the opposite, in fact. In the *Daily Express* (London) on 17 September 1936 Lloyd George, who Hitler praises in his book for being a great propagandist, is quoted as saying:

There is for the first time since the war a general sense of security. The people are more cheerful. There is a greater sense of general gaiety of spirit throughout the land. It is a happier Germany. I have never met a happier people than the Germans and Hitler is one of the greatest men.

Marching for Marxism

The *Communist Manifesto*, written by Karl Marx and Friedrich Engels in 1847 and published a year later, opens with the famous promise:

> *Let the ruling classes tremble at a communistic revolution. The proletarians have nothing to lose but their chains. They have a world to win!*

Alas, of course, real life is never so simple, as many failed communist societies could testify, not to mention failed anti-communist dictatorships. But for a century at least, from the middle of the 19th century up until the fall of the Berlin Wall in 1989 it certainly seemed as though the grand predictions of Marx and Engels were right and the world really was involved in a straight fight between the workers' forces on one side (calling for common ownership of the means of production), and an increasingly beleaguered and unpopular elite clinging to private ownership – *their* ownership, of course.

So what's Marxism all about? Karl Marx (1818–1883) and Friedrich Engels (1820–1895) wrote a great deal, of a largely rather turgid quasi-economic variety. You have the three voluminous parts of *Das Kapital*, but also the *Critique of Hegel's Philosophy of Right*, in which Marx and Engels declare that religion is 'the opium of the people', and the *Theses on Feuerbach* where they observe that 'philosophers have only interpreted the world in various ways – the point is to change it'. But for the workers of the world, Marxism is essentially encapsulated in just one document – the short and colourful manifesto for the embryonic Communist party. This was originally written in German, printed in London and finally speedily translated into French in order to inspire the workers' uprising in Paris of June 1848.

The Communist Manifesto

The year the *Communist Manifesto* was published was the 'Year of Revolutions' in Europe. Protests rocked not only Paris, but also in Rome, Berlin, Vienna, Prague and Budapest. The Paris Insurrection itself started as a street protest against royal interference in civil government inflamed by resentment at the perceived betrayal of the principles of France's first, 1789, revolution. The earlier revolution, the crowds knew only too well, had promised them not only liberty and fraternity (comradeship) but equality as well. The last part of the deal had never been delivered; hence the riots. Troops fired on the crowds, the government fell in the scandal following and a new government came in – which promptly cracked down on the protesters even more harshly than the first one had done.

The other revolutions of that year also fizzled out in failure for the working class, beaten back by the bourgeoisie (the upper-middle class, if you like; educated types who own things like factories and farms), much to Marx's and Engels' frustration. Nevertheless, this was the revolutionary backdrop to the *Communist Manifesto* – a chaotic time in which there seemed to be a new class of worker, facing a new type of exploitation. These workers had already the choice of another new political movement – socialism. Nowadays people use the terms *communism* and *socialism* as if they mean the same thing. Literally, communism is a political system where as much as possible is owned 'in common', and socialism is a system of social organisation in which property and the distribution of income are subject to social control, which pretty much merge together. One 'ism' would do! But back then neither Marx nor Engels ever had much time for socialism, which they considered a middle-class concern, respectable to the ruling classes and bourgeoisie where any decent doctrine should have been intolerably dangerous and subversive. Communism, they felt, was much better: the unacceptable face of working class power, presenting a totally alien face to the capitalist class.

The fundamental proposition of the *Communist Manifesto* is that in every historical epoch the prevailing 'mode of economic production and exchange' and 'the social organisation necessarily following from it' determine the political structures of society, along with the intellectual beliefs and ideas. That is, economics determine social life, and that decides political positions. In one of the *Manifesto*'s more memorable phrases, Marx and Engels argue that it therefore follows that 'the whole history of mankind has been a history of *class struggles*, contests between exploited and exploiting, ruling and oppressed . . .' This idea, as Engels ambitiously puts it in the preface to the English version of the *Manifesto*, is comparable to Darwin's theory of evolution. Marxism is the theory of the evolution of societies. It's as impersonal and its conclusions as inevitable as Darwin's biological model of the development of species.

In the 1850s, the *Manifesto* describes society as a whole already increasingly 'splitting up into two great hostile camps, into two great classes directly facing each other: *bourgeoisie* and *proletariat*'. The bourgeoisie (the upper-middle class, if you like, anyway, educated types who own things like factories and shops and, as opposed to the people who work in them for a wage, who are the proletariat) has established itself as the supreme power in the modern state, running the government, turning it into 'but a committee for managing the affairs of the whole bourgeoisie'. The *Manifesto* says:

> *The bourgeoisie, wherever it has got the upper hand, has put an end to all feudal, patriarchal, idyllic relations. It has pitilessly torn asunder the motley feudal ties that bound man to his 'natural superiors', and has left remaining no other nexus between man and man than naked self-interest, than callous 'cash-payment'. It has drowned the most heavenly ecstasies of religious fervour, of chivalrous enthusiasm, of Philistine sentimentalism in the icy water of egotistical calculation. It has resolved personal worth into exchange value and, in place of the numberless indefeasible chartered freedoms, has set up that single, unconscionable freedom – free trade.*

'In one word', adds Marx ungrammatically (by my count it's five), 'for exploitation, veiled by religious and political illusions, it has substituted naked, shameless, direct, brutal exploitation'.

Under industrial society, the *Manifesto* continues, the workers have themselves become mere extra (human) appendages attached to machines, of whom only the most simple and monotonous activity is required. Add to which, Marx says, the 'lower strata' of the middle class, the shopkeepers and trades-people are sinking gradually into the proletariat, as the capitalists render their skills irrelevant by the might of their new methods of production.

In fact, the *Manifesto* says that industrial society not only creates but requires constant change, as opposed to the tranquillity of the feudal and other epochs. It warns, 'Constant revolutionising of production, uninterrupted disturbance of social conditions, everlasting uncertainty and agitation distinguish the bourgeois epoch . . .'

The trouble with capitalism

The Marxists see another problem with capitalism in that it relies upon exploiting ever-new markets, a claim the Scottish philosopher Adam Smith made earlier in his widely read analysis of the creation of wealth (*The Wealth of Nations*, published 1792; see Chapter 17). The Marxist prediction is that industries must obtain raw materials from ever more obscure and remote sources, and must persuade consumers of new and exotic needs, in the process creating a world market. The same logic applies in the intellectual sphere, with the rise of a 'world literature'. Legal systems, governments and methods of taxation must transcend any frontier. The 'most barbarian' nations have to be dragged into the impossible equation, and the cheap prices of commodities are the 'heavy artillery' with which the bourgeoisie forces the barbarians to capitulate. All nations, on pain of extinction, are compelled to adopt the capitalist mode of production. The *Manifesto* again:

> *Modern bourgeois society with its relations of production, of exchange, and of property, a society that has conjured up such gigantic means of production and of exchange, is like the sorcerer who is no longer able to control the powers of the nether world whom he has called up by his spells.*

The trouble for capitalism is that, by creating the proletariat, the bourgeoisie has already 'forged the weapons that bring death to itself'. Well, that's what Marx and Engels hoped it had done anyway. The nearby sidebar 'Marxist ideals' offers a few more of their aspirations.

Marxist ideals

Marx and Engels unveil their practical response to the problems of poverty and social injustice in 19th-century Europe in the *Communist Manifesto*. They present their manifesto as a series of short points, simple to remember:

- Abolition of land ownership and rents.

- A heavy progressive income tax.

- Abolition of all inheritance rights.

- Confiscation of the property of all those who no longer live in the state, or who rebel against the new government.

- Centralisation of all capital and credit in a state bank.

- Central state control and ownership of the means of communication and transportation.

- Increased state production through factories and farming; development of under-used land.

- 'Equal liability of all to labour'; new armies of workers, especially to work the land.

- Disappearance of the distinction between town and country: population distributed evenly over the country.

- Free education for all in state-run schools, preparing the children for work in the new industries.

That's the programme after the communists are in power. Before that, the *Manifesto* concludes, communists should support every 'revolutionary movement against the existing social and political order, bringing to the fore, as the main issue, the property question'.

Marxist economics: Predictions of doom

Marxism is an economic theory that predicts capitalism must fail, because capitalism is based on the ever-increasing exploitation of the workers by the owners of the means of production – land, factories and machines. As the conditions of the workers deteriorates, resentment increases against the bosses, and revolution is inevitable.

But as to the crucial, factual claim of increasing absolute poverty, Marxism has simply been wrong. Marx and Engels didn't perceive the almost inexhaustible ingenuity of the capitalist system in increasing production through technical progress, and generating within itself apparently unlimited financial resources, making possible high standards of living not only for the tiny minority of mill owners and the ever-expanding ranks of the petty bourgeoisie, but for the workers too.

Then again, there are those, such as the French former Marxist André Gorz, who've suggested in recent years that the truly oppressed class of modern capitalism isn't that of the workers any more, but of the 'unworkers' – the old, the unemployed and the very young (such as the street children of South America), who can't work and must rely on state handouts or charity (or crime) for their sustenance. But these people are very weak – they don't have the option of withdrawing their labour by going on strike – and thus can be ignored by governments, bourgeois or otherwise.

Marxism insists that capitalism inevitably lurches from periods of boom to periods of bust, and because it's by its very nature short-sighted, in the downturns unemployment can spark revolutions. And certainly, even bourgeois economists accept that capitalism has its cycles, with recurrent troughs and adjustments – in bad cases, economic depressions. But again, capitalism has proved itself able to add on socialist elements (welfare benefits, job creation programmes) to see it through these busts.

Marxism and human psychology

Marxism is also a theory of psychological and social relationships. It invokes a kind of *anomie* or alienation as a central feature of life in industrial society (to use the terms coined by the 19th century's new breed of social scientists; for more on this see Chapter 17). Marx and Engels therefore believe that the key to reforming social life, whether its problems are material or spiritual, is to abolish property . With no property, there can no longer be two classes. With no classes, conflict no longer exists.

The *Communist Manifesto* (like anarchism, the rival ideology at the time) requires of its adherents a great deal of blind faith. In this, it's more of a religious doctrine than a scientific theory. For this reason, it's not surprising that where the words of the *Manifesto* actually took root was among the preindustrial societies of Africa, China, South America and Russia – among the 'rural idiots', as Marx and Engels used to refer to people who worked on the land. Indeed, as the last years of the 20th century showed, the industrialisation of Russia and China that proceeded under communism actually brought about the collapse of the command economy (where goods and services and even prices were regulated by the government rather than market forces) and the return of capitalism.

Signing Up to the Social Contract

Aristotle thought that people, being rational, would be naturally inclined to organise themselves voluntarily in societies. Thomas Hobbes (1588–1679), writing nearly 2,000 years later, thought that people, being rational, wouldn't.

Hobbes considers that social life is only a mixture of selfishness, violence and fear, topped with a healthy dollop of deceit, the last there to make things work more smoothly. Hobbes calls this the 'State of Nature', a shocking phrase calculated to arouse the wrath of the Church that conflicted head-on with the rosy biblical image of Adam and Eve in the Garden of Eden before the Fall – that naughty episode in the Garden of Eden involving eating the forbidden fruit.

In the State of Nature, Hobbes writes, 'Life itself is but Motion, and can never be without Desire, nor without Fear, no more than without Sense.' In consequence:

> . . . there is no place for Industry; because the fruit thereof is uncertain: and consequently no Culture of the Earth; no Navigation, nor use of the commodities that may be imported by Sea; no commodious Building; no instruments of moving, and removing such things as require much force; no Knowledge of the face of the Earth; no account of Time; no Arts; no Letters; no Society; and which is worst of all, continual fear, and danger of violent death; And the life of man, solitary, poor, nasty, brutish, and short.

To those of his contemporaries who dispute this nature for humans, perhaps asking why God should create such a race, Hobbes challenges them to go to sleep with their doors and money chests unlocked. Anyway, he says, he's not accusing people's nature so much as their actions. 'The Desires, and other Passions of man, are in themselves no Sin.' This is because, in the:

> . . . war of every man against every other man, this also is consequent; that nothing can be Unjust. The notions of Right and Wrong, Justice and Injustice have there no place. Where there is no common Power, there is no Law: where no Law, no Injustice.

Notions of justice or fairness and rights are 'Qualities that relate to men in Society, not in Solitude'. Morality requires society. The solitary man isn't moral. Only through society can 'the solitary man' achieve any relief from fear, any peace and security: 'Fear of oppression, disposes a man to anticipate, or to seek aid by society: for there is no other way by which a man can secure his life and liberty.'

However, even if justice doesn't exist, the other laws of nature are real enough. The most fundamental of these laws is that every living thing struggles to survive. Because the best way of doing this is for there to be peace, and not war, the requirement is to seek peace.

Worrying about Hobbes' wicked world

Hobbes' view is that people are just machines, moved by what he terms appetites and aversions. Everyone seeks to fulfil their appetites, varying only in degree and particular taste. Hobbes says the 'human machine' is programmed to direct its energies selfishly. He doubts if it's ever possible for human beings to act altruistically, and even apparently benevolent action is actually self-serving, perhaps an attempt to make people feel good about themselves. Instead, for human beings, in the first place, he puts 'a general inclination of all mankind, a perpetual and restless desire of Power after power, that ceaseth only in Death'.

Hobbes says you can only stop people fighting each other to death by forcing them to behave; hence the social contract. Here is how he introduces the term:

> *Transferring the right to use force to the sovereign authority, by the people, 'the mutual transferring of Right' is 'that which men call Contract'.*

The only way, Hobbes continues, to do this, is to:

> *. . . confer all the power and strength upon one Man, or upon one assembly of men, that may reduce all their Wills, by plurality of voices, unto one Will . . . This is more than Consent, or Concord; it is a real Unity of them all, in one and the same Person, made by Covenant of every man with every man . . .*

And this new creation, the state (or, as Hobbes calls it, the Commonwealth) is 'that Great Leviathan' (which is one of those biblical terms for a giant sea monster) that only comes about after either one man 'by War subdueth his enemies to his will', or when 'men agree amongst themselves, to submit to some Man, or Assembly of men, voluntarily, on confidence to be protected by him against all others'.

Hobbes presents his ideas in a book which he calls *Leviathan* or *The Matter, Forme and Power of a Common Wealth Ecclesiasticall and Civil* (1651). Much of the *Leviathan* is legalistic in tone, as befits a theory based on constructing order out of anarchy. Crucially, even restrictions on the all-powerful sovereign exist. No man 'can be obliged by Covenant to accuse himself' much less to 'kill, wound, or maim himself'. On the other hand, covenants (legal obligations) entered into out of fear are obligatory, just as, Hobbes says, if someone has agreed to pay a ransom, then he or she must pay it. He says there:

> *The final Cause. End or Design of men, (who naturally love Liberty, and Dominion over others,) in the introduction of that restraint upon themselves . . . is the foresight of their own preservation and of a more contented life thereby; that is to say, of getting themselves out from that miserable condition of War, which is necessarily consequent . . . to the natural Passions of men, when there is no visible Power to keep them in awe, and tie them by fear of punishment to the performance of their Covenants . . . Covenants without the Sword are but Words.*

And the sword has great range and freedom in Hobbes' civil society. To begin with, any man who fails to consent to the decrees of the Leviathan (the all-powerful state) may 'without injustice be destroyed by any man whatsoever' (with the exception of 'natural fools, small children and madmen, who do not understand the injunction in the first place'). At the same time, anyone who has what Hobbes calls 'sovereign power' (like kings and presidents) can't justly be punished, for whatever he or she does is by definition just. It's not even acceptable to question the sovereign's actions, for that's to superimpose a new authority over him or her.

What of social policy in the commonwealth? Hobbes thinks that the state should help and look after those incapable of work, but compel those who are unwilling. His egalitarianism extends to the distribution of 'Things that cannot be shared out': the state must hold these in common (or else distribute them by lot).

Another key idea (still an important part of the British constitution) is that the state and the Church should be united – and then the laws will be unambiguous.

Hobbes finishes the *Leviathan* by saying that he hopes that there's nothing too controversial in his views and with the respectful wish that some day in the future a sovereign may adopt his book as a partial guide:

> *I ground the Civil Right of Sovereigns, and both the Duty and Liberty of Subjects, upon the known natural Inclinations of Mankind, and upon the Article of the Law of Nature; of which no man . . . ought to be ignorant.*

Challenging Hobbes

Writing a century after Hobbes, John Locke says that because of the arbitrary powers it gives to the sovereign, Hobbes' social contract is actually worse than the state of nature it's supposed to help them to rise above. Who, Locke asks, would sign a contract to escape from 'polecats and foxes', if the result was to be put 'at the mercy of lions'?

Philosophers have fluttered over many of the ideas in the *Leviathan* (as Hobbes describes, disparagingly, such learned types as being in the habit of doing). In the 19th century, Nietzsche misappropriated the 'will to power'; in the 20th century John Rawls borrowed the idea of a social contract to explain moral decision making; and today *social determinism* (the view that people think and act in ways determined by outside forces greater than them) in general is often echoed, for example in talk of 'the selfish gene' that scientists sometimes claim explains human behaviour.

Hobbes' idea that you could deduce and derive individual rights from a supposed fundamental right to self-preservation has taken root in many legal systems in many states. In fact, together with the works of the Dutch lawyer and politician, Hugo Grotius, he both set the style and laid the foundations for future work in the areas of political theory, social ethics and international law.

Hobbes' interest in the methods of geometry and the natural sciences also brought a new style of argument to political theorising that's both more persuasive and more effective. And finally, from Hobbes there comes a warning that because social organisation originates in a struggle between its members, however committed to fairness and equality it may intend to be, it inevitably creates inequalities and becomes authoritarian.

Applying Machiavelli's Social Glue

The Italian political philosopher Machiavelli, sometime civil servant in Milan, has an unsavoury reputation. Indeed, people today use his name as a kind of adjective meaning cunning, amoral, scheming, tricky or wicked. But in fact, his reputation – his nickname was Doctor of the Damned – is far worse than he deserves. (Actually, much of Machiavelli's notoriety probably relates to his attacks on the Roman Church, the body that he blames for the political ruin of Italy, as it seemed to him at the time.)

Ironically perhaps, for one who offers his political theory for the benefit of princes, Machiavelli (1469–1527) was the first writer to move away from the paternalism of traditional society towards something closer to today's notions of democracy. In his writings, the masses, ignorant and vulgar though they may be, are better guardians of stability and liberty than individuals can ever become. Machiavelli argues that because people are all a mixture, none much superior to the other, and no system is perfect either, so even a good prince can become corrupt, it's best to design the state with a series of checks and balances. And because the state is only as good as its citizens, the rulers must be aware of the dangers of allowing civic spirit to wane.

Despite his reputation for cynicism, Machiavelli reminds people that injustice threatens the foundations of society from within, and urges that people must always combat it – wherever it appears and whoever it affects. His reputation comes from two of the most notorious political works ever written, *The Prince* (1532) and *The Discourses* in 1531 (*Discourses on the First Ten Books of Titus Livy*, to give the full title).

Prior to Machiavelli, medieval writers had based legitimacy on God, who expressed His will through the hierarchy of pope, bishops and priests, or alternatively through the emperor and the royal families of Europe. Machiavelli, in contrast, has no doubt that power is available to all and any who are skilful enough to seize it. Popular government is better than tyranny not for any over-riding moral reason, but by reason of its success in bringing about certain political goals: national independence, security and a well-rounded constitution. This means sharing power between princes, nobles and people in proportion to their real power. Machiavelli is the first major European figure to praise freedom as a primary virtue, writing that 'all towns and all countries that are in all respects free, profit by this enormously'.

Unfortunately, people have rarely read Machiavelli thoughtfully – or even read his work at all – before condemning him.

Chapter 15

Looking Out for Liberty

. . . .

In This Chapter

▶ Exploring liberty, American style

▶ Examining Locke's contradictions

▶ Outlining classical liberalism with J. S. Mill

▶ Encouraging selfishness with Adam Smith

▶ Addressing inequality with Rousseau

. . . .

> *We hold these truths to be self-evident, that all men are created equal*
>
> — The Declaration of Independence

The opening line of the Declaration of Independence seems unambiguous. Freedom, at least as we understand it as members of a democratic society, is a condition we take for granted. The history of the concept of liberty is a complicated one, however, in which ideas of the rights and responsibilities of human beings within a society have undergone considerable change.

In this chapter I examine the various takes on liberty, starting with the most famous one of all, The Declaration of Independence, while calling in on the most important thinkers on the subject along the way.

Praising Liberty: The American Declaration of Independence

The world's only superpower (as the Americans now like to call themselves) owes much of its military, economic and cultural dominance to a political recipe. This recipe is set out in just a couple of documents drafted at the time of the American Revolution – in particular the American Declaration of Independence and the Constitution of the United States.

One slogan in particular has made an indelible mark on political philosophy. It's from the Declaration of Independence, which asserts that all 'men' (but alas, not women, not Indians, not black people) are equal:

> *We hold these truths to be self-evident, that all men are created equal, that they are endowed by their Creator with certain unalienable Rights, that among these are Life, Liberty and the pursuit of Happiness. That to secure these rights, Governments are instituted among Men, deriving their just Powers from the consent of the governed, That whenever any Form of Government becomes destructive of these ends, it is the Right of the People to alter or to abolish it, and to institute new Government, laying its foundation on such principles and organising its powers in such form, as to them shall seem most likely to effect their Safety and Happiness.*

The contemporary political commentator Simon Jenkins, writing in the *Guardian* newspaper (London) in 2007, surely reflected a commonly held view when he declared, 'the noblest testament to freedom is the American Constitution'. Yet, in fact the Constitution is quite the opposite. It's a remarkable document, indubitably both far-sighted and successful, but its aims weren't at all to protect individual liberties, let alone freedom. It left black Americans as slaves, and indigenous Americans on reserves. It left women without civil rights. Instead, it reflects its origins in reconciling various points of views in constructive compromises. Its central aim seems to have been to create checks and balances against the dominance of one point of view.

The US Constitution is a remarkable document, but it's philosophically neither innovative nor original. Its aim is to create a society that revolves around money, and its style is legalistic – full of legal clauses necessary for setting up a big enterprise like the new United States. No room for philosophical observations, let alone ethical discussions. Rather, its success is in that it's very business-like – simple and efficient.

Making amends

So what happened to the individual citizen's rights that sparked the War of Independence and that Americans so celebrate the US Constitution for protecting? These, and all the other contentious issues, had to be left for later politicians to incorporate in the document as amendments. Because the Founding Fathers (the revolutionary leaders who drafted the documents) were initially concerned to balance the powers of the states, they had to leave the protection of individual rights to one side. And because almost all of the individual states had already written up constitutions containing bills of rights, people saw the the federal Constitution as potentially undermining or conflicting with those rights.

So you have to look for the famous United States citizens' rights from the amendments, not the Constitution itself. It's only the First Amendment that offers individuals freedom of religious choice and freedom of speech. It states that:

> *Congress shall make no law respecting an establishment of religion, or prohibiting the free exercise thereof; or abridging the freedom of speech, or of the press; or the right of the people peaceably to assemble, and to petition the Government for a redress of grievances.*

However, religion in America, as elsewhere, continues to be a divisive issue. Over the years the pendulum has swung from the religious conservatives to the secular reformers, often meeting in battle on the terrain of otherwise obscure legal points in the Supreme Court, which is the United States highest court with a special responsibility for guarding the spirit of the US Constitution (see the later section 'Guarding the Constitution: The Supreme Court' for more).

Many of the other amendments are controversial too. Take the Second Amendment, which says that 'A well regulated Militia, being necessary to the security of a free State, the right of the people to keep and bear Arms, shall not be infringed'. This gives Americans the right to have their own guns. They're big ones like machine guns and rocket launchers too. Is that a good idea? Certainly, counting only since the end of the Second World War, a staggering one million Americans have been shot dead by their fellow countrymen! And like many of the ideas of the Constitution's authors, it doesn't seem to matter that the amendment clearly says that the right to carry guns is only there in order to allow individual states their militias – kind of military police.

People have likewise always contested other key protections of the Constitution. The US government has regularly violated the Fourth Amendment, which protects the 'right of the people to be secure in their persons, houses, papers, and effects, against unreasonable searches and seizures', most recently as part of the so-called 'War on Terror', with tapping of phone calls, bugging homes and of course reading emails.

But a more deadly example of why rights matter was shown by what happened in the early years of the United States to America's unfortunate Cherokee Indians. These were one of the continent's original races, who had on paper become a recognised partner in the newly United States. The Americans confiscated the Cherokee's land under a special law called the Indian Removal Act, and whose idea was that? None other than Thomas Jefferson who'd written those glowing words for the Declaration of Independence that I start the section with!

Protecting the right to have your own slaves

In 1781, at the time the Founding Fathers wrote the Constitution, the census of 1790 records that slaves existed in nearly every state. Of a total national population of 3.8 million people, 700,000 of them, or 18 per cent, were slaves. Only Massachusetts and the districts of Vermont and Maine had none. In the southern states, with economies based on cultivating cotton, rice and tobacco, the proportion was far higher. Their representatives considered slavery to be not only sanctioned by the Bible, but what was more, an economic necessity. So what did the authors of the Constitution, the Founding Fathers, do about the slaves?

Even Benjamin Franklin, a scientist and writer, not a farmer, held several slaves during his lifetime. In 1789 he said, 'Slavery is such an atrocious debasement of human nature, that its very extirpation, if not performed with solicitous care, may sometimes open a source of serious evils.' His compromise was to set one of his slaves free after his death, but even this slave never saw freedom because he died before his master – lazy fellow! The practical result was that despite the freedoms claimed in the Declaration, the Constitution and later amendments to it, slavery wasn't only tolerated in the Constitution, but was incorporated into it.

As for the Fifth and Sixth Amendments, which offer various legal rights, notably a right to trial by and impartial jury, black Americans have often found themselves being tried by prejudiced white jurors. But then, the historical origin of this provision was that politicians thought juries should comprise 'one's peers' – a protection intended more for the aristocracy than for the commoner. A similarly well-intentioned but ineffectual protection is offered in the Eighth Amendment, which sought to outlaw 'cruel and unusual punishments', but nonetheless has never been able to prevent the routine application of various cruel and unusual punishments including forms of execution.

Guarding the Constitution: The Supreme Court

If the Amendments haven't been as effective as those who proposed them hoped, who's to blame for that? Today, as part of the doctrine of the division of powers, the Supreme Court is seen as overseeing and guarding the Constitution. But none of this is written into the Constitution. For example, back in 1832, when the Cherokee Indians successfully persuaded the Supreme Court that the Indian Removal Act (which confiscated their lands and obliged them to relocate to the West) was unconstitutional, the then president simply ignored it, saying, 'Let the Court enforce its rulings', and ordered the Army to move against the Indians.

Being ignored is a problem. But so is being stuffed – the practice used, for example, in court cases when the jury is stuffed full of sympathetic jurors. In the United States, presidents are able to stuff the Supreme Court because although judges are appointed for life, nowhere does it state how many judges they can appoint at any one time. The President has the power to appoint judges subject to approval by the senate. In consequence, the political make-up of the Court has been regularly influenced by expanding the total number of justices.

The Constitution and politics

Finally, strange though it may seem, the US Constitution doesn't have anything to say about politics. This is because, at the time of the Articles of Confederation, (which was, in a sense, the first constitution of the United States, drafted in 1777 by and establishing a "firm league of friendship" among the then just13 states) political parties didn't exist. There were regional blocs and temporary affiliations, but nothing like political groupings around shared manifestos. For this reason, details of how to vote, how parties choose their candidates, and even how to arrange things like congressional districts aren't part of the Constitution. The Founding Fathers weren't interested in democracy as people understand the concept today, with everyone choosing a president, but rather in how to balance the powers of the individual American states within the union. They never imagined that one day the president would effectively run everything.

The US Constitution created both the world's richest and most innovative nation, and its most powerful. But if power is every politician's goal, policy is often their later downfall. The authors of the documents of the American Revolution were more concerned with power than with its application. As a result, the United States is a country where 'the pursuit of happiness' has led to extremes of wealth and power, where 'might is right' and the government is continually waging wars around the world at the prompting of what a conservative – not a radical – president dubbed the 'military-industrial complex'.

Profiting from the Slave Trade with John Locke

Should the people who drew up the American Constitution (see the preceding section) have listened more to the English (even as they were throwing them out of the States) – at least the English philosophers? But in fact the political theory that Englishman John Locke (1632–1704) set out in the *Two*

Treatises on Civil Government (1690) is credited with inspiring both the American and the French Revolutions in the name of fundamental rights and freedoms. Locke's influence is there in the American Declaration of Independence, in the American constitutional separation of powers and the Bill of Rights. It's also there in the doctrine of natural rights that appears at the outset of the French Revolution, and in the revolution's *Declaration of the Rights of Man* which asserts that the rights of Man are universal: valid at all times and in every place. Or as Locke put it, firmly, in his book: 'All being equal and independent, no one ought to harm another in his life, health, liberty, or possessions'.

John Locke as political visionary

The French philosopher Voltaire called Locke a man of the greatest wisdom, adding, 'What he has not seen clearly, I despair of ever seeing.' A generation later, in America, Locke's reputation had risen still higher. Benjamin Franklin thanked him for his 'self-education', Thomas Paine spread his radical ideas about revolution and Thomas Jefferson credited him as one of the greatest philosophers of liberty of all time. Here are a few of Locke's memorable sayings:

On limiting the power of the state:

Whenever the power that is put in any hands for the government of the people, and the protection of our properties, is applied to other ends, and made use of to impoverish, harass or subdue them to the arbitrary and irregular commands of those that have it; there it presently becomes tyranny, whether those that thus use it are one or many.

The legislature acts against the trust reposed in them, when they endeavour to invade the property of the subject, and to make themselves, or any part of the community, masters, or arbitrary disposers of the lives, liberties or fortunes of the people.

On children and marriage:

Adam and Eve, and after them all parents were, by the law of nature, under an obligation to preserve, nourish and educate the children, they had begotten.

On crime and punishment:

Besides the crime which consists in violating the law, and varying from the right rule of reason, whereby a man so far becomes degenerate, and declares himself to quit the principles of human nature, and to be a noxious creature, there is commonly injury done to some person or other, and some other man receives damage by his transgression. In which case he who hath received any damage, has besides the right of punishment common to him with other men, a particular right to seek reparation from him that has done it.

On freedom:

He that in the state of nature, would take away that freedom, that belongs to anyone in that state, must necessarily be supposed to have a design to take away everything else, that freedom being the foundation of all the rest.

Everyone's equal (well, almost)

Everyone is equal; well, except slaves. Because, curiously, the philosopher whose name inspired others to demand liberty had another, more sinister side.

It was while working as secretary to a diplomat that John Locke met Lord Shaftesbury (Anthony Ashley Cooper). The noble lord was charmed by Locke's wit and learning, and immediately invited him to join his household as his personal physician-cum-philosopher. Ashley, later to become the First Earl of Shaftesbury, was a key player in English political life, and under his influence Locke soon started work, alongside the *Essay Concerning Human Understanding*, on his *Essay Concerning Toleration* and his *Two Treatises of Government*. The celebrated latter work reflects his patron's interest in trade and the colonies.

Lord Shaftesbury had important business interests in the American colonies already. He was one of the leaders of the Lords Proprietors of the Carolinas, a company that a Royal Charter to found a colony in what's now North and South Carolina, in the New World. Locke became the secretary (literally, general manager and supervisor) to the company from (1668–71), as well as secretary to the Council of Trade and Plantations (1673–4) and member of the Board of Trade (1696–1700). In fact, Locke was one of just half a dozen men during the Restoration (the period following the English Civil War when the monarchy was restored under King Charles II) who created and supervised both the colonies and their iniquitous systems of servitude. And one of his most important jobs involved writing a constitution for the new colony, thus putting his philosophical principles into practice. So where did his principles lead him?

The preamble to the Constitution for Locke's mini-state states specifically that in order to 'avoid erecting a numerous democracy', eight lords proprietors (including Earl Shaftesbury himself) would become an hereditary nobility, with absolute control over the citizens. These would feudal serfs, or what he calls *leet-men*.

One legal clause explains that 'Any lord of a manor may alienate, sell, or dispose to any other person and his heirs forever, his manor, all entirely together, with all the privileges and leet-men there unto belonging . . .'

Another rule notes that all the leet-men shall be:

> . . . *under the jurisdiction of the respective lords of the said signory, barony, or manor, without appeal from him. Nor shall any leet-man, or leet-woman, have liberty to go off from the land of their particular lord, and live anywhere else, without license from their said lord, under hand and seal.*

Lovely money to be made from the slave trade

Slavery had existed in Africa prior to the colonisation of America. Plenty of accounts record that slaves used to be sent across the North African desert to the Berber kingdom, along with gold. These were people generally enslaved following their capture in wars, or sold to settle debts – occasionally even to amend for crimes such as murder or sorcery.

However, historians consider that the practice was originally not only on a much smaller scale, but also much less malevolent. Salve owners may treat African slaves as part of the family. The owner may work alongside of slaves and share the same food and shelter. In the Americas, by contrast, the trade represented what's been called a new 'industrial slavery'. Slave owners kept huge anonymous gangs of slaves in camps and used them to produce labour intensive crops such as sugar cane, tobacco and cotton. The owners didn't work alongside their slaves, but lived in mansions and employed overseers with whips to force the slaves to work 'until they dropped'. Conditions were inhumane and horrific in the plantations of the New World.

Conditions on the way to America in the slave ships were pretty bad too. After being picked up in the ports of the western coast of Africa, the prisoners were crowded together in chains below decks and held in unsanitary and inhumane conditions for long weeks. Their ship followed a long route dictated by what's come to be know as 'the triangular trade'. This typically involved sailing from British ports, such as Liverpool or Bristol, to the western coast of Africa, carrying the products of the new industries such as ironware or cotton goods, which were then exchanged for the slaves. When the slaves were on board, the ships would set sail for the West Indies or other ports in the Americas – the second side of the triangle. On arrival, xxx would sell the surviving slaves, and take on board products such as sugar cane, rum or tobacco for the third and final leg of the trip back to England. It's no wonder that in 1723 John Houstoun described the slave trade as 'the hinge on which all of the trade of the globe moves'.

Astonishingly, by 1820 more slaves lived in America than colonists – five times more! (Not for nothing was the first president of the Unted Staes, George Washington himself, a slave owner - the country was built on slaves and their labour) The indigenous Indians had largely died out too (by wars, by eviction from their territories and by disease). But both in cruelty and bureaucratic attention to details and cost, the only parallel to the slave trade is the transportation of Jews and the other 'inferior races' by the Nazis during the 1930s and 1940s to the concentration camps.

Europeans greatly expanded the already existing African slave trade by offering money and other commodities for larger and larger numbers of slaves. These inducements led Africans to go on raids to capture other Africans to sell. The raids themselves also added to destitution, thus encouraging people to sell their children into slavery (perhaps ignorant of the full consequences) to buy food for the remaining members of the family.

What's more, 'All the children of leet-men shall be leet-men, and so to all generations.' As for the Africans (arriving there in chains), the Constitution gives each colonist 'absolute power over his Negro slaves'.

The transatlantic slave trade was just beginning as Locke wrote the Constitution. In time it would become one of the largest involuntary migrations of peoples in the modern era. During the three and a half centuries of the trade, nearly 9 million black Africans were transported to the Americas – and that's not even counting those who died along the way. The bulk of the slaves were transported between 1700 and 1850 and the British set the pace, counting for at least a quarter of all the slave ships.

If Locke, like Shaftesbury, had public responsibilities to fulfil, he also had his views in private. In 1671 he bought shares in the profitable slave traders the Royal Africa Company (which used to brand each of its slaves with the letters *RAC*) as well as, one year later, in The Bahama Adventurers.

Slave-owning: It's all right, philosophically

Philosophy has long thought slave-owing to be alright. For Aristotle in particular, (see chapter 2) the domestic slave was defined as the possession and property, or, as it were, the 'separable part of the master', even if he thought people should use slaves not merely according to the their interest or caprice, but for the general good and according to reason. Likewise, Aristotle defined the slave as a person 'naturally' fitted to be such, writing in his book, the Nicomachean Ethics:

> *Those men, therefore, whose powers are chiefly confined to the body, and whose principal excellence consists in affording bodily service; those, I say, are naturally slaves, because it is their interest to be so. They can obey reason, though they are unable to exercise it; and though different from tame animals, who are disciplined by means merely of their own sensations and appetites, they perform nearly the same tasks, and become the property of other men, because their safety requires it.*

That's an outrageous view, but politically a useful one, and sure enough, in the *Second Treatise*, Locke himself writes:

> *. . . there is another sort of servants, which by a peculiar name we call slaves, who being captives taken in a just war, are by the right of nature subjected to the absolute dominion and arbitrary power of their masters. These men having, as I say, forfeited their lives, and with it their liberties, and lost their estates; and being in the state of slavery, not capable of any property, cannot in that state be considered as any part of civil society; the chief end whereof is the preservation of property.*

Nowadays philosophers don't talk much about Locke's view of slaves. But that doesn't mean the subject is irrelevant. Because in Locke's philosophy, property is the key to civil society, and the key to property is labour.

However, Locke's position on liberty is, in fact, ambiguous. In the *Essay Concerning the True Original, Extent, and End of Civil Government*, Locke urges that slavery is 'so vile and miserable an Estate of Man' and 'so directly opposed to the benevolent temper and spirit of the nation' that it was 'hardly to be conceived that any Englishman, much less a Gentleman, should plead for't'. The natural liberty of man here represents an inalienable freedom from absolute, arbitrary power. However, in order to justify the economics of slavery, Locke thought it necessary to strip some people of their reason and thus their freedom.

In fact, it was only by locating slaves outside the social contract and creating new concepts of cultural and intellectual inferiority that Locke could reconcile his belief in a person's inalienable rights over his or her person to the personal advantages of playing a key part in the institution of slavery.

Taking the Democratic Turn with J. S. Mill

John Stuart Mill (1806–1873) was born in London, son of James Mill, and worked at the East India Company with a brief spell as a member of parliament. He was particularly interested in women's rights, constitutional reform and economics. In 1830 he met Harriet Taylor, to whom, he says in his autobiography, he owes none of his 'technical doctrines' but all of the liberal ideas, in 1830.

Mill holds that allowing people to decide for themselves as much as possible increases the general happiness, thereby arriving at a philosophy arguing in favour of liberty of thought, speech and association. And it's these ideas on the roles of individuals and society, set out in *On Liberty* and *The Principles of Political Economy (with Some of the Applications to Social Philosophy)*, that created a new political philosophy in Western democracies: classical liberalism.

Mill wrote *The Principles of Political Economy* in 1848, around the same time as Marx and Engels were attempting to foment proletarian revolution. Mill's writing is essentially an attempt to emulate his illustrious Scottish predecessor, Adam Smith (see the following section), in setting out the workings of the modern state.

For example, he writes, following Smith, that it's the element of cooperation that's the key to modern societies. From such cooperation a great 'flowering of co-operatives' and joint-stock companies can follow, Mill suggests enthusiastically. But he also adds that:

> *Whatever theory we may adopt respecting the foundation of the social union, and under whatever political institutions we live, there is a circle around every individual human being which no government, be question: the point to be determined is, where the limit should be placed; how large a province of human life this.*

This is the essence of classical liberalism. Mill's variety is grounded in the utilitarian ethic adopted from Jeremy Bentham (see chapter 7), rather than on the appeal to fundamental rights of that other great liberal Englishman, John Locke. Yet despite different starting points, both arrive at the characteristic set of individual rights and freedoms.

Still evidently in the spirit of Smith, Mill offers some grand advice to governments about money. He says that only labour creates wealth, but that capital is stored up labour and may be accumulated – or even inherited – quite legitimately. Inheritance is acceptable, even when initially based on an injustice, when a few generations have passed, because to remedy the injustice would create worse problems than leaving the situation alone. On the other hand, the state should prevent the inheritance of wealth, beyond the point of achieving 'comfortable independence', by intervening and confiscating assets. People who want to live more than 'comfortably' should work for it.

Mill thought that this 'Benthamite' or at leat Bentham-flavoured, part of his book would cause more than a little stir, and indeed hoped to become notorious for it. However, tucked away in nearly half a million other words, it attracted little interest.

So what is Mill's influence? He's one of the first writers to consider himself a social scientist, and was firm in his conviction that the social sciences were justly related to the natural sciences, and that you could pursue them using similar methods. Mill distinguished between the study of individuals, which would be largely psychology, and of societies, which would be largely economics and politics.

Voting for Life, Liberty and the Pursuit of Wealth

Adam Smith (1723–1790) is a much more radical philosopher than he's usually given credit for. Where earlier philosophers, such as Plato and John

Locke, thought society should be based on altruism, or at least the suppression of selfishness, he allows that selfishness is actually a very useful thing and society should encourage it more! Or as he puts it, it's not out of the benevolence of the butcher or the baker that you can expect your supper; it's from their enlightened notion of their own self-interest. Don't scorn self-interest, he says, because

> . . . it could never have imposed upon so great a number of person, nor have occasioned so general an alarm among those who are the friends of better principles had it not in some respects bordered up on the truth.

Alongside *The Wealth of Nations*, published in the same year as the American Declaration of Independence (1776), and still a popular read with right-wing politicians, Adam Smith penned another significant work, *The Moral Sentiments*, written rather later and based on the observation of others. (For more on both books, see chapter 17). Upholding justice becomes the key task of governments, even as economic forces are allowed to let rip.

The first edition of *An Inquiry into the Nature and Causes of the Wealth of Nations* cost 1 pound and 16 shillings, and sold out within six months. It was a barnstorming success because *The Wealth of Nations* isn't, despite the title, merely concerned with economics. It's a much more comprehensive vision of society, and in its pages economics is merely a by-product, albeit a necessary one, of social life. In the book, Smith is concerned not only with money, but also with justice and equity. And nowadays if those of a different disposition adopt his findings (Smith was the darling of right-wing governments at the end of the 20th century), that's not his fault.

Searching for Equality of Outcome or of Opportunity

Jean-Jacques Rousseau (1712-1778) roots his political philosophy in questions of justice too, in particular, the issue of the origins of inequality, and starts by distinguishing between two kinds of inequality:

- **Natural or physical inequality:** Differences of age, health, strength and intelligence

- **Moral or political inequality:** 'The different privileges that some enjoy to the prejudice of others' – things such as wealth, honour and power.

His essay, Discourse on the Origin and Basis of Inequality Among Men, written in 1754 as an entry to a prize competition of the Academy of Dijon, did not win the prize but makes many original points. He writes:

Those who talked ceaselessly of 'greed, oppression, desire and pride', Rousseau says, failed to realise that they were introducing into nature ideas that only originated in society. This is the favoured notion at the heart of Rousseau's alternative philosophy. But what of all the other supposed advantages of civilisation? Rousseau deals unceremoniously with them. They are but

> . . . *the extreme inequality of our ways of life, the excess of idleness among some and the excess of toil among others.*

Rousseau says one of the great mistakes Hobbes made (Chapter 14) is to have imagined that the savage shared civilised man's greeds and passions. Instead, Hobbes should've realised that the state of nature is a happy one. It requires a sophisticated, rational knowledge of good and evil to make civilised man so wicked.

Instead, Rousseau says that the first people lived like animals. He says this not in any derogatory sense, merely in the sense that the original people sought only simple fulfilment of their physical needs. They would've had no need for speech, nor concepts, and certainly not property. Rousseau points out that much of the imagery in both Hobbes and Locke belongs to a property-owning society, not to the supposed natural state prior to the invention of property rights. By realising this, 'we are not obliged to make a man a philosopher before we can make him a man'. The first time people would've had a sense of property, Rousseau thinks, is when they settled in one location and built huts to live in.

Even sexual union, Rousseau notes pragmatically – as well as reflecting on his own experience (he had five illegitimate children whom he left neglected in orphanages) – is unlikely to have implied any exclusivity, but was more likely to have been just a lustful episode no sooner experienced than forgotten, remembered least of all in terms of the children. Neither the father nor the mother is likely to know whose children they beget, he argues, assuming that paternity is the defining characteristic and minimising the mother's very definite knowledge!

Because this primitive state is actually superior to those that followed it, Rousseau goes on to suggest that the only reason why this early society ever changed must have been as a result of some sort of disaster, perhaps one causing shortages of food or other hardship. This would've forced people to start identifying certain areas as theirs, and maybe to start living in groups. This in turn would imply increased communication, and the development of language. And a second dimension to these changes exists: people began to

judge themselves by a new criterion – how others thought of them.
To Rousseau, this last is a change of the utmost significance, for it's self-consciousness that was the downfall of Adam and Eve in the Garden of Eden, and it's this self-consciousness that makes humankind permanently unhappy with its lot, and resentful or fearful of others.

After this, most unfortunately, 'the whole progress of the human race removes man constantly further and further from his primitive state'. According to Rousseau (at this point following Thomas Hobbes), society necessarily leads people to hate each other, in accordance with their different economic interests. But Hobbes' so-called social contract is, in fact, made by the rich as a way of doing down the poor. Actually, not even the rich benefit from the contract because they warp themselves and become increasingly out of touch with nature's harmony, raised needlessly above their own proper state, just as the poor are pushed below theirs.

For Rousseau, justice is not crude equality, but rather the correct placing of individuals according to their talents and abilities – according to their merit. Unfortunately, society disrupts this balance (which is also the problem Plato discusses in his *Republic*). And Rousseau considers the very notion of the social contract to be flawed:

Rousseau suggests instead just two laws, or principles, that you could say are 'antecedent to reason', antecedent being the posh way of saying 'came before'. The first (as with Hobbes) is a powerful interest in self-preservation and personal well-being; the second, however, is 'a natural aversion to seeing any other sentient being perish or suffer, especially if it is one of our own kind'. The only time 'natural man' would hurt another is when his own well-being requires it. In saying this, Rousseau is drawing a parallel for humankind with the animals who – unlike their masters – never harm each other out of malice alone.

Rousseau's version of the origins of the division of labour is similarly perverse and even bizarre. Instead of the use of iron (for ploughs and so on) improving agriculture by making farming easier and more efficient, he sees the new technoglies as a burden on the producers of food. 'The more the number of industrial workers multiplied, the fewer hands were engaged in providing the common subsistence, without there being any fewer mouths to feed.' Then, he says, you must consider all the unhealthy trades of modern society – labouring in mines, preparation of certain metals (such as lead) – and the general migration to the cities, before you can claim society has improved people's lives. Not that Rousseau is saying people should return to 'living with the bears', a conclusion he hastens to forestall.

However, Rousseau says that people outside society won't tolerate subjugation, 'as an unbroken horse paws the ground with its hooves' and rears at the approach of the bit, or animals break their heads against the 'bars of their prisons' – yet civil society reduces all to slaves. And Rousseau dismisses the explanation offered by such as John Locke (see the earlier section 'Profiting from the Slave Trade with John Locke') that the government is like a father, for 'by the law of nature, the father is master of the child only for such time as his help is necessary and that beyond this stage, the two are equals, the son becoming perfectly independent of the father'. In fact, by giving up liberty, a man degrades his being.

Moving from the small picture to the larger, one, Rousseau offers a 'hands-off' state. After all, he says, the only way that the sovereign and the people can have a single and identical interest, so that all the movements of the civil machine tend to promote the common happiness, is for them to be one and the same – which isn't going to happen. Actually, in later writings, notably *The Social Contract*, Rousseau suggests that maybe a way around the selfishness *does* exist, through a system of majority voting in which each individual's wishes become instead part of a general will, rather than reflecting directly anyone's particular desires. But his earlier claim is more insightful.

Another important implication is that no one can be outside the law, for when some people are, all the other people are left 'at their discretion'. Furthermore, society should have few laws, and introduce new ones only with the greatest circumspection, so that 'before the constitution could be disturbed, there would be time enough for everyone to reflect that it is above all the great antiquity of the laws that makes them sacred and inviolable'.

Chapter 16

Aesthetics and Human Values

. . . .

. . . .

> . . . each thing has its own characteristic beauty, not only everything organic which expresses itself in the unity on an individual being, but also everything inorganic and formless, and even every manufactured article.
>
> – Schopenhauer

This chapter is about matters of taste in art and beauty. Aesthetics is a particular kind of ethics, concerned with judgements about what is good and what is not so good, and what is out and out bad. Deciding things like that is a political matter too, and aesthetic judgements are often highly controversial. Some of the fiercest arguments are put forward by people who think something really is great 'art' (or literature) and opponents who see the same things as mere paint marks or money-minded kitsch. And just to make matters more complicated still, aesthetics relies on notions of authenticity and originality that are very hard to pin down. But in this chapter, we'll have a pretty good try.

So, Just What Is Art?

What is art? What's the difference between a brilliantly dashed-off character sketch and a mere scribble? When is a pile of bricks a sculpture, and when is it a pile of bricks? What quality is it that can make a painting, a work of music, a piece of rock into *art*?

Art is, if you think about it, rather an odd thing that can work across so many different areas. In fact, the most likely explanation is that art has nothing to do with the painting, music or sculpture itself, but rather is to do with the person, the artist, who creates it. It's the artist's imagination, feeling and originality that people celebrate when they hail something as a work of art. And in that sense, a forger who makes rather a good copy of a particular work of art, or even creates a new work in the style of a famous artist, is producing works of less merit because the work no longer represents originality or passion.

'What is art?' is the kind of question the branch of philosophy rather dauntingly called *aesthetics* asks. Aesthetics is all about appreciating art. But here's a funny thing – the word *aesthetic* comes from the Greek for *perception*, and originally applied to things that you experience via the five senses, as opposed to the more esteemed objects of thought that philosophers especially appreciate. However, these days philosophers of art use the term to talk about judgements of taste and the appreciation of the beautiful – exactly the sort of abstract judgements that use of the word was supposed to rule out in the first place. Confused? That's art for you.

One question often raised in aesthetics is whether beauty is objective (something out there not just something to do with your own personal tastes), in which case people really ought to learn to appreciate great art and indeed listen to long works of classical music, or whether it's subjective and emotional, in which case one person's view is as good as anyone else's. Time to frame the tennis-girl poster and on with the rap music! Because, indeed, such things are popular, and if beauty is subjective, you have to accept the authority of general opinion.

Two Russian artists, Vitaly Komar and Alexander Melamid, provided an interesting perspective on this question in 1996 when they challenged notions of 'high' and 'low' art by polling various citizens of various countries on a range of artistic preferences and producing pictures to fit. So, for example, the artwork for the American buyer featured a (clothed) couple strolling leisurely through a soothing lakeside landscape while a couple of deer frolicked in the background.

Take that interestingly shaped piece of wood that I found in the forest. It would look great in a glass case with a spotlight on it. But is it art? And what about that particularly impressive splatter picture made by swirling pots of runny paint around a huge canvas in the middle of the room? Or does art have to be the carefully planned and deliberate communication of some eternal human ideal, like truth or beauty? That sounds plausible and certainly plenty of art experts say it.

But the trouble is, for the person looking at the eventual product, painting, poem, concert or whatever, what the audience of the art receives isn't necessarily what the artist intended to send. It's true that monkeys or Mother Nature herself don't intend to create great paintings, but that doesn't mean that what they produce looks any different to someone who finds it later on. But if the difference is in the intentions, then plenty of artists intend to produce great works and never manage to, so what went wrong there? Or consider again the curious case of some of the most respected names of art in the 20th century, like Jackson Pollock – he of the infamous splatter paints.

Arguing about Art and Intentions

All the art experts, all the big galleries, if not maybe quite all of the humble folk who look at them, agree Jackson Pollock's splatter paintings do indeed count as great art. And JP intended it to be art too. But what's curious about most of the most radical artists of the post-Second World War period is that they came from nowhere to prominence with the support of . . . the CIA! Yes, the American secret services actively promoted (through books, funding schemes, newspapers and of course galleries) radical art as part of a labyrinthine strategy to undermine the Soviet Union.

This was all part of a special strategy to win over intellectuals – including philosophers – described as 'the battle for Picasso's mind' by one former CIA agent, Thomas Braden, in a television interview in the 1970s. Tom Braden was responsible for dispensing money under the heading Congress for Cultural Freedom. Naturally, most of the people he gave money to had no idea that the funds, and hence the artistic direction, actually came from the CIA. Intellectuals and great artists, after all, hate being told what to think.

And what was the communist empire doing meanwhile? They were promoting, through galleries, public funding and so on, a very different kind of art supposedly reflecting communist political values. 'Soviet realism' was a kind of reaction to 'Western Impressionism' (all those dotty – *pointilliste* the art-experts call them – landscapes and swirling, subjective shapes) and ensured that people in the paintings looked like people, decent, hard-working types too, and what's more were doing worthy things – like making tractors or (at least) looking inspirationally at the viewer. When Soviet art wasn't figurative (as this sort of stuff is called), it was very logical and mathematical, full of precise geometrical shapes and carefully weighted blocks of colour.

And all this prompted the CIA to throw money at hippy artists – people they normally wouldn't have liked very much (left-wing, anti-Americans, often) who were producing ugly images of a world gone mad. Nowadays, happily, connoisseurs everywhere enjoy and appreciate both the works of Soviet realism and the Western subversion as art. But the philosophical question raised is just whose intuitions mattered in the making of the images and sculptures – the individual artists' ideas of the social values or the political schemes of the people who commissioned, paid and effectively directed them?

Figuring out forgeries

No one likes forgeries. The trouble with forged money, for example, is that you can get into trouble paying with it. The trouble with fake designer goods is that they may fall apart, and that's not why you just paid three times as much as normal for them. But the trouble for philosophers about forgery is much more metaphysical.

Typically, the debate tends to focus on things like forged paintings. If the real painting and the forgery look the same, what's the difference? When galleries (as they've started to do) ask the public to visit and admire exact copies of their most famous paintings (while the gallery keeps the real ones locked safely away elsewhere), it certainly seems like a cheat. But why exactly? The picture looks exactly the same! As scientists would say, the visual perception is identical and so the pleasure should be indistinguishable. Many humble people will have queued up (and paid too!) to see great works, and maybe even sensed for a moment a feeling of seeing and sharing a special experience obtained from contact with truly great art, but then later on someone tells them that what they marvelled at was actually a security copy. And in general, if a painting, a sculpture or even a recording of a musical performance has been widely admired, has given delight to many, yet is then revealed to be a forgery or a copy, everyone feels cheated. Yet why? The object itself hasn't changed, so what has?

Then again, remember the cheat in the competition for the most authentic artificial (plastic) flower – he's the person who used a real flower to fool the public and the judges. Clearly, intentions matter. The story behind the picture or sculpture or music matters.

Many famous pictures aren't original in the absolute sense – the artist may be copying a set style or have done a number of very similar studies. In this age of high-tech copying, the distinction between a copy and an original is becoming increasingly hypothetical!

African art or high street kitsch?

Consider the case of ethnic art, like African masks or sculptures. These by their very nature can be both crudely made and crude in appearance – because they're linked to sexual rites and traditions in simple societies where elaborate and delicate works have no role. As such, they're easily and cheaply mass-produced for tourists too – maybe in a garage in your neighbouring town. So how do you tell which is a work of art and which is a work of complete cynicism?

Obviously, you turn to experts – people like Bernard Dulon, who pays good money for such works and has his own ethnic art gallery in Paris. Bernard has said that he can tell 'straight off it's the real thing', because every work of ethnic art has its own 'aesthetic, emotional and ethnological language'. Or, take another contemporary French art dealer, Renaud Vanuxem, who says he can always tell a fake from a genuine artefact because 'although it might look right, it doesn't feel right, it doesn't have soul'.

This is pretty metaphysical stuff. Lots of people no longer think human beings have souls – let alone that pictures or African masks have. Yet now philosophers of art want you to accept that works of art have soul and forgeries (or just lesser works – bad art, like I might create) don't. But can the experts justify such distinctions to the rest of us? Denis Dutton, Professor of Philosophy at the University of Canterbury in New Zealand, editor of the well-known website 'Arts and Letters Daily' and author of a book called *The Art Instinct*, once tried to explain the difference with regard to one of the art world's most famous scandals – how for decades experts praised the works of the 20th-century forger Hans van Meegeren, who made increasingly implausible copies of a much-valued 17th-century Dutch painter, Vermeer. The curious thing about these fakes, cheats, copies, call them what you will, is that they weren't copies of actual paintings but were fakes in that Hans van Meegeren passed off his work as being previously unknown, rediscovered works of the Old Master.

As Professor Dutton puts it (and he would know) the fakes all had their own style, and didn't actually look like the rest of the known works of Vermeer. But because van Meegeren's first fake had become part of the supposed catalogue of Vermeer, all his later works seemed to match too. Of course they did! In fact, the fakes looked more like 20th-century German expressionist paintings than they ever looked like 17th-century Vermeers. So the fraud wasn't in lack of style or lack of originality, but simply in using a fake name. It seems indeed that the fakes did have soul, but maybe not the one expected.

Well, Hans van M. shouldn't have borrowed a famous person's name. That's why his art is a definite fake. And for economists and art dealers, that's enough of an answer to the question 'What is real art?'.

But what about if you consider the case of tribal art? This case has no famous names, only mysterious objects and unknown traditional meanings. Indeed, some art experts think that the key to separating real tribal art from the stuff made down the road for tourists is that the real things aren't made with any interest in the Westerners who later come across them, but rather serve a special, esoteric purpose – a purpose known only to those in the special circle of the tradition. In short, as French gallery owner Denis Dutton has put it, the very finest works of tribal art, New Guinea art or African art 'have a lack of any interest in our perception at all; they're sort of in another world'.

Yet African witchdoctor masks or whatever are also said to be art because they do express something important for their makers and the original audience, with shared values. Like Western paintings, they're supposed to also be the expression of something unique by one human being.

It's easy to say that the work of art reduced by an artist for quick sale to the local bar owner to pay the beer bill is inauthentic, because it doesn't represent a deep and profound attempt to convey some important message. The existentialist view of authenticity is often linked to the notion of authenticity used by philosophers and artists in debates on aesthetics. Existentialists like – Jean-Paul Sartre and Edmund Husserl (see Chapter 12) – put a priority on authenticity, but it's not very clear what this adds up to beyond the slogan. To make matters worse (more complicated), Sartre himself insists that 'the real is never beautiful' before adding, 'Beauty is a value applicable only to the imaginary . . . that is why it is stupid to confuse the moral with aesthetic.' Literally, to be authentic is to be real, and not fake.

Most unfortunately, though, many of the great artists have been reduced to operating in rather inauthentic ways – obliged to dash off pictures and sketches for landlords and rich benefactors just to keep the debts at bay. Only recently have artists enjoyed the luxury of being just able to create!

Art experts today rail against what they sometimes call *kitsch* – art that borrows the superficial aspects of great art, adds expensive frames and conveys simplistic messages. Surely here you can agree that this sort of stuff is never going to be art? Yet, equally, most of the great works of art were paid commissions – for the Church or for the local landowner. Many examples of great painting started off very plainly as portraits commissioned by rich aristocrats to record their success in life. Yet this money-minded origin hasn't stood in the way of people accepting these works.

Do artists need to look right too?

With tribal art, Aboriginal paintings and African masks and such like, another knotty issue (with racist undertones) is whether art has a racial component. For instance, can a white Australian paint Aboriginal art? Certainly it seems more plausible that the direct descendant of 40,000 years of Aboriginal ancestors can convey the spiritual significance of the dreamtime though an image better than a newly arrived Western artist. Yet what sort of logic is this? After all, a white Australian could be more deeply aware of Aboriginal culture, maybe more so than an authentic but resolutely modern Aborigine who paints just to make money to support a taste in rap music. Who can judge which person is authentic?

Censoring books

Anyone who's brought up a young child knows that it's very important to control the influences that he's exposed to. Why? Otherwise he'll turn out like you. Similarly, Plato is notorious for being very keen on censorship. In his plans for his ideal state, he wanted to control as many of the influences on people as possible – censoring art and cultural matters in general not just for the better (safer) upbringing of children but for all the citizens in his idealised republic. And at least people have taken up that part of his political philosophy, because certainly censorship is alive and well all over the world. Computers and the Internet in particular are also introducing all sorts of notions of privacy and control. As the long-anticipated information society becomes a reality, policy makers and legislators have been struggling to retain control.

Internet users in China have been obliged to send their communications through special ports and filters that are under the government's watchful eye. Vietnam, Iran, Saudi Arabia and several of the other Gulf states have developed similar systems of filtration. The French government is trying to curb the use of English in its national cyberspace, and in the United States, Germany and Japan legislators are constantly fighting against indecent material. In the UK, children are protected from a wide range of unsuitable material, much of it nowadays coming via email.

But, interestingly, few countries agree on just what it is that they need to protect their citizens from. Take the case of one well-intentioned library in Britain, which swiftly responded to complaints by parents about a book featuring baby-battering and the murder of a policeman that had somehow sneaked into its young children's section! Yet that book was also one of the traditional children's favourites – called *Punch and Judy* and about funny puppets that children have laughed at for centuries. This illustrates a key fact about censorship: it's not so much the book or programe that the authorities need to control – it's the reaction of the reader or viewer.

Appreciating the Aesthetic Sense

Philosophers agree very little on a definition of beauty, which isn't in itself a very unusual thing (they also agree very little on what makes a table a table, on the colour of snow, and so on . . .). In classical times people held the key elements of beauty to be harmony, proportion and unity. Some say assessing beauty is an aesthetic judgement; others say not. Some say beauty is both capable of definition and objective, like Plato with his 'form of the beautiful'; others say it's entirely subjective and beneath serious consideration.

If beauty is the former, then it's a quality out there just as, say, a colour is; if it's the latter then it's purely a matter of emotional response. Thomas Aquinas thought the former and defined beauty as 'that which pleases in the very apprehension of it', whereas Immanuel Kant thought it was basically a matter of personal task, although he offers that beauty has 'subjective universality and necessity' by which he intends to give it some sort of solid foundation in people's understanding of the world.

Nowadays, with artistic interest in the grotesque and the violent, the distinction is often lost, but beauty used to have an ethical element: to be beautiful was (in that respect) to be good, to be better than ugly. It's because of this that you can describe actions as *beautiful*, or indeed ugly people whose character is kind as *beautiful*.

Considering Aesthetics, Art and Beauty

The Ancient Greeks linked beauty to goodness. Their phrase *kalos kai agathos* (beautiful and good) was the standard description of the Homeric heroes, people like Odysseus who the Ancient poet Homer had described doing great things like biting the heads off monsters. Plato also linked beauty to truth, generating the historic philosophical trilogy of truth, beauty and goodness. But what is beauty's relation to truth and virtue? Christians have often resented the way that 'beauty' seems to trump these values – and certainly beautiful people can get away with more failings than ugly bods. Despite that, paintings of religious scenes invariably make God, Jesus and all that side very handsome – and the Devil, Judas and all that crowd grotesque and ugly. Casting directors making crime dramas likewise seem to have pretty fixed ideas about who 'looks like' a villain, and who looks like an innocent victim. Some have suggested that beauty has its beautiful that can do this, and not what is merely ordinary or even ugly?

In his *Enquiry Concerning Beauty, Order, Harmony, Design* (1725), Francis Hutcheson (1694–1746) argued that recognising an object as beautiful was a matter of distinguishing its special aesthetic qualities from factual or empirical ones. He thought the beauty of an object was essentially a matter of its capacity to affect an observer in some particular way. But different kinds of arts (genres) produce different responses: comedy versus tragedy, exotic art versus music, and so on. That suggests that a person's emotional or aesthetic response depends not only on the object itself, but on what aspect of it the observer is looking at or focusing on.

Immanuel Kant discussed beauty and taste in his heavyweight and influential *Critique of Judgement* (1790), saying there that beauty depends on appearance and within that on form and design. In visual art, he said, it's not the colours but the pattern that the colours make; in music, the relation between the sounds, not timbre or pitch that matter. And the English art critic John Ruskin (1819–1900) asserted that beauty has a spiritual core.

Such accounts of art were influential in the 19th century, but the 20th brought a greater concern with matter over form and a challenge to the idea of art and beauty as moral concepts.

Ten shockingly arty events

What arty types like to call a 'creative tension' exists in art and music, about working right at the limits of public taste. Plus, there's money to be made there. Here's ten examples reflecting both motivations.

✔ Painting: Manet's *Breakfast on the Lawn*, featuring a group of sophisticated French aristocrats picnicking outside, shocked the art world back in 1862 because one of the young lady guests is stark naked!

✔ Painting: Balthus's *Guitar Lesson* (1934), depicting a teacher fondling the private parts of a nude pupil, caused predictable uproar. The artist claimed this was part of his strategy to 'make people more aware'.

✔ Music: Jump to 1969 when Jimi Hendrix performed his own interpretation of the American National Anthem at the hippy festival Woodstock, shocking the mainstream US.

✔ Film: In 1974 censors deem *Night Porter*, a film about a love affair between an ex-Nazi SS commander and his beautiful young prisoner (featuring flashbacks to concentration camp romps and lots of sexy scenes in bed with Nazi apparel), out of bounds.

✔ Installation: In December 1993 the 50-metre-high obelisk in the Place Concorde in the centre of Paris was covered in a giant fluorescent red condom by a group called ActUp.

✔ Publishing: In 1989 Salman Rushdie's novel *Satanic Verses* outrages Islamic authorities for its irreverent treatment of Islam. In 2005 cartoons making political points about Islam featuring the prophet Mohammed likewise result in riots in many Muslim cities around the world, with several people killed.

✔ Installation: In 1992 the soon-to-be extremely rich English artist Damien Hirst exhibited a 7-metre-long shark in a giant box of formaldehyde in a London art gallery – the first of a series of dead things in preservative.

✔ Sculpture: In 1999 Sotheby's in London sold a urinoir or toilet-bowl-thing by Marcel Duchamp as art for more than a million pounds ($1,762,000) to a Greek collector. He must have lost his marbles!

✔ Painting: Also in 1999 *The Holy Virgin Mary*, a painting by Chris Ofili representing the Christian icon as a rather crude figure constructed out of elephant dung, caused a storm. Curiously, it was banned in Australia because (like Damien Hirst's shark) the artist was being funded by people (the Saatchis) who stood to benefit financially from controversy.

✔ Sculpture: In 2008 Gunther von Hagens, also known as Dr Death, exhibited in several European cities a collection of skinned corpses mounted in grotesque postures that he insists should count as art.

Glossing Kant's sublime view

And so to the less than fully appreciated Kantian treatise on the beautiful and the *sublime*. Pronounced, to be arty, 'soooblime', as in 'darling, while we're in the Jacuzzi listening to Bach, pass me a glass of that sublime, light and bubbly, humerous but philosophical, chateau Martin premier cru'. In my example, some posh folk are talking about wine, but the point is that sublime things don't have to be just art objects, but that somehow high art and being sublime does seem often to be a bit posh – Classical music is art, rap songs are not. But back to Kant, who wrote before there was such a sharp distinction between high and low, classical and popular culture. And he asks, what is the sublime? Before answering: night is sublime, day is beautiful. The sea is sublime, the land is beautiful; men are sublime, women are beautiful – and so on. Lots of professors wrote treatises like that at the time Kant was having a go; it was almost compulsory.

The sublime, a word which comes from Latin and means 'exulted' and unspeakably great, has been a big part of aesthetic theory in Western art and philosophy, ever since an otherwise unknown aesthete called Longinus praised it to the skies in the first century CE, and all the more so following its more explicit formulation in the early 18th-century Europe.

That first study of the value of the sublime is a treatise called *On the Sublime* and in it Longinus describes at length how hearing Ancient Greek poetry produces sublime sensations in him like deep emotion mixed with pleasure and exaltation. Longinus's best guess for explaining art was that it was all about the skill of metaphor – a point that Plato and Aristotle had also made. Actually, although his book was written as long ago as the first century AD, it was only properly published in 1554. (Mind you, they only invented the first decent printing presses around then, give or take 100 years.)

Despite the delay in reaching the bookshelves, Longinus's influence on the new arty theme of the sublime extended well into the 17th century. He was thus was able to influence both a radical French literary establishment and more conservative English types, such as the writer John Dennis and the philosopher Anthony Ashley Cooper. All rather sublime, or 'beyond explaining in words'. As it seemed were the hikes that Lord Cooper, and later John Dennis, took in the European Alps. Nonetheless, it was on these walks that many of the new *aesthetes* (beauty-lovers) experienced the sublime for themselves. In records of their travels, they commented on the horror and the harmony of the experience, and the raw tumult of nature's beauty.

Indeed it was John Dennis who specifically launched the notion of the naturally sublime, or the sublime as it appears in the natural world. John Dennis published his comments at the end of the 17th century, giving an account of his crossing of the Alps where, contrary to his prior feelings for the beauty of nature as a 'delight that is consistent with reason', the experience of the journey was at once a pleasure to the eye as music is to the ear, but 'mingled with Horrors, and sometimes almost with despair'. Shaftesbury's writings reflect more of a regard for the awe of the infinity of space – the 'space astonishes', he gushed – and the sublime appearance of the mountains was of a grander quality and higher importance than mere beauty.

Another British philosopher, Edmund Burke, took an important next step in the development of the concept of the sublime in a book called *A Philosophical Inquiry into the Origin of Our Ideas of the Sublime and Beautiful* (1756). For the first time someone posed a philosophical argument to suggest that although the sublime may inspire horror, you can also receive pleasure from the experience. This argument released the aesthetic experience from its traditional safe home of the realm of beauty.

When Immanuel Kant published his book *Observations on the Feeling of the Beautiful and Sublime* (1764), philosophers generally agreed that being sublime was quite different from being beautiful. It was, in fact, better.

This was all a great contrast to the classical notion of the aesthetic experience described by Plato and Saint Augustine. For them, *beauty* was purity of form, and *ugly* was simply the absence of beauty – lacking form and non-existent. Ugliness couldn't create special feelings.

Yet in his learned account of the 'Analytic of the Sublime' (part of his book, the *Critique of Judgement*), Kant distinguished between the 'remarkable differences' of the beautiful and the sublime, noting that beauty 'is connected with the form of the object', having 'boundaries', but the sublime 'is to be found in a formless object', and is without boundaries.

In a chapter headed the 'Analytic of the Beautiful', part of Kant's book *Critique of Judgement*, he states that beauty isn't a property of artwork or natural objects, but instead a consciousness of the state of feeling the pleasure derived from having made a judgement of taste. It may appear that you're using reason to decide what's beautiful, but the judgement isn't cognitive (involving ideas and principles), 'and is consequently not logical, but aesthetical'. In fact, Kant says, judgement of taste is purely subjective and is based upon nothing but 'a feeling of satisfaction derived from the presence of an object'. On the other hand, this is a disinterested pleasure (that is, an objective judgement) and in as much as people share awareness of what's good, it's universal.

What's more, where beauty relates to understanding, Kant says the sublime is a concept belonging to reason, and 'shows a faculty of the mind surpassing every standard of Sense'. You experience the sublime when your imagination fails to comprehend the vastness of the infinite and you become aware of the ideas of reason and their representation of the boundless totality of the universe. The sublime makes you conscious of your own *finitude* (knowing how small and mortal you are), and also aware of the overarching superiority of the moral law.

No, no! Stop, Professor Kant! All I want to know is how to tell good art, good music and good films from bad. Or indeed, whether it matters. Feelings of finitude scarcely seem to come into it. Maybe a walk in the Alps can bring them on, but many of the new 'ugly' forms of art seem to be moving in the opposite direction – making the world small and the artist feel important. Kant (fortunately for him, no doubt) wasn't around to see where artists took the sublime later.

Recognising the beauty trap

In the United States people spend more money on so-called beauty than on education or on social services. In countries like Brazil the army of Avon ladies selling make-up is larger and more numerous than the usual ugly assemblage of military types. Beauty openly makes or breaks products via advertising, and decides success or failure in films, television newscasts, popular music and increasingly real-world activities such as politics, sport and business too.

Beauty isn't just a kind of evolutionary mechanism, but is essential to social and political life, the cognitive researcher and author of books like *Survival of the Prettiest* (2000) Nancy Etcoff says. To ignore its power is to order the tide itself to 'go back' and obey your will. Instead, she says, 'How to live with beauty and bring it back into the realm of pleasure is a task for 21st-century civilisation.'

In a rather dull book called the *Primacy of Perception* (1976), the 20th-century French philosopher Maurice Merleau Ponty also places 'bodily self-image' firmly at the centre of his philosophy, arguing that the body 'forms our point of view on the world' and is 'the visible form of our intentions'. When this self-image goes awry the consequences are profound. You can attribute all sorts of malign effects to notions of beauty (eating disorders, anxiety, stress, low self-esteem, sexual harassment, incest and rape) – and refuse to allow any good ones.

Similarly, writing more recently, Naomi Wolf describes in *The Beauty Myth* how historically people have esteemed several types of beauty, and how 'the qualities that a given period calls beautiful in a woman are merely symbols of the female behaviour that that period considers desirable'. Naomi Wolf thinks that the reason people do this is that they've been programmed by millennia of evolution to identify the most fertile partner. Men look for women who have the hourglass shape because this maximises the chance of the woman being old enough to bear children, but young enough not to be either pregnant already or breast-feeding (in which case she's not fertile). After all, women, equally, look for square jawed, tall, dark and handsome men, who thereby (she argues) illustrate not only their masculinity but their ability to help bring up children. And the reason why many women wear make-up and are constantly dieting is that they've been taken in by a kind of cult religion – the cult being that of the body beautiful.

Respecting Nietzsche's nasty view

Plato thought that art should try to reflect – mimic – beauty in the world. This indeed was the view of most European artists up until the time of Nietzsche. Philosophers sometimes say the fact that artistic fashions changed, with the impressionists and later surrealists changing the world to fit in with their values and priorities, had much to do with the influence of Nietzsche.

In his writing, Nietzsche argues that art should make you think (so you shouldn't receive it passably) and any example that doesn't make you think isn't true art.

In a celebrated passage in *Human, All Too Human*, Nietzsche explains:

> *Art is above and before all supposed to beautify life, thus make us ourselves endurable, if possible pleasing to others: with this task in view it restrains us and keeps us within bounds, creates social forms, imposes on the unmannerly rules of decency, cleanliness, politeness, of speaking and staying silent at the proper time. Then, art is supposed to conceal or reinterpret everything ugly, those painful, dreadful, disgusting things which, all efforts notwithstanding, in accord with the origin of human nature again and again insist on breaking forth: it is supposed to do so especially in regard to the passions and physical fears and torments, and in the case of what is ineluctably or invincibly ugly to let the meaning of the thing shine through.*

> *After this great, indeed immense task of art, what is usually termed art, that of the work of art, is merely an appendage. A man who feels within himself an excess of such beautifying, concealing and reinterpreting powers will in the end seek to discharge this excess in works of art as well; so, under the right circumstances, will an entire people. Now, however, we usually start with art where we should end with it, cling hold of it by its tail and believe that the art of the work of art is true art out of which life is to be improved and transformed – fools that we are! If we begin the meal with the dessert and cram ourselves with sweet things, is it any wonder if we spoil our stomach, and even our appetite, for the good, strengthening, nourishing meals to which art invites us!?*

Choosing between Banned and Approved Art

Nowadays many parents are put off by Japanese Manga comics – full of both sex and violence. But such concerns are an old story. Pretty disgraceful carvings and cave paintings exist that go back tens of thousands of years. No one knows if our predecessors regulated access to these artworks or not, and if so, for what reasons. But certainly more recent risqué art has caused controversy – such as in the 19th century with the arrival of the new one penny comics, the penny dreadfuls. These were full of exciting stories about highway robbers and murders.

But the penny dreadfuls, with their stories of sex and violence, shocked and worried the Victorians. They feared (like Plato, but unlike Aristotle who, clinical as ever, thought such stories cleansed the watcher) that violent plays encouraged violent thoughts, and so thought that it was their duty to prevent the pollution of the young from stories of sewer dwelling boys battling the bluebottles (policemen, not flies, that is, of course) and salvaging corpses. 'When it is remembered that this foul and filthy trash circulates by the thousands and tens of thousands week by week amongst lads who are at the most impressionable period of their lives, it is not surprising that the authorities have to lament the prevalence of juvenile crime', warned one commentator in 1890. Evidence existed to support the Victorians' fears too: the almost respectable story of Werther's unrequited love for the lovely Lotte in Wolfgang von Goethe's (1780–1833) *Dr Faust*, which ends in the tragic suicide of the hero, led to a whole spate of copycat suicides at the start of the 19th century.

So it was that responsible social commentators decided to dedicate themselves to the task of eradicating what they saw as the plague of poison literature. One such commentator, such as James Greenwood, said:

> There is a plague that is striking its roots deeper and deeper into English soil chiefly metropolitan week by week, and flourishing broader and higher, and yielding great crops of fruit that quickly fall, rotten-ripe, strewing highway and by-way, tempting the ignorant and unwary, and breeding death and misery unspeakable.

Popular titles (perhaps reflecting the paucity of ideas) included *Sweeny Todd, the Demon Barber of Fleet Street*, *Spring-Heeled Jack, the Terror of London* and *Three-Fingered Jack, the Terror of the Antilles*, not to mention the Hounslow Heath Moonlight Riders or the king of the Boy Buccaneers, Admiral Tom. 'Nasty-feeling, nasty-looking packets are every one of them, and, considering the virulent nature of their contents, their most admirable feature is their extremely limited size,' wrote Greenwood in 1874.

Nonetheless, both H.G. Wells and Noel Coward were avid consumers of such savoury titbits, praising the genre highly. They willingly wandered among the lonely tarns and stagnant weed-covered pools, slept in whispering hollows in secluded woods, saw the moon shine on the swiftly flowing waters even as they glimpsed heading serenely downstream the white hand of a corpse, not to forget the waiting condemned cell and the creaking gibbet on the lonely common.

You might think it all very tame stuff today, what with contemporary technologies immeasurably increasing the scope for the voyeuristic to sample horror or to witness 'nightmares of depravity', as one presidential candidate put it as recently as 1995. Today's censors wouldn't look twice at the highwaymen stories.

Instead, today, many of the concerns people have relate not to what's depicted but what may be involved in the production of the sex, violence or horror images. In so-called *snuff movies* unpleasant things (such as being killed) actually happen to people or animals, and the fact that the making of the images involves criminality only adds to the appeal. That a market exists that appears to prefer unpleasant events to be real rather than just the result of technical sophistication is a fact that television networks know only too well . Meanwhile, sexual activity, which in a way sits strangely alongside crime and violence in the censors' library, has always attracted a disreputable premium for being real as opposed to faked. *Romance* in 1999 and the radical French film *Baise Moi* (2002), with its story of how a rape triggers two women to go on a rape and maiming spree, challenged this tendency and confused censors who weren't sure whether to ban the films for the glamourless, real sex scenes, or the run-of-the-mill, intermittent fake violence.

Hollywood and violence

In the 1930s an American-inspired series of films apparently glorifying gangsters caused a very similar moral panic to that of the penny dreadful *Moonlight Riders*. One typical US story, *The James Boys as Guerrillas*, described the (at least partially) true story of how the boys took on the Feds. And it was published in the context of an ongoing hunt for the boys. Then, too, there were the tales of Bonny and Clyde, and even Robin Hood, continuing to set a bad example.

A new code drafted by Will Hays, a US film mogul with political connections, helped. It resulted in filmmakers adding additional scenes depicting concerned citizen groups or the chief gangster dying in a grisly fashion at the end. But for many Americans, just portraying gangsters as the main characters was too much.

Happily, by the middle of the decade Hollywood, propelled by organisations like the 'Legion of Decency', thought to reinvent the genre with a law officer carrying out all the exciting car chases and shootings that previously had been the responsibility of the gangsters, thereby making the violence completely ethical.

Censorship is part of social life – inevitable and desirable. For example, the rules on where people can and can't be naked are a form of censorship. You don't want to find the milkman standing outside the door with no clothes on (even if you may want to find him standing inside the bedroom with no clothes on). Where people widely agree with the rules, they're hardly even noticed, but where a minority opposes the rules, the censor is unlikely to be able to find a rational argument to justify his position. As Bertrand Russell wrote in one of his 'Sceptical Essays': 'It is obvious that 'obscenity' is not a term capable of exact legal definition; in the practice of the Courts, it means anything that shocks the magistrate.'

Nowadays violence is pretty *de rigeur*, but views on the acceptable degree of nudity in church (thinking more of the decorations than the parishioners) has fluctuated. The artist Michelangelo battled on artistic grounds for his view that the human form was divine and needed no covering, particularly not in heaven. But, in fact, ever since fig-leaves have been regularly added to his statues and frescoes.

Today, feminists and others continue to argue that so-called classical art depicting women in sexually suggestive roles or simply as naked forms, should be suppressed – removing this art from display in public institutions such as universities and libraries. Very little consensus on what constitutes exploitative or degrading representations exists. Censorship of the female form ranges from almost total prohibition in some Islamic countries to almost complete legality in some secular jurisdictions.

It seems that societies that protect women from being made into sexual objects by imposing strict rules about clothes and social intercourse (limiting their rights to talk to people, or to go into buildings with men) are very slow to protect women from violence – real violence, like being killed by family members. The rallying cry that images ranging from the barely skin-revealing to the pornographic are all a form of violence against women that appears to offer a straightforward justification for censorship contrasts with the violence of the censors in administrations such as Afghanistan under the Taliban, dedicated to promoting virtue and rooting out vice. In fact, given the reduced role of women in societies that 'protect' them from such violence, other feminists decry censorship of the female form as reactionary and oppressive.

When a fundamentalist religious state was set up in Afghanistan in the 1990s, one of its first acts was to create a Ministry for the Propagation of Virtue and the Prevention of Vice. Its edicts included the banning of all television, music, photographs of living people, shaving and the showing of flesh in public. As well as forcing women to wear top-to-toe garments to hide themselves (and even then confining them to the home except when accompanied by a male) the men were also required, for example, to wear long trousers when playing football.

Britons and sex

In the famous *Lady Chatterley's Lover* trial of 1959, lawyer Mervyn Griffith-Jones asked the British court to consider whether the book of that name by the very intellectual and respectable D.H. Lawrence was the sort of thing, as he put it, that 'Englishmen would want their wives and servants to be reading'?

That rhetorical question fell on unappreciative ears in the courtroom, and the jury decided that Griffith-Jones was over-stressing the dangers to society of D.H. Lawrence's sexy book. This was indeed a low point for campaigners against what they perceived as the ever-rising tide of filth, because the case was lost and D.H. Lawrence went on to become the standard bearer of artistic freedom. In fact, public opinion simply refused to accept that the book was filth, and half a century on it's a respected part of the literary landscape.

But in 1993 an independent bill in the House of Commons did manage to fight back against a new tide of so-called video nasties, such as *Driller Killer, I Spit on your Grave*. The minister responsible (David Mellor) supported the bill in the strongest terms, saying: 'No one has the right to be upset at a brutal sex crime or a sadistic attack on a child or mindless thuggery on a pensioner if he is not prepared to drive sadistic videos out of our high streets.' Together with a later Criminal Justice Bill, the bill marked nothing less than 'a return to responsible censorship' by popular demand, cheered that trusty guardian of UK morals the *Daily Mail* newspaper.

Diotima on Greek Sex

Indeed, although few women philosophers are recorded in the history of the subject, you find one important female philosopher, Diotima, in Plato's *Symposium* making a rare lecture to Socrates, who's temporarily listening and learning for once! Socrates asks Diotima to explain about beauty, and she says that the attraction to beauty, specifically in the naked body, is fundamental but only a preliminary stage to something else. She even argues that an entirely natural link between seeing a beautiful body and wanting to have sex with it exists – it's the subconscious desire to make the beauty last for ever. In this way, sexual attraction and beauty are irrevocably linked.

Diotima then advises Socrates that although a wise philosopher may indeed 'fall in love with the beauty of one particular body', he'll then discover that the quality of beauty that attracted him in the first place to one lover is in fact the same thing that attracts him to another – that the beauty of his lover is only part of some greater, eternal beauty. In fact (and Diotima here offers the famously ugly Socrates a glimmer of hope), the philosopher will realise that the beauty of mortal bodies is nothing compared to the beauties of the soul, 'so that wherever he meets with spiritual loveliness, even in the husk of an unlovely body, he will find it beautiful enough to fall in love with . . .'. She goes on to say the philosopher finds beauty in laws, institutions and human artefacts too, and thus 'by scanning beauty's wide horizon', the philosopher is saved from 'a slavish and illiberal devotion to the individual loveliness' of a single lover, or a single human construction. Turning his eyes towards 'the open sea of beauty', the philosopher finds instead 'a golden harvest of philosophy' centred around knowledge of the good.

Testing the limits of Free Speech

The limits of free speech with the evergreen example of the woman who shouts as a joke 'Fire! Fire!' in a cinema and watches people stampede and some of them die underfoot. The words are also deeds, and the deeds are what the public defends itself from. But then again, that's exactly what the Victorian moralists were arguing too.

In 2002 the US Supreme Court, charged with upholding the rights of the citizen, was asked to mark out the boundaries for this sort of issue, specifically to rule whether freedom of expression includes the burning of crosses by the Ku Klux Klan, part of the KKK's campaign to intimidate black Americans. The Court was guided by a decision in 1919 when it had ruled that where there was a 'clear and present danger' of criminality, even words wouldn't be tolerated. Satisfactory? Well, that ruling was in relation to pacifists campaigning against conscription in World War One.

Banning nasty pop music

Most people are quite comfortable with footballers wearing short trousers – but what about pop songs encouraging violence towards minorities? In October 2001 German police swooped (as is their wont) on one of that country's best-known, if not most popular, pop groups.

The group were called Landser, which is the old-fashioned word for a German soldier, hinting at the 'good old days' of the First and Second World Wars. The group had actually already had a brush with the censors (which it lost) over its first choice of name, Final Solution – which you may assume was a none-too-empathetic reference to Hitler's attempts to kill millions of European Jews and Slavs. At least the group was allowed its choice of title for its first CD, which was named *The Reich Will Rise* and called for attacks on foreigners, Jews, gypsies and political opponents (just like old times). But one of the songs brought upon it the censors again.

Despite being neo-Nazis, the group argued that they had a right to express themselves, and indeed that the song was quite good, maybe even to them a 'work of art'. Not surprisingly, they lost the case, but as with many other battles between censors and rebels they greatly benefitted from the publicity.

Getting Back to Nature

Many of the philosophers we rely on to represent little oases of good sense and rationality in a disorganised world disappointingly turn out, on closer inspection, to be not only rather eccentric but also downright irrational. David Henry Thoreau, an anarchist who eked out a living by making pencils while living in a shed by a pond, on the other hand, appears even at first glance to be rather eccentric.

Thoreau (1817–1862) was born in Concord, Massachusetts, which for ecological purposes means in the temperate forest zone of the eastern coast of North America. Some people call him the poet laureate of nature writing.

In his journal entry for 7 January 1857, Thoreau says of himself:

> *In the streets and in society I am almost invariably cheap and dissipated, my life is unspeakably mean. No amount of gold or respectability would in the least redeem it – dining with the Governor or a member of Congress! But alone in the distant woods or fields, in unpretending sprout-lands or pastures tracked by rabbits, even in a bleak and, to most, cheerless day, like this, when a villager would be thinking of his inn, I come to myself, I once more feel myself grandly related, and that cold and solitude are friends of mine.*

> *I suppose that this value, in my case, is equivalent to what others get by churchgoing and prayer. I come home to my solitary woodland walk as the homesick go home. I thus dispose of the superfluous and see things as they are, grand and beautiful . . .*

Walking in the woods with Thoreau

Being a political radical, Thoreau naturally studied at Harvard, and then, having acquired the foundations for a very conventional philosopher (rhetoric, classics, mathematics and so on), returned to his native town where he became part of a group of writers that included Ralph Waldo Emerson, the leading light of a movement called New England transcendentalism. This cult-like movement held that it's through nature that you get in touch with your essential soul.

It was in 1845 that Thoreau relocated himself about half an hour's walk from his home to a small wooden shed, which he fondly but inaccurately called a 'log-cabin', on the shores of Walden Pond, which isn't a pond but a lake set in some forest (ponds, after all, are defined by being small, and this one the locals said was bottomless). Thoreau can at least be allowed this small contribution to human knowledge – he found the lake at its deepest point was 100 feet. Whatever his motives for moving there, it wasn't particularly secluded, being very close to the town, and indeed Thoreau praises not only wilderness in some supposed pure state but also 'partially cultivated countryside'. In his 1 November 1858 journal entry he writes:

Take the shortest way round and stay at home. A man dwells in his native valley like a corolla in its calyx, like an acorn in its cup. Here, of course, is all that you love, all that you expect, all that you are. Here is your bride elect, as close to you as she can be got. Here is all the best and all the worst you can imagine. What more do you want? Bear her away then! Foolish people imagine that what they imagine is somewhere else.

The experience of living alone in his shed in the 'wilds' inspired his next book, *Walden, or Life in the Woods*, which combines complimentary descriptions of the woods with disparaging observations on human nature and society such as that the 'mass of men lead lives of quiet desperation'. *Life in the Woods* starts by saying that most people waste their time by trying to acquire material goods, instead of living simply (which is Plato's ancient lament too) and that even those who rise above that waste time reading modern fiction instead of Homer and Aeschylus. That is the Harvard influence. Fortunately, as the story unfolds, Thoreau begins to find nature in all her mystery and splendour even more interesting than the Greek classics. For this reason, more important than his books are his daily journal entries.

Each entry was a two-step process. First, Thoreau would carefully record his observations, such as the weather for the day, which flowers were in blossom, how deep was the water of Walden Pond and the behaviour of any animals he saw. But then, after this, he'd attempt to identify and describe the spiritual and the aesthetic significance of what he'd seen. Thoreau recalls approvingly the story that when a traveller arrived and asked the poet Wordsworth's servant to show him her master's study, she showed him a room saying, 'Here is his library, but his study is out of doors.' So it was with Thoreau.

Valuing the wonders of Nature

Scientists say that humans are actually in the middle of the sixth great extinction, as it's called. The last one was 65 million years ago and saw the disappearance of the dinosaurs. This time, the world is losing all types of creatures, especially fellow mammals. This extinction began as the inevitable consequence of the success of one species some 50,000 years ago, which began to multiply and spread across the face of the earth, killing and destroying as it did so. Alfred Russell Wallace, forgotten co-author of the theory of natural selection, wrote 'we live in a zoologically impoverished world from which all the largest, and fiercest, and strangest forms have recently disappeared'. Creatures such as the flightless birds, of which the dodo is the only one we remember, are its victims, along with the woolly rhino, mammoth and elk, and giant varieties of kangaroos, sloths, goannas and even car-sized tortoises. Then there's the sad examples of the pygmy hippos and elephants, despatched from the last few places in the Mediterranean where they'd survived up to perhaps 10,000 years ago.

One environmental philosopher with a strong aesthetic sense, Holmes Roysten, recently put it thus:

> *Several billion years worth of creative toil, several million species of teeming life, have been handed over to the care of this late-coming species in which mind has flowered and morals have emerged. Ought not those of this sole moral species do something less self-interested than to count all the produce of an evolutionary ecosystem as rivets in their space ship, resources in their larder, laboratory materials, recreation for their ride?*

> *. . . If true to their specific epithet, ought not Homo Sapiens value this host of species as something with a claim to care in its own right? . . . There is something Newtonian, not yet Einsteinian, besides something morally naïve, about living in a reference frame where one species takes itself as absolute and values everything else relative to its utility.*

Dodos are just birds – how many of them do you need to have? Maybe just enough to keep the zoos going, next to the last few pandas and cuddly koala bears – enough to provide something for future generations to look at and, if we ever got another chance, to even return to the wild. Nowadays, scientists are trying to develop ways to stockpile the DNA and genetic codes of rare animals so that if (when) they die out scientists can resurrect them later; in which case no animals need be left, but plenty of test tube samples.

Equally, these DNA samples reveal that animals are actually all much of a muchness. Human beings are very closely related not only to monkeys but to things like spiders and marigolds. People are just carbon-based living organisms, when you get down to it. So what's all this fuss about saving species about? Probably it's got more to do with aesthetic priorities than anything else. Certainly, the world doesn't need any dodos as long as Trafalgar Square is still full of pigeons. As Darwin himself remarks in *Origin of Species*:

> *Many years ago, when comparing, and seeing others compare, the birds from the separate islands of the Galapagos Archipelago, both one with another, and with those from the American mainland, I was much struck how entirely vague and arbitrary is the distinction between species and varieties.*

What people today are living through, or more accurately, participating in, is a cyclical process of the reduction in biodiversity. Previous extinctions were due to climatic change, perhaps triggered by geological or celestial events. This one is just due to humanity's approach to nature – basically, people destroying whatever they find for the immediate satisfaction of their wants.

Saving the Spotted Quoll

Half of all the mammal species that have become extinct worldwide (in historical times) disappeared for ever from just one wealthy country, Australia. Australia is the original sanctuary island, where many animals to be found nowhere else in the world uniquely survived and flourished – until the last 100 years or so.

In total, 126 species of plants and animals have died out of existence in Australia in just 200 years. Now extinction is part of the natural world. But a rate like this would normally take a million years. Not just the dodo, but the great auk and the thylacine (which died a lonely death in Hobart zoo in 1936) are extinct, while the Toolache wallaby, which used to be abundant in the swampy grasslands of south Australia, and the desert rat kangaroo now exist only in photo albums. And the spotted-tailed quoll, the torrent tree frog, the golden bandicoot, the woylie, the double-eyed fig parrot and Boyd's forest dragon are all waiting in the last few shrinking remnants of their habitats for fires, chainsaws and bulldozers to catch up with them too.

Yet is there really so little space left on earth for other species? Aldo Leopold wrote of the insatiable demands of development:

> *If in a city we had six vacant lots available to the youngsters of a certain neighbourhood for playing ball, it might be 'development' to build houses on the first, and the second, and the third, and the fourth, and even the fifth, but when we build houses on the last one, we forget what houses are for. The sixth house would not be development at all, but rather it would be mere short-sighted stupidity. 'Development' is like Shakespeare's virtue, 'which grown into a pleurisy, dies of its own too-much'.*

Part V
Philosophy and Science

'I'd like you to meet Pythagoras Johnson, Aristotle Sutton, Plato Hinks, Democritus Wilford, Hegel Smith, Descartes Mitchell......'

In this part . . .

'I didn't get a book on philosophy to read about boring old science' said one of my fan letters the other day, but equally, a lot of people these days want what they read to do just that. Only they want the latest bang-up-to-date theories of the universe – the scientific worldview – and not this history of ideas stuff! But in this part, both tastes are amply catered for, because we put the two halves of philosophy – often separated off – back together again. The result? By the end of the book, we really do have a 'theory of everything' and have everything sorted out and cleaned up and organised. Everything, I promise you. And if this part doesn't make you sceptical about someone's ability to do that, nothing will.

Chapter 17

From Ancient Science to Modern Philosophy

> *The strongest arguments prove nothing so long as the conclusions are not verified by experience. Experimental science is the queen of sciences and the goal of all speculation.*
>
> – Roger Bacon

You hear a lot about ancient philosophers, but not much about ancient scientists. At least, that's what it seems like. But words can mislead! Until late in the 18th century, what you now call science *was* the central theme of philosophy. Equally (if confusingly) what was *then* called science was really philosophy, or 'knowledge of what's necessarily true'. It was only after Isaac Newton, who set out on paper a new way of naming and defining things, that we had not only 'physiks' but science too. The philosophy of nature (as it was called then) was studied as much by Aristotle, Kant and Descartes, on the philosophers' team, as it would later be by Copernicus, Kepler, Galileo, Bacon and Newton, on the newly re-badged scientists' team.

This chapter starts with a look at early attempts to make sense of events and processes in the everyday world around us, from gravity to light, and atoms and empty space – or 'nothing'. It also covers a bit of more conventional 'science', such as Newton's and Darwin's efforts to make sense of nature by supposing new laws and underlying mechanisms.

Theorising on Everything with Early Greek Philosophers

The central assumption of science is that the world follows rules – rules that you can identify and investigate. The most important of these rules is that of *cause and effect* – if something happens, then something must have caused it. And if you can find out the cause, you can either stop things happening – or make them happen, exactly when and as you like. Linked to that is the belief that the world is orderly and consistent, and the assumption that identical conditions will produce identical outcomes. Notice anything about these? They're all philosophical ideas, and you can't prove them in a scientific way!

So when philosophers today look at what the Ancients thought, it's not just a historical diversion. Their views order and continue to frame today's views. *For better or for worse.*

Seeing water everywhere with Thales

Thales of Miletus is sometimes called the first true philosopher. But if that's so, he's also the first true scientist. He probably lived around 2,600 years ago, and was considered to be one of the Seven Wise Men of the Ancient World on account of his mathematical and astronomical knowledge, which he applied to practical issues.

Among Thales's achievements was predicting the eclipse of 585 BC, which was almost total and took place during a battle – well 'weirding' the killing. Another story (told by Aristotle) describes how his science led him to anticipate a very good olive season, and so he hired in advance all the olive presses in Miletus. That summer indeed saw a bumper crop and so, having cornered the olive press market, he was able to rehire the presses out at a tidy profit.

No doubt this windfall funded several years of Thales's less profitable speculations on the *study of essences* – the search for the defining features of things over and above their unreliable surface appearances. This is the problem that Plato harks on about all the time. However, Thales, like Plato's contrarian (always disagreeing with the boss!) student Aristotle, went about things by investigating and observing nature, rather than by a process of theoretical reflections leading to the creation of new, abstract properties.

Thales decided that the human soul must be a kind of magnet, because only magnets could make things move by an invisible force (as people thought souls were able to do). Similarly, practical investigations led him to conclude that the world was, in essence, water. Why say the world is made of water rather than, say, of rock? Well, Thales saw that water can turn into air (steam) and likewise freeze into rocks – ice. And you can crush plants into (greeny-browny) water. His isn't such a silly idea, and it leads towards the possibility people hold dear today, of everything being made up of the same thing – atoms.

So Thales was no fool, even if Plato (with his own different theories to promote) makes fun of him in his playlet, the *Theaetetus* (with that story of the wise man so busy staring up at the stars that he fell down a well).

Breaking everything down into atoms with Democritus

If Thales started the quest for the essence of matter (see the previous section), the great Leucippus originally came up with the first theory of atomism. But because Leucippus left only a few scraps of writing, it's his pupil (circa. 460–370 BC), comparatively well served with some 50 fragments of his writings left, who gets most of the credit.

Atomism theorises that the world around, with all its diversity of appearance, is fundamentally created out of tiny (invisible) building blocks that are all exactly the same. Part of the ancient theory was that nothing can split these blocks. Nowadays atoms are split all the time to make electricity. Either way, atoms are both a very modern idea and one that was kicking around several thousand years ago. And kicked around it was too, because the problem with atoms is that between one atom and another either something else must exist (which upsets the theory, because what is that something?), or there's nothing – a void – which is an even worse problem than the missing something, for how could any serious philosophers say that nothing existed?

Leucippus did precisely that, saying romantically that atoms meet in the void and join together to form compounds with different properties, before separating again. Democritus added on to this his own idea that certain particularly high-quality and smooth atoms make up people's souls, and interact with the slightly cruder world atoms, thereby giving rise to sensations. That bit of the ancient science has fallen by the wayside, however.

Carving Up the World with Natural Philosophers

Philosophers like talking about nothing, and the best form of nothing is, of course, space. Right back at the beginning of (recorded) philosophy, Democritus said simply the void is what 'is not'. But Plato, who's the definitive word on this as on so many other matters, thought that space is actually a very special kind of thing, neither made of matter like the rest of the universe nor yet entirely abstract, like the forms themselves. (Plato's mysterious 'Forms' are explained in Chapter 2). Space is something in between: 'an invisible and characterless thing, that receives all things and shares in a perplexing way all that is intelligible,' or so Socrates' friend, Timaeus, explains in the dialogue of the same name. The only way to investigate its properties is by 'a kind of bastard (that is, separated from its origins) reasoning that does not involve sense perception', such as in a dreamlike trance.

Plato's idea is more sophisticated than those of other philosophers and indeed physicists up to and perhaps including Einstein. (But not the latest batch of sub-atomic theorists.) Certainly, most of the rest, following Aristotle and Newton, even thought that space was amenable to empirical and experimental investigation, and ended up with a highly theoretical *absolute space*, absolute in that it was eternal, fixed and very, very regular – which didn't even fit the facts.

And Plato's approach has elements of relativity in it. When objects are impressed onto the flux, as he puts it in his playlet, the *Timaeus*, it in turn changes, and in changing affects the objects again. 'It sways irregularly in every direction as it is shaken by those things, and being set in motion it in turn shakes them.' Matter acts on space, and space acts on matter. This is pretty much Einstein's Theory of General Relativity in a nutshell, more than 2,000 years before he lived.

Non-being and nothingness

'Nothing shall come of nothing, speak again' advised King Lear to his daughter (that's my literary reference for the book over with, folks!), but like many philosophers before and since, she heeded him not. You can trace controversy over whether nothingness really exists back to the pre-Socratic philosophers in Ancient Greece or, to be more precise, to Asia Minor, southern Italy and Sicily. Foremost amongst them was Parmenides of Elea, who warned in the early fifth century BC that to speak of not being was to take a 'wholly incredible course, since you can not recognise Not Being (for this is impossible), nor speak of it, for thought and Being are the same thing'.

Lucretius on the nature of things

De Rerum Natura, which is the posh Latin name for 'On the Nature of Things', is a kind of epic poem. It would be an unusual book, let alone poem. Lucretius (circa, 95–54 BC) describes it as a honey-coated pill containing some unpalatable truths about the universe – truths discovered by the great philosopher Epicurus, such as that everything in the universe is made up of just two things: empty space and tiny, invisible particles that you can neither create nor destroy. His celebrated thought experiment of the spear is intended to demonstrate that the universe is infinite and contains all possible things and all possible worlds:

Suppose for a moment that the whole of space were bounded and that someone made their way to its uttermost boundary and threw a flying spear. Do you suppose that the missile, hurled with might and main, would speed along the course on which it was aimed? Or do you think something would block the way and stop it? You must

assume one alternative or the other. But neither of them leaves you so much as a loophole to wriggle through. Both force you to admit that the universe continues without end. Whether there is some obstacle lying on the boundary line that prevents the spear from going farther on its course, or whether it flies on beyond, it cannot in fact have started from the boundary.

In fact, the view set out in Lucretius's poem was far and away the best description of the universe at least up to the 20th century, and for all today's sophisticated models it still, perhaps, remains in some ways superior to present thinking. For example, Lucretius (or rather Epicurus) specifically added a little swerve to the movement of the fundamental particles, so as to allow for the possibility of freewill in human lives. Otherwise, without this the universe and everything in it is no more meaningful than the ceaseless playing of the tiny motes of dust in a sunbeam.

Parmenides and his followers, the Eleatics (like Zeno of the tortoise race fame), were challenging the teachings of Pythagoras, who claimed that nothing, a kind of not-being, does indeed exist. But others – such as Democritus of Abdera who's remembered for his theory that the world is made up of atoms – who were tracing a few decades after Parmenides, insisted, like Pythagoras, that not-being must in fact be, whatever Parmenides' reasoning.

And so it is too that you find Plato, in the playlet called the *Sophist*, coming down on the side of nothingness and saying that what's not in some sense also is. For Plato, not-being is a necessary part of creating distinctions in the first place. If it weren't possible to have nothing in the cupboard it wouldn't be possible to have something in it either! This is the same thought that persuaded medieval theologians, such as Thomas Aquinas, to say that it's necessary that God brings things into being from nothing, and prompted Leibniz to insist on the nothingness of empty space as a preliminary stage to arranging his monads within it. If existentialism is the pinnacle of abstract philosophy, its origins are here in the Ancients' musings over the physical structure of the universe.

Nasty modern existentialism

Even the Nazi existentialist philosopher Heidegger (who was long an enthusiastic member of the Nazi party and even cherished hopes of being its leading philosophical theorist) has a place for nothingness in his system, saying that '*das Nichts selbst nichtet*', which is German for 'Nothing noths' (*noths* is a made-up word; Heidegger liked to do that). What did Heidegger mean? No one knows. The logical positivist Rudolf Carnap (1891–1970) used this as one of his examples of metaphysical nonsense. But it's not true to say that everybody agrees that nothing doesn't exist. Many of the 20th-century existentialists wanted to sort out nothingness as much as the Ancients had. Sartre writes that it's only through awareness of nothing (or nothingness, if you prefer) that freedom is possible. Nothingness causes anxiety, but in choosing something you define yourself. Heidegger's something, though, was service to the Führer in the project of 'purifying' German culture. So beware of nothing! It noths!

Fighting it out over science: Aristotle and Plato

Aristotle considered the origins of philosophic inquiry to stem from people's innate desire to understand the causes behind the natural world. For him, it was common sense to link the gods of mythology and the 'true essences' of philosophy because they both attempt to explain the forces of nature.

Since the dawn of the scientific age in the 17th century, philosopher-scientists have insisted that people should put aside beautiful but irrational stories of poets, artists or mystics, and accept instead only scientific explanations of the natural world that you can defend through argument and demonstration.

Yet this new concept of truth isn't so new. Aristotle engaged in extensive biological studies of living, breathing organisms, but still had to frame his studies within a theory – which is always every bit as imaginary as anything in myth. In Aristotle's science, both the individual parts of organisms and all its activities contribute towards a single ultimate end. Everything has one purpose or function. Darwin challenged that in a way, by making much of nature random. But he still conjures with a general purpose for all things – in this case, the need to survive (see the later section 'Explaining evolution with Darwin'). Darwin's theory has great explanatory power, of course. But so did Aristotle's. And so too do the foundational tales of the Ancients.

In fact, a generation before Aristotle, in one of Plato's little playlets – a woeful account known as the *Apology* – Socrates disapproves of explanations based either on traditional stories and myths or on bang-up-to-date science. He moans about the inability of the poets to defend or explain their conceptions of nature:

> . . . *they do not make their work by wisdom, but by some kind of talent and by inspiration, like the seers and the 'oracle-mongers'. These people, too, say many things, wonderful things, but they know nothing about what they are saying.*

Opening up the book of nature with Isaac Newton

Sir Isaac Newton is such a great philosopher he's been conspicuously banned from most books on the subject, in order, I suppose, not to make the rest of the philosophers look useless. Every bit of philosophy he studies, after all, turned into a science – the menace! Only the things he didn't get around to doing are left as philosophy for today's philosophers.

The most famous scientist of them all, Newton 'invented' the laws of gravity and many other very useful things that I won't describe here in maths, optics (the science and mysteries of light), theology and alchemy too.

He was particularly interested in something called salnitrum – a strange mineral compound that was made out of an acid (ideally nitric acid, for home alchemists reading this), an alkaline salt (like bicarbonate of soda, a white powder you can clean your teeth with, amongst other useful things) and, last but by no means least, a 'volatile salt' (like ammonium carbonate) liquids which were known to be just the job for reviving people who had fainted. Mix all these ingredients together correctly, and (Newton and other alchemists thought) you can create a kind of magical ingredient which enabled metals to grow like plants. And why not, they thought, when plants can grow in the soil. In fact, because it contained salnitrum, Newton and others thought that the Earth itself was a great animal, or more precisely, an enormous animate vegetable. Nutty? Perhaps. Yet it was through ideas like this that Newton explained the law of gravity. Gravity was for Newton not only an invisible force, like others that chemistry revealed, but also, in effect, the very hand of God.

Yet out of all his many interests, it's to philosophy he always returns.

And why not, because before he was born (in 1642), philosophers didn't make any distinction between the kinds of knowledge philosophers sought, and the kinds natural scientists did. For instance, in his great book *Principia*

Mathematica he acknowledges that you can trace the mathematics of the laws of gravity back to Pythagoras. Newton recalls of the Ancient Greek that:

> . . . *by means of experiments he ascertained weights by which all tones on equal strings were reciprocal as the squares of the lengths of the string . . . The proportions discovered . . . he applied to the heavens and . . . . by comparing those weights with those of the planets and the lengths of the strings with the distances of the planets he understood by means of the harmony of the heavens that the weights of the planets towards the Sun were reciprocally as the squares of their distances from the Sun.*

In philosophy, just as in everyday discourse, the term *nature* is loose and elastic. It's covered pretty much everything, from the ultimate nature of the universe, to the living world, to the non-human world, to (at its broadest) everything that exists.

The idea that things that people like John Locke used to call *ideas* are really *brain states* – phenomena created by chemical reactions in the tissue of the brain – is a 20th-century elaboration of an older doctrine, perhaps spelt out best by the 17th-century British philosopher Thomas Hobbes. Nowadays 'consciousness' or 'what goes on in people's heads' may also go under rather grand-sounding titles such as the *contingent mind-brain identity hypothesis* or the *central state mechanism*. Locke indeed writes in the second book of his *Essay Concerning Human Understanding* that 'perception, thinking, doubting, believing, reasoning, knowing' are all aspects of a kind of 'internal sense', not in principle different from those of smell, touch, taste and so on.

Making friends with Nature

To most Ancient Greeks, including Plato and Aristotle, natural laws are revealed by both of the disciplines that the modern age calls philosophy and science – and indeed by religion as well. Viewed like this, nature has a kind of intelligence, a mind of its own, which you need to tune into in order to understand the subtle regularities of its workings. To understand nature is, in this sense, to understand the patterns of the intentions of God. This is one influence on the association of nature with things of value, whether ethically or aesthetically speaking. The natural is good: true art represents this goodness, or taps into its rhythms; true morality captures the goodness in people and provides principles by which humanity might flourish. This general hunch surfaces in different ways down through Western history, from medieval theology to the Romantic poets.

Reductionism and *eliminitativism*

How does the mind work? Is this a question for philosophy – or for science? After all, you can't see thoughts (even if nowadays scientists claim to see electrical traces of them in brain scans). Thoughts are indisputably invisible, intangible. That said, maybe we don't need them? *Reductionism* is the view that thinking is best reduced to a purely physical or chemical process of stimulus/response, and that behaviour is merely a complicated reaction to a stimulus.

Another recent theory called *eliminitativism*, which sounds like it might be something to do with toilet training small children, is actually intended to flush the notions of mind and thought down the water closet of knowledge as outmoded expressions relating to a superstitious pre-scientific era. And you don't want those, do you! The idea behind eliminitativism, (sorry, I should say the chemical stimulus propelling more chemical reactions) is that many and perhaps all of the everyday, commonsense notions of mental states (such as beliefs, or views or desires) are misleading fictions that bear no relationship to anything in 'reality'.

Nature stands in contrast to the artificial world: that is, things made by human beings. It refers to the whole universe, and to the whole of time. Philosophical views of nature have fluctuated, with people sometimes seeing it as random, messy and imperfect. The Romantic writers and philosophers such as Shelley reacted against the recent taming of nature by Newton (reducing the planets to mere lumps of rocks circling the Sun) and suggested that nature, instead, has a higher state that determines all values.

For many philosophers from Descartes down, to be human is to be capable of transcending the constraints of nature through reason. For existentialists like Sartre, the idea that nature, human or otherwise, might have any bearing on the value of people's lives, or the decisions people make in shaping them, is both wrong and morally degrading. Viewed this way, nature is a kind of threat to human freedom – a mechanistic system from which you need to escape in order to be truly yourself.

But what is nature, in and of itself? If you look at the natural world, you find that (for better or worse) it's everywhere shaped and changed by human influence. You're *part* of nature.

A CLOSER LOOK

As Henri Poincaré put it nicely in the 19th century, 'Science is facts; just as houses are made of stones, so is science made of facts; but a pile of stones is not a house and a collection of facts is not necessarily science.'

Explaining evolution with Darwin

Charles Darwin (1809–82) was born in England, or Shrewsbury to be precise, but people don't remember him for his fossil hunts around Wenlock Edge there. Rather, he's famous for his travels in the good ship Beagle to exotic places like the Galapagos Island, full of giant tortoises and other rare species like Lava Lizards, and Blue or Masked Boobies (or little birds to you or me) and dolphins, as well as to Tierra del Fuego where he was more struck by the locals, of whom he noted in his diary:

> . . . *how little must the mind of one of these beings resemble that of an educated man! What a scale of improvement is comprehended between the faculties of a Fuegian savage and a Sir Isaac Newton! Whence have these people come? Have they remained in the same state since the creation of the world?*

Eventually he wrote it all up, expanding on an already existing scientific theory in his celebrated account *On the Origin of Species*, with its sub-title, *By Means of Natural Selection or the Preservation of Favoured Races in the Struggle for Life* (1859).

In the work he used examples of the newly discovered or little- known species peculiar to these remote islands to try to demonstrate that related species had at some point had a common ancestor, and that by a process of either successfully adapting to circumstances and therefore flourishing, or failing to adapt and therefore dying out, species evolved into the myriad forms he saw at the time.

Darwin extended his theory to cover the human race, and this challenged many deeply-held social, ethical and psychological assumptions. Moral values, even, were just another form of randomly generated behaviour whose effect was to improve the chances of species preservation.

This is what Darwin had to say, for example, in the book on the link between morality and evolution:

> *The moral nature of man has reached its present standard, partly through the advancement of his reasoning powers and consequently of a just public opinion, but especially from his sympathies having been rendered more tender and widely diffused through the effects of habit, example, instruction, and reflection. It is not improbable that after long practice virtuous tendencies may be inherited.*

Darwin then continues to say that 'with the more civilised races' belief in God has had a profound influence on the development of moral codes. However, he concludes:

> '...the first foundation or origin of the moral sense lies in the social instincts, including sympathy; and these instincts no doubt were primarily gained, as in the case of the lower animals, through natural selection.

Some philosophers, particularly those who think God has a role in morals, resist the reduction of ethics to a survival strategy, arguing that because evolutionary theory rests on this random principle, applying the theory to human society and culture is inappropriate. But that seems to be missing the point. Darwin is indicating how a simple mechanism may result in complex behaviour – even moral behaviour.

Discovering relativity with Galileo

Galileo Galilei was born in Pisa, where he studied medicine and later mathematics. From 1592–1610 he was professor of mathematics at Padua, applying his mathematics to the mysteries of motion, both the celestial and the earthly kind. From 1610 he became 'first philosopher' (as opposed to various lesser philosophers, presumably) and private mathematician to the Grand Duke of Tuscany, a position that enabled him to set about communicating his ideas through a series of books that changed the direction of both philosophy and science.

Challenging the Ancients

Galileo's direction was something long overdue, because ever since Aristotle philosophers had been promoting positions that weren't only wrong (such as that heavy objects fall proportionately faster than light ones), but were also cumbersome and unproductive. In a book called *The Assayer* (1623) Galileo particularly concentrates on analysing Aristotle, separating out his notion of movement that allowed, for example, plants to move towards the sun, in the same way that you or I might move towards the biscuit tray during a discussion of the philosophy of science.

Analysing the world

Galileo offers a more precise definition that separates in the physical and psychological worlds. Doing this makes the physical world open to mathematical analysis. *The Dialogue Concerning the Two World Systems – Ptolemaic and Copernican* (1632) sets out, in addition to the well-known arguments for the Sun-centred solar system, a more original one for the relativity of motion and space.

Galileo throws his weights around

Galileo simply says imagine that before you carefully drop a large iron weight and a small lead weight over the side of a tower like the conveniently leaning one at Pisa, you tie a string between them. Will the little weight try to fall less slowly than the big one, and so hold it up – acting like a little lead balloon? If so, would tying ten little weights to one big weight make it fall even more slowly?

Yet one big weight plus ten little weights is actually an even bigger mass, and so, seen like that, the whole lot ought to fall even faster than before! This is a contradiction, and the only way around it is to assume that all things fall at the same speed. If you sort of still doubt it, you're probably remembering that air resistance causes light things to float about a bit rather than fall straight down. Hence Galileo is always throwing metal weights around.

The book featured Galileo's celebrated ship thought experiment, in which two friends discuss whether they'd be able to tell the difference between whether they were in the cabin of a boat sailing steadily 'in any direction you like', but smoothly, from being in a motionless boat. Would they be able to detect the boat's movement, for example, by taking a goldfish bowl with them and watching to see whether the fish were affected, or by throwing a ball across the cabin to each other?

This thought experiment, like the much misunderstood one of dropping the two balls off the leaning Tower of Pisa, proves its point logically, not experimentally. The ship experiment proves motion is relative to the frame of reference, while the Tower of Pisa one demonstrates that all objects must fall at the same speed – or as posh folk put it, that everything must be subject to the same acceleration effects from gravity.

The *Dialogue* caused the Vatican to condemn Galileo, a year after its publication – confining him to his (actually rather nice) Italian farmhouse and obliging him to recant. But the reason for that censorship seems to have been less to do with the debate concerning the two rival astronomical systems and more about a very blunt insult included by Galileo (who was nothing if not arrogant) to the sagacity of the Pope himself. In his elegant and witty *Dialogue*, Galileo put the Pope's well-known views into the mouth of an imaginary character – a buffoon – whom he called Simplicio.

As well as a great writer and a bit of a satirist, Galileo was also a careful empirical scientist, who made systematic and effective observation part of his method, most famously, using his new telescope. But it was he who wrote that the book of nature is written in mathematics.

Chapter 18

Investigating the Science of Society

Man's characteristic privilege is that the bond he accepts is not physical but moral; that is, social. He is governed not by a material environment brutally imposed on him, but by a conscience superior to his own, the superiority of which he feels. Because the greater, better part of his existence transcends the body, he escapes the body's yoke, but is subject to that of society.

– Émile Durkheim

*I*s there really a science of society? No one's quite sure. They're not even sure what to call it: *social science*, *sociology* or maybe something quite different like *cultural studies*. But don't get hung up on all that. In this chapter, I look at this branch of philosophy, made popular by the pioneers of sociology such as Auguste Comte, Max Weber and even Karl Marx.

Understanding the Science of Society

Auguste Comte coined the term *sociology* in the 19th century. Pioneers or founders of the new science of society include Jean-Jacques Rousseau, Alexis De Tocqueville and Karl Marx. Marxism made social class the key to understanding human relationships, and Max Weber introduced different categories of rationality as a way to understand what motivates people and completed Marx's theory of class conflict by adding a symbolic element, the social status. But it's Émile Durkheim's study on suicide that's the classic example of the sociological approach. In it, the French philosopher demonstrates that suicide isn't just an individual phenomena, but a social phenomenon that changes according to religious beliefs and social structures. (For more on Durkheim, see the section 'Socialising with Durkheim', later in this chapter.)

Judging behaviour or giving advice isn't the aim of social scientists, who focus rather on the roots and origins of opinions, representations and ideologies.

To study society and not just individual motivations is necessary to make sense of human life. Political philosophy, in particular, can't ignore the influence of shared ideologies and systems of beliefs. Anthropologists also observe and analyse rituals, myths, magic and various forms of belief, interpreting them as primitive examples of thoughts that all societies have, however apparently modern and developed they appear to be.

Keeping Positive with Comte

The science of society really starts with Auguste Comte (1798–1857), a middle-class French intellectual. He was inspired by his study of medieval Catholic scholars into attempting to produce not only a new religion of humanity but a blueprint for a new social order.

Comte wrote out the six volumes of his *Cours de Philosophie Positive,* which translates as *Course in Positive Philosophy,* between 1830 and 1842. Like René Descartes and many philosophers since, Comte starts from a position of deep admiration for the precision and authority of the natural sciences, characterised (at least in the public mind) by the advances in physics and chemistry. His positivist idea was that the methods of natural science were the only way to understand human nature, both in individuals and collectively. Hence the only way to find out how to organise society was to actually apply these scientific, quantitative (that is, measuring things) methods to society itself, dissecting it to discover the laws and the principles governing it.

The social construction of reality

Karl Marx and Friedrich Engels described society as split between two warring classes – the workers and owners or bosses. However, even if social scientists are themselves Marxists (as a lot of them seem to be), most of them think it's more complicated than that.

The French philosopher Louis Althusser (who strangled his wife to death – how would social scientists explain that?) has influenced both political science and sociology with his theory about dominant ideologies and the 'state apparatus' that splits society up between bureaucrats and politicians on one side, with workers and business owners lumped together on the other. Althusser says that, in a bid to maintain power, the state has to make sure that all the institutions in society (the TV and media, schools and colleges, industry and big business) project only the picture they want people to see of social reality.

Philosophers argue over exactly what is meant by the term *positivism*, (maybe Comte didn't know exactly either, as he borrowed the notion from another French philosopher and economist called Claude de Saint-Simon, who he worked for as secretary for a number of years) but basically it's rooted in this kind of attempt to apply practical, scientific methods to old philosophical mysteries previously investigated largely by the power of thought and reflection.

Comte's great discovery (well, it sounds important anyway) was of a Law of Human Progress. According to this, all societies pass through three stages: the theological, the metaphysical and the scientific or positive.

The defining feature of each stage is the mental attitude of the people:

- ✔ During the *theological stage*, people seek to discover the essential nature of things and the ultimate cause of existence, interpreted as God. Philosophers, Comte thought, were stuck at this stage, perpetually but fruitlessly pursuing these sorts of questions.

- ✔ Most people, however, were at the next, the *metaphysical stage*, which involves increasing use of abstract theory.

- ✔ The final stage – the so-called *scientific* (or *positive*) *stage* – comes only when enough people in a society put aside the illusions of opinion (Comte echoes Plato more than a little here) and confine themselves to logical deduction from observed phenomena.

The stages are also supposed to correspond to periods of human history:

- ✔ The theological stage relates to the bad old days before recorded history and on into the medieval world.

- ✔ Comte compares the metaphysical stage to the 16th, 17th and 18th centuries, a time when monarchies and military despots gave way to political ideals such as democracy and human rights, including, most importantly for social life, property rights.

- ✔ The last stage in history, Comte thinks, will be a scientific, technological age when people rationally plan all activity and moral rules have become universal. At this final stage the science of society – sociology – comes into its own.

The stages even apply to individuals. Comte rather unconvincingly declares

> *Now each of us is aware, if he looks back on his own history, that he was a theologian in his childhood, a metaphysician in his youth and a natural philosopher in his manhood.*

But then, remember, Comte was an idealist who also wrote of love as the guiding principle and of bringing 'feeling, reason and activity into permanent harmony'.

Socialising with Durkheim

Born the year after Comte's death (see the preceding section), Émile
Durkheim attempted to take Comte's bid to develop a science of society
a whole lot further. Durkheim tried to use the methods of natural science
(especially physics and chemistry) to understand social phenomena that
people took to be essentially just another part of the natural world. The
data relating to the structure of society he found not in a test tube but in the
shelves of official files containing statistical information on suicides, on the
labour force and census details recording people's religion and education.
But, unlike Comte and like his fellow social scientist and German contemporary Max Weber (1864–1920), Durkheim also wanted to build upon this logical
structure a more profound, metaphysical theory of social life.

His grand theory of society was that

- ✔ Individual morality and indeed consciousness are created from social
  life and the collective consciousness.
- ✔ Social life is created out of a vast symbolism.

What's more, unlike Marx's theory of class conflict (discussed in Chapter 14),
Durkheim wanted to try to find a way to achieve this new social consensus
without losing the benefits of individual emancipation and freedom.

Rules and society

Durkheim centres his recipe for a just society around what he calls *the collective consciousness* and the notion of *social facts*. These are 'ways of acting,
thinking and feeling, external to the individual' – such as the customs and
institutional practices, moral rules and laws of any society.

Although these rules exist in the minds of individuals, Durkheim says
that you can find their true form only when considering the behaviour of
the whole – of society itself. In this, not for the last time, he's echoing the
words of Plato and Socrates 2,000 years before. Like Plato (see Chapter 14),
Durkheim considered society to be essentially a moral phenomenon, created
within a framework of over-arching eternal values. And, like Plato, he rejected
efforts to build social structures out of human atoms, saying society creates
individual characters – not the other way around. In his book *The Division of
Labour in Society* (1893) he reminds the reader that, in Comte's words: 'cooperation, far from having produced society, necessarily supposes, as preamble, its spontaneous existence', and then continues:

> *Collective life is not born from individual life, but it is, on the contrary, the
> second which is born from the first . . . Co-operation is . . . the primary fact
> of moral and social life.*

For this reason, Durkheim rejects Thomas Hobbes's rough old vision of the world in the state of nature (where life is 'nasty, brutish and short', described in Chapter 14), saying that if society really were based, for example, solely on selfish calculations of interest and social contracts, then the key social relationship would be the economic, 'stripped of all regulation and resulting from the entirely free initiative of the parties'. Society would simply be the situation 'where individuals exchanged the products of their labour, without any action properly social coming to regulate this exchange. If this were so, we could with justice doubt their stability. For if self interest relates men, it is never for more than some few moments', he says, meaning that people thinking of their own interests make fickle allies. Taking up Hobbes's literary style too, Durkheim goes on:

> . . . *where interest is the only ruling force, each individual finds himself in a state of war with every other since nothing comes to mollify the egos and any truce in this eternal antagonism would not be of long duration. There is nothing less constant than interest. Today, it unites me to you: tomorrow, it will make me your enemy.*

Durkheim's conclusion is that you have to look elsewhere for an explanation of the solidarity of society. He recommends what he calls the organic approach. This approach isn't to do with lots of hens laying their eggs in the open air and making chocolate without any pesticides, but rather is the one used by Comte 50 years earlier, in which everything relates to a whole in the same way that, for example, a beehive works. Seen this way, you can then explain the division of labour only as something that evolves in the midst of pre-existing society. As Durkheim explains:

> . . . *It is thought, it is true, that everything takes place through private conventions freely disputed. Thus it seems all social action is absent. But this is to forget that contracts are possible only where a juridical regulation, and consequently a society, already exists. Hence the claim sometimes advanced that in the division of labour lies the fundamental fact of all social life is wrong.*

> *Work is not divided among independent and already differentiated individuals who by uniting and associating bring together different aptitudes. For it would be a miracle if differences thus born through chance circumstance could unite so perfectly as to form a coherent whole. Far from preceding collective life, they derive from it. They can be produced only in the midst of a society, and under the pressure of social sentiments and social needs. That is what makes them essentially harmonious.*

Durkheim's point is that societies are built up out of shared beliefs and sentiments, and the division of labour emerges from the structure created. Because, he reminds his readers, your very awareness, your consciousness, isn't an individual but a social phenomenon. Consider practical things like national flags and other shared symbols; or moral codes such as notions of basic rights; and even unwritten, generally accepted, beliefs such as the idea that you should give young children toys to play with or that swimming in the sea should be free. It's these sorts of shared things, written and unwritten rules, 'collective representations', that together create a collective consciousness.

Or think about crime and society's reaction if, for example, someone breaks into a house and steals the TV or framed photo of grandpa. Such things are wrong not because of the affront, the offence to the householder, but because of the affront *to the collective consciousness itself*. Seen this way it follows that, more generally, self-interest, or even considerations of the interests of the majority (the goal assumed by utilitarianism, see Chapter 7), cannot produce moral behaviour. Instead, it's the collective consciousness that functions as a kind of watchdog for its own well-being and presses a position based on certain principles. Durkheim says:

> It has often been remarked that civilisation has a tendency to become more rational and more logical. The cause is now evident. That alone is rational which is universal. What baffles understanding is the particular and the concrete . . . the nearer the common conscience is to particular things, the more it bears their imprint, the more unintelligible it is.

For Émile Durkheim, the essence of and the key to social life is symbolism. It's through symbols that individuals communicate most effectively, and their social values are preserved and embodied in the sacred symbols.

Simple and complex societies

Durkheim makes a special distinction between two types of possible society:

- ✔ **Simple societies:** These are held together by traditions that operate uniformly on the various members, who are like little atoms with no differences between themselves and fully interchangeable.

- ✔ **Organic societies:** This way of organising society is more complex. It involves a range of parallel institutions and traditions, with individuals falling into increasingly distinct sub-groupings, each with its own traditions and social norms. Within each grouping individuals can become specialised and fulfil a particular function in the social whole. Durkheim sees the division of labour (which Marx sought to abolish, seeing it as creating inequality) as a desirable aspect of this evolution.

But a particular disease of complex societies exists. Durkheim calls the disease *anomie*. This is the sense of futility and alienation. In *Suicide: a Study of Sociology*, Durkheim takes the discovery that self-destruction is more prevalent amongst certain religious groups – Protestants – than amongst others, notably Catholics. In this most celebrated (for want of a better word) study, Durkheim looked at the number of people committing suicide and found that it wasn't just an individual activity (tragedy) but an action directly linked to and reflecting a general breakdown in social cohesion.

Being Bureaucratic with Weber

Like Durkheim, Max Weber (1864–1920) also finds important links between religious beliefs and apparently unrelated aspects of social life. But his particular insight, set out in his best-known work *The Protestant Ethic and the Spirit of Capitalism*, is to do with economics.

According to Weber, the industrial revolution in Europe was linked to the rejection of traditional and elaborate Catholic religious practice in favour of a Protestant ideology that emphasised the virtue of a lifetime spent working hard with no greater aim than serving God. Being rich was *good*.

This was a huge contrast to the established view of the time. After all, in the Bible didn't Saint Matthew specifically warn that 'You cannot serve both God and Money'? The Catholics certainly knew that. Yet the new approach made making money okay. Not to forget, it also, very conveniently, justified reducing paying workers to the absolute bare minimum required for them to survive, in order to maximise those holy and virtuous profits.

Weber argued, in particular, that the development of capitalism occurred first in Holland and England, out of all the world's societies, because these two countries were Protestant powers. All the economic changes and scientific discoveries associated with the time flowed from this pre-existing fact, rather than vice versa. In this way, Weber's view harmonises with Durkheim's approach, by putting the social before the economic.

Capitalism

Capitalism is the economic system based on the production of goods, ultimately for consumption, by means of capital (money capable of hiring people and buying land and machines). Marx and Engels used the term as an insult. They predicted that capitalism must finally dramatically implode, due to its 'fundamental contradictions', and would then be replaced by communism. Certainly, even bourgeois economists do accept that capitalism has its cycles, with recurrent troughs and adjustments – in bad cases, economic depressions and slumps. But nowadays, communism itself looks pretty unlikely to replace capitalism. (See Chapter 14 for more on why.)

Max Weber's career was largely spent in several professorial positions in respectable German universities, churning out his heavy-handed theories. But he was actually involved too, for a period, as a bureaucrat himself – as a hospital administrator during the First World War. His idea is that it's not enough to explain activity in terms of causes and mechanisms – a purpose and bureaucracies must exist. Weber favours government according to rules, rather than mere authority. The government is the best guardian of social life because it operates in the interests of rationality. But what exactly is that?

For Weber, the best form of *rationality* is when the choice of means and ends either:

- ✔ Accord with the canons of logic, the procedures of science or of successful economic behaviour.

- ✔ Constitute a way of achieving certain ends, when the means chosen to achieve them accord with factual and theoretical knowledge.

Otherwise, if the ends are motivated by values, be they religious, moral or aesthetic, or if values influence or determine the means employed, then the behaviour is 'value-rational'. That sort of behaviour, for Weber, isn't nearly as good.

Sometimes tradition may decide the ends. Tradition is another kind of value, and again Weber thinks it's one that gets in the way of economic progress. Worst of all, sometimes emotions and passions affect behaviour. This he calls 'affectual action', and of course that is also opposed to rational behaviour.

In fact, Weber says you should only seek to be goal-rational (he calls it *zweckrational*), which is properly logical. For example, if someone wishes to buy a gold watch, they will (if they're goal-rational) realise it's necessary to start doing overtime at work to save money for the purchase. Weber thinks that capitalism is very rational, being made up of lots of little decisions like this. Workers move to find jobs, or lower their wages, and capitalists choose whether or not to invest their money in new factories, and to make people redundant (or maybe just shuffle them around) to increase profits.

Treating People as Economic Entities

Although economists like to portray their study as a precise kind of mathematical science, it remains firmly rooted in both social and individual psychology, as moulded by political institutions and norms. At the heart of economics is the notion of human rationality and choice, and as in theories of utilitarian ethics, economists arbitrarily consider judgements to be of equal merit: it's not important why someone buys a tin of beans, only that they do so. Yet economics is inextricably entwined with judgements of value. It both influences and is influenced by ethics.

The word *economics* comes from the Greek *oikonomia*, which itself is a combination of *oikos* meaning house and *nemein* meaning manage.

But this view of economics is a very different conception from the insatiable thirst for new goodies – products – endorsed in modern economies. Instead, the ancients believed that nature places a natural limit upon the extent of necessary riches. Aristotle distinguishes natural acquisition from what he sees as the perverse and unnatural desire to pursue wealth as an end in itself. He would've been influenced by the very Ancient Greek Xenophon (who lived around 430–350 BCE and knew Socrates) who'd earlier written a book on economics (aptly titled *Economics*) that includes an account of Socrates' views on such matters:

> . . . for the base mechanic arts, so called, have got a bad name; and what is more, are held in ill repute by civilised communities, and not unreasonably; seeing they are the ruin of the bodies of all concerned in them, workers and overseers alike, who are forced to remain in sitting postures and to hug the loom, or else to crouch whole days confronting a furnace. Hand in hand with physical enervation follows apace enfeeblement of soul: while the demand which these base mechanic arts makes on the time of those employed in them leaves them no leisure to devote to the claims of friendship and the state.

In fact, although cities may come into being to facilitate trade and preserve life, the ancients thought that the ultimate goal of the political association was to promote virtue and the good life.

It was only nearly 2,000 years later that naughty Englishman John Locke was prepared to defend unlimited acquisition against the teachings of the ancients, in this case based on his conception of the labour theory of value. Following in the footsteps of Thomas Hobbes (see Chapter 14), in his *Second Treatise of Government* Locke says human beings possess an inalienable claim to their body, and this grants each of them a right to take possession of property in which they've invested their labour:

> The labour of his body and the work of his hands, we may say, are properly his. Whatsoever, then, he removes out of the state that Nature hath provided and left it in, he hath mixed his labour with it, and joined to it something that is his own, and thereby makes it his property.

Rather than understanding riches as a tool for achieving a definite and limited set of ends, Locke recognises money's ability to overcome nature's bounds. The farmer can only profit from hoarding excess produce as long as he prevents it from spoiling. If he exchanges his surplus for money, he can acquire without needing to ever again concern himself with spoilage. The body dies but wealth lives on.

Within this framework, human action is increasingly determined by simple calculations of anticipated costs and benefits – without regard for any ethical consequences. No wonder John Locke and his boss invested so much of their money and efforts in the slave trade!

Feeling Adam Smith's hidden hand

Writing a century later than Locke (see the preceding section), the Scottish philosopher Adam Smith allows society to be determined by an entirely greater, non-human force – economics. He says it's self-interest that makes the world go round.

As he famously explains in his barnstormer of a book, *The Wealth of Nations* – published in the same year as the American Declaration of Independence (1776) and still a popular read with right-wing politicians (one of the best-selling books of all time) – it's not out of the benevolence of the butcher or the baker that you can expect your supper, but from their enlightened notion of their own self-interest. People are just cogs in a beautifully functioning, money-making machine. Smith says:

> The wheels of the watch are all admirably adjusted to the end for which it was made, the pointing of the hour. All their various motions conspire in the nicest manner to produce this effect. If they were endowed with a desire and intention to produce it, they could not do it better. Yet we never ascribe any such intention or desire to them, but to the watchmaker, and we know that they are put into motion by a spring, which intends the effect it produces as little as they do.

Although the name Adam Smith is synonymous with the economics of *laissez faire* (leave it alone!), where the business of running society is left to the 'hidden hand' of the market (see sidebar) this isn't out of any lack of concern for the weakest in society, but rather out of a conviction that this is simply the best possible arrangement for everyone. Smith himself lived very simply and gave most of his wealth to charity.

Like Freud, Smith sees moral behaviour as built up in the mind from the influence of parents, teachers, school fellows (peer group, you might say today) and society in general. The conscience acts as a kind of 'impartial spectator', watching and judging you. Where Freud (as discussed more in Chapter 10) would allow the unconscious to still lead you astray, Smith makes his an impartial spectator, similar in role to that of the Freudian superego and quite capable of leading you towards the light. In his book *The Moral Sentiments* he says:

> . . . *it is chiefly from this regard to the sentiments of mankind that we pursue riches and avoid poverty. For to what purpose is all the toil and bustle of the world? What is the end of avarice and ambition, of the pursuit of wealth, of power, or pre-eminence? . . . To be observed, to be attended to, to be taken notice of with sympathy, complacency, and approbation, are all the advantages which we can propose to derive from it. It is the vanity, not the ease or the pleasure, which interests us.*

Smith goes on: 'To judge your own behaviour requires you to – at least for a moment – to divide into two people, and one be the spectator of the actions of the other. Nature had endowed each of us with a desire not only to be approved of, 'but with a desire of being what ought to be approved of'. (Which is rather harder).

Four factors determine people's respect for others: personal qualities, age, fortune and birth. The first is open to debate, so age is a better yardstick. Fortune or wealth is, Smith notes, in a way a surprising source of respect. Rich people are admired and benefit in terms of social esteem just by their wealth, and equally, poor people lose out both ways.

Smith is aware of the possibility of self-deception, and curses it as the source of 'half of the disorders of human life'. If only, he wrote in *The Moral Sentiments*, people could see themselves as others see them, 'a reformation would be unavoidable. We could not otherwise endure the sight'.

The hidden hand

The hidden effects of economic forces and the workings of the market, become in Smith's phrase 'the invisible hand'. As he puts it in his barnstorming account, *The Wealth of Nations* (1776).

> . . . *every individual necessarily labours to render the annual revenue of the society as great as he can. He generally, indeed, neither intends to promote the publick intent, nor knows how much he is promoting it . . . he intends only his own gain, and he is in this, as in many other cases, led by an invisible hand*

to promote an end which was no part of his intention.

Notice he doesn't say 'hidden hand', but invisible hand. Funny how these quotes take on a life of their own. But the idea, which is influential, is that economic forces can be trusted to guide people's actions, and lead them towards making the right decisions both for themselves and everyone else around them. Is that true? A lot of governments assume it is, and a lot of other people disagree. But to decide who is right requires less economics than philosophy.

Manipulating the market with J. K. Galbraith

What motivates people to consume? What's the cultural significance of consumption? How are patterns of consumption woven tightly in with patterns of social inequality? And just what drives the choices consumers make when they 'consume'?

In the early part of the 20th century, economists spent considerable effort trying to understand household needs and expenditures, and looked at consumption expenditure trends by income class. But fashions change, and so they did in economics – by the middle of the century no one wanted to study this. Instead, economists discussed grand theories of how economic forces drive money and states. Two of the grandest were the economic theories known as 'general equilibrium theory' and 'Keynesian macroeconomics'. Not for these economists grubby research into suicides (like Durkheim conducted) or individual purchasing habits.

In fact, economists in the tradition of the 18th-century liberal political philosophers (such as J.S. Mill and Adam Smith) felt it almost intrusive to look at what individual consumers did or didn't do. They rested on the duty of liberal politics to enable everyone to exercise as much free choice as possible – typically by spending money and making purchasing decisions.

Consume more to be happy

Mainstream economics assumes that everyone makes their decisions independently of everyone else – that preferences are independent of the likes and dislikes of others. Mainstream economists assume society is made up of lots of independent individuals – not groups, let alone classes.

Yet, as customer research specialists know only too well, people fit into very easily identified and surprisingly rigid categories. The man (and it is a man) who buys a Ford Escort car reads a certain newspaper, likes fluffy dice hanging from the rear-view mirror, thinks bumper stickers saying 'Honk if you hate noise pollution' are funny, watches certain programmes on a certain kind of TV and of course votes a certain way. These are statistical trends. Exceptions are anticipated. But economics is about averaging out all the individual choices, and such patterns ought to be central to the theories.

And economic theory remains deeply wedded to the idea that higher consumption corresponds to increased well-being – that the higher the gross national product, the better. (The *gross national product* is the measurement economists use of all the money, be it physical goods or intangible services, that people in a country generate, one way or another.)

Economics has also retained another 19th-century bias – about usefulness. Making steel or fertiliser is, of course, very useful (never mind about pollution), but making music or saving the wilderness aren't useful, in this sense. Economists prefer goods and services to meet what they perceive to be practical needs. As an example, in the US a car provides the practical value of transport, as well as being a heavily laden, symbolic consumption item.

John Kenneth Galbraith's 1958 book *In Praise of the Consumer Critic: Economics and The Affluent Society Consumption in Mainstream Economics* (*The Affluent Society* for short) was perhaps the most influential philosophical account of consumption in the period following the Second World War. A multi-faceted and sweeping look at consumer society and consumerism (with forays into psychology, sociology and other fields), it helped define a new counter-culture against consumerism. Galbraith's book fed into the radical views of the 1960s and went on to nourish new perspectives such as those behind the environmental and feminist movements of the 1970s.

Money as the route to happiness

The last two decades of the 20th century saw a political backlash, and a reassertion of consumer culture and money as the routes to happiness. Economists and politicians alike decided consumers are sovereign, that advertising is of limited effectiveness and that you can understand consumption as effective action to create identity, meaning, value and well-being in individuals' lives. *The Affluent Society* makes three major claims about consumption:

- ✔ The production side creates consumer desire.

- ✔ The relationship between consumption and utility has become weak or perhaps even negative.

- ✔ The structural pressures to increase private consumption drive out the provision of public goods.

Galbraith rejects the usual view that relates production and consumption, which is that consumer desires (or preferences) arise from somewhere outside the economic system, and that firms simply then respond to the desires. The economy's success is then measured by its ability to satisfy these consumer desires. In *The Affluent Society*, Galbraith says it's the other way around. He argues that consumers' desires are no longer urgent, or intrinsic, because when a society is affluent, urgent needs have been met and it's the sales and marketing efforts of corporations that create wants. Advertising creates the craving for more and more powerful cars, more songs for iPods, more exotic food, more erotic movies – more *Dummies* books, even! It's advertising that creates 'the entire modern range of sensuous, edifying and lethal desires'.

And yet economists, Galbraith says, 'have closed their eyes (and ears) to the most obtrusive of all economic phenomena, namely modern want creation'. Worse still, the emphasis on private consumption is crowding out public goods – the public interest. Galbraith is especially prescient on the natural environment:

> *The family which takes its mauve and cerise, air-conditioned, power-steered and power-braked automobile out for a tour passes through cities that are badly paved, made hideous by litter, lighted buildings, billboards and posts for wires that should long since have been put underground. They pass on into countryside that has been rendered largely invisible by commercial art. (The goods which the latter advertise have an absolute priority in our value system. Such aesthetic considerations as a view of the countryside accordingly come second. On such matters we are consistent.) They picnic on exquisitely packaged food from a portable icebox by a polluted stream and go on to spend the night at a park which is a menace to public health and morals. Just before dozing off on an air mattress, beneath a nylon tent, amid the stench of decaying refuse, they may reflect vaguely on the curious unevenness of their blessings. Is this, indeed, the American genius?*

More manipulation of poor consumers

The Cold War and rise of psychological warfare helped feed fears of corporate brainwashing through ads. This warfare came in books like Vance Packard's 1957 *The Hidden Persuaders*, and even a contribution from philosophy from Theodor Adorno and Max Horkheimer, whose classic 1944 piece *The Culture Industry: Enlightenment as Mass Deception* became the standard text for academic critiques of consumerism for 20 years in both the US and Europe.

In these accounts, the powerful and active agents are corporations, not individuals. This perspective was dominant until roughly 1980. At that point a marked ideological shift on consumerism began, spearheaded by the economist Milton Friedman and his political supporters, Mrs Thatcher and Ronald Reagan, respectively the British prime minister and the US president for most of the 1980s.

Being a consumer came to be seen as more active than passive. The public were supposed to be able to see through the tricks of advertisers to their own interests, and even to be busy doing their own kinds of manipulating by using their purchasing choices as part of a sophisticated exercise of asserting and creating their own personal identities.

Paternalist state policy (that is, the state acting as a nice sugar daddy) and Keynesian economics (with its assumption that the government can make better economic judgements than the individuals and companies that make up the 'market') combined with a new right-wing celebration of the individual to produce a bit of a social paradox. The growth of huge companies operating around the world almost beyond national laws, with turnovers the size of whole nations, was accompanied by an ideology that talked of just the reverse – of individual consumers who were kings with corporations at their mercy.

So what was really going on? Are people collectively (at least) 'consumer kings' or corporate victims? Certainly, people are trained from the earliest ages to be consumers and identity is deeply bound up with consumption choices.

And social science is right to point out that individuals can't escape their class positions, in much the same way that they can't avoid being part of the consumer system. If economists insist on the (by definition!) 'goods are good' mantra, perhaps because it's superficially democratic and anti-elitist, they're also taking a very political stance. Consumption has always had both symbolic and utilitarian aspects.

Classical economics minimises social motivations – the dictates of fashion and the desire to look like other similar people (your peers) – in order to make the individual king. But in so doing, economics fails to understand – or predict – what people's choices are going to be.

Consumption also reflects and reproduces other categories, such as national identities and rural culture. The reality behind consuming is that virtually all goods and services have social meanings and effects. The liberal philosophy that cordons off this particular sphere as purely private, as having nothing to do with society and therefore not a legitimate subject for analysis, is taking a political not a scientific stance.

In fact, standard economics rests on three planks, none of which economists like to debate:

✔ Consumption brings about well-being.

✔ People make free and rational choices.

✔ Consumption has a practical purpose and is rational – it is utilitarian.

After all, if reducing consumption could enhance people's general well-being, then the calculations of the economists fall apart. Hence they prefer not to consider the possibility!

The unworking class

The sociologist and former Marxist André Gorz and the contemporary philosopher Zygmunt Bauma criticise conventional Marxist interpretations of society. Both of these redefine the exploited class, not in terms of ownership or wages, but rather as individuals *who can't consume.*

Why not? Too full of cream cakes? No room for any more DVDs in the rack? No, simpler than that. No money.

As Gorz puts it, the truly oppressed class of modern capitalism isn't that of the workers any more, but of the 'unworkers' – the old, the unemployed and the very young (such as the street children of South America) who can't work and must rely on state handouts or charity (or crime) for their sustenance.

Even at the time that Marx and Engels were writing, Mikhail Bakunin (1814–76) was expressing this view in Russia. He foresaw an uprising of the 'uncivilised', driven by their instinctive desire for equality. Bakunin predicted, in contrast to Marx, that civilisation would enfeeble the revolutionary instinct, and that violence was part of a primitive urge.

Discrediting Ayn Rand's capitalist hero

Ayn Rand (1905–82) was born, rather more grandly, Alisa Zinov'yevna Rosenbaum in Saint Petersburg, Russia. There she studied social sciences, but far from becoming a learned researcher or professor, she went off to be a screenwriter, a career that almost inevitably took her to Hollywood. Here she odd-jobbed for a number of years, including appearing as an extra in Cecil B. DeMille's film, *The King of Kings*. The film features author Ayn Rand as a face in a crowd.

The founder of objectivism

Rand's fame doesn't rest solely on her film work, impressive though it is. She's nowadays celebrated as the founder of the quasi-philosophical movement called *objectivism*. What's that then? Something to do with being objective and rational, perhaps – just like Max Webber recommends? Something like that, certainly. If there's more to the theory, then no one knows what it is. However, there's a US postage stamp featuring Rand, and a video game called *BioShock* built around her writings.

Rather, Ayn Rand's sociological contribution is to argue for a particular ethic of rational self-interest and libertarian, hands-off capitalism. Weber's protestant work ethic is about a personal belief amongst Protestants about the heavenly value of hard (see the earlier section 'Being Bureaucratic with Weber'). Rand's ethic is also about the very personal and down-to-earth advantages of hard work (or any work really) that makes you rich.

Admirers describe Rand as a philosopher, but she most certainly isn't one. Even if her books advance a certain philosophy of life, they do so not by offering any arguments (which is the hallmark of philosophy) but only via large amounts of assertion. These range freely (or some might say, ramble haphazardly), looking for targets to criticise, such as homosexuals, whom she considers 'disgusting'. Despite all this, or perhaps because of it, some US schools and at least 30 US colleges nowadays study objectivism.

And for these serious students, Rand sets out the objectivist philosophy in her third novel, *The Fountainhead*, which appeared in 1943 and rapidly found a mass market, and is today claimed to have sold over 6 million copies. That's not quite a million times more than my books!

Rand's nightmare vision of a world without big business

Then Rand's book struck a very characteristic American note, that of 'the entrepreneur as hero', and this was also the theme developed in due course by her best-known literary effort, *Atlas Shrugged* (1957). The plot involves a dystopian US in which industrialists and other creative individuals (Ayn Rand, anyway) decide to go on strike and retreat to a mountainous hideaway where they build an independent, free economy.

Naturally, the country dedicated to the pursuit of wealth lapped this up. After the popular success of *Atlas Shrugged*, Rand started a newsletter devoted to updates about objectivism, and a book on the origins of the 'philosophy', *The Ayn Rand Lexicon: Objectivism from A to Z*. This says

> *Aristotle's philosophy was the intellect's Declaration of Independence. Aristotle, the father of logic, should be given the title of the world's first intellectual, in the purest and noblest sense of that word. No matter what remnants of Platonism did exist in Aristotle's system, his incomparable achievement lay in the fact that he defined the basic principles of a rational view of existence and of man's consciousness: that there is only one reality, the one which man perceives – that it exists as an objective absolute (which means: independently of the consciousness, the wishes or the feelings of any perceiver) – that the task of man's consciousness is to perceive, not to create, reality – that abstractions are man's method of integrating his sensory material – that man's mind is his only tool of knowledge – that A is A. If we consider the fact that to this day everything that makes us civilised beings, every rational value that we possess – including the birth of science, the industrial revolution, the creation of the United States, even of the structure of our language – is the result of Aristotle's influence, of the degree to which, explicitly or implicitly, men accepted his epistemological principles, we would have to say: never have so many owed so much to one man.*

This is, of course, nonsense. But splendidly profitable nonsense! Similarly, her book *Atlas Shrugged* offers a little bit of philosophical content, built around a speech by its hero, John Galt. Galt echoes Nietzsche's contempt for the Christian virtues of sacrifice, offering that this 'is an age of moral crisis, brought about by the doctrine of sacrifice' and complaining that the 'essence of previous moral codes is to demand that you surrender your mind and your life to the whims of God or society'.

In place of this, Rand offers an argument rooted in a first principle of self-ishness: 'If you must act to benefit others, why is it acceptable for others to accept such benefits? Because they did not earn them.' Far better, Rand thinks, here following Adam Smith, to leave the free-market to arrange things:

> *In a society of trade, there is no conflict of interests among men at different levels in the pyramid of ability. The most talented people, who make new discoveries and invent new products and technologies, contribute the most to others; while those at the bottom, who are engaged in mere physical labor, benefit the most.*

The speech, which like the book is very long, spanning around 50 pages, reveals the key idea in the 'philosophy' of objectivism eventually. Will I spoil the plot if I tell you it now? Good, then I will. Here it is. John Galt says:

> *You will win when you are ready to pronounce this oath: 'I swear – by my life and my love of it – that I will never live for the sake of another man, nor ask another man to live for mine.'*

Atlas Shrugged was reviewed by *National Review* in 1957. They called the book 'sophomoric' and 'remarkably silly', and said it 'can be called a novel only by devaluing the term'. Despite this, the book has acquired a cult-like following including quite a few influential public figures such as Alan Greenspan, sometime head of the US Federal Reserve; Hugh Hefner of *Playboy* fame; Angelina Jolie, the female Rambo or action woman film star; and Jimmy Wales, the business entrepreneur (also curiously, involved in porno – great business model!) behind a rather successful but not exactly profitable online encyclopaedia called Wikipedia, which treats Ayn Rand respectfully and at length.

Discovering markets and chaos theory

Have you ever looked at the charts showing the movements of stocks and shares? They invariably go up and down. And at any particular time it's impossible to predict whether they're about to go up – just a bit more please! – or plunge violently downwards. You'll certainly have noticed that if you've actually put any money into buying stocks or shares.

Economists assume that while a buzz of random short-term changes happen in stocks and shares, the long-term trends are determined by sensible, macro-economic (that is, large-scale) factors such as changes in technology or productivity or wars or new inventions. Economic theory traditionally assumes that prices change smoothly, rather than in abrupt jumps – an assumption borrowed from the physics of movement. Yet in fact prices jump around in response to news or rumours.

At one time, it was thought (oh, simple people!) that the Sun, the moon and the stars were kinds of deities controlling human lives. Indeed, there are still people (that make today's kind of philosophers very cross) who take astrology and such like very seriously. But clearly, ever since Newton, people have been able to not only predict the motions of the Sun and moon, and the stars and the planets, but also the movements of falling apples and assorted lead weights. Because, ever since Newton, people have known that the natural world obeys laws.

Only, it turns out it doesn't, or at least, only when it wants to (which comes to about the same thing). In fact, the movements of the heavenly bodies remain inherently unpredictable, owing not merely to the vast complexity of the forces that influence them but also the inter-relatedness of these forces. Astronomers can only give an approximation of where the moon will be tomorrow. They might well be out (by a couple of inches).

In many real-world situations, tiny factors multiply themselves, causing profound changes. In geological time, scientists know that the magnetic poles of the Earth have flipped, changing at a stroke the Earth's climate and weather systems. Yet this nothing more than an electrical spark can trigger this massive change. Collosal effects caused by tiny changes is the essence of what mathematicians and physicists call _chaos theory_.

Today, impressively powerful computers are fed vast amounts of facts, programmed with a range of rules for interpreting them and can churn through incomprehensibly large numbers of calculations before spewing out predictions for the future. They attempt to act out the vision of the French philosopher Pierre Laplace (1749–1827), who predicted very firmly that one day (at least in theory) a great intelligence (a super-super-super-computer, as you may nowadays put it) able to calculate the movements of everything in the universe would be able to predict the future.

> _Such an intelligence would be able to embrace in the same formula the movements of greatest bodies of the universe and those of the lightest atom, of it nothing would be uncertain and the future, as the past, would be present to its eyes._

Typical of the super-computer people is the task of predicting global warming. They take millions upon millions of measurements of air, sea and ground temperatures, wind speed, tides, dust levels, sunspot patterns, rainfall and so on. Then the computer applies the rules, which the climate experts grandly declare to be (like Newton's ones) accurate descriptions of how the world works.

But weather, indeed climate, isn't so easily tamed. It's the epitome of a complex system accountable to no one. This is because, in fact, maths is less tidy than non-mathematicians know. Take that complicated sort of maths you use to measure the changes. *Calculus* is a triumph, but you can't solve most differential equations at all because most things vary in unpredictable ways, non-linear ways. (Plot a graph and you can't make the dots fit on a line.) Yet it's human nature to always look for patterns, scientists and stockmarket investors alike, even if the pattern may not be there.

In social science, theoretical and mathematical modes try to explain the way societies work. By a 'model' is meant a mathematical construct, a set of mathematical rules supposed to accurately capture the way things are relayed in the world that, with the addition of certain verbal interpretations, describes observed phenomena. The justification of such a mathematical construct is solely and precisely that it's expected to work, as the respected 20th-century mathematician John von Neumann once put it.

And although in natural science you imagine the models really do match reality, they're equally just abstract theories, with no more justification than that they seem to work. These are the three traditional rules of science that people pretty much universally believe:

- ✔ Simple systems behave in simple ways.

- ✔ Complex behaviour must have a complex cause.

- ✔ Different systems follow different rules.

Chaos theory reminds people that the truth is the opposite:

- ✔ Simple systems can behave in complex ways.

- ✔ Complex behaviour can arise in simple systems.

- ✔ Different systems can follow the same rules.

That's why chaos theory itself can apply to biology, weather or even stock markets.

Chapter 19

Exploring Scientific Truth and Scientific Fashions

Pursue this investigation further and you will see that science has now become as oppressive as the ideologies it had once to fight. Do not be misled by the fact that today hardly anyone gets killed for joining a scientific heresy. . . . Heretics in science are still made to suffer from the most severe sanctions this relatively tolerant civilization has to offer [It seems that] science has become rigid, that it has ceased to be an instrument of change and liberation.

– Paul Feyerabend

How many of people are brought up on a neat and eminently satisfactory picture of science as a steady progression from crude guesses to ever-more sophisticated knowledge, propelled by ingenious techniques and machinery? It seems as if science, like the ocean waves approaching the shore, moves in only one direction, and if foolish humans attempt to stop the flow of progress, it's only a matter of time before their obstructions are swept aside and the great tide of discovery flows on.

This chapter looks at the origins of science as a particular way of making sense of the world around us, at the way scientists say they work – and at the way they actually seem to operate, which turns out to be rather different.

Setting the Scene: Reason and Science

The grandest figures of Western philosophy assume the steady progression of science. Descartes, considered by many to be the pivotal figure in the development of modern, rational thinking, firmly asserted that only those able and willing to put aside their false beliefs (and note instead what was left clearly and distinctly behind) could accurately identify knowledge. His idea was that as long as philosophers made sure to base their theory on a firm foundation at the very outset, they could then develop the rest of their theory without needing to worry about one or two of the later bits added on to it were in fact faulty. The firm foundation would allow dodgy parts to be replaced without the lot collapsing. This view of science as basically very solid with maybe just one or two details needing refining is psychologically pretty appealing. And it's the way most of us view it. But philosophers of science warn that it just ain't true.

Ptolemy and the spheres

Ancient philosopher-mathematicians like Ptolemy demonstrated that you can make powerful calculations as long as you start with clear principles (or *axioms*) and then allow nothing else to sneak into the calculations (or theory) unless you can logically deduce it from these axioms. What better model for science! No matter that Ptolemy's astronomical system fixed the Earth immovably at the centre of the universe while the stars rotated around it on crystal spheres, making divine music as they turned – because although it certainly sounds like nonsense today, Ptolemy's system made an excellent foundation for other theories, both scientific and philosophical.

Ever since Ptolemy, mathematical ideals have guided philosophers and scientists firmly towards grand schemes based on simple principles and away from the complexities and inconsistencies of real life.

Kant: Reason and the unreasonable

Kant's original concerns were all scientific. Although many remember him nowadays for logical rules he derived from his activities as a very dry and pure philosopher, in his lifetime he also came out with many strange deductions from his 'scientific' research. For example, he says all the planets in the solar system have life on them (with the intelligence of the life on them increasing the farther away the planet is from the Sun) and that people have only a fixed amount of sleep in them at birth (and die early if they use it up by lying in bed too long; my Dad still believes that one!).

Or take the case of Gottfried Leibniz, the philosopher-cum-inventor (See alsdo Chapter 5) who deduced a universe made up of a single substance without parts that he called *monads*. Like Descartes, Plato and so many scientists before and since, Leibniz preferred to fit the universe into his theory than allow the universe to spoil his theories. So, for example, Leibniz explains that although these monad-atom-thingies don't appear to the senses ('they are colourless', he says, but *invisible* is a better way to put it, and is what he means), you can still deduce the monads' existence – in fact you have to – in order to explain reality. Today's quantum physicists do much the same thing, making their mysterious, invisible particles conscious of each other, able to communicate instantaneously across the entire length of the universe, and generally blithely ignoring all the rules of classical mechanics as set out in physics textbooks.

In fact, whatever you might like to think, scientists often start, as Jean Jacques Rousseau advised people to do, 'by putting the facts aside, as they will not affect the question'. Sounds weird? But in practice, in science, experiments don't lead to new theories, because all historically significant theories (and quite a few insignificant ones too) agree with the facts. Rather, as every politician and spin-doctor knows, lots of facts exist and you can choose the right one to bolster your theory. Scientists are political animals, and their methods are no different. *Even if scientists think their methods differ.*

Causing Science Problems with the Problem of Causation

It's not only philosophers who seek out causes to explain mysteries, but scientists too. Knowing what'll happen if you do something is useful, but knowing what caused it to happen is better. That Ancient Greek Democritus (460–370 BC) once said that he'd rather discover 'one true cause' than gain the kingdom of Persia, by which he meant that to understand what really causes something is powerful knowledge.

Comprehending cause and effect

Within philosophy, the nation of *cause and effect* (I hit my thumb with a hammer and sure enough, a moment later it hurts!) is central to theories of perception, decision-making, knowledge and how the mind works. Indeed, Samuel Alexander (1859–1938) once suggested that causation was the *essence of existence* itself. He thought that it's the ability to cause things to happen that separates fact from fiction, the real world from the imaginary one.

Or take philosophical debates over free will. These often have as their starting point the question of how you can be free if something else, maybe biochemical or electrical, caused your thoughts and wishes. Debates in the metaphysics of mind often revolve around the problem that the mind must itself be in some sense physical in order to be able to influence – cause – physical events.

Being challenged by Hume

This all demands an explanation of what exactly philosophers mean when they talk about something *causing* something else – what kind of word is this? The framework for the philosophy of causation really starts with David Hume. Hume (who is described in more detail in Chapter 5) was a great iconoclast - by which I mean he was the kind of person who took great pleasure in demolishing everyone else's favorite theories. Despite being brought up by devoutly religious parents, he was himself an atheist, and had theories to back it up too. (His book describing them however, *Dialogues Concerning Natural Religion*, was not published until several years after his death, because he feared it was too controversial!)

When Hume examined the notion of cause and effect, which Descartes had classed as a *necessary truth* (that is, it was true not as a matter of fact, but something that simply *couldn't* be otherwise), he decided it could yield only probable knowledge. He realised that when you see an event constantly followed by another, you only infer (assume) that the first event caused the second. However, Hume says 'we cannot penetrate into the reason of the conjunction'. For instance, if you eat an apple, you expect it to taste a certain way; if you take a bite if the apple and it tastes, say, of banana, you'd consider that anomalous. My apple's gone bananas! But Hume says that this response is sloppy thinking: 'The supposition that the future resembles the past is not founded on arguments of any kind, but is derived entirely from habit.'

From the apple/banana example you may conclude that all knowledge is flawed, and that you can believe nothing. Hume saw this, but in the manner of the gentleman philosopher he was, suggests that carelessness and inattention offer a remedy – recommending that you should neglect the flaws in your arguments and continue to use dodgy reasoning whenever you find it suits you! Philosophy remains, then, only as an agreeable way to pass the time (well, he found, anyway), not a reason to change your views.

Hume's practical bent meant that he thought the only evidence worth having about the way causes and effects relate must ultimately be good old measurable evidence from the senses. But you can't sense or directly experience causal relations; instead you always deduce them from observations of one event following another. These are events linked in space and time. You press a button on the front of the TV and, after a short delay, the screen lights up, and you assume you caused the tele to come on. But the button *might* have been broken and your 2-year-old *might* have helpfully operated the remote instead from behind the sofa. You'd never know the difference! But the difference is there, and it's fundamental.

The tidy and convenient expectation people have of things actually having simple causes that always produce the same effects is simply a by-product of memories of the regular and predictable succession of events in the past. But remember what happened to Bertrand Russell's chicken in Chapter 1!

JARGON BUSTER

Causation

Many different kinds of causation exist. David Hume thought most about events that are you expect to always follow the causes – it's the philosophical favourite, if A then B. But plenty of other kinds of causal relationships in the world (like clouds and rain) exist that are merely probable – if it's cloudy then a 25 per cent chance of rain exists.

Another useful kind of causation is the *counter-factual*, which historians use to interpret the significance of past events, and lawyers use as a way to distribute blame. For example, historians may say that if the Luftwaffe had decided to bomb all the airbases instead of the cities in World War II, then Hitler would easily have been able to invade Britain and the world would now be under a Nazi dictatorship. One event would have caused another.

Never mind that in this case it's all imaginary, because for philosophers it's by no means settled whether causation is really built into the fabric of the universe or merely a feature of the particular way people's brains chop up the kaleidoscope of everyday sense experience and organise it in their heads.

Hume sees humans as essentially animals, with the additional facility of a sophisticated language. Reason is merely a product of people's use of language, and animals too can reason, albeit in simpler ways. He offers accounts of both emotions and ideas as if people were essentially machines, motivated by pleasure and pain, or as Thomas Hobbes had put it earlier, by appetites and aversions. His observation that an *is* doesn't imply an *ought* also stresses that, sooner or later, everyone falls back on their feelings in order to make any choices.

GREAT IDEA

In his later writings Hume accepts the label *sceptic*, and certainly that's how his contemporaries saw him. The first victim of his approach was consciousness, or the self, as an entity. Hume observed that consciousness is always of something – of an impression of some sort, being hot, cold or whatever – and so you can understand the self as a kind of bundle of perceptions. No one can perceive the self as such, not by looking inwards and certainly not by looking at anyone else. Hume, thus, went one step further than Bishop Berkeley (see chapter 5), who'd demonstrated that no matter existed by proving that no mind existed either.

In many people's estimation, Hume is Britain's greatest philosopher. Yet he never got a job in a university there, partly due to the controversy raised by his debunking of religion. Even his great friend (and the then much more famous philosopher) Adam Smith, while acting as a referee for Hume's candidature for the post as professor of Ethics and Pneumatic Philosophy at Edinburgh, wrote advising against the appointment! It would've been upsetting for Hume to imagine that his best friend had caused him to not get the job, so it's just as well he'd already come up with his strange theory about causation being imaginary.

THOUGHT EXPERIMENT

How tin hats cause head injuries

Here's an example of cause and effect in practice that perplexed people during the First World War.

The number of soldiers arriving at the rudimentary field hospitals with bits of shrapnel lodged in their heads was a very serious matter. The number of patients was very high, the soldiers took a long time to recover (if they ever did) and it cost a lot of money to treat them. Now, at the beginning of the war the soldiers had been smartly kitted out with cloth hats to wear, of the kind that looked smart but only protected from bright sunshine. So, seeing the dreadful figures for head injuries, some pen pusher in Whitehall decided that getting soldiers (like motorbike riders or building site workers today) to wear strong, protective helmets made of steel would reduce the number of injured soldiers arriving at the field hospitals with bits of shrapnel in their brain. But on the contrary, after the introduction of tin hats the number of such injuries to the head *increased* dramatically.

So what was going on? How on earth could wearing tin hats have caused more injuries?

Was it another example of those health and safety know-nothings making things worse, making the soldiers less good at dodging bullets, perhaps? Or could it have been that wearing the tin helmets made the soldiers more careless?

Actually, at first, no one could explain the rise in injuries despite the protective headgear. But then some bright spark realised that the medical figures recorded only those soldiers requiring treatment, and not those who'd died before they could reach a hospital (let alone reach a statistician). It turned out, on closer examination, that the number of soldiers *dying* from being shot in the head had dropped dramatically, but the number of injuries had gone up because more soldiers were surviving.

This demonstrates two things: that in statistics, as in philosophy, the question is often more important than the answer; and secondly, that effects can appear very different when you change your view on their causes.

Letting Black Swans Destroy Favoured Theories

Karl Popper (1902–94) is counted as one of the key philosophers of science of the 20th century. (Well, there aren't so many so not a lot of competition exists . . .) Nevertheless, he was never welcomed into the academic citadel, never quite accepted in the poishest academic circles.. He described himself as a *critical rationalist*, the *rationalists* being thinkers such as Descartes, Leibniz and, above all, Immanuel Kant with his rules and categorical imperatives who thought the path to true knowledge was via careful mental reasoning. Popper chose the term to signal his rejection of *classical empiricism*, or attempts to find out about the world through practical investigations and experiment that the logical positivists of the so-called Vienna Circle in the 1930s were reviewing and refining at the time. And he wasn't simple-minded follower of fashion either – against all the enthusiasts for scientific method,

Popper argued that no theory-free, infallible observations as empiricists ask you to assume, but rather all observation is theory-laden and involves seeing the world through the distorting glass (and filter) of pre-existing conceptual assumptions.

Karl Popper was also a social and political philosopher advocating what he called the *open society* (where governments have no secrets and individuals take all the important decisions for themselves) , and an implacable opponent of *authoritarianism* or what's nowadays sometimes called centralised, big-government. Having slipped out of Austria in the 1930s to avoid the Nazis, he was a particularly staunch defender of liberal democracy (and the principles of social criticism and debate upon which liberal democracy is based). His arguments against the conventional view of scientific methodology, based on *inductive reasoning* (drawing general conclusions from a limited number of cases), along with his championing of the principle of falsifiability as the way to distinguish real science from fake, non-science have greatly influenced the way the public in general see scientists – even if many specialists in the business of examining how science actually works reject Popper's work as simplistic.

Falsifiability is simply the idea that scientists conduct experiments aiming to confirm theories, and when they find the results contradict their expectations they realise that their theory must be false.

Conventionally speaking, people suppose that when experiments are conducted to test theories in reality, and that when the results don't accord with those anticipated, the theory is disproven. Karl Popper preferred the term *falsified* in his *Poverty of Historicism*, directly taking issue with Descartes who (as I mention in the earlier section 'Setting the Scene: Reason and Science') thought that it was enough to be very pleased with your theory (to see it clearly and distinctly).

Of course, you can get around an inconvenient result in many ways – notably scrumpling up the findings and throwing them in the wastepaper basket, and the history of science is full of scientists doing this. For example, Galileo, credited with 'proving' that the Earth goes around the Sun and not vice versa, and Louis Pasteur, saluted for discovering that tiny germs are everywhere (and hence pioneering ways to avoid them) both refused to have their theories falsified by experiments that came to results that contradicted their theories. In these cases, you have to salute their determination, but that's with hindsight. As far as rational, scientific debate went, Galileo and Pasteur lost – at the time! If scientists regularly prefer their hunches – or their religious convictions – to their findings, a gap between what people think scientists do and what they actually do seems to exist.

Shifting Paradigms and Causing Scientific Revolutions

In his writings (notably *The Logic of Scientific Discovery*, 1935) Karl Popper accepts an alliance with the great 17th-century sceptic David Hume, to challenge the entire basis of science. That is what's known as the principle of induction, as opposed to deduction, which is what philosophers and Sherlock Holmes are, at least in myth, supposed to do. *Deduction* can be logical and reliable. The opposite, *induction*, can only ever be illogical and unreliable.

Yet even though it's logically impossible to ever prove a universal statement, inferring general laws from particular cases is the basis of scientific method. Take a claim like 'All swans are white', for instance. Scientists can find plenty of evidence to support the theory – a white swan in the lake at Regent's Park, a white swan in London Zoo, a pair of nice white swans in the Pells Pond in Lewes – but none of that actually proves the theory *universally*, meaning everywhere and for all time. No, not even the two white swans at the Pells. Because, no matter what you know today, the future may be different. Science might find some black swans living somewhere. And indeed, that's exactly what happened in 1697 in Australia, where some explorers found a previously unexpected variety of black swan. Right up until then, Europeans were pretty sure that all swans were white.

Because all scientific theories are like the black swan example, vulnerable to the next case that comes along despite making universal claims for their truth, they ultimately rely only on faith. 'Me, I believe in gravity and the laws of thermodynamics!'

However, Karl Popper differs with David Hume, who in a way was more radical, because he clings to the belief that every counter-instance *is* decisive. The theory that earth was flat was demolished after someone siailded successfully right around it, the idea that all swans were white was demolished by the discovery of black swans. This is the rock Popper proposes to rebuild the structures of science upon.

Hume himself concluded that science and philosophy alike rested less upon rock – let alone the rock of logic and method – than they do upon the shifting sands of scientific fashion and aesthetic preferences. And the 20th-century American philosopher Thomas Kuhn took up Hume's view, rather than Mr Popper's.

Remember the Ancient Greek theories of how the heavenly bodies might be on crystal spheres? It's probably the paradigm example of how falsification doesn't seem to take place, let alone decide the survival or otherwise of a theory. As observational evidence piled up against their crystal spheres, the Ancients simply increased the number of spheres each time a new problem came up. But then, one day, the old theory suddenly fell out of fashion and a new orthodoxy took its place. It's this process that the American philosopher of science, Thomas Kuhn, named the *paradigm shift*. Once out, the term soon spread, virus like, from the physical sciences to the social sciences, and on to the arts and even business management courses! It became so popular that people began to describe the idea as itself a kind of paradigm shift.

Analysing how scientists really work: Thomas Kuhn

In his 1962 book *The Structure of Scientific Revolutions*, Thomas Kuhn offered a way to see behind the apparently lofty and impregnable fortress of scientific consensus – revealing it as really just a shifting facade. Kuhn writes that 'a scientific community cannot practise its trade without some set of received beliefs' and that these beliefs form the foundation of the 'educational initiation that prepares and licenses the student for professional practice'. The nature of the rigorous and rigid preparation helps ensure that the received beliefs exert a deep hold on the mind of each new member of the community.

What people consider to be normal science, Kuhn says, is built upon the assumption that the scientific community knows what the world is like, and responsible scientists take great pains to defend that assumption. You must suppress new ideas, new paradigms/theories, 'because they are necessarily subversive' of basic commitments. To do otherwise would require you to reconstruct existing assumptions and re-evaluate accepted facts. This would be a huge task: possibly dangerous; possibly impractical; certainly time consuming. Thus sensible members of the established scientific community should strongly resist new ideas. As Kuhn put it, in sciencenovelty emerges only with difficulty, manifested by resistance.

Nor can the scientists function without a set of beliefs, for a paradigm is essential to scientific inquiry. Kahn says that 'no natural history can be interpreted in the absence of at least some implicit body of intertwined theoretical and methodological belief that permits selection, evaluation, and criticism'.

He also says that evidence alone doesn't decide theories. He notes that philosophers of science have repeatedly demonstrated that you can put more than one theoretical construction upon a given collection of data. Put another way, you can often rearrange facts to come up with quite different explanations. Even if problems and weaknesses with a theory begin to accumulate, he says, it's often easier for the establishment, be it scientific, religious or political, to either modify the original idea or suppress the conflicting information than to abandon their established orthodoxies.

Given all that you might wonder, how and why do paradigms ever change? Thomas Kuhn links the process that he calls paradigm shift that takes place within the scientific community to the process of *perceptual* (conceptual) *change* in an individual, where you resist change at first, but after making the 'jump' you find it impossible to return to the old ways of thinking. Here's a little example of perceptual change. Look at the picture of the rabbit in Figure 19-1.

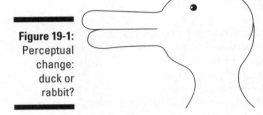

Figure 19-1:
Perceptual
change:
duck or
rabbit?

Pretty, isn't it? But oops! I've put included a picture of a duck with a long beak by accident. Look at the picture again. This little visual trick may not be entirely convincing as an example, but you probably know cases in real life of perceptual shifts. Perhaps you thought you recognised a friend some way off because - lots of things fitted in with your impression, such as her long yellow hair. But suddenly the woman's a bit nearer and she doesn't look anything like your friend at all! It's a stranger wearing a yellow scarf instead.

Another way to look at it, Kahn suggests, is to liken a paradigm shift to a political revolution. Afterwards, all the old rules, all the old certainties have changed.

Abolishing method with Paul Feyerabend

Paul Feyerabend (1924–94) was a philosopher of science best known for his anarchistic view of science and his rejection of the existence of universal rules. Like Hitler, Wittgenstein and the logical positivist movement, Feyerabend was Austrian by birth. All three of those shared a conviction that science was a kind of applied logic, and very powerful too.

But not Feyerabend! Instead, he advocates what he calls a radical *epistemological anarchism*, in which he goes further than Karl Popper and Thomas Kuhn. Anarchists refuse to accept other people's rules,a nd Feyerabend refused to accept other people's views about what counts for knowledge. He says that there's actually no such thing as scientific method, and that the scientific world view is no better than any other (for example, he offers views based on astrology, or voodoo). He says that the various scientific world views of the past were all quite rational within their own framework, and only fall apart when you examine them from outside.

Paul Feyerabend worked for most of his career as a professor of philosophy – not a scientist – at the University of California (1958–89). At various times he also lived in Britain, New Zealand, Italy and Switzerland. His best known works are *Against Method* (1975), *Science in a Free Society* (1978) and *Farewell to Reason* (1987). His writings bring wit and humour where many of philosophers and scientists fail to do so. His writings are fresh, lively and clear even if not *entirely* persuasive.

Taking on scientific method

Feyerabend challenges the comfortable view of scientists of their own activity and the 'crude and superficial' critique of philosophers generally. In an article called *How To Defend Society Against Science* (1979) he says:

> *Methodology has by now become so crowded with empty sophistication that it is extremely difficult to perceive the simple errors at the basis. It is like fighting the hydra – cut off one ugly head, and eight formalizations take its place. In this situation the only answer is superficiality: when sophistication loses content then the only way of keeping in touch with reality is to be crude and superficial. This is what I intend to be.*

His style is to ask apparently ridiculous questions, to disconcert his opponents. For example, he takes up the pseudosciences of astrology, of alternative medicine and of magic generally, saying that they're no more irrational than science itself, equally rooted in human traditions and what he calls myths.

> *You say we can criticize myths by comparing them with a 'bulk of sound scientific knowledge'. I take this to mean that for every myth you want to criticize there exists a highly confirmed scientific theory, or a set of highly confirmed scientific theories that contradicts the myth and belongs to the 'bulk'. Now if you look at the matter a little more closely you will have to admit that specific theories incompatible with an interesting myth are extremely hard to find. Where is the theory that is incompatible with this idea that rain-dances bring rain?*

Going against scientific orthodoxy

In Feyerabend's sceptical account, scientific 'facts' are taught at a very early age and in the very same manner in which children were taught religious 'facts' only a century ago. Teachers make no attempt to awaken the critical abilities of the pupil so that she may be able to see things in perspective. At universities the situation is even worse, for indoctrination is here carried out in a much more systematic manner. Criticism isn't entirely absent. Society, for example, and its institutions, are criticised most severely and often most unfairly and this already at the primary school level. But science is exempted from the criticism. Society at large receives the judgement of the scientist with the same reverence as it accepted the judgement of bishops and cardinals not too long ago. The move towards *demythologization* (the attempt to remove all the mysterious or mythical aspects from daily life) , for example, is largely motivated by the desire to avoid any clash between Christianity and scientific ideas. If such a clash occurs, then science is certainly right and Christianity wrong.

Comparing Quantum Mechanics to Common-or-Garden Mechanics

Quantum science is the science of eeeny weeny tiny things, or *quanta* – things too small to see, even with the best electronic microscopes. Quantum physics defies the rules about how science is supposed to operate – that is in a 'commonsense' way, amenable to experimentation, with no mysteries, no invented elements allowed to explain the inexplicable. Instead, he quantum world as *indeterminate* (impossible to specify exactly).

Yet the great relativist himself, Einstein, would have none of this, saying that 'God does not play dice', and that it's people's understanding of the quantum world that's at fault; a position also taken by Karl Popper, for example.

Querying quantum theory

Philosophers have a soft spot for quantum mechanics, because it sounds impressive and supposedly within normal rules don't apply. For example, the law of cause and effect which is embedded in fundamental laws of physics such as Newton's law of gravitation and other boring ones about mechanics, like cause and effect – the billiard ball hits the other billiard ball and causes it to move off with a velocity – zzzz! Thank goodness none of it's true. That is, at the quantum level . . .

And then you have that *indeterminacy principle* (see the following section), which makes it impossible, even in theory, to know either the exact energy state or the exact position of a particle.

Have I lost you already? But that's another feature of quantum physics – as one of its founding figures, Richard Feynman, put it in a quotable quote: 'I think it is safe to say that no one understands Quantum Mechanics.' Mind you, I think he meant the whys of the science, not the hows. Although he wrote a book called *Quantum Mechanics*, and sure enough, that doesn't explain the science either. After all, as he says in the book, 'One does not, by knowing all the physical laws as we know them today, immediately obtain an understanding of anything much.'

Professor Feynman agrees with Paul Feyerabend that although most people are very pleased with scientific explanations, scientists themselves (let alone philosophers) shouldn't be, saying, 'The more you see how strangely Nature behaves, the harder it is to make a model that explains how even the simplest phenomena actually work. So theoretical physics has given up on that.'

In another tract called *The Distinction of Past and Future, from the Character of Physical Law* Feynman elaborates, saying that in all the laws of physics that found so far no distinction between the past and the future seems to exist. He says, 'The moving picture should work the same going both ways, and the physicist who looks at it should not laugh', because in quantum mechanics it makes no sense to talk of past and future. But what will you do with all your clocks and watches if there's no longer any point to time! This sort of physics undermines your understanding of the world. Should physicists be doing stuff like that? But in *The Pleasure of Finding Things Out*, Feynmann thinks yes, most certainly:

> *Science alone of all the subjects contains within itself the lesson of the danger of belief in the infallibility of the greatest teachers in the proceeding generation . . . Learn from science that you must doubt the experts. As a matter of fact, I can also define science another way: Science is the belief in the ignorance of experts.*

Having said that, the big task for quantum science is still to find out what the universe is made of. Isn't it basically stars and planets and specks of dust swirling in a perfect vacuum? Yet the doubters aren't going along with that, not at all. Only a tiny part of the universe is made of this sort of familiar material; the other 96 per cent is still a mystery. So you have to infer its presence instead from astronomical observations and the laws of gravity.

The Swiss astronomer Fritz Zwicky is credited with first noticing that there seemed to be most of the universe missing, back in the 1930s. He realised that the gravitational attraction of a huge amount of unseen material – dark matter, dark energy or dark fluid, call it what you will – seemed to hold together the universe and galaxies. In the 1970s more detailed astronomical observations by Vera Rubin (a woman astronomer – at last a woman's *acknowledged* for influencing philosophy!) of the size, shape and spin of galaxies made the problem worse. So today, physicists spend many billions of euros hunting for dark-matter particles with the Large Hadron Collider at the European Organisation for Nuclear Research in Geneva.

Dark energy was a challenge to Einstein's theories, which didn't allow for such mysterious entities. But the idea of an invisible, unifying medium goes back many thousand of years before either Zwicky or Einstein. Every science has its demons, and this one has appeared in a multiplicity of forms from ancient times through the Enlightenment and right through to the latest theories of quantum mechanics. Electricity, gravity, atomic matter and even spiritual life have called upon the services of an 'invisible medium' to fill certain theoretical gaps in their make-up. Usually they've called it the 'aether', an ancient Greek word meaning 'thing that shines'. Not that it does shine, of course. Anyway, ever since Einstein's Theory of General Relativity, scientists have banned the topic from conversation, only returning to it occasionally in disguise and under a different name. Because dark matter or dark energy is actually only what the Ancients as far back as Aristotle called *the aether* and counted as the fifth element, alongside fire, earth, water and air.

The Ancients liked thinking up new names for things they didn't understand. We don't do that any more, of course, except in quantum physics where scientists name new particles almost every day. Sounds like a dodgy science! But the aether has hung on because it fills a pretty big black hole in physics.

Wondering about indeterminacy

With so much science around, threatening to make sense of everything, no wonder the uncertainty principle is very popular with philosophers, seeming as it does to offer a little hole in the edifice of science. Coined by the physicist Werner Heisenberg (1901–76), generally credited as the co-founder with Erwin Schrodinger of modern quantum physics, the *uncertainty principle* puts a limit on the accuracy with which you can specify the position and momentum of subatomic particles, loosely speaking of course. Heisenberg allows you might be able to specify one precisely, but not the other. Heisenberg saw this as affecting people's ability to predict the future behaviour of particles, and hence the future generally. The phenomena of atomic physic are still 'real', but the elementary particles themselves are shadows. They're merely potentialities and possibilities in a world of probabilities.

Heisenberg intended the principle to refine the semi-classical model of Einstein and his brainy chums, Planck and Bohr. *Classical* refers to the nice, sensible physics of Isaac Newton, where apples fall off trees at predictable velocities, not to the ideas of the Ancient Greeks, of course, who 'Classical' usually does refer to . Anyway, back to Heisenberg, In a series of lectures in the 1950s, later published as *Physics and Philosophy* he says

> *In the experiments of atomic physics we have to do with things and facts, with phenomena that are just as real as any phenomena in daily life, but the atoms or the elementary particles themselves are not as real; they form a world of potentialities or possibilities rather than one of things or facts.*

The theory of incompleteness

Kurt Gödel (1906–84) was born in Austria but spent most of his career in the United States, where he met Einstein and later counted him as a great friend. His name is synonymous with his *incompleteness theorem*, which may sound airy but is in fact very mathematical and precise.

Please undelete this - my style has been edited out.In the 1930s he produced a logical proof demonstrating the completeness of what dull philosophers call *first-order predicate calculus* – that is, the logic of sentences such as 'Eric is an apple', 'Socrates is mortal', 'God is dead' and so on. But as a by-product of his proof he opened up a nasty can of worms, because he realised that all the logical systems being explored by his contemporaries – philosophers like Gottlob Frege in Germany or Bertrand Russell and Alfred North Whitehead in Britain – were incomplete. Well, you may say 'Give the lads time and they'll surely finish'! But not at all: Godel means the systems are *incomplete* in the much worse sense of being *necessarily* unprovable. This indicates that mathematics itself, in as much as it depends on logic for its certainty (or consistency), is also incomplete. You can put Gödel's Theorem (if you want the posh name) like this, that is more 'formally':

> For any consistent formal system (**S**) containing a certain part of arithmetic, you can construct a sentence in the language of **S** that you can neither prove nor disprove within **S**.

How's that, Granddad! Or, indeed, what does that mean? Well, Granddad or Grandma would surely say, 'My child, what your friend Mr Goddle has here has implications for mathematics and logic that are profound, in that he means that no system exists in which you can prove, hence justify, every mathematical truth. He's saying that mathematics contains claims that you can neither prove nor disprove by considering the original axioms.' Er . . . and what does that mean? 'Well, let's just say that maybe Zeno was right after all when he set out that early problem for physicists with his famous race, when he said that, in theory at least, Achilles wouldn't be able to catch up with the tortoise.'

Strange forces being invented to link the atoms back together again

Another crazy feature of quantum mechanics is that it allows particles to affect each other – to *communicate*, as it's put, instantaneously across the whole width of the universe! No causal mechanism is either possible or needed, yet the science is all very respectable and scientific. And if that's okay, why not astrology too - why not allow cosmic influences on people that defy 'causal' (indeed rational) explanation?

Astrology's origins are lost in antiquity, but for centuries it was as much part of philosophy as logic or ethics is today, a crucial part of educated people's intellectual apparatus. Ancient Rome relied heavily on its court astrologers for warnings of natural or political disasters, exercising an influence that the Roman writer Tacitus denounces in his *History* as a 'deceitful attempt to run the affairs of State'. People understood the stars and planets to be part of the same great system that human beings struggled along in, and they felt that understanding their movements could shed light on human affairs too – without there necessarily existing a simple, causal connection, as anti-astrologers today like to derisively allude.

The heyday of astrology was from about 1300 to 1700 in Europe, where the study guided medicine, farming, chemistry, navigation, warfare and indeed all areas of life. Even the Pope (like US President Ronald Reagan more recently) asked astrologers for advice. Alas, over the last 3–400 years, astrology has fallen out of favour with philosophers, with little remaining but the superficial popular and psychological forms. But even Isaac Newton grew up in a world where astrology ranked as one of the great studies of mankind. Medieval universities taught it as one of the core subjects, and it was part of a sophisticated system of medical knowledge involving the different parts of the boy and different herbs.

Early astrologers needed to examine the heavens for signs, such as shooting stars, that might portend culture events – usually calamities. A Babylonian sect built *ziggurats* — pyramids with the edges not smooth but stepped – to better examine the heavens and find the link between the heavenly bodies above and the human ones below. Their research inspired the Ancient Greeks to develop the methods of personal horoscopes – the 12 signs, like Aquarius and Leo – although it's the Roman names that have survived.

The Christian Church of course thought all this very pagan, and in the year 333 AD the Emperor Constantine forbade the study in Europe in the name of Christianity. As recently as 2005, the newly elected Pope particularly cited belief in astrology as one of the evils he'd be working to root out, so astrology still has some influence. On the other hand, despite its official disapproval the Church continued to wax lyrical about the 'heavenly sign' of the 'star of Bethlehem', and if you look carefully you might be surprised how many old churches contain astrological symbols in their masonry, stained-glass windows and even paintings.

The next low point in the subject's fortunes came with the problem, pointed out by the saintly philosopher Augustine as well as quite a few others, of twins. I'm one myself, and we share many more details in our zodiacal charts than seems likely given our totally different personalities. Scientists trotted this problem out regularly, as well as the supposed flaw in astrology that the planets aren't actually in the same positions as they used to be, and relate differently in space to the constellations and so on, which for linear thinkers implies that the learned astrological talk about the conjunction of this and that seems to be just philosopwaffle. No wonder that in 1975 nearly 200 self-styled 'leading scientists' paid good money to newspapers to present their objections to astrology. This group was later debunked by Paul Feyerabend in his book *Against Method,* as part of a surpringly 'logical' case he manages to make for the ancient study. Indeed, 'astrology' is a key battle ground for philosophers of science, pushing their various viewpoints.

Another regular appearance in the 'science wars', as the philosophers sometimes like to these debates, is 'alternative medicine', which simple-minded and evidently unphilosophical pundits (waving scientific credentials though) decry all forms of medecine that seem to them, to be irrational and to defy the principles of experimental science. Homopathy, for instance, where people are given infintessimally small doses of a mineral or somesuch (so small, that as the saying goes, you'd need to drink a whole ocean full to be sure to get even one active molecule!) defies all 'rational' explanation'. Hence orthodox thinkers consider it to be a fraud on a credulous public - and even 'dangerous' as it may delay patients from seeking more conventional medical advice. The fact that homeopathy has no negative side-effects (unlike conventional drugs, of which indeed, a great deal of 'blind faith is often required, as the number four cause of death in the United States these days (that's well over 100 00 people a year) is from prescription drugs, correctly given out by doctors) and does seem to cure at least some people (indeed, in countires like India, there are 200 000 registered homeopathic doctors and homeopathy is one of the 'National Systems of Medicine') has not stopped it being the *Bête noir*, the bugbear, of many self-proclaimed defenders of science.

The traditional understanding of the workings of astrology, as put forward by Ptolemy some 200 years BC, sets out all the knowledge of the astrologers and provides details of how to create personal horoscopes. For him, the system involved questions of time, objectivity and, above all, symbolism. And although astrology doesn't seem to match modern notions of science, it does seem to offer an incredibly rich and subtle array of cultural, aesthetic and psychological insights. The descriptions of astrological types are all ambiguous, containing within each sign opposite tendencies.

Capricorn (my sign), for example, actually *isn't* a farmyard goat with a bad temper and a tendency to be too stubborn, but a wonderful, mythical creature with a fish tail, giving it great sensitivity and creativity! The goat half gives people born under the sign the characteristics of being steady, hard-working and materialistic, and the fish tail makes them dreamy, imaginative and spiritual. Given how neatly that fits my personality astrology must be true! (Funny how other people born the same month are so different though. . . .)

Mind you. astrologers say that as Capricorn comes at the beginning and the end of the Zodiac – it starts the cycle, and ends it – it's an especially ambiguous sign, but all the signs contain the same paradoxes. You can't understand such contradictions by logical, linear thinking at all, and so people often briskly dismiss the subject despite it being a treasure trove of ideas and insights, philosophical and scientific (well, scientificky).

But logic and rationality only get you so far, both in philosophy and in life. There still remains a little space for wonder and mystery.

Part VI
The Part of Tens

'These should be easy to mug – just
a lot of old nerds studying Greek.'

In this part . . .

Philosophy books can be kind of hard going. That's why hardly anyone reads them. Not even book reviewers and philosophy professors read philosophy books. (I've cut a few corners myself – but hey, no one knows that.) Anyway, for those of you who don't quite have time to plough though the 'real thing', this part contains a short guide to the classics.

Reading or dozing off over philosophical classics is all very well, but it's a rather passive way to do philosophy, and this book is an encouragement to think for yourself and actively *do* philosophy. So we end with (but equally, you can start with) ten totally refreshing and stimulating philosophical puzzles to keep you pondering.

Chapter 20

Ten Famous Philosophical Books – and What They Say

▶ Taking a bite out of some of the classics

▶ Picking up some tips for reading philosophy

Although the classics can be awfully long and dull when compared to watching TV, true philosophy fanatics shouldn't overlook them. In this chapter, I describe ten books that true fans ought to know about, and put on their coffee table, if not actually plough through. These books aren't *really* the best philosophy books, but they're all ones that have a curious cachet – the author sounds important, the title sounds imposing, you know the sort of thing. If you want just a wee taste, just a *wee drappie*, of the classics, this chapter is for you.

The Critique of Pure Reason, by Immanuel Kant

Kant's big idea is to assume people's ideas and concepts shape reality, rather than suppose that reality is somehow out there and people's ideas and concepts latch onto it to a greater or lesser extent.

Kant was one of the first philosophers to actually be paid for his trouble, one of the first professors of the subject in a university. However, his income depended on people coming to his lectures, and if you read this book, you can see why he made very sure to keep his other, 'scientific', interests going too. When he was wearing his scientific hat (so to speak) Kant said that the everyday, physical world around us exists, but when Kant was wearing his philosopher's hat, the cone shaped one with a D on it, of course, he said that the everyday world is all an illusion, and that we can never directly know about underlying reality.

The Republic, by Plato

Plato's Republic is the biggy! This is nowadays Plato's most read playlet (in the past it was probably the *Timaeus*). Anyway, the thing about the *Republic* is that includes a fairly long discussion of the Theory of Forms, which is Plato's big idea. (See Chapter 2 for more on the Forms.) Plato finishes with a reassuring comment on the survival of the soul after death. Just before that, he also gives quite a decent discussion of the nature of art. In fact, the book is full of ideas. That's why it remains the philosophical classic to beat.

The Forms themselves are crucial. The whole of philosophy revolves around them. But no one has managed to work out quite what they are, or if they really exist. But this is the book where it all started.

Fear and Trembling, by Søren Kierkegaard

Say what you like, but Kierkegaard can write. Philosophise too? Well, maybe. Anyway, his argument is that reason can only ever undermine faith, not support it. Authentic belief is an act of faith – a leap in the dark. Religious types who philosophise are wasting their time.

Well, maybe. The thing about Kierkegaard – like Descartes, like Spinoza, like rather a lot of philosophers, let alone the monkish ones, Anselm, Aquinas and Augustine (and why do they all begin with *A* anyway?) – is that their supposed free-wheeling philosophy remains tethered to a personal search for reasons to believe in God. So, whether their quest is original and thought-provoking or rambling and incoherent, it's a philosophy that bends over backwards to accommodate a pre-existing personal commitment to God.

Ethics, by Baruch Spinoza

First few and last two lines. All set out very methodically, of course.

'I understand that to be CAUSE OF ITSELF *(casua sui)* whose essence involves existence and whose nature cannot be conceived unless existing.'

That's enough. You've already lost me, Baruch! Spinoza wasn't a priest, but he seems to have been pretty devout. And he's on message saying that only one God exists, but unfortunately he says that this God is the entire universe. People are just bits of the universe, no more significant than, say, ants or rocks or plants or pants.

The whole book is set out in pseudo geometrical style, as definitions, axioms and theorems or, as he puts it, propositions. The full title of the book, often neglected (as I just have) is after all *Ethics Proved in Geometrical Order*.

Spinoza has some style. He writes 'Love, pleasure et cetera, I shall not stop to consider, for they have nothing to do with what we are now dealing with.' Mind you, that's what people say about his book as a whole, for even if it proves geometrically the existence of , it's a pretty sad sort of God who has no interest in individual people or indeed any of the properties religious folk normally attribute to their deities. Spinoza's God is a kind of cosmic ghost instead.

Discourse on Method, by René Descartes

First of all (to impress people and catch them out), make a note that the full title is *Discourse on the Method of Properly Conducting One's Reason and of Seeking the Truth in the Sciences*. Notice the word *sciences*. The *Discourse on Method* is really just the preamble to a collection of Descartes' scientific papers on the nature of light and on meteors! Descartes at one point even cuts up some poor monkeys – the rotter! – to see whether they have souls in them. He finds no evidence of any, unlike when he cuts up some dead people and discovers an apparently useless gland in the neck.

What's Descartes going on about? God? No, the book is really about Descartes (or at least his scientific work). In fact, Descartes, you really ought to know, was a very stuck up and pompous chap. Highly rated by the Brits, less so by his own people – the French. Could it be a cultural conspiracy to promote one of France's *worst* philosophers?

Yet by making philosophy more methodical – like science – Descartes has been very influential.

A Treatise of Human Nature, by David Hume

Or 'By Anon'. Because, although philosophers now know Hume wrote the book, originally he published his book anonymously. And then he praised it also anonymously. Nice try! The book begins:

'All the perceptions of the human mind resolve themselves into two distinct kinds, which I shall call IMPRESSIONS and IDEAS. The difference betwixt these consists in the degrees of force and liveliness, with which they strike upon the mind, and make their way into our thought or consciousness.'

In the book, Hume is very clever, and he's a hypocrite. He mocks those who claim to have solved all philosophy's problems with their own new system – and then produces his own new system to do just that! He says he'll be brief and goes on for hundreds of pages. He says all notions of cause and effect are faulty, but you should carry on using them anyway. He says that he'll turn the science of ethics – the study of right and wrong – into a practical matter like, say, the study of beer-making or gardening, but ends up with a theory of human nature that has nothing left because the core of each person is invisible to himself, and certainly invisible to anyone else.

Hume writes clearly, methodically and plainly. He works his way through all of the concerns of philosophy in turn, solving most of them. And no wonder he was always a controversial figure for doing it!

Leviathan, by Thomas Hobbes

Hobbes writes, 'I put for a general inclination of all mankind, a perpetual and restless desire of Power after power, that ceaseth only in Death.' It is because of this, that an absolute power is required to control them.

Despite his humble origins as the son of an unemployed vicar in back-country England (his father disappeared shortly after quarrelling with another pastor at the church door, indeed blows had been exchanged) Thomas Hobbes somehow managed to rise to the top of the English social hierarchy, hobnobbing with dukes and living off a personal income courtesy of the king himself.

But then, by the time he'd left this school at age 14, he'd already translated Euripides' *Medea* from Greek into Latin verse, a feat that continues to impress philosophical commentators today (perhaps rather more than it should).

Modern societies today reflect and accept Hobbes' view that people are basically motivated by self-interest and left to their own devices they always come into conflict. Of course lots of other people thought that already, but Hobbes puts it rather nicely in this book, saying amongst other things that the human machine is programmed to spend its energies selfishly and that he doubts if it's even possible for human beings to stop being selfish. Even, say, helping an old lady across the street is actually self-serving, perhaps an attempt by someone to feel good about himself. Hobbes says that for human beings, the real aim is always to gain power.

Three Dialogues between Hylas and Philonous, by George Berkeley

'Can there be a pleasanter time of day, or a more delightful season of the year? that purple sky, those wild but sweet notes of birds, the fragrant bloom upon the trees and flowers, the gentle influence of the rising sun', starts the book. This is fine stuff! Berkeley is about to prove to Philonous that nothing in the garden exists.

Berkeley's big idea was that what philosophers were beginning to call sense perceptions weren't created by some strange interaction with matter, as everyone around him assumed, but were placed directly in your minds by God. This cuts out the middle man, so to speak.

Berkeley formed a student society at Trinity College, Dublin, to discuss the scientific philosophy, and announced his new principle to overcome the threat of the materialism that already seemed to be rapidly reducing the world to a kind of complicated machine. In place of the mathematically tidy and predictable world of Newton and Locke, he came up with a kind of *radical immaterialism*, in which the world loses its objective reality and instead becomes intricately connected with whoever's looking at it. *Esse est percipi*, or 'to be is to be perceived'. Sounds daft, doesn't it? Yet that's also what modern physicists are saying. At least, at the quantum scale of the very, very small . . .

I should also note that the Berkeley is a bit of sceptic. He thinks most philosophy is just waffle. What about his own writing then? Many philosophers have tried to mimic Plato's celebrated dialogues, and most of their efforts are, frankly, dire. But Berkeley's aren't bad!

Ethics, by Aristotle

Aristotle's idea was that the difference between a good person and a bad person is that one is good and the other is bad. There are two steps to the argument, though. Good is good and bad is bad, and that bit is is Aristotelian logic. The other bit is about people's attitudes and behaviour, and this bit – brilliant isn't it! – was revived (particularly by Professor Alasdair MacIntyre) in the sunset years of the 20th century as virtue ethics. Many philosophy courses now teach the theory. So if you're on one, better keep this summary close!

Here are the first few lines:

> *Every art and every investigation, and similarly every action and pursuit, is considered to aim at some good. Hence the Good has rightly been as 'that at which all things aim'. Clearly, however, there is some difference between the aims at which they aim . . .*

And to close:

> *Book 10. Pleasure and the Life of Happiness*
>
> *The student of ethics must therefore apply himself to politics.*

Well, you know, there's some good sense there. Or if not exactly good sense, sense anyway. Pity about the details – woman are domestic cattle, some men are born to be slaves, that sort of thing.

Existentialism and Humanism, by Jean-Paul Sartre

Sartre's book is short and stylish. Great to carry on le Metro. That's what the French value! Pretentious – moi? Oui! Long boring books are for the Anglo-Saxons . . .

Here are the first few lines:

> *Atheistic existentialism, of which I am a representative, declares with greater consistency that if God does not exist there is at least one being whose existence comes before its essence, a being which exists before it can be defined by any conception of it. That being is man or, as Heidegger has it, the human reality. What do we mean by saying that existence precedes*

essence? We mean that man first of all exists, encounters himself, surges up in the world – and defines himself afterwards.

That's not actually the literal first few lines. Although this is a very short book (just 50 pages!), Sartre still manages to pack in quite a lot of waffle – but hey, you should see his *magnum opus*, *Being and Nothingness*!

Anyway, this is how the book ends:

> *Existentialism is not atheist in the sense that it would exhaust itself in demonstrations of the non-existence of God . . . existentialism is optimistic. It is a doctrine of action, and it is only by self-deception, by confining their own despair with ours that Christians can describe us as without hope.*

Sartre's point is that people should take responsibility for their actions, and not make excuses. For example, a believer in God might say that exploitation of the workers is all right because in heaven God will see that their hard work and virtue is rewarded. Belief in God is used as an excuse not to correct wrongs on Earth. No wonder Sartre calls all such attitudes 'bad faith'!

Chapter 21

Ten Philosophical Puzzles to Keep You Thinking

1 love philosophy problems and thought experiments, or to be precise, philosophical puzzles and science fiction. Because traditional philosophy problems aren't much fun. They're things like 'Is freewill ever really possible?' or 'How can you be certain that your sense impressions reflect a physical reality that really is out there?'. You know the sort of thing – they discuss it on philosophy courses – but then, people are being made to discuss these questions. No one says they're interesting.

But philosophical puzzles and mad science are fascinating. Curiously, they overlap with the boring problems too. Here are ten fairly typical ones just to whet your taste buds!

Probing Protagoras's Problem

Protagoras's problem is a classic problem, indeed a classical problem, such as the Ancient Greeks liked to discuss. This philosophical thought experiment isn't a trick – or if trickery does exist, no one's discovered it yet.

The story goes that Protagoras has trained a bright young fellow called Euathlos to be a lawyer, under a very generous arrangement whereby Euathlos doesn't need to pay anything for his tuition until or unless he wins his first court case. But much to Protagoras's annoyance, after giving up hours of his time training Euathlos, the pupil decides to become a musician and never takes any court cases!

Protagoras demands that Euathlos pay him for his trouble, but Euathlos refuses, saying he has no money apart from for his music. Ha! So here's where it gets riddlesome. Protagoras decides to sue his former student in court. Protagoras thinks he has what's known in legal circles as a cast-iron case because:

- ✓ If Euathlos loses the case, Protagoras will have won, in which case he'll get his money back.

- ✓ If Euathlos convinces the court and wins the case, Protagoras will then be able to make Euathlos pay him, because his student will then have won a case, despite his protestations about being a musician now, and will therefore have to pay up under the terms of their agreement.

Looks pretty straightforward, no?

But, however, Euathlos reasons very differently:. If he loses, he thinks, then

- ✓ If Euathlos loses, he will have lost his first court case, in which event the original agreement releases him from having to pay any tuition fees.

- ✓ If Euathlos wins, Protagoras will then lose the right to enforce the contract, so he will not be able to make him pay anything.

That's the riddle. They can't both be right. So who's making the mistake?

The paradox is that both ways of thinking seem to be correct, but they lead to two opposing conclusions. You can't fault either Euathlos or Protagoras on their logic, but both of them can't be right, which tends to undermine logic and with it the basis for most reasoning.

Anyway, that's the short answer. The longer answer is that the statements sort of refer back on themselves, so the first one is true if the second one is false, but the second isn't false if the first one is true, so the first one must be false, so the second one . . . have I lost you? Think about this then.

- ✓ The statement below is true.
- ✓ The claim you just read above is false.

Playing in the Sandpit with the Sorites Problem

The Ancient Greeks were perplexed by the problem of definitions. For example, when is a heap of sand a heap? They called this philosophical thought experiment – wait for it – the problem of the heap, or the Sorites problem (their word for all heaped up). But I can do better than that.

Take, for example, a pre-school that advertises its services to parents on the promise that the children will have a sandpit to play in. The teacher gets a spade, constructs a rectangular box and fills it with sand. Now the children have a sandpit. But each day, as the little children play in the sandpit, a few grains of sand disappear. After one week, the sandpit still looks pretty full, but after three months, the level of sand is noticeably lower. However, the teacher has no doubt that the school still has a sandpit for the children. Nonetheless, after one year, the sandpit has only a few handfuls of sand left in it. It's clearly no sandpit now. The parents feel cheated. But at what point did the sandpit cease to be a sandpit?

The problem is that most judgements are vague. A sandpit isn't defined as containing at least 100,000 grains of sand, and even if it were, would you notice if someone fobbed you off with one made of 99,999 grains instead? But on the other hand, somewhere in the weeks and months since it was made, the sandpit did stop being a sandpit.

When it comes to reasoning, even humans rely on one iron distinction – that between what is and what's not. So, if it's impossible to say how many grains of sand make a sandpit, it's also impossible to say when blue isn't green, when an inch is really an inch, a spade a spade and so on. It's worse than saying all reasoning relies on approximations – because what are the approximations being compared to?

Related to this is the question of whether a sandpit is one thing or many – a million things, maybe, if you count all the grains of sand. Or take a tree – is it one thing or many? If you divide a tree into branches, roots, bark, leaves, twigs and so on you have a situation very like with the Sorites problem. In the autumn the tree loses its leaves, but still remains a tree. In the winter, a foolish gardener then chops all the tree's branches off, so it becomes a stump. But it's still the tree. However, in mid-winter the neighbour chops the stump down to one foot and takes the wood to burning on a fire. All that's left is the roots of the tree! And maybe it never grows again.

Identifying Locke's Sock

John Locke, the great English liberal philosopher once came up with an interesting thought experiment.

Locke proposed a scenario regarding his favourite sock that had developed a hole. He pondered whether his sock would still be the same after he applied a patch to the hole. If yes, then would it still be the same sock after he applied a second patch or even a third? Indeed, would it still be the same sock many years later, even after he'd replaced all of the material of the original sock with patches?

It's not a very original thought experiment, bearing rather too close a resemblance to the various ancient ones known as Sorites problems (see the preceding section), using things such as dwindling piles of sand or ships that have had their timbers replaced one by one. But nevertheless, Locke's sock has produced its own batch of new approaches to the problem of identity.

One response to Locke's paradox, helpfully proposed, is to use the concept of *four-dimensionalism*, or so say contemporary American philosophers such as David Lewis and others. Their idea is to think of objects not merely as three-dimensional spatially-defined things but as things that also extend across the fourth dimension of time. From this new 4-D perspective, Locke's sock starts off as a ball of wool, undergoes some curious spatial manipulations and ends up travelling around England and Holland, usually either on or just above the ground, leaving the odd tiny fibre on the floors of bedrooms. Of course, starting off with wool is rather arbitrary, so you might want to consider the wool on the back of the sheep too, or the atoms in the grass that became the wool, or . . .

In fact, the solution seems to upset notions of identity even more than having a hole in your sock does.

Knowing Your Own Mind with Swampy Things

The original Swamp Thing appeared in a science-fiction comic book written by Alan Moore. Swamp Thing is an elemental entity created upon the death of a scientist, Alec Holland, which mysteriously retains Holland's memory and personality intact. Swamp Thing is 'a plant that thought it was Alec Holland, a plant that was trying its level best to be Alec Holland'. Swamp Thing is also an elemental creature who uses the forces of nature and wisdom of the plant kingdom to fight the polluted world's self-destruction.

No wonder then that Alan Moore's 1980s comic book saga *Swamp Thing* is counted by aficionados as a cornerstone of American comic books. And it's only slightly less unremarkable that the story inspired a thought experiment for Professor Donald Davidson, which he wrote up in a learned 1987 paper entitled 'Knowing One's Own Mind'.

In Professor Davidson's philosophical version, it's his good self who goes hiking in the swamp and is vaporised by being struck by a bolt of lightning. At the same time, another lightning bolt strikes nearby in the swamp and spontaneously rearranges its swampy molecules so that, entirely by coincidence, they take on exactly the same form that Davidson had at the moment of his untimely death. This, of course, is impossible.

Not in the least bothered by that, Professor Davidson says that his imaginary Swampman will have a brain absolutely identical to that of the departed hiker, and will thus, presumably, behave exactly as he would have. Swampman will walk out of the swamp, return to his family and place of work and (says Davidson) will interact with colleagues and friends and family apparently just as before.

Now here's the interesting bit, assuming that the comic isn't very interesting. Professor Davidson says that Swampman appears to recognise people yet, as he puts it, 'it can't recognise anything, because it never cognized anything in the first place'!

Anyway, that's the paradoxical bit for Davidson.

These considerations led Professor Davidson to deny that the Swampman's utterances refer to anything in particular, but are rather just programmed responses like an alarm clock going off. Philosophers shouldn't even construe utterances (in the style of a horror movie) like 'Urrgh, me, Swampman!' as referring to anything in particular. When Swampman says to his wife, 'Darling, I had a strange experience while in the Swamp', he's being insincere as he has in fact never met the woman before; he just thinks he has. Davidson goes so far as to say that because Swampman has no past he may not be a real person at all!

This much-discussed thought experiment is flawed because:

- ✔ The scenario is evidently implausible

- ✔ The electrical activity that governs thoughts and memories in the brain is generally understood to be impossible and not merely implausibly difficult to replicate, by lightening strikes or whatever

- ✔ It all seems to be devised to pose a much more mundane philosophical question that you could address much more simply, for example by imagining someone whose memory malfunctions so that she thinks she remembers things that, in the everyday sense, she doesn't

Losing Your Marbles with Professor Davidson

Buoyed up by the success of his Swampman thought experiment (see the preceding section), Professor Davidson offers another effort, this time wisely eschewing the literary flourishes.

Professor Davidson asks you to suppose that at some point the previous day he'd looked at a glass marble on a shelf. Now, he argues, suppose someone swaps the marble for another visually identical one, without him knowing anything about the exchange. Then, when Professor Davidson looks again at the marble, a sort-of paradox would exist. Because surely his internal state after looking at the other marble would be identical – yet the marbles, in a sense, are different!

Worse still, Davidson says his utterances could refer to different marbles. This proves, he says, that you can have no grounds to attribute *any meanings or thoughts* to him at all! Case proven!

Squabbling over the Plank of Carneades

The plank of Carneades is an exciting thought experiment attributed to Carneades of Cyrene.

The story starts by supposing that two sailors, let's call them Robin and Crusoe, are shipwrecked. After their ship runs into a storm and sinks, they're left splashing in the water until they both see a plank a short way off – a plank big enough to support just one person. Swimming energetically, Robin gets to the plank first, and Crusoe arrives just after. Fearing (correctly) that if he doesn't get control of the plank he'll drown, Crusoe tips Robin off the plank and paddles away on it, leaving the other sailor to a watery grave!

Not long afterwards, a ship spots Crusoe and rescues him. Now the question posed by Carneades, and doubtless the shipmaster too, is should Crusoe be put in the ship's brig pending trial for his selfish behaviour?

Philosophically you can debate this experiment, but legally speaking, in the real world the precedents go against Crusoe. Because he upset the plank and tipped Robin in the sea, English law would hold him to have killed Robin. As the case of Her Majesty the Queen v. Dudley and Stephens (1884) established, an argument of necessity is no defence. On the other hand, if Crueso had waited for a wave to temporarily dislodge Robin from his perch, he would've had every right to both grab the plank and defend it. But perhaps that's tactics, not philosophy.

Giving Up Reality with the X-perience Machine

Here's a story that's both an exciting yarn and science fiction! Oh yes, and a bit philosophical . . .

People rushed to try out the first X-perience machines as they were made available.

The machines, at least at first, were fiendishly expensive, but at least in Dysutopia, the Social Services department offered anyone feeling a little bit depressed or down the opportunity to pop into a refresh booth, lie on the couch, put the experiences helmet on, and relax while the machine stimulated her brain. It created the absolutely compelling impression that you were (like the best possible dream) flying over the Himalayas, or lying on the beach in Torquay, or having karmic sex . . . any option from a previously selected experiences menu.

Naturally, the machines were very popular and time on them had to be strictly limited. No one was allowed more than ten minutes a week without a doctor's note.

What could be wrong with that? – wouldn't you want to try such a thing? But then suppose someone suggests that the machines be made available commercially, so that anyone who wants can have happy experiences whenever she wants, for as long as she wants?

There was a rush to order the X-machines (as they were called now), and the ten minute safety limit seemed a very silly old anachronism. People connected themselves up for days on end, emerging eventually from the dream world tired, haggard and very thirsty.

Some rich owners got around this by arranging to have trained teams of nurses and doctors put them on drips and so on, so that the experiences could be extended for weeks, even months on end. But nothing could get around the psychological shock of awakening from the dream world to find themselves back in the evidently all-too inferior real one.

So some X-machine owners told their doctors that they didn't ever want to reawake from their dreams. They'd rather programme the machines, lie down and live in the virtual world until their bodies, twitching occasionally and attached to the life-support drips, eventually aged and died.

Now the philosophical (ethical really) question is, assuming you had enough money, would you still do try the machiens?

X-machines are known in philosophy circles as *Robert Nozick's Experience Machines* after the contemporary US philosopher, but the idea is an old sci-fi favourite. One example is the short story 'The Chamber of Life', published in the magazine *Amazing Stories* in October 1929. Unlike many imaginary scenarios involving the mind, if no such machines exist today, that doesn't mean they may not exist soon. Indeed, you can easily make comparisons with the effects of certain drugs – and the decisions of their users.

As far as Mr Nozick's machine goes, the claim is made that most people wouldn't want to substitute reality for irreality – no matter how much more enjoyable the latter might be. This, the philosophers claim, shows that truth is more important to people than pleasure.

Jumping Up for the Cosmos

One of Ptolemy's influential arguments is designed to show that the Earth must not only be at the centre of the universe, but also completely motionless – steady as a rock. To support this argument, Ptolemy asks his listeners to consider the fact that that if the Earth moved, as some earlier philosophers had suggested, then certain bizarre consequences would have to follow. In particular, if the Earth rotated once every 24 hours, was it not intuitively obvious that an object thrown vertically upwards would not fall back to the same place, but would fall back, if ever so slightly, to one side? Try jumping up and down in the air and see whether the Earth moves, even if only very slightly, underneath you!

Ptolemy's record isn't encouraging, although it's still true that his theory outlived many other (better) ones, but then his experiments weren't truly thought ones. He forgot the lesson of the other ancients, that those wishing to understand phenomena in the natural world should recognise that experience of events can be a poor guide.

Worrying about What Happens After the Sun Goes Out

Suppose something rather sudden and final happens to the Sun, so that one day it suddenly disappears. – not so much, of course, in a puff of smoke but, say, down a wormhole or tear in the fabric of space-time itself. Anyway, it disappears. Opinions differ on exactly what would happen afterwards to the Earth.

Ptolemy thought that the world would gradually become very dark, and maybe rather cold, but would otherwise remain unmoved. After all, Ptolemy thought that the Earth was fixed immovably at the centre of the entire universe, so the disappearance of one sun was hardly likely to shake it. And anyway, Ptolemy used crystal spheres, not gravity, to hold the sun and planets in their proper place.

Some time later, Copernicus returned to the problem. Although he agreed that the world would become dark – and what's more, do so instantly – he thought that (having looked through a telescope at Jupiter and seen four little moons obediently circling the planet) if the Sun disappeared, the Earth would fly off at a tangent from its heavenly circle – like a stone on a string that suddenly breaks.

Nowadays everyone knows that light takes a little bit of time to get from the Sun to the Earth, so it's easy to chuckle indulgently at Copernicus for imagining that were the Sun to disappear, daylight back on Earth would end instantly. Clearly you'd have plenty of time (about eight minutes, in fact) to set up emergency lights.

But now what about gravity? How long does gravity take to reach the Earth? Does it need eight minutes too? In fact, gravity has long puzzled both philosophers and scientists. Because one of the peculiar properties of gravity is that it appears to act instantaneously over a distance. Newton and Leibniz exchanged many unkind letters with each other on the subject, as Newton tried to balance all the cosmic gravitational forces within his static and unchanging system.

The thought experiment is intriguing, as in a sense you'd expect, like Copernicus, gravitational forces to act instantaneously, with the Earth immediately leaving its orbit. But if you think about it a bit more, this would create a slightly paradoxical situation, with the earthbound observers noting the lurch of the Earth towards Deep Space being able to deduce that the Sun had just disappeared (down a wormhole) a good eight minutes before the light itself went off.

Einstein's conclusion was that gravity couldn't operate faster than light and so, were the Sun to disappear, you'd not only get time to switch the lights on but for sailors to batten down the hatches in anticipation of some pretty big waves caused by miscellaneous gravitational effects. Mind you, in both cases, you'd have to predict the Sun's disappearance because, obviously, by the time an observer reported its disappearance the gravitational effects would have arrived too.

Does the experiment work? Yes, and it points to the fundamental truths of the inter-relatedness of space, time and energy.

Getting Relativity in Einstein's Elevator

Imagine a physicist who's drugged (or maybe he just had too big a lunch and dozes off) and wakes up to find himself in a box being pulled steadily upwards by a rope (I embellish a little) dangling from a hot air balloon. What will the physicist think is happening when he wakes up?

And the answer is that, although he'll be cross to be trapped in a box (which he'll probably think is the Physics department store cupboard), he probably won't realise that he's being pulled upwards (let alone by a hot air balloon). At least, he won't realise as long as the movement is entirely regular, just as if you travel up a skyscraper in a lift it's only at the beginning and end of the trip that you feel anything.

Yet now suppose the box (which is well soundproofed) has risen so high into the atmosphere that suddenly the hot air balloon bursts! (Which is a bit of physics in itself.) Locked inside the windowless, sound-proofed box, what will the physicist think is happening? 'Ah ha!' he says. 'They've taken me in a rocket to outer space! Excellent!' Because, in fact, as the box quickly reaches its escape velocity of 9.8 metres a second, the physicist will have become weightless. It will appear to him that gravity has disappeared. Indeed, the physicist can try various simple experiments, such as dropping a coin in midair, to see if it stays gently floating alongside him in the box. In fact, for the physicist inside the box, no matter what experiment he conducts, nothing will help him distinguish between being in a state of zero gravity (in space) or being in a situation where rapid acceleration towards the ground is cancelling out the gravitational force.

The lift is designed to demonstrate this equivalence between acceleration and gravitational field effects. From this, Einstein built his Theory of General Relativity, which overturned Newton's tidy but mysterious gravitational force that was so good at explaining falling apples and replaced it with a new, counterintuitive and almost unobservable notion of curved space-time.

Index

• F •

• *G* •

• *U* •

• *V* •

• *W* •

Notes

Notes

Notes

FOR DUMMIES®

Do Anything. Just Add Dummies

UK editions

BUSINESS

Starting a Business **DUMMIES**
A Reference for the Rest of Us!
978-0-470-51806-9

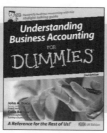

Understanding Business Accounting **DUMMIES**
A Reference for the Rest of Us!
978-0-470-99245-6

Lean Six Sigma **DUMMIES**
John Morgan
Martin Brenig-Jones
978-0-470-75626-3

FINANCE

Investing **DUMMIES**
Tony Levene
A Reference for the Rest of Us!
978-0-470-99280-7

Tax **DUMMIES**
Sarah Laing
A Reference for the Rest of Us!
978-0-470-99811-3

Sorting Out Your Finances **DUMMIES**
A Reference for the Rest of Us!
978-0-470-69515-9

PROPERTY

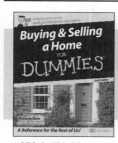

Buying & Selling a Home **DUMMIES**
A Reference for the Rest of Us!
978-0-470-99448-1

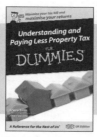

Understanding and Paying Less Property Tax **DUMMIES**
A Reference for the Rest of Us!
978-0-470-75872-4

DIY & Home Maintenance ALL-IN-ONE **DUMMIES**
Jeff Howell
A Reference for the Rest of Us!
978-0-7645-7054-4

Backgammon For Dummies
978-0-470-77085-6

Body Language For Dummies
978-0-470-51291-3

British Sign Language
For Dummies
978-0-470-69477-0

Business NLP For Dummies
978-0-470-69757-3

Children's Health For Dummies
978-0-470-02735-6

Cognitive Behavioural Coaching
For Dummies
978-0-470-71379-2

Counselling Skills For Dummies
978-0-470-51190-9

Digital Marketing For Dummies
978-0-470-05793-3

eBay.co.uk For Dummies,
2nd Edition
978-0-470-51807-6

English Grammar For Dummies
978-0-470-05752-0

Fertility & Infertility For Dummies
978-0-470-05750-6

Genealogy Online For Dummies
978-0-7645-7061-2

Golf For Dummies
978-0-470-01811-8

Green Living For Dummies
978-0-470-06038-4

Hypnotherapy For Dummies
978-0-470-01930-6

Available wherever books are sold. For more information or to order direct go to www.wiley.com or call +44 (0) 1243 843291

13902_p1

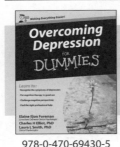

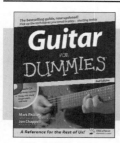

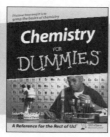

FOR DUMMIES®

Helping you expand your horizons and achieve your potential

COMPUTER BASICS

978-0-470-27759-1

978-0-470-13728-4

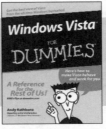

978-0-471-75421-3

Access 2007 For Dummies
978-0-470-04612-8

Adobe Creative Suite 3 Design Premium
All-in-One Desk Reference For Dummies
978-0-470-11724-8

AutoCAD 2009 For Dummies
978-0-470-22977-4

C++ For Dummies, 5th Edition
978-0-7645-6852-7

Computers For Seniors For Dummies
978-0-470-24055-7

Excel 2007 All-In-One Desk Reference F
or Dummies
978-0-470-03738-6

Flash CS3 For Dummies
978-0-470-12100-9

Mac OS X Leopard For Dummies
978-0-470-05433-8

Macs For Dummies, 10th Edition
978-0-470-27817-8

Networking All-in-One Desk Reference
For Dummies, 3rd Edition
978-0-470-17915-4

Office 2007 All-in-One Desk Reference
For Dummies
978-0-471-78279-7

Search Engine Optimization For
Dummies, 2nd Edition
978-0-471-97998-2

Second Life For Dummies
978-0-470-18025-9

The Internet For Dummies, 11th Edition
978-0-470-12174-0

Visual Studio 2008 All-In-One Desk
Reference For Dummies
978-0-470-19108-8

Web Analytics For Dummies
978-0-470-09824-0

Windows XP For Dummies, 2nd Edition
978-0-7645-7326-2

DIGITAL LIFESTYLE

978-0-470-25074-7

978-0-470-39062-7

978-0-470-17469-2

WEB & DESIGN

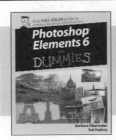

978-0-470-19238-2

978-0-470-32725-8

978-0-470-34502-3

Available wherever books are sold. For more information or to order direct go to www.wiley.com or call +44 (0) 1243 843291

13902_p4